LITERACY AND POPULAR CULTURE

ENGLAND 1750–1914

DAVID VINCENT
University of Keele

CAMBRIDGE
UNIVERSITY PRESS

Published by the Press Syndicate of the University of Cambridge
The Pitt Building, Trumpington Street, Cambridge CB2 1RP
40 West 20th Street, New York, NY 10011–4211, USA
10 Stamford Road, Oakleigh, Melbourne 3166, Australia

First published 1989
First paperback edition, 1993

British Library cataloguing in publication data

Vincent, David, 1949–
Literacy and popular culture: England
1750–1914. – (Cambridge studies in oral and literate culture; 19)
1. England. Literacy, 1660–1880
I. Title
302.2′0942

Library of Congress cataloguing in publication data

Vincent, David, 1949–
Literacy and popular culture: England 1750–1914/David Vincent.
        p.   cm. – (Cambridge studies in oral and literate culture; 19)
Bibliography.
Includes index.
ISBN 0-521-33466-7
1. Literacy – England – History. 2. Reading (Adult education) –
England – History. 3. Education – England – History. I. Title.
II. Series.
LC156.G72E58 1989 88–34697 CIP
374′.942 – dc19

ISBN 0 521 33466 7 hardback
ISBN 0 521 45771 8 paperback

Transferred to digital printing 1999

For Charlotte

CONTENTS

List of figures and tables   *page* ix
Preface   xi

1 Introduction   1

2 Family   21
   Family literacy   22
   The status of literacy   29
   The post   32
   Conclusion   49

3 Education   53
   The domestic curriculum   54
   Becoming literate   66
   Official schooling   73
   Conclusion   92

4 Work   95
   Occupational literacy   96
   Occupational learning   104
   Occupational recruitment   119
   Labour relations   134
   Conclusion   153

5 The natural world   156
   Knowledge   159
   Authority   171
   Time   180
   Conclusion   193

6 Imagination   196
   Transition   197
   Commercialisation   210

Conclusion   226

7 Politics   228
   The State   229
   The press   241
   The earnest worker   258
   Conclusion   268

8 Literacy and its uses   270

   Appendix A   Marriage register sample   281
   Appendix B   Literacy networks   283

   Notes   286
   Bibliography   328
   Index   356

FIGURES AND TABLES

Figures

2.1	Balance between male and female literacy rates	25
2.2	Literacy by generation, 1859–1914	27
2.3	Literacy by age, 1839–1914	27
2.4	Social and educational mobility at marriage, 1839–54	31

Tables

2.1	Highest and lowest per capita postal deliveries, 1863	40
2.2	European postal flows and comparative development in 1890	47
4.1	Occupational literacy of grooms, 1839–1914	97
4.2	Occupational literacy in industrial districts, 1754–1914	98
4.3	Literacy of brides by occupation of father, 1839–1914	102
4.4	Literacy of grooms by occupation, of sons by occupation of father, of daughters by occupation of father, 1839–1914	102
4.5	Occupational literacy by groom and bride's father for selected districts, 1839–1914	103
4.6	Social mobility, groom's father to groom, 1839–1914	129
4.7	Social mobility, groom at same, higher or lower class than father, by period	129
4.8	Literacy and mobility of sons of working-class fathers, 1839–1914	130
4.9	Literacy and mobility of sons of unskilled labourers and miners, 1839–1914	131
4.10	Destinations of upwardly mobile sons of working-class fathers	133

PREFACE

This book is based on the premise that the consequences of the coming of mass literacy in England must be sought in the diverse areas of activity in which the skills of reading and writing were practised. It is argued that the often discrete categories of education, family, work, popular beliefs, the imagination and politics must be studied together, and that statistical data should be integrated with the many forms of literary evidence. As is ever the case, such objectives are easier to prescribe than implement. The research has taken me into unfamiliar areas of material and analysis, and for this reason I have been more than usually dependent on the advice and assistance of colleagues and friends at Keele and elsewhere.

I was helped in the construction of the sample of marriage registers and the use of computer facilities at Keele and the University of Manchester Regional Computer Centre by Alan Branthwaite, Paul Collis and David Sherwood. Alice Belcher, Peter Belcher, Nesta Evans and Charlotte Vincent shared with me the often agreeable task of visiting record offices and parish vestries in different parts of the country to abstract entries from the registers. The coding of over 30,000 occupations was undertaken by Michael Pearson Smith. This section of the research was supported by a grant from the Nuffield Foundation.

I greatly benefited from discussions of various aspects of the work with John Briggs, Bob Bushaway, Marjorie Cruikshank, Patrick Joyce, Miles Kitchener, Andrew Miles, David Mitch, Robert Poole, Roger Schofield, John Sloboda, Charles Swann, Joan Vincent, Richard Wall, Bob Woods and Chris Wrigley. I am particularly grateful to Gill Sutherland for the care with which she read the complete text. Margaret and Peter Spufford once more provided hospitality and encouragement. Johanna Reilly relieved the burden of typing the chapters. My wife began this book with me as we went out in search of signatures and marks, and at the end was there to correct my own illiteracy as I wrote up the findings. And finally my best thanks to Anna, Rebecca and Michael Vincent, whose first encounters with reading and writing have taught me more about this subject than all the reading and writing I have done myself.

1

INTRODUCTION

Joseph Mayett was born in 1783, one of ten children of a farm labourer in the vale of Aylesbury. The poverty of his family caused him to spend his childhood making lace rather than attending school:

> however notwithstanding this my mother being able to read and write a little though in some instance hardly legible yet she taught me to read at a very early age I cannot Remember learning the Alphabate but when I was four years of age or there about my Godmother presented me with a new book it was the reading made easy it had many pictures in it which I Remember I was much delighted with this takeing my attention there was nothing suited so well as my book and by this means I was sone able to read it without spelling . . .[1]

He received further assistance from his grandmother, and from a Sunday school, where he made progress in 'Learning hard names'; and in his early twenties, whilst serving in the Royal Bucks. Militia against Napoleon, he persuaded a fellow soldier to teach him to write, so that he could correspond with his parents. Over the century and a half covered by this study, Mayett's laborious acquisition of the skills of literacy became an increasingly common experience in English popular culture. In the middle of the eighteenth century, three hundred years after the invention of printing, half the English population could not write.[2] By 1914, over 99 per cent of brides and grooms had gained sufficient command over the technology of communication at least to sign the marriage register.[3] England, together with a handful of advanced Western countries, had for the first time in history achieved a literate society. This book seeks to understand how and why literacy spread into every interstice of English society, and what impact it had on the lives and minds of the common people.

Literacy in history presents a more than usually difficult problem of perspective. At one level the nineteenth-century drive to mass literacy could amount to little more than groups of ill-clothed, ill-disciplined children gabbling through incomprehensible paragraphs in the Bible or

sterile vocabularies in primers before the demands of their family economies thrust them into a labour market largely indifferent to their barely
grasped skills. At the same time we are dealing with a practice which, at
least since the twin events of the Reformation and Counter-Reformation,
has been seen as ever more central to the salvation or advancement of man
and society. As Furet and Ozouf discovered when they traced the spread
of reading and writing in France, it is virtually impossible for even the
most dispassionate account to avoid the language of growth and success.[4]
Literacy became a consequence, a cause, a guarantor, and eventually the
very epitome of progress.

Today the transition from orality to literacy is attracting increasing
attention from scholars in a wide range of disciplines. The most recent
survey of the literature claims that 'More than any other single invention,
writing has transformed human consciousness.'[5] It is argued that in the
ancient world, the dichotomy between 'primitive' and 'advanced' countries can best be explained in terms of the discovery of writing.[6] The
invention of printing in the fifteenth century has been identified with the
emergence of the spirit of innovation and individualism in Western
Europe.[7] The more recent arrival of the electronic media has served only
to intensify the concern with the relationship over time between the
technology and content of communication.[8] In more practical terms,
around a hundred countries have launched mass literacy campaigns which
have reduced the world illiteracy level from 44 per cent to 29 per cent in
three decades.[9] 'The right of all to education' is now considered 'an
integral part of human rights as a whole'.[10] In decolonisation struggles,
literacy and liberation have gone hand in hand, if only because, as
Guinea-Bissau reported to Unesco, 'proficiency in reading arithmetic was
seen during the war of liberation as a condition for using some of the more
sophisticated weapons'.[11] Amongst those countries thought to have con-
quered reading and writing generations ago, successive economic crises
have forced attention on the attainments of the workforce, and led to the
discovery of 'functional illiteracy' and to demands for reform and
extension of the system of elementary and adult education.[12]

The distance between ambition and performance was never greater than
in the industrialising countries of the eighteenth and nineteenth centuries.
Any historian of literacy is faced with a yawning gap between the hopes of
the educators and the experience of the educated. A number of recent
studies, in particular Harvey Graff's work on North America,[13] have
successfully demolished many of the claims made on behalf of reading and
writing by those bent on civilising the labouring poor. Yet the subject
cannot be confined to the category of myths or false ideologies. The way in
which individuals communicate with each other, the means by which they
acquire and transmit bodies of knowledge, skill, imagination and belief, lie

at the heart of their culture. The spread of literacy raised a series of major questions about how the common people thought about their world, and how they performed in it. If the transformation of their mental outlook was less immediate and dramatic than the reformers had hoped, there were in the end few areas of popular culture left untouched by the shift from restricted to full literacy which had taken place by 1914.

The scope of this study is defined in the first instance by the availability of the principal source of statistical evidence, the marriage registers of the Church of England. Prior to the middle of the eighteenth century, there exists no single long-term set of data for any country except Sweden,[14] and levels of literacy can only be established by means of educated guesses based on an assortment of wills, depositions and other documents. However, in an effort to correct abuses which had crept into the system, Hardwick's Marriage Act of 1754 established that no wedding would be valid unless it was entered in the parish register and signed with a signature or a mark by the bride and groom and two witnesses. Henceforth there was created an orderly body of evidence on the distribution of basic literacy skills in every parish in the country. Until the Registration of Births, Deaths and Marriages Act of 1836 the data were collected locally, but thereafter the system became the responsibility of the Registrar General, who published aggregate literacy tables in his annual reports. The period up to 1839 has been the subject of a major research project by Roger Schofield, who has established the general movement of literacy levels, and the more important social and economic factors which lay behind them.[15] Little systematic analysis of the registers for the remainder of the century has yet been made,[16] and for this study the evidence of the Registrar General's reports has been supplemented by a sample of 10,000 marriages taken from ten registration districts in different parts of the country between 1839 and 1914.[17] This has made possible a closer examination of the forces which wiped out illiteracy levels of 33 per cent for grooms and 49 per cent for brides in no more than three generations.

All the analysis of the marriage registers suggests that the single most important correlation was between literacy and occupation. More than any other factor, how the child's father earned a living determined its chances of learning to read and write. In broader terms, the achievement of full literacy has been a characteristic goal of every society undergoing an industrial revolution, and recently much attention has been focused on what is claimed to be the key role played by literacy in the loosely defined process of 'modernisation' in the developing countries. The connection between literacy and work will be the subject of a separate chapter, but the broader question of the relationship between the technology of communication and the economic and social upheavals of the Industrial Revolution will inform the entire study, and for this reason the middle of the eighteenth century, which saw the first signs of the transformation in modes of production, is an appropriate point of departure.

The outbreak of the First World War is an obvious destination. England managed to ensure that all its young men could read and write just in time to send them to their deaths in the trenches. The official illiteracy level first dropped below 1 per cent in the last full year of peace,[18] although, as we shall see, there remained a gap between the attainments of the marriage cohort and those of the population as a whole. And whilst the uses of reading and writing have continued to multiply throughout the twentieth century, it was in the first two decades, at the very moment of its triumph, that literacy began to be challenged by radically new forms of mass communication. Whilst almost all the competition to the printed word still came from traditional oral sources of knowledge and imagination, by 1914 the important innovations in cinema and radio had already been made. Today the average English child spends twenty-five hours a week watching television, exactly the same length of time that it attends lessons at school.[19]

The concern here is with England and not with the remainder of the United Kingdom.[20] The evolving relationship between the cultural traditions of the nations of the Union still awaits a proper examination, but in this context the fact that England alone possessed only one language is sufficient to confine us to its borders. Elsewhere in Great Britain and Ireland, as in much of Europe and North America, the spread of literacy was intimately connected to the struggle for supremacy of competing tongues, which in turn raised major questions of national identity.[21] England itself, however, was as much divided as united by its common language, and later chapters will examine the part played by reading and writing, especially as taught by schools, in the conflict between regional and class-based codes of communication.

Elsewhere, the limits of this book are less easy to establish. Culture is here taken to refer to what Clifford Geertz has described as 'the informal logic of actual life',[22] the patterns of meaning which make sense of experience, and the artefacts and practices in which they are embodied. Literacy plays a dual role in the evolution of culture. As a mechanical skill it is a means by which thought is generated, stored and transmitted, and at the same time it is a crucial element in the system of values by which social groups define themselves or are subject to definition by those in power over them.[23] Thus the growing abandonment of 'popular' by 'polite' culture throughout early modern Europe, which has been charted by Peter Burke,[24] was founded on the assumption that the common people could make little or no use of the printed word. Their subordination was both caused and measured by their relation to reading and writing. In turn the arrival of mass literacy, which is the concern of this study, embodied a two-fold challenge to the identity of popular culture. The increasingly widespread employment of the new modes of communication threatened the structures of authority which kept the cultures apart, whilst the meanings attached to literacy itself, and to associated concepts such as learning, rationality, science and literature, were at the heart of the debate about the boundaries between the cultures.

The task of assessing the impact of literacy on popular culture over time appears at first sight to possess one major advantage. In contrast to the notion of culture, literacy would seem to be an uncontentious term. Indeed it may be argued that one reason why its promotion became the object of so much public investment and private demand during the Industrial Revolution was precisely that it was so easy to recognise and measure. Year after year the Registrar General's reports seemed to provide an exact statement of the success of the schools, and, by extension, of social progress in general; and parents could see in their children's increasing ability to read and write a direct return for expendi- ture on education or the reduction in family income.

However, as soon as we move from possession to use, difficulties arise. The problem of perspective which lies at the heart of the topic stems from the absence of any accepted criteria for measuring the power of literacy. The strength of the steam engine, with which this technology of communi- cation was so often compared, could be objectively calibrated. But the horsepower of the schoolmaster, the consequences of his labour for the community which supported him, was and has remained a matter of intense debate.

The accumulation of research in recent years has done little to resolve the confusion. Too often literacy has been the battlefield rather than the meeting place between the wide range of disciplines which now have an interest in the subject. Psychologists and sociologists, historians and economists have introduced a variety of methods and concepts which those who argued over the issue in past centuries could never have anticipated. The language of 'psychic gaps' and 'mass modernity', 'human capital' and 'generalised cognitive transformations' belongs very much to the twentieth century. It is, however, possible to detect a certain pattern in the competing claims of modern scholars which bears a more than passing resemblance to the range of hopes and expectations of those who first attempted to democratise the capacity to read and write.

Throughout the period of this study, the vocabulary of aspiration was derived directly or indirectly from the Church. The earliest theories of the uses of literacy were formulated in response to the danger of heresy or disbelief. We owe the term 'oral tradition', the notion that the character of a whole structure of thought could be determined by the role of the written word, to the seventeenth-century puritan Bishop Joseph Hall. He argued that the strength of 'Romish Traditions' which still flourished outside educated society was derived from their means of transmission. Where Anglicanism was taught and defended by the Bible, Catholicism relied upon the spoken word: 'As for orall Traditions, what certaintie can there be in them? What foundation of truth can be layed upon the breath of man? How doe they multiply in their passage, and either grow, or dye upon the breath of man?'[25] At the centre of the discovery of popular culture a century later lay the same axis between religion and literacy. John Brand's edition of Bourne's *Antiquitates Vulgares*, which was the foundation text of the folklore movement in England, began with the assumption that 'Few, who are desirous of investigating the popular Notions and vulgar Ceremonies in our Nation, can fail of deducing in them in their first Direction from the Times when Popery was our established Religion.'[26] The ability of Catholicism to survive the Reformation was explained by the immunity of the culture of the 'Common People' to the transforming power of print; superstitious beliefs and practices, 'consecrated to the Fancies of Men, by a Usage from Time immemorial, though erazed by public Authority from the *written Word*, were committed as a venerable Deposit to the keeping of *oral Tradition*'.[27] Form and content could not be divorced. The two cultures owed their separate identities to their respective modes of communication.

By the end of the eighteenth century, revolution was replacing Rome as the chief enemy of the established order. Whereas the charity school system had been founded to reinforce the authority of the Church of England, Sarah Trimmer could now claim that in the face of the threat of France, 'no less than the safety of the nation probably depends upon the education of those children who are now growing up to maturity'.[28] Increasingly the weapons of the Enlightenment were employed to counteract its influence. As in the United States, Evangelical Protestantism and new theories of social development combined to create a powerful ideology of literacy.[29] Within the primers and teaching manuals there was a gradual shift to more secular forms of knowledge and morality, and at least some of the newly equipped readers used their skills to emancipate their minds from the claims of both religion and the capitalist order. Yet embedded in the ideology was the constant assumption that literacy would have a profound impact on the mental and moral character of the individual and by extension of his society. Thus, for instance, Sir James Kay-Shuttleworth, the leading educational administrator of the middle third of the nineteenth century, conceived the purpose of the Government's reforms as the provision of an education 'calculated to develope the entire moral and intellectual capacity of the whole nation'.[30] For their part, those who employed their education to set down an account of their lives write of their first encounter with 'book knowledge' in terms which amount to a secularised conversion experience. 'It was in every sense a new light to me', recalled the weaver Ben Brierley; for the shepherd Robert Story, 'the effect on my mind was magical'; and when the cabinet maker Henry Price discovered the world of literature, 'my eyes were opend it seemd for the first time in my life'.[31]

In the face of such expectations, it was a brave man who questioned the claims which were made on behalf of literacy and the institutions which promoted it. As early as the 1720s we find Bernard Mandeville complaining of the new Charity Schools that 'The generality are so bewitched with the Usefulness and Excellencey of them, that whoever dares openly oppose them is in danger of being Stoned by the Rabble.'[32] Yet he had a case to make. It was not only that, as so many teachers were later to discover, 'such as are so Ungovernable, that neither Words nor Blows can work upon them, no Charity School will mend'.[33] Nor was his critique confined to his well-known fears about the implications of education for the provision of a deferential labour force. His fundamental argument was that far too much was coming to be expected of the acquisition of literacy. It was not schooling, but the 'Precept and the Example of Parents, and those they Eat Drink and Converse with, that have an influence upon the Minds of Children',[34] and as for the central relationship between literacy and the Church, 'those who complain ... that they cannot imbue their Parishioners with sufficient Knowledge of what they stand in need of as Christians, without the assistance of Reading and Writing, are either very lazy or very Ignorant and Undeserving themselves'.[35]

The fears and hopes generated by the French and Industrial Revolutions eventually overwhelmed such doubts, but as the elementary education system began to consume an ever larger proportion of the State's resources, new dissenting voices began to be heard. The catalyst of the debate was the Revised Code of 1862, which in its crude attempt to ensure that the Government received value for money stimulated a wide-ranging debate about the relationship between the basic skills of literacy and the wider structures of knowledge and morality within the working-class community. Although they reached some of Mandeville's conclusions, the more thoughtful critics were now looking forward to the development of modern child psychology. In a paper delivered to the National Association for the Promotion of Social Science in 1867, the educationalist W. B. Hodgson launched a sweeping attack on the orthodox view of the learning process:

> The radical fallacy is in supposing that no knowledge or improvement is obtainable except from books, and the result is a

confounding of means with ends. A child is a living, restless, never ceasing interrogator, 'perpetually wanting to know, you know', perpetually asking, What? and how? and when? and where? and above all (as I have observed with some surprise) why? perpetually putting all around it 'to the question'.[36]

In this activity literacy played only a limited role. Reading and writing, he argued, 'are no more knowledge or education . . . than a knife, fork and plate constitute a dinner'.[37] Such skills were at best 'mechanical means', 'tools for gaining knowledge; they are not crop, but plough and harrow'.[38]

Set in its historical context, the scope of the debate among contemporary observers becomes more comprehensible. It is easier to associate literacy with progress than progress with the study of literacy. As one recent survey concluded, 'Despite a vast amount of study since the end of the nineteenth century, reading and literacy are still very confused research areas.'[39] The claims made on behalf of these skills continue to range between the extremes of ambition and caution.

The tendency to attribute transformative powers to literacy has been most notable in studies of developing nations, where mass education programmes have been taking place. In the first of these, completed by Stalin as part of collectivisation, A. R. Luria found that 'only a year or two of schooling' produced a fundamental reorganisation of cognitive activity amongst hitherto illiterate peasants.[40] More recently, reading and writing have been placed at the centre of the creation of 'modern man', whose attitudes, values and behaviour have been counterposed to the passive, isolated, fearful, inward-looking 'traditional man', whose horizons are confined by his continuing dependence on oral means of acquiring and transmitting information.[41] The technology of communication becomes not just a characteristic but the very engine of change. As Daniel Lerner put it in his influential study, 'Literacy is the basic personal skill that underlies the whole modernising sequence.'[42] Most recently, Emmanuel Todd has concluded that 'Literacy – associated with a rise in age at marriage – may be considered the central element in any region's or any nation's attainment of modernity.'[43] Those particularly concerned with industrialisation have sought to establish a literacy threshold, below which economic take-off cannot take place.[44] The disciplines of anthropology and psychology have come together to put forward a series of generalisations about the way in which the acquisition and employment of these skills promote new ways of classifying, reasoning and remembering, transforming the thought processes of the individual, and by extension, of his culture. Whether they attempt to explain the present or the past, these theories rest on a basic dichotomy between 'oral' and 'written' cultures, which can be located in every society in which the victory of print is incomplete. The encounter with books produced a fundamental change in the mind of the reader, who undertakes a one-way journey to a rational, purposive, participatory way of life. From being God's chosen instrument, literacy comes close to replacing the role of religion altogether. We are presented with a new form of spiritual conversion, as profound and irreversible as any described by those who found salvation through reading the Bible.

Reaction to this approach embraces both the conceptual framework and the methodology of the study of the connections between literacy and culture. In the midst of increasing doubts about the substance of notions of social progress inherited from Victorian liberals and Marxists, it is tempting to dismiss out of hand the claims made for literacy within both bodies of thought. If individuals and cultures display no general pattern of advancement, whether unilinear or dialectical, the function of reading and writing may be both slight and inconsistent. Studies of the subject have been attacked for their failure to establish a convincing measure for the changes which are said to take place. In practice it has proved extremely difficult to set up a satisfactory relationship between theory and evidence in this field. As Scribner and Cole discovered, 'It is striking that the scholars who offer these claims for specific changes in psychological processes present no direct evidence that individuals in literate societies do, in fact, process information about the world differently from those in societies without literacy. They simply make assumptions about changed modes of thinking in the individual as the mediating mechanism for the linguistic and cultural changes which are the object of their inquiry.'[45] The challenge is to find a means of interrogating these assumptions without losing sight of the scale and complexity of the processes which they seek to explain. On the one hand there is a proper mistrust of what one hostile critic has termed 'the wide-sweeping pseudo-sociological generalisations of the mass-culture theorists'.[46] On the other there is, at the very least, the testimony of those who have directly experienced the spread of literacy, either in the previous century or in our own times. There is a substance about their accounts of the impact of reading and writing which cannot be discounted by attributing false consciousness to them, or inadequate scholarship to outside observers. What is required is a way of understanding the power of literacy in its specific historical context which will permit a cautious appraisal of the body of claims and counter-claims which now surround the issue.

The way forward is to go back to the critique which began to be mounted in the heyday of Victorian confidence about the consequences of mass education. As he sought to restore a sense of proportion to the subject, W. B. Hodgson turned to agriculture rather than industry for a metaphor.

Reading and writing were not the 'crop' but the 'plough and harrow'. His insistence that literacy should be regarded essentially as a simple tool anticipated much of the more successful recent research. It is an approach which throws into sharp relief the characteristics of the skills with which this study is concerned.

In the first instance, as Hodgson himself recognised, literacy is a double- rather than a single-edged tool. The relationship between reading and writing is far from constant either over time or between cultures. Differing levels of possession and application are determined by a number of factors, including methods of education, availability of raw materials, and the perceived value of each skill. Reading has traditionally taken precedence over writing partly because it is technically easier to learn, and certainly easier to teach in a situation where time and resources are at a minimum. A labourer's home was much more likely to possess reading matter, even if it was no more than an old handbill or a fragment of newspaper, than writing materials, although the determined child or autodidact could always improvise, with chalk replacing pen and ink, and the wall of a barn a sheet of paper. The early schools taught reading first, and it has been calculated that in the seventeenth century, a child of average ability would have mastered that skill by the age of seven and would only learn to write if it stayed at school for a further year.[47] In the charity schools writing took a back seat, and it was not until the arrival of the monitorial system of Bell and Lancaster in the early decades of the nineteenth century that teaching manuals began to recommend that the two skills be taught simultaneously.[48] The evidence presented to the Newcastle Commission would suggest that the Church schools were slow to respond to this initiative, and the private day and Sunday schools slower still. However, the gap was closing. Webb has calculated that during the first half of the century, the ratio between those who could read and those who could also write ranged from three to two to two to one,[49] but the records of the examinations conducted under the Revised Code from 1862 indicate that almost all children who gained some proficiency in reading could also attain what were considered to be comparable standards in writing.[50]

The changing emphasis owed much, as we shall see in chapter 3, to an altered conception of the functions of each skill, with writing in particular undergoing a major revaluation. As the two processes were brought together and linked with the third 'R', arithmetic, there was a danger of losing sight of the very different roles reading and writing play in the development and exercise of the individual's capacity to acquire and generate knowledge. Yet the slow convergence should also warn us against accepting the absolute dichotomy between the impact of the skills that Furet and Ozouf insist upon in the context of

France, where reading continued to be taught before and apart from writing.[51]

Arithmetic, the final member of the triumvirate which came to dominate English elementary education in the nineteenth century, will not be discussed here. This is a matter of some regret, for not only is the spread of numeracy itself a matter of great interest, but also the significance of the first two 'R's was partly contained in their relationship to the third. However, both the causes and consequences of the teaching of arithmetic raise too many issues to be coped with here, and must await a separate and much-needed history.[52]

As a tool, literacy was a form of pre-industrial technology. The spread of reading and writing was so closely bound up with the economic and social transformation of the Industrial Revolution that it is easy to lose sight of the antiquity of the practices concerned. The codification of language and the development of the skills of written communication are as old as civilisation itself. The major innovation in book production took place in the late fifteenth century, and little changed in the printing industry for three hundred years. Despite a series of innovations during the nineteenth century, commencing with Stanhope's iron press in 1800 and the introduction of steam power at *The Times* in 1814, printers successfully resisted attempts to undermine their handicraft traditions.[53] The transformation in the availability of the printed word which began during the early decades of our period owed more to a revolution in demand than supply. By the 1790s, the publication of new book titles was running at four times the level of the beginning of the century, and during the first half of the nineteenth century it was to increase by a further 600 per cent to reach 2,500 a year by 1853.[54] Steam power played its part in expanding the centres of population in which the literature was to be read, and in the production and distribution of newspapers, but the making of books still relied on techniques which Caxton would have recognised, with the advanced scientific developments largely confined to ancillary matters such as the reproduction of illustrations. The relationship between industrialisation and the possession and use of literacy was complex, with the impact of the factory system mediated by a range of institutional and intellectual processes which will be discussed in later chapters. But at the outset it is necessary to recognise that we are dealing with a hand tool, which has more in common with the scythe or the cobbler's awl than with the spinning jenny or the blast furnace.

The tool was not only old in itself, but its presence in the world of labour long pre-dated the Industrial Revolution. Studies of Consistory Court depositions have established that by the end of the sixteenth century more than half the tradesmen and craftsmen could sign their names,[55] and in Stuart England around 15 per cent of the least literate section of the male population, the common labourers, displayed an ability to write and therefore to read as well.[56] By the third quarter of the eighteenth century, the threshold of the period covered by this study, at least one labourer and servant in three could sign the marriage register.[57] If these proportions are translated into absolute numbers, and account is taken of those who could read but not write,[58] the extent and vitality of the seventeenth-century almanac and chapbook trade becomes easier to understand. In the pre-industrial society there may well have been as many labourers as traders and shopkeepers who were capable of entertaining and instructing themselves through the medium of the printed word.

Amidst the story-telling and the folk-songs, alongside the customs and rituals, reading and writing had entered the fabric of popular culture.[59] Outside the towns, the literate were a small minority in any community, but always they could be found. The 1642 Protestant Return revealed that even in the most backward parishes, there were at least a handful of men who could sign their names.[60] Everywhere there were parents prepared to buy an education for their sons or provide one themselves. Schools and teachers were becoming more numerous, and the dense network of chapmen ensured a constant supply of cheap literature.[61] Whilst most men and virtually all women continued to rely on traditional means of communication in their daily lives, they lived and worked alongside those who had access to wider bodies of knowledge and imagination.[62] The literate blacksmith or miller, the occasional farm worker who was known to be a reader, formed a bridge between the worlds of the educated and the uneducated. The connection was reinforced by the new translations of the Bible and Prayer Book which caused the most unlettered of labourers to make some contact with the language and concepts of polite discourse.

The long history of reading and writing in the towns and villages of pre-industrial England meant that the impact of mass literacy in the nine-teenth century was a great deal more subtle than appeared to many contemporary observers. The folklore movement, for instance, was founded on the assumption that until the invasion of the railway and the board school, there survived, as Cecil Sharp put it, a 'common people . . . whose mental development has been due not to any formal system of training or education, but solely to environment, communal association, and direct contact with the ups and downs of life'.[63] English missionaries arriving in New Zealand in 1815 found a totally unlettered population, who lacked even their own written language,[64] but back home, such enclosed communities, if ever they had existed, had long since disap-peared. The undefiled oral culture was a victim not of the steam engine but the Reformation.[65] Whilst it is important to retain the distinction between oral and written means of creating and transmitting ideas and informa-tion, in practice the two modes of communication had been an active presence in the mental universe of the labouring poor for generations before the period of this study.[66] The literate and non-literate, and their respective structures and artefacts, had already formed a complex series of conflicting and mutually reinforcing relationships. The process of change was consequently uneven both in pace and direction. The educational reformers had some cause to place themselves in the vanguard of modernisation, to view literacy as the cutting edge of the drive against pre-industrial modes of thought and behaviour, but equally there were ways in which literary forms could act as a means of carrying into the new society older traditions and belief systems. Print could both accelerate and retard progress, simplify and intensify the long-established heterogeneity of popular culture.

All tools are by definition artificial. In mental, as in physical labour, a range of cultural and material factors determined whether, when and how the individual gained control over the implements which were needed. No matter how humble its background, how confined its prospects, every child had to acquire an intricate range of skills which were deeply influenced by their position in the continuing process of learning and living. In this sense, reading and writing increasingly stood apart both from the other main tool of communication, speech, and from the range of occupational and domestic techniques which the children of the labouring poor had to absorb as they grew up.

The first known primer, *The ABC Both in Latyn & English*, was published within half a century of the introduction of printing,[67] and by the middle of the eighteenth century a wide range of aids to learning were available to those engaged in the transmission of basic literacy. A central theme of chapter 3 will be the rapid growth in the market for alphabets, grammars, spelling books and school manuals as the theory and practice of instruction became increasingly elaborate. By contrast, throughout the period studied, little guidance was offered to parents as they faced the inescapable task of teaching their children to speak. Learning to talk was assumed to be as natural as learning to walk. The subject only became a matter of pedagogic concern when defects in vocabulary and especially in pronunciation were thought to endanger the work of the schoolmaster.

It is now accepted that the young child develops and employs sophisticated cognitive skills as it extends its powers of communication from simple words to what is likely to be a wide range of sentence structures by the time it reaches school age.[68] Inside the classroom, advancing language competence in oral and advancing language competence in written forms interact with each other throughout the child's education. Given that language training commences as soon as a parent first speaks to a baby, and that reading and writing demand a specialised ability to respond to the abstract qualities of symbolic representation, it will always be more difficult to appreciate the quality of intellectual activity which takes place as a child begins to talk. However, whereas recent educational theory has tended to emphasise the complementary nature of the cognitive processes involved in acquiring command over the two forms of communication, the increasing professionalisation of teaching literacy in the eighteenth and nineteenth centuries led in the opposite direction. As parents and private adventure schools were denied a role in elementary education, so the notions of 'learning' and 'knowledge' became the prerogative of the classroom. A child who could participate in the speech community of its neighbourhood but who could not read was considered 'ignorant' and such faculties as it could display were likely to be written off as 'vices' which the schoolmaster was charged to eradicate. Reading and writing were abstracted from and opposed to the training which had taken place in the home.

A similar divergence occurred in relation to the pattern of learning which every working man underwent in his occupation. Even the most 'unskilled' of labourers had to acquire particular habits and attitudes and a substantial body of information about the customs and operation of his trade, together with varying degrees of manual dexterity. Whether it was a matter of progressing from bird-scaring to walking at the plough tail, or of advancing from marking-up a piece of wood to making a complete piece of furniture, the education continued throughout much of childhood and adolescence. The essence of the training had always been its integration with practice. Inside or outside the institution of apprenticeship, the tools of the trade were mastered as they were used. Whilst the stages of the education might be celebrated by long-established rituals, the skilled artisan took pride in his inability ever to finish it. 'It is a business that is never learned', explained one millwright; 'it requires a long servitude; a man can never come near to perfection.'[69]

Despite the removal of protective legislation, and ever more intense pressure from the factory system, existing methods of acquiring occupational knowledge remained remarkably resilient throughout the period.[70] Within the child's world of learning, the major change took place in the comparative status of modes of training which had less and less in common with each other. In relation to the other tools required for participation in the affairs of the community, reading and writing were comparatively simple skills, yet it was the transmission of literacy which became the object of elaborate theory from the late eighteenth century onwards, whilst the transmission of occupational techniques remained largely a matter of custom and practice. Whereas perhaps only one or two men in a community could instruct a boy in the art of thatching or shoeing a horse, many parents or neighbours could manage to teach a child its letters, yet reading and writing became the only skills which had to be acquired in a specialised building from a specialised teacher. With few exceptions, occupational training remained embedded in productive activity, whilst literary training was increasingly isolated from its influence. Alone of the tools a child would need, reading and writing were to be gained away from the company of adults and apart from every other process of daily life.

The degree of artificiality attached to the separate tools raised important questions about their function in popular culture. In predominantly oral conditions, the means of communication were acquired as an integral element of the general pattern of socialisation. Every child learned to speak and to understand the speech of others; few were conscious of doing so. Problems of exclusion only arose in the case of competing languages or dialects. But the democratisation of access to the hitherto restricted technology of written communication had the effect of creating new lines of demarcation, which were a consequence less of the intrinsic characteristics of reading and writing and more of the historically specific set of material and social relations within which these skills were mastered and employed. The process of achieving mass literacy widened the gulf between childhood and adulthood, and gave a modern form to dichotomies between education and training, ignorance and knowledge, intelligence and skill, and above all between mental and manual labour.

The utility of any tool depends on its state of repair. If it is ill made or ill maintained, it may be as much a liability as an asset to its owner. In this sense, reading and writing could be the sharpest or bluntest of instruments; they could gleam with constant use or lie rusted through prolonged neglect. There was little in common between the bridegroom nervously wielding a pen for perhaps the first and last time in his life and the self-taught artisan obsessively reading and writing in every spare minute of his time, and still less between the eighteenth-century blacksmith laboriously preparing a customer's account and the twentieth-century unemployed steelworker coping with the intricacies of a Supplementary Benefits form. Divisions can be imposed, but in reality command over the skills of literacy varies infinitely from individual to individual, within and between societies.

In response to this difficulty, the concept of functional literacy has gained increasing currency since the Second World War. A person cannot be considered literate, Unesco decided in 1956, until he 'has acquired the knowledge and skills in reading and writing which enable him to engage effectively in all those activities in which literacy is normally assumed in his culture or group'.[71] The essence of the definition is the notion of participation. In Unesco's work in the underdeveloped world, this meant engagement in productive activity, but recently the emphasis has broadened to embrace all forms of human endeavour.[72] The strength of this approach is its recognition that levels of literacy only acquire meaning in relation to the demands of the society in which the individual lives. At every point, questions must be asked about the needs and aspirations of those who have learned to read and write, and about the relevance of their skills to prevailing economic and political structures. The concept is essentially historical; it implies that little can be gained by considering the statistics of literacy in isolation from their context.[73]

Yet the problem of measurement remains. If it draws attention to the relativity of reading and writing, the notion of functional literacy greatly complicates the task of specifying change over time. Like its sister concept, relative deprivation, it suffers from the basic paradox that improvements in standards automatically depress levels of possession. Every rise in welfare benefits enlarges the population in poverty; every advance in the use of literacy increases the numbers defined as illiterate. Thus, taken at face value, official statistics indicate that seventy years of educational endeavour since 1914 have left at least two million adults unable to read or write adequately.[74] In the United States 90 per cent of the population was deemed literate in 1860, but in 1975 research revealed that 15 per cent of adults 'lacked the competencies necessary to function in society'.[75] The danger is that in adjusting the categories in response to change, it becomes impossible to establish the scale of change or sometimes even its direction. The most thorough study of the acquisition of literacy in Britain since the Second World War, the Bullock Report of 1975, failed to reach a definite verdict on the basic issue of progress or regress because the evolution of standards frustrated the creation of a 'firm statistical base for comparison'.[76]

It is therefore necessary to turn back to older and cruder definitions of literacy. During the period under review, there were occasional attempts to measure degrees of competence and use. Surveys were made of the possession of books in the 1830s and 1840s, but these recognised that although ownership was surprisingly widespread, literature was more often inherited than bought, and more often neglected than read.[77] Statistics of school attendance were notoriously unreliable in themselves, and bore no necessary relationship to literacy levels. From 1836 onwards, records were kept of standards of literacy amongst the prison population, but their value was undermined by a lack of rigour in the collection and categorisation of data.[78] The examinations conducted under the Revised Code provided more reliable evidence of variations in attainment during the last third of the nineteenth century, but even here several revisions of criteria complicated their analysis. Thus we are left with signatures on marriage registers, which on the face of it could scarcely tell us less about function and context.

The limitations of this category of source material have been well rehearsed.[79] It offers no direct evidence of an ability to read, and the capacity to inscribe two words on just one occasion in an individual's life provides the slightest possible indication of command over the skills of writing. However, when set against alternative forms of measurement, the registers can be seen to possess a number of abiding virtues. Firstly, they are unique in providing a standardised body of evidence over the whole of the period, for the whole of the country, and for every level of society, although the introduction of civil registration in 1837 caused problems of coverage which are discussed at greater length in appendix A. They also permit comparison between countries over time, in spite of variations in the forms of marriage. The only other measure of international development is statistics of postal flows, which began to be kept on a systematic basis with the formation of the Universal Postal Union in 1875.[80] Unlike signatures, letter writing is a clear reflection of the employment of literacy, and I will make use of British and European evidence later.

Secondly, the registers are at least an objective test. Many contemporary studies, and also the North American censuses which recorded literacy,[81] relied on unverified self-assessment by the subject. There was some concern that the pressures surrounding the marriage ceremony might cause a literate bride or groom to make a mark out of nervousness, or out of fear of embarrassing an illiterate spouse.[82] At most the uncertainty would lead to a slight under-representation of literacy levels, but the Registrars General did not think the problem serious,[83] and the frequency of literate/illiterate marriages (discussed below in chapter 2) suggests that the issue of embarrassment was not as acute as observers sometimes assumed. Thirdly, if the registers lack the wealth of detail to be found in the census, the requirement to give information on age, occupation, marital status and residence does permit analysis of some of the more important determinants of literacy.[84]

Finally there are grounds for arguing that the evidence of the signatures is not quite as limited as at first appears. In spite of the increasing attention paid to the teaching of writing during the nineteenth century, most children learned to read first, and it is probably that the proportion of signatures understates the numbers who could make some minimal use of the printed word. Although there is the possibility that a bride or groom may have acquired the meaningless trick of drawing two words on a special occasion, in practice the quality of writing indicates a more substantial command of the skill. Of the 180 signatures in the register of St Peter's, Stoke-on-Trent in 1839, all of them legible and none of them printed, only 5 per cent were so shaky as to indicate extreme unfamiliarity with a pen.[85] Those who could sign were likely to have gained the basic ability to form letters, which was the summit of a school's ambition until composition was introduced to the sixth standard in 1871, and to have reached this in writing, they would possess at least a limited fluency in reading.[86]

The terms 'literate' and 'illiterate' must therefore be approached at two levels. Despite their manifest shortcomings, there is a real if restricted meaning in the marriage register signatures, and throughout this study the statistical framework will be derived principally from this source. In some cases it was possible that basic and functional literacy coincided. The inscription of a name after the wedding was a use of writing, and for some brides and grooms may have been its first and last employment outside the classroom. But for most of those who laboriously acquired the ability to participate in the world of written communication, the bare figures are an increasingly inadequate guide to the significance of their achievement. It is necessary to integrate the statistics with complementary qualitative evidence.[87] The concept of functional literacy must be introduced not as an alternative form of measurement, but rather as a way of giving meaning to the data which can be quantified. The signatures constitute not the end of this study, but its point of departure.

Hence we return to Hodgson's plough and harrow. Just as the value of an agricultural implement depends on how it is used, on the soil that is tilled and the seed that is sown, so it is with the ancient hand tools of reading and writing. What matters is not possession but practice.[88] The impact of the skills on individuals and their community depends on whether and for what purpose they are employed. If, for lack of incentive or opportunity, tools lie dormant, they will lose their edge. Literacy will not affect the way individuals think unless they use literacy in order to think. It will not alter their identity unless it is seen to have a specific function in the society in which they live. The consequences of the spread of literacy must therefore be sought in the various contexts in which practice might take place and be given meaning. This study will concentrate on the application of reading and writing in six areas. It will begin with the family, within which literacy was gained and first used, and succeeding chapters will consider its place in the classroom, the workplace, the response to the natural world, the imaginative life of the community, and finally in the development of political ideology and movements throughout the period.

Literacy was a tool for communication. It replaced oral forms of learning and oral forms of expression. Each chapter will be concerned with the transition to new ways of acquiring knowledge and new ways of transmitting it. Reading and writing transformed the nature of learning, by providing new means of storing and retrieving the mental product of a culture, and set up a new mode of discourse between communicator and audience. The consequences of the application of this tool were diverse in the extreme, but for the purposes of this study we can isolate three related issues of particular importance.

Firstly there was the problem of coherence. The artificiality of the instrument of literacy was at once its greatest strength and its greatest weakness. Language is by its nature a construction, a symbolic representation of reality, but the written form permits a far higher level of abstraction than the oral. Once knowledge can be stored and thought distanced from its immediate context, analytical inquiry into the present and the past becomes feasible for the first time. The transition from orality to literacy dramatically extended the mental resources of popular culture, but at the same time constantly threatened it with fragmentation. It was no easy matter to integrate inherited bodies of thought and ways of thinking with the limitless possibilities of intellectual exploration proffered by the printed word. Those who mastered the new technology of communication faced a constant struggle to establish a working relationship between book learning and day-to-day experience.

Secondly there was the problem of community. Where the oral tradition depends for its existence on face-to-face contact, reading and writing are essentially solitary activities. A feeling of group membership is naturally reinforced by the preservation and reproduction of information by speech, and is always challenged by the use of literacy. The more intense exploitation of the printed word in English popular culture during the late eighteenth century generated a new level of individual self-awareness which was most strikingly manifested in the emergence of a fertile genre of working-class autobiography.[89] The capacity to distance personality from communal structures and to pay articulate attention to interior development made possible the emergence of a much more objective conception of change. Again the prospects were ambiguous. In one direction lay a heightened consciousness of collective identity and historical purpose, in another the withdrawal of the reader from collective traditions and practices.

The final problem was that of power.[90] Speech is a common possession, whereas print is a species of private property. There are complex structures of authority within the oral tradition, with those who remembered the most claiming precedence over those with the most to learn, but these are informal and are policed by the community. The wider employment of literacy in English popular culture after 1750 closely paralleled the final attack on customary property rights on the land. Cultural resources were mapped out in a pattern of freeholdings as the means of producing and preserving knowledge were subject to legal ownership. Thus the issue of control became increasingly important, with more to lose and more to gain. As forms of capitalism, wide areas of literary discourse remained small scale in this period, and the common people were frequently able to gain possession or influence the possession of others. But as the newly literate sought to exploit the potential of these more powerful tools of expression, so they faced an unprecedented threat to the remaining independence of their ways of thinking and acting.

2

FAMILY

Until the introduction of the Revised Code in 1863, the task of signing the marriage register was the only examination the great majority of the population would ever face. Those who signed displayed both their identity and their independence; those who did not remained anonymous until the register was completed by another hand. As with most examinations, success might be qualified, but failure was absolute. A signature said little about educational standards. Only the gentry and the occasional lawyer drew attention to their learning by the elaboration of their writing; few adopted the twentieth-century conceit of cultivated illegibility. A mark, on the other hand, was evidence of undivided ignorance. To contemporary observers, the tables which the Registrar General began to compile in 1839 split England in two.[1] In every county, and later in every registration district, a precise calculation could be made of the proportion of the population which lay outside the boundary of civilised society. The figures defined the problem and over time displayed its solution. By 1914 England could claim a homogeneous culture.

Yet even at the time, those responsible for compiling the statistics recognised the danger of over-simplification. It was not just that the returns of the individual registration districts revealed an immense range of standards within and between different parts of the country. It was also that the very nature of the event which generated the figures challenged the divisions which at first sight they created. A wedding was a family affair. As individuals a bride or groom could only sign or not sign, but as couples there were four possible combinations of literacy and illiteracy. If the focus was widened to include the two relatives or friends who had to complete the register as witnesses, and then the other relatives in the congregation and the subsequent offspring of the marriage, the range of patterns was virtually unlimited. In response to this problem, tables were published from 1847 onwards displaying the proportion of weddings in which one or both partners made a mark, but little was read into the figures. It may be argued, however, that it is with the weddings, with the families from which the brides and grooms came and with the families which they were now to create, that the study of literacy should begin.

Here we may trace the basic fissures in popular culture created by the distribution of the skills of written communication, and examine some of the ways in which their dissemination and application could open up new lines of connection and demarcation in the social networks within which individuals lived out their lives.

Family literacy

In the sample of registration districts undertaken for this study, literate and illiterate England were almost exactly balanced at the end of the 1830s. During the subsequent seventy-five years, illiteracy fell to 1 per cent, leaving an average for the period of 25 per cent. The immediate impact of setting these aggregate returns in the context of the family is to increase the presence of both literacy and illiteracy. Taking the partners together, literacy was to be found in 85 per cent of marriages, and illiteracy in 36 per cent.[2] As we pursue the increasing presence and use of the tools of literacy in the coming chapters it is essential to realise that those who could sign their names and those who could not, those who were learning their letters and those who were forgetting them, those unable to decipher a shop sign and those at ease with Shakespeare were not strangers to each other. The separate columns in the Registrar General's returns were statistical abstractions. In practice the patterns of educational attainment were more complex and the issues of status and stigma were less stark than a casual glance at the published returns would suggest.

At every point during this period of rapid change, the simple averages are reshaped. If we take, for instance, the first quarter of the period, the sample years 1839–54,[3] a return of 52 per cent literacy means in practice that only just over one marriage in three contained no illiteracy, whereas at least one partner could sign his or her name in almost two families in three. At the other end of the scale, the years from 1899 to 1914, when the overall illiteracy rate was reduced to one in forty, the proportion of marriages in which at least one partner still could only make a mark was almost twice as high.

If the witnesses to the marriages are included, the transformation is still more dramatic. It is, of course, impossible to establish the identity of all those who acted in this capacity. By convention, bride and groom each had a witness of his or her own sex. Some were evidently a parent or a close relative; others had either gained different surnames through marriage or were unrelated. However, the proximity of the witness literacy rates to those of the partners, which will be examined later, suggests that as might be expected, those who were chosen to add their signatures or crosses to the register were members of the bride and groom's immediate social group. In taking the sample, a check was kept on the names of the witnesses, and on the rare occasions when an individual acted in a series of marriages, the entries were excluded from the sample. Throughout the survey period, the proportion of ceremonies in which all four participants signed with a mark was only one in fifteen, about a quarter of the mean for brides and grooms. Conversely, illiteracy was to be found somewhere in as many as 44 per cent of the ceremonies. Similar recalculations increased the literacy in the first phase from 52 per cent to 85 per cent, and quadrupled the presence of illiteracy in the final phase.

Few people lived alone in the eighteenth and nineteenth centuries, and fewer still lacked either relatives or close friends. In households, in the informal relationships in the neighbourhood, literate and illiterate were everywhere in each other's company. Only amongst the middle class had the centuries of educational progress come close to expelling illiteracy from the basic social networks. Whereas almost all the ceremonies involving middle-class grooms were fully literate by the middle of the nineteenth century, only a quarter of contemporary ceremonies involving grooms from the skilled working class displayed a similar standard. At the bottom of the scale, just one unskilled labourer in thirteen was able to arrange a wedding in which all the participants could sign their names. Yet these same labourers were by no means isolated from the literate. Although only three in ten could sign their name in the first phase, no fewer than three in four managed to include at least one literate individual at their wedding, and in almost half the marriages of unskilled labourers which began at this time, at least one partner could display a basic command of writing. Given that the literacy rate of labourers at the beginning of the sample was much the same as Schofield's returns for this group over the preceding ninety years,[4] it is likely that the patterns displayed here had been present since at least the mid eighteenth century. Whether looked at in the dimension of the family and its surrounding social group, or of the parishes which were examined for this survey, the distribution of signatures and marks denies the existence of ghettoes of illiteracy, complete sections of the community cut off from those able to make use of the printed word.[5]

Once the rates began to move upwards in the second third of the nineteenth century, the patterns of literacy created by the weddings had the general effect of both accelerating and retarding the process of change. The proportion of ceremonies in which at least one individual was literate passed 90 per cent thirty years before the average for brides and grooms in the sample, and conversely, the proportion of fully literate ceremonies did not reach 50 per cent until 1879, forty years after the mean rate had been as low. At the end of the century, one ceremony in six and one couple in eight contained at least one illiterate member. Everywhere the simple graph of improvement is qualified, and in two areas in particular the received account of the distribution of literacy over time is subject to major revision.

As far back as calculations can be made, the differential between husbands and wives had been one of the most consistent features of the literacy rates. Progress had been made since the sixteenth and seventeenth centuries, when 'women were almost universally unable to write their own names',[6] but they were still twenty points behind men in 1750, and had narrowed the gap by only four points by the 1840s. However, as the pace of change accelerated, it ceased to be a simple matter of one half of the population striving in vain to catch up with the other.

In the early reports of the Registrar General, and in the first two years of the sample survey, women were everywhere behind. The discrepancy in the first five years of the official returns ranged from one point in Surrey to twenty-four points in Lancashire. Thereafter the pattern began to break up. As soon as the long period of stagnation came to an end, a challenge was mounted to male dominance. By 1864, rapid advances in the female rates in the South and South-East, combined with a sluggish performance by men in East Anglia, meant that women were now ahead in almost all the counties south of a line from the Wash to Dorset (see fig. 2.1), and also in Rutland and Herefordshire. Year by year more areas were added to the redoubt which had been established, until in 1884 the counties in which women were ahead just outnumbered those in which men retained their superiority. During the final ten years of the period there were more literate brides than grooms in two English counties in three. If the focus is narrowed to the registration districts, much the same picture is revealed. Whilst there were pockets of male resistance in the counties where women were leading the aggregate returns, there were patches of female success in other areas. By 1864 brides were ahead in 41 per cent of the 575 districts, and in 1884, the final year for which this detail is available, grooms could gain the upper hand in only 45 per cent.[7] See fig. 2.1.[8]

For reasons which will be explored in chapter 4, women continued to fare less well in the towns and in particular in the heavily populated manufacturing centres of the Midlands and the North. As a consequence, the aggregate returns continued to display them in second place. Yet by the 1860s communities in which brides were more literate than grooms were becoming commonplace in the South, and within twenty years disticts could be found in which brides were level with or ahead of their partners in every county in England. The differentials were sometimes marginal, but in 1884 there were almost twice as many illiterate grooms as brides in Oxfordshire, Suffolk and Sussex. Amongst Suffolk's seventeen districts, the discrepancies ranged from Ipswich, with thirty-nine illiterate men to thirty-one illiterate women, to neighbouring Woodbridge, where

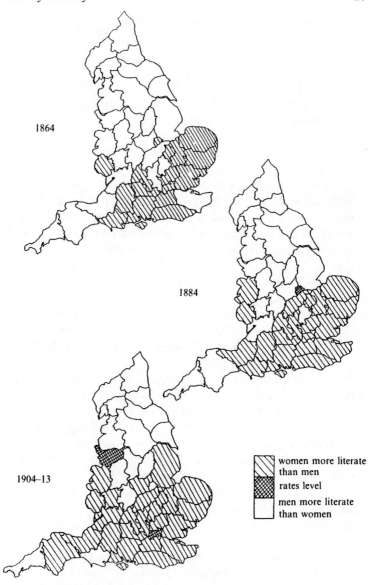

Fig. 2.1. Balance between male and female literacy rates

in 1884 twenty-five grooms and just four brides made a mark in the marriage register. The transition was particularly clear in the sample district of Samford in south-east Suffolk, where the survey was extended back to 1754. For ninety years the men remained the more accomplished half of the population, but eventually they were overtaken, and by the

1880s the district possessed a tradition of literate brides which extended over four decades. The inhabitants of these parishes will have known little and cared less about the national rates. From their perspective it had become natural to encounter heads of households who had to look to their wives to spell out a letter or read a newspaper. In terms of basic attainments, the progress of Victorian England had caused a widespread subversion of the established hierarchy of the sexes.[9]

The next most obvious agent of differentiation within the family was age. In the absence of a full-scale family reconstitution exercise, it is not possible to identify the precise patterns of literacy displayed by separate units of parents and children, but a number of general features can be distinguished. At a time of stasis in the overall rates, children should on average achieve at the same level as their parents.[10] This is not to say, however, that within each family, the children necessarily reproduced the standards of those above them. Aside from the fact that at the end of the period of stability, a third of working-class marriages in the sample contained one literate and one illiterate spouse, such detailed work as has been undertaken suggests that it was far from automatic for all children to reproduce the attainments of their parents.[11] The interaction of a wide range of normative and material pressures, which will be examined in chapter 3, introduced a significant element of chance to the process of cultural transmission. No matter how consistent the intention of parents, it was impossible to guarantee that all children would acquire, or, for that matter, fail to acquire, some ability to read and write.

Whilst the increasing systemisation of education from the 1830s onwards reduced the degree of randomness in the literacy of children, the consequent growth in the aggregate rates increased the distance between parents and their children. Fig. 2.2 indicates that by the middle of the century, a gap of twenty points had opened up between one generation and the next.[12] The children educated in the forties and fifties displayed a clear lead over their parents' age-group when they came to be married fifteen years later, and they in turn were to be overtaken by their own children later in the century. In the sample period as a whole (see fig. 2.3), young brides and grooms outperformed those in middle age, who in turn looked down upon the elderly.[13] The natural order of the family was challenged. Parents had to learn from their children; the old had to borrow knowledge and skills from the young. At the end of the period, as fig. 2.3 demonstrates, the balance had yet to be regained.

This much was evident to contemporaries, and indeed educational reformers deliberately set out to reverse the flow of values and information within the family. Less obvious was the fact that the triumph of the Victorians was distorting the yardstick by which it was measured. The returns of the Registrar General reflected the attainments of a sector of the

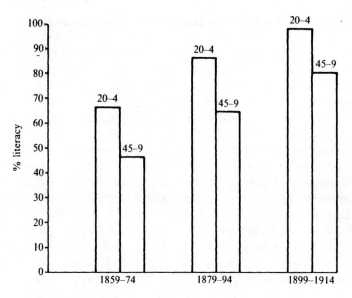

Fig. 2.2. Literacy by generation, 1859–1914

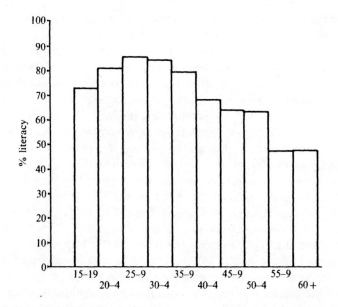

Fig. 2.3 Literacy by age, 1839–1914

population which was heavily biased towards the young. True love could strike at any age, and always there were widows or widowers starting anew, but for the most part the registers were signed by those with the major part of their adult lives in front of them. In the sample, 84 per cent of brides and 78 per cent of grooms were under thirty. At the outset of the sample period, this caused little difficulty. The rates had been dormant for so long that one cohort was much like another. Thereafter, the official figures become increasingly unreliable.

The task of redressing the balance was hampered by the fact that even with over 10,000 marriages, the number of elderly brides and grooms could become dangerously small when the sample was subdivided. However, by grouping the sixteen sample years into four bands it was possible to recalculate the aggregate returns by weighting the rates for each cohort according to its size in an adjacent census. In the first phase, 1839–54, there was virtually no change. But in the next phase the reworking reduced the average rate of grooms from 68.7 per cent to 62.6 per cent, and of brides from 61.3 per cent to 51.0 per cent. The larger change amongst women is explained by the greater distance their rates had to travel. In the third phase, 1879–94, there was again a gap of six points between the apparent and true rates for men, but amongst women, dramatic advances by the young increased the distortion to thirteen points.

The reworking of the final phase called into question the very existence of the pre-war victory over illiteracy. In 1900, the first generation to feel the benefits of Forster's Education Act was just reaching middle age, and those children who had finally been forced into school by Mundella's Act of 1880 were only in their twenties. The men and women whose childhood had been passed without the benefits of universality or compulsion still comprised a substantial proportion of the adult population. Their numbers were sufficient to render the achievement of the period less comprehensive than at first appeared. Again, it was the rates for brides which suffered the largest revision. By this time the aggregate returns suggested that for the first time in history, women had achieved parity with men throughout the country, but it was to take longer to overcome the legacy of past failings. As Lady Bell noted in 1905, 'More than one would expect of the women between fifty and sixty cannot read, and even some of those of forty.'[14] Whereas the rate for men dropped by only four points, from 97.8 per cent to 93.4 per cent, women fell back from 97.5 per cent to 86.2 per cent. If the figures are taken together, and allowances made for the greater number of women in the population, it is likely that during the period from 1899 to 1914, at least one adult in ten still lacked a minimum command over the basic skills of literacy.[15] 'Among the lower class', wrote Robert Roberts of Edwardian Salford, 'a mass of illiterates,

solid and sizeable, still remained.'[16] This small but significant minority will
have lived on into inter-war England, and cannot finally have disappeared
until the 1940s.

The status of literacy

In itself, the more complex distribution of literacy which emerges from
this reworking of the official statistics tells us very little. If we are to
appreciate the significance of the divisions that have been identified,
questions must be asked about the status of the ability to sign a name, and
about the function of the skill in family life. It will be necessary to go
beyond the registers to answer the second of these questions, but the
ceremonies can be made to yield some evidence on the first.

The patterns of marks and signatures produced by the weddings were a
consequence partly of necessity and partly of free-will. If, as was the case
in the first year of the sample, there were only forty-four literate brides for
every fifty-seven literate grooms, 13 per cent of the marriages had to be
mixed. But here, as throughout the period, the proportion of mixed
marriages was significantly greater than it needed to be. In fact in 1839 one
literate groom in five courted an illiterate bride, and perhaps more
strikingly, one literate bride in twelve walked down the aisle with a groom
who would be unable to sign the register. The element of choice was even
greater in the nomination of witnesses, where a wider pool of candidates
resulted in a still more variegated pattern of marks and signatures. The
pattern of discrimination reflected in the ceremonies can tell us something
of the value that was given to nominal literacy by different sections
of the community, and conversely, of the stigma attached to those who
were unable to display a basic proficiency in the tools of written
communication.

There is little enough evidence available to the historian on the factors
which influenced the selection of marriage partners amongst the labouring
poor. Few of those who left an account of their private lives excluded
material considerations from their description of courtship, but at the
same time most claimed to have fallen in love with their future spouse.[17]
They felt that they had exercised some freedom of choice and that their
subsequent marriage was founded on a genuine compatibility between
husband and wife. Beyond physical health, the attributes a suitor looked
for, and which in turn caused a proposal to be accepted, are never
explicitly described, and we are left to make inferences from the detail in
the marriage registers. It is clear that spatial and social distance played a
role in circumscribing the field of possible partners; at issue here is
whether educational attainments or their absence also limited the range of
individuals who might prove attractive to each other.

We might begin with the least literate section in the sample, the unskilled labourers in the early years of the period. For the years 1839–54, the literacy of brides and grooms was evenly balanced at 31.4 per cent and 31.6 per cent respectively. In theory, virtually every marriage could have been wholly literate or wholly illiterate; conversely, had partners been selected on a purely random basis, taking no account of educational attainments, 43 per cent of marriages would have been mixed. In practice, 36 per cent of the marriages were a consequence of a literate groom choosing an illiterate bride or vice versa. Over half of those who possessed sufficient skill to sign the register were content to go through the ceremony with a partner who would only be able to make a mark.

It is perhaps to be expected that in a section of the community where illiteracy had been so widespread for so long, there should be few signs that lack of education was a handicap in the formation of relationships. However, the situation was not substantially different in contexts where illiteracy was much less of a commonplace. If, for instance, we take the unskilled labourers forward forty years, to a time when illiterates comprised less than a quarter of partners, the proportion of mixed marriages is still as high as 26 per cent. Equally the skilled labourers, who had a long tradition of high literacy, were still prepared to countenance frequent matches between individuals of uneven attainments. The most striking indication of the general outlook amongst this group is to be found in the second phase, 1859–74, where in spite of the fact that women lagged twelve points behind men, one literate bride in seven found herself marrying an illiterate groom. Only when the overall illiteracy rate fell into single figures did the incidence of mixed marriages become so rare as to draw attention to itself. Even then, the individuals in this shrinking minority were not forced to associate with each other. On the contrary, to take the sample as a whole, in the final phase from 1899 to 1914 almost all the remaining illiterates were to be found marrying those who could now sign their name.

Given the close association between social class and literacy rates, it is conceivable that the incidence of mixed marriages was merely a reflection of individuals marrying above or below themselves. Although the absence of consistent information on the occupation of brides in the registers prevented a direct comparison between the two partners, the entries for the fathers of the bride and groom permitted a tabulation of the incidence of sons and daughters marrying into families of a higher, lower or equivalent social standing. Fig. 2.4 suggests that the influence of social mobility through marriage on patterns of literacy was at best marginal. In the first phase of the sample, when the choice of a literate or illiterate partner was greatest, there was only a slight tendency for downwardly mobile brides and grooms to marry less literate partners, and conversely

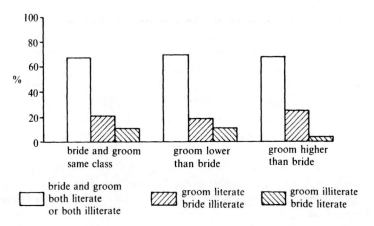

Fig. 2.4. Social and educational mobility at marriage, 1839–54

for those making progress up the social scale to take a more educated husband or wife. Chi-square tests confirmed that in terms of the crude indicators which are available here, social mobility provides only a small part of the explanation of educational mobility at marriage.[18]

Further evidence on the perceived significance of nominal literacy is supplied by the witnesses. In some respects these subordinate actors in the ceremony are more relevant to this issue than the principals. Whereas the completion of the register was an incidental if necessary task for the bride and groom, it was the sole function of the witnesses. Most marriage partners, particularly in the early part of the sample period, would be able to choose between literate and illiterate relations and friends. In cases of difficulty the services of the parish clerk or even a total stranger could be called upon. If real status had been attached to a signature, if a mark had been regarded as an inferior authority, we would have expected to find literate brides and grooms doing everything possible to avoid an illiterate witness, and illiterate partners striving to recruit educated acquaintances to enhance the standing of the ceremony. Equally, if making a mark had been a cause of serious embarrassment, we would have expected to find illiterate candidates declining a duty which would have exposed their shortcomings before the entire parish.

In general terms, the pattern of witness signatures reinforces the impression given by the marriage partners. For the sample as a whole, the literacy of witnesses was just three and a half points higher than the mean of brides and grooms. For the most part the marriage partners seem to have paid little attention to how their witnesses could perform their duty. Where both bride and groom were literate, the register tended to be signed throughout, but even so, one in seven of these couples chose at least one illiterate witness, and one in fifty watched two marks entered alongside their signatures. Elsewhere, over half the wholly illiterate couples found at least one witness who could write his or her name, and couples of mixed literacy had witnesses of equally mixed ability.

One group, however, does seem to have been sensitive to the issue. The literacy of witnesses to the marriages of unskilled labourers in the first quarter of the period was half again as high as the rate displayed by the principals in the ceremony.[19] Whereas skilled labourers at this time were content with witnesses of broadly similar standing, those below them seem to have made a serious effort to seek out the better educated of their friends and relatives. Only when this section had begun to achieve respectable rates during the third quarter of the period did they relax their attitude.

The examination of the patterns of choice revealed in the registers thus offers little confirmation of the widespread belief amongst contemporaries that real stigma was attached to an inability to sign the register. Where literacy was only one amongst many attributes to be taken into account, it does not seem to have been a matter of great significance. The mixture of signatures and marks was too great to support the notion that comparable educational attainments were a necessary, still less a sufficient, basis for a marriage. Whilst the more literate groups amongst the lower orders and over time displayed slightly greater coherence, the variation was not large enough to confirm the hypothesis recently advanced 'that the greater the degree of illiteracy in a society, the less will be the concern of the illiterates about being illiterate'.[20] Indeed the least literate was the only group to display any real concern about the matter at all. However, there does seem to be an important distinction to be drawn here between being illiterate and the practice of literacy. When it came to forming relationships, the most illiterate showed little interest in the literacy of their partners, but they did think it of some importance that as many signatures should be made at their wedding as possible. Those who could not write attached status to writing rather than to writers.

The post

The completion of the registers was one use of literacy, but in the families which started life at the ceremonies, the function of reading and writing remained to be determined. The newly married couples were faced with a familiar problem of using and responding to the use of unfamiliar skills. As the pattern of marks and signatures indicated, even the least educated sections of society had long been accustomed to households in which literate and illiterate lived out their lives together. At the same time the rapid advances during the latter two thirds of the nineteenth century produced a veritable turmoil of shifting standards. If the official returns understated the heterogeneity of popular culture, they also underplayed the scale of the transformation which was taking place in individual communities. Amongst the more backward sections of the population it was not uncommon for levels of literacy which had taken centuries to achieve, and which had remained unchanged since the mid eighteenth century, to be doubled within the space of a single generation. The grooms sampled in the iron-making centre of Dudley, for instance, increased their literacy from 44 per cent to 94 per cent between 1869 and 1894, whilst in the nearby rural parishes of Cleobury Mortimer, the rate rose from 42 per cent to 82 per cent between 1839 and 1879. Women and the unskilled suffered the greatest upheavals. Amongst the grooms in social class 5 the rate rose from thirty-two in the first quarter of the sample period to fifty-six in the second to eighty in the third. In Macclesfield, the literacy of brides was transformed from 39 per cent in 1849 to 84 per cent in 1874, and in the village of Samford in Suffolk a rise of similar proportions took place between 1834 and 1864.

In family after family husbands and wives had access to new means of communication, and in turn faced new responsibilities in educating their offspring. The pace of change raised questions about both the general conduct of family relations, which will be the concern of the remainder of this chapter, and the specific matter of raising children, which will be examined in chapter 3. In each case it is necessary to concentrate on how the new skills were employed, which in turn entails an examination of expanding opportunities. These took many forms, but in the present context perhaps the most striking area of growth was in letter writing. In 1840 the cost of a letter was reduced from an average of 6d to a flat rate of 1d. During the subsequent seventy-five years the volume of correspondence increased nearly fifty-fold, from an estimated 76 million items in 1839 to 3,500 million in 1914.[21] Like the registration of marriages, the Penny Post was the work of the Whig Reform Government, and it was of similar value in providing for the first time an official statistical return. Whilst the range of information in the annual reports of the Postmaster General was more limited, occasional attempts were made to analyse the postal flows by district, and with the establishment of the Universal Postal Union in 1875, systematic international comparisons became possible. Unlike the marriage registers, however, the post was a direct reflection of practice. A letter had to be written, by or on behalf of the correspondent, and it had to be read, by or to the recipient.

From the beginning, the expansion of the postal system was closely associated with the use of literacy by the working-class family. The proponents of penny postage faced strong opposition. Although its revenue had stagnated since the Napoleonic Wars, the Post Office remained an immensely profitable state monopoly, which produced a net income in 1839 of £1.5 million, a margin of 70 per cent on turnover and equivalent to fifty times the Government grant to elementary education.[22] To put at risk so secure a source of income it was necessary to demonstrate the existence of a massive untapped demand for correspondence, and to indicate how its fulfilment would benefit a society then in the throes of a major economic and political crisis. Both lines of argument led directly to the homes of the labouring poor.

The initial premise upon which the reformers based their case was that the four-fifths of the population who worked with their hands made little or no use of the existing facilities. 'We are justified in saying', wrote Rowland Hill's brother Matthew, 'that, for the great mass of our countrymen, the Post Office does not exist.'[23] 'The entire communication by post', stated a witness before the 1838 Select Committee on Postage, 'is limited to the higher classes at present.'[24] The subsequent increase in postal flows served only to confirm this impression. In 1874, Andrew Wynter surveyed the period of change: 'As long as there was no public post in existence, the relations of the mass of Britons extended no further than their own towns and villages, where any communications they required to make were made orally.'[25] At the end of the nineteenth century, the postal reformer J. Henniker Heaton took stock of progress under Queen Victoria: 'It need not be hastily inferred that our grand-fathers were barbarians. But certainly the masses were almost as much restricted to oral communication and local commerce as their native ancestors were under the Stuarts, or as the Turks are under Abdul Hamid.'[26]

Those with a more direct knowledge of popular culture in the 1820s and 1830s tended to avoid such sweeping generalisations. Correspondence was not unknown in the working-class community, and its more literate members, including the Nottinghamshire framework-knitters' leader Gravener Henson, occasionally acted for those unable to write a letter or read one they had received. But as Henson stressed, the cost of the service imposed severe restrictions on its use:

> When it is considered that in our business many of the workmen work for as low as 4s a week, and that in most instances they cannot earn above 10s, the postage of a letter of 10d is a great object. They have generally complained to me when writing the letters, that it was not the paying of the postage, but they were afraid of the answer coming when they had not sufficient money to release it.[27]

The problem was not only the scale of the charges, which from 1812 ranged from 4d for fifteen miles to 1s for three hundred miles and 1d for each additional hundred, but also the mode of payment.[28] For all but the most prosperous artisan the cost of a letter represented a major burden on a hard-pressed family economy, and charging on delivery made it impossible to save against such an expense. A correspondent could not foresee whether the distant relative would be able to pay for the letter the day it arrived; neither could he or she be certain that the surplus cash would be available whenever the letter carrier called with a reply. Douglas Jerrold observed that

> The Postman rarely knocks at the doors of the very poor, and when, perchance, he stands at the threshold of the indigent, it is too often to demand a sacrifice. The letter that he proffers must, perhaps, be purchased at the price of a dinner: at any cost, however, the letter must be purchased; for it comes from one who, it may be, has been silent for years; a far off son, a married daughter. To thousands a letter is a forbidden luxury: an enjoyment, not to be bought by those who daily struggle with the dearest necessities, and who, once severed from a long distant home, are mute because they cannot fee the post, and will not, must not, lay the tax on others wretched as themselves.[29]

Anecdotes abounded of elderly parents pawning clothes to read a letter from a distant son, and of would-be correspondents adopting ever more ingenious methods of avoiding payment altogether.

It remained to be shown that reform would release the necessary flood of correspondence. 'I have asked many of the working classes upon the subject', said Henson, 'and they are quite of the opinion that were the postage lowered to 1d., 10 letters would be sent where one is now sent, and that no such thing as evading the post would be attempted by anybody.'[30] Rowland Hill was confident that at the very least demand would generate the five- or six-fold increase required to maintain the existing level of revenue. There were three general reasons for supporting these claims. Firstly the success of the special penny post during the Napoleonic Wars could be cited as a precedent. The use made by soldiers and sailors of this privilege had helped to maintain morale at home and in the forces.[31] In addition, local Penny Posts were operating in 356 towns in England and Wales by the mid 1830s.[32] Secondly, the increasing mobility of labour throughout the economy was splitting up working-class families as never before. Domestic servants, tramping artisans, rural migrants into the expanding industrial centres, to say nothing of immigrants from Ireland and emigrants to the New World, all left behind them parents, spouses and sweethearts with whom they would wish to retain contact. It was strongly argued that as Thomas Davidson put it, 'the working classes have the social and domestic feelings as strongly as the middling or upper classes, particularly in the younger part of life'.[33] The desire to maintain family relationships would promote the use of literacy.

Finally it was asserted that the working-class community possessed a sufficient level of skill to make possible correspondence with distant relatives. It is interesting that the argument here rested not on the crude literacy rates which were just becoming available, but rather on the distribution of literacy within the family. Although it could not yet be proved statistically, a thoughtful observer could form a general impression. 'Are the operative classes in general sufficiently educated to be able to write?' Richard Cobden was asked by the 1838 Select Committee. 'Not so much educated as one could wish', he replied. 'But still the operatives living so much together, and generally having families, there is usually one in the family or connection who can write.'[34] In this context, practice was a group rather than an individual matter.[35]

Not everyone welcomed the idea of a growth in domestic correspondence. 'Will clerks write only to their fathers and girls to their mothers?' asked the Tory J. W. Croker, 'Will not letters of romance or love intrigue or mischief increase in at least equal proportion?'[36] There were, however, a wide range of potential benefits to be set against such dangers. It was not just that opening up the postal system would reduce the 'anguish' and 'misery' caused by the inability of separated families to keep in touch with each other. Such correspondence would generate major social, economic and political gains. Most obviously it would be the means of realising the objectives of the elementary education system to which the state was now formally committed. At present the absence of sufficient opportunity to make use of literacy was obstructing the work of the schools. Skills learnt in the classroom were decaying through neglect. 'Those who have learned to write a copy at school', argued a Cirencester businessman, 'have lost it; they have had no accounts to keep; and the consequence is, they cannot write, nor read writing, the great majority of them.'[37] Furthermore the prospect of finding an application for literacy would encourage working-class parents to educate their children. As a promoter of schools for the poor in Liverpool put it,

> if they could correspond with their friends, who, from various causes, are removed from them to a distance, it would stimulate parents to be more attentive in sending children to school to acquire a knowledge of writing, that they might have that luxury within their reach, but which the high rate of postage now, even if they could write, precludes.[38]

It was in fact the perfect Liberal reform, social advance obtained by a reduction in the role of the state, a point not lost on Rowland Hill: 'it calls on Government for no factitious aid, for nothing in the shape of encouragment, still less of compulsion; but merely for the removal of an obstacle, created by the law, to that spontaneous education which happily is extending through the country'.[39]

The campaign for the Penny Post reached its climax as the economy entered the worst slump of the nineteenth century. The widespread unemployment and consequent strain on the recently introduced New Poor Law served only to strengthen the case of the reformers. Throughout the Industrial Revolution the only structural solution to unemployment the State was prepared to countenance was mobility of labour, within or beyond the national economy. Here it could be argued that promoting the use of literacy would help to overcome the reluctance of the unemployed labourer to travel in search of work. Cheap postage would assist the Poor Law in its ambition to free the labour market. At present paupers clung to their parish, 'chiefly from their inability to pay the cost of communicating by post with the relatives and friends they might leave behind'.[40] More generally it would facilitate migration from the countryside into the towns, and emigration would become more attractive if there was regular correspondence with those who were already experiencing the delights of a new life in the colonies.

Partly as a consequence of the economic crisis, a major challenge was now being mounted to the political system. In this context, as elsewhere, the relevance of using literacy was to be found in the home. As older forms of maintaining discipline decayed, increasing attention was being paid to the family as the bedrock of social order.[41] The Post had a particular role to play in counteracting the tendency of urbanisation to weaken parental authority. 'May we not presume', asked Rowland Hill,

> that many young persons of both sexes, who are continually drawn into this metropolis from distant parts of the kingdom, and are thenceforth cut off from communication with their early guardians, might, under different circumstances, be kept from entering upon vicious courses, to which the temptations are so great, and against which the restraints, in their case, are so few?[42]

Domestic relationships and rational discourse would reinforce each other and in turn serve to strengthen the judgment of the working man. The cotton manufacturer Thomas Davidson hoped he had found a means of checking the rising tide of discontent amongst his workforce:

> From the very limited range of their enjoyments, whatever the object of political or social character they take up, they throw into it a feeling of excitement and intensity which appears to me to be injurious to their general moral and intellectual happiness. Hence the excitement for politics at one time, at another for

trades' unions and combinations of various kinds; and it appears to me, that to furnish them with the means of frequent epistolary intercourse would tend to modify and let down in some degree those feelings of over-excitement in their minds upon the subjects just mentioned.[43]

The arguments put forward in favour of postal reform provided a conspectus of the hopes which were entertained for the use of literacy by the working-class family. By the same measure, the subsequent failure of the Penny Post to meet the goals set by its promoters raised fears that the households of the labouring poor were incapable of making the transition from possession to application of the skills of written communication. The first Parliamentary return on 12 March 1840 revealed that instead of the expected five- or six-fold increase, postal flows had merely doubled.[44] In the first complete year, gross revenue fell by almost 50 per cent, and with costs rising sharply, profits fell by nearly 75 per cent, costing the Treasury nearly £1.2 million in lost revenue.[45] The volume of post did not reach its original target until the mid 1850s, and it was not until the mid 1870s that profits finally regained their pre-1840 level.

Rowland Hill now found himself on the defensive, and in the ensuing post mortem all the evidence pointed away from the working class and towards middle-class correspondence. The business community, which had been eager for reform, was now quick to make use of the new opportunity. Pickford and Company, for instance, reported that in the year ended March 1843, it had dispatched 240,000 letters, an eight-fold growth since 1839.[46] A London wholesale grocer was cited as sending out an extra 10,000 price lists, and Charles Knight claimed that the book trade had been transformed by the new arrangements.[47] In the political sphere, the immediate beneficiary had been the Anti-Corn Law League, which had taken part in the campaign for cheap postage, and now lost no time in exploiting its potential for mass communication. In 1844 it sent out 300,000 letters together with over two million 'stamped and other publications',[48] and Cobden wrote to Hill thanking him for a reform which had been 'a terrible engine for upsetting monopoly amd corruption: witness our League operations, the *spawn of your penny postage*'.[49] By contrast, only the vaguest claims could be made on behalf of the mass of the population, and it seemed difficult to resist the verdict of a hostile pamphlet published in 1844:

> Thus, where the poor man receives, say eight letters, from his sailor-son, or his daughter in service in the capital, or in some distant town, and thus gains a shilling in the year by cheap postage, let any one consider how much is gained and saved by this Penny Postage in such houses such as Loyd, Jones and Co.,

Baring Brothers and Co., Morrison and Co., &c. Indeed, the point is too plain for argument, that Penny Postage is a boon to the rich instead of the poor and is a sacrifice of national revenue to swell the coffers of a class which does not require it.[50]

Not for the last time, the middle class was taking the lion's share of a flat-rate benefit designed for the underprivileged.

The reformers pleaded for time, and indeed the passing years did appear to vindicate their optimism. Per capita deliveries of letters in England and Wales increased from an official figure of four in 1839, to eight in 1840, and thence to thirty-two by 1871 and sixty by 1900.[51] At the end of the nineteenth century Great Britain had the heaviest deliveries of letters and postcards in the world.[52] Yet there was no guarantee that this expansion represented an extension rather than an intensification of the use of the facilities. The standard histories of the postal services are virtually silent on the key question of who actually wrote and read the proliferating correspondence, which reflects the uncertainty of the Post Office itself. Successive Postmasters General could do little more than list the possible causes of growth. Contemplating a nine-fold increase in letters since 1839, the annual report of 1864 concluded that 'It would be hard to determine what proportion of the marked increase in correspondence which is exhibited in the foregoing pages is attributable to the improvements effected by the Post Office, and what to the growth of trade and commerce and the more general diffusion of education.'[53] Short of opening the letters,[54] they may have felt there was little more that could be said; however, it is possible to use their own and other statistics and reports to make some attempt to weigh the factors which lay behind the increase.

'Improvements effected by the Post Office' clearly played some part in the growth of letter writing. Those wishing to use the post in 1840 faced many difficulties. A quarter of all registration districts lacked their own post office;[55] there were no letter boxes in doors, no post boxes in the streets.[56] During the subsequent twenty-five years, strenuous efforts were made to extend the facilities. Doors were mutilated, experimental pillar boxes introduced in 1855, and by 1864 the Postmaster General could claim that after adding 10,000 places to the delivery network in ten years, only a few 'thinly populated, isolated and remote' communities were outside the system.[57] Through the use of literacy the nation was to be fully integrated for the first time in its history.[58]

To celebrate this achievement, the Post Office took the trouble to compile a table comparing per capita deliveries in 1854 and 1863 in every Postal District in the country.[59] These calculations, which were not repeated in the nineteenth century, produced enormous disparities, the

Table 2.1. *Highest and lowest per capita postal deliveries, 1863*

Malvern	103	Bolton	11
Leamington	57	Colchester	11
Southport	52	Durham	10
London	48	Blackburn	10
Brighton	48	Wigan	9
Margate	44	Burnley	8
Stamford	44	Bury	7
Ramsgate	42	Dudley	7
Scarborough	42	Oldham	6
Windsor	40	Ashton-u-Lyne	6

figures in 1863 ranging from six letters a year for each inhabitant of Ashton-under-Lyne and Oldham to 103 for Malvern Wells. Table 2.1 reveals a striking pattern. With the exception of London and the market town of Stamford, the Districts with the highest returns were all resorts; with the exception of Colchester, those with the lowest were northern industrial towns.

The resort returns were in fact somewhat inflated by the method of calculation. The per capita figures were based on the preceding census, and were distorted by the influx of visitors in the summer months. Nonetheless they were evidence that, as might be expected, middle-class families were making extensive use of the new facilities. With similar census populations, the District of Brighton had 4,590,349 deliveries in 1863, and Wigan just 831,831. Those who could afford to take holidays in the spas or at the seaside were whiling away their time exchanging letters with their friends and relatives.[60] As in most of the aggregate returns made by the Post Office in this period, the figures are for incoming rather than outgoing mail. However, a comparison of the one occasion when letters posted were given for 1891 with returns in other years for deliveries confirms that the volume of letters received does reflect the general level of correspondence.[61]

At the other end of the scale, few qualifications need to be made. In 1863, as in 1854, the rapidly growing industrial communities were receiving the smallest number of letters. Only the cities and the major ports in the region, which were capable of generating substantial commercial and administrative correspondence, achieved respectable rates. Where there were merely large numbers of factory workers, Rowland Hill's missionary endeavours had made little impact. In Oldham, for instance, whose population had grown by 441 per cent during the first half of the century, the Post Office delivered an average of just three letters to each resident in 1853, and provided one receptacle for every 23,533 inhabitants wishing to make a reply. The population figure of course includes children, but when account is taken of the higher correspondence of the town's manufacturers, businessmen and public officials, it is clear that the arrival of a letter in a working-class home was a rare event. In poorer neighbourhoods, this state of affairs showed little change throughout the century. Walter Southgate remembered Bethnal Green in the 1890s: 'No one could boast of a letter box so that the "rat a tat tat" of the postman was indeed an event everyone knew about. There would be enquiries as to whether it was good or bad news. Letter boxes were a sign of affluence and status in those days.'[62]

As the Postal Districts were not co-extensive with the Registration Districts, it is not possible to make a precise correlation between the possession of literacy and its employment, but a general impression can be gained by grouping both sets of figures into counties. This indicates that there was some association between the two factors. London, for instance, with 86 per cent literacy and forty-eight letters per head in 1863 remained near the top, and Staffordshire, with 57 per cent literacy and fifteen letters, near the bottom. Across the range, the capacity to read and write varied less than the desire to use the skills, although in the middle the two indexes often moved together. Cambridge, for example, had rates of 69 per cent and twenty-three respectively, and Suffolk, 67 per cent and twenty-two. The comparison emphasises the significance of commercial activity. In Lancashire the high level of correspondence in Manchester and Liverpool counterbalanced the poor performance of the smaller factory towns, so that the overall rate of postage was only marginally lower than in the more literate but sleepier county of Hereford.

It was evident the hopes of the reformers that migration would promote and in turn be sustained by letter writing were not being fulfilled. So far from increasing the level of use, the rapid growth of a town appears to have held down the postal rate. The most that can be said is that almost all the meagre flow of letters in Ashton, Oldham and Dudley was from outside. It was not until the urban community reached the size of Manchester or Birmingham that it began to generate a substantial proportion of its own mail.[63] By 1863, 47 per cent of London's 161 million letters came from within the capital, and were delivered in the inner area no fewer than twelve times a day. The northern mill towns tended to be too compact to require much internal communication by letter. Most information continued to be exchanged through conversation.

The extension of the facilities and the more sophisticated measurement of their use largely confirmed the initial verdict on the Penny Post. Those with money to spend or money to make were the chief beneficiaries of the reform. Alongside the rapidly growing resort correspondence, new species of commercial activity had been called into being. The introduction of the book post in 1848, its extension to cover circulars in 1856, and the arrival in 1863 of the pattern post for samples of no intrinsic value, made possible for the first time nation-wide mail-ordering and advertising. In 1863, for instance, the drapers of London despatched 1,690,000 letter circulars and 282,000 book circulars to customers all over the country.[64] By 1871, every Postal District from Accrington to York had substantial weekly deliveries of book packets, circulars and samples.[65] In Oldham this category comprised a fifth of the mail coming into the town. Even tiny Sawbridge-worth in Hertfordshire, which consistently boasted the smallest volume of mail in England, received 201 commercial items in its weekly total of 1,618. Providing profits for proprietors and information for educated readers, the newspaper post, now free of the Government stamp, was running at over a quarter of a million items a week in 1871, and in addition there was the Money Order Office, which, as the Postmaster General put it, having been 'established in the first instance for the purpose of facilitating the transmission of small sums by poor persons, has gradually become the bank of the entire trading community'.[66]

The most obvious reason why poor persons appeared not to be gaining greater benefit from the expanding postal services was the handicap under which they entered the world of mass correspondence. They had a good deal of ground to make up, and it is important not to lose sight of how far they had come by the 1860s. Oldham's six letters a head may have looked derisory when set against the more sophisticated cities in 1863, but it was double the rate achieved in 1854, despite a population increase within the Postal District of 23 per cent. Taking a longer view, Burnley, another of the low-scoring Districts, had increased its deliveries from an estimated 828 paid and unpaid letters in a sample week in 1838 to 12,372 in a week in 1861.[67] In the absence of a further official calculation of per capita rates it is impossible to arrive at a precise measure of the relative progress of different communities over the century. But if allowance is made for the growth of population in the central towns of each Postal District, it would seem that the low-scoring areas in the aftermath of reform subsequently made much faster progress than those which had established an early lead, in much the same way that, as we have seen, literacy rates showed the most dramatic advances amongst originally backward groups. Between 1842 and 1901, which saw a five-fold increase in per capita deliveries in England and Wales, Oldham, bottom of the table in 1854, expanded its use by at least twice the national average.[68]

A separate problem was the initial unfamiliarity with the practice of letter writing. Whilst correspondence had taken place before 1840, it would take a major domestic crisis to force a labourer to engage directly or by proxy in this form of communication; 'my experience in writing letters for them', stated Gravener Hensen on behalf of the framework-knitters of Nottingham, 'has satisfied me that they never write unless it is almost upon life and death'.[69] The later extension and systemisation of elementary education made little impact. Under the Revised Code of 1862, which was explicitly designed to focus attention on the basic elements of literacy, 'writing' meant, as it always had done, copying, not composing. The development of teaching methods will be discussed at greater length in the next chapter, but it is important to note here that 'composition' only became an element of the official syllabus in elementary schools in 1871. Even then the subject was not encountered until the sixth standard, where no more than 2 per cent of pupils a year received a little instruction in how to set out a letter. Throughout the period, the great majority of the 'literate' working class had never been taught anything more than a basic manual dexterity, the 'ballet with the pen' as Furet and Ozouf aptly call it.[70] Only those whose occupation or whose involvement in some form of working-class organisation had forced them to make the enormous transition from imitation to the formulation of sentences and paragraphs were in a position to respond to the reduction in postal charges, either for themselves or on behalf of those for whom self-expression through writing remained an unknown art.

The traditional perception of community also stood in the way of a large-scale exploitation of the new opportunities. Oral transmission of information depended upon and in turn helped to define a sense of belonging. A mutual knowledge of people and a place made conversation possible, and the continual exchange of news, opinions and gossip created a shared identity. The occasional letter might cross the boundary of the known world, but the correspondence was likely to be between close relatives on matters of private family interest. This association of communication with locality was now challenged by the introduction of a flat-rate pre-paid charge for letters which, it was hoped, would eliminate the dimension of distance in contact between individuals and thus overcome the barriers which stood in the way of the emergence of a new sense of nationhood.

The machinery of large-scale posting demanded a new level of impersonality. If costs were not to rise in proportion to volume, the efficiency of sorting and delivery had to be transformed. This entailed not only organisational improvements, but the introduction of the ready-gummed envelope which had to be properly addressed. For the letter to reach its destination with a minimum of delay, the correspondent had to distinguish with much greater precision between the recipient and his or her family, between the home and the street, and the street and the village or town. The traditional methods of finding an individual would not suffice. John Sykes recalled of his West Riding village that 'Bill o' Ben's o' Bob's o' Will's o' th' Hill was a fair sample of the way they had of identifying a man in those days, before the streets and house numbers had been invented.'[71] Previously the letter carrier worked on the basis of personal contact; letters were so infrequent that each addressee had to be sought out, and once found a charge had to be made which often involved prolonged explanation and negotiation.[72] Small wonder that most letters remained in the post office to await collection. Now every inhabitant was to be described in such a way that he or she could be located by a total stranger. Much trouble was caused to the Post Office in the early years of the new system by writers unwilling or unable to differentiate between individual and community. On one sample day in July 1843, 3,557 letters were sorted bearing only a name and 'London'.[73] Three quarters of the two million returned letters in 1861 were 'Owing to the letters being addressed either insufficiently or incorrectly; more than 10,000 letters having been posted without any address at all'.[74] Not until the 1880s was the Postmaster General able to report a decline in the business of the Returned Letter Office, 'attributable probably in part to the increase of education, which causes letter writers to exercise more care and accuracy in addressing letters than was formerly the case'.[75]

By this time the postal flow was reaching a rate of fifty letters a head and there was some evidence that correspondence was beginning to play a larger part in the family life of the labouring poor. The most striking examples of the use of the post in creating or sustaining relationships were to be found not in everyday letter writing, but rather in specialised forms of communication relating to particular events and ceremonies. Of these the earliest, and until the last quarter of the nineteenth century the most important, was the sending of valentines.

The observance of 14 February underwent a metamorphosis during the eighteenth century which was later to befall many other customs. What had begun as an exchange of gifts, with many local variations of obscure origin, was gradually transformed into an exchange of tokens and letters, which in turn began to be replaced by printed messages from the end of the century.[76] As the gifts were translated into writing and then into print, so profits accrued to both the Post Office and commercial publishers. And as the price of both postage and the valentines came down, so larger sections of the population entered the market. By 1835 the Secretary of the Post Office was recording 'that on or about St. Valentine's Day there is a most extraordinary influx of many thousand letters',[77] and with the coming of the Penny Post, which amongst much else relieved loved ones of the necessity of paying for the compliments they received, the practice boomed. Rowland Hill calculated that 400,000 valentines were sent in 1841,[78] and by 1850 the flow had passed half a million, 'gorging the general as well as the local posts with love epistles'.[79] In London alone the extra mail on 14 February rose from 430,000 in 1863 to one and a half million in 1871.[80]

'Cupid's Manufactory', as Dickens called it, which at its peak employed as many as 3,000 women, catered for all tastes, and, most important, for all levels of income and literacy.[81] The quality of the poetry and spelling of the penny cards issued by firms such as the great broadside publisher James Catnach suggested that they were composed, bought and read by those with only a limited command of written English.[82] For those who retained some literary ambition of their own, 'Valentine Writers' were on sale, providing specimen verses and replies which could be adapted to the particular romance. Given that most courtship took place within walking distance of the couple's home, it is possible that hand-made and hand-delivered valentines flourished well before penny postage. We find, for instance, the young weaver Samuel Bamford exchanging home-produced 'love billets' with his sweetheart at the end of the 1790s.[83] The arrival of the printed card tended to stereotype and ultimately to vulgarise the expression of affection, but at the same time it increased both the number of those able to engage in this form of communication and the distance over which contact might be made. The Post Office's calculation that 'those sent from London to the country were more than twice as numerous as those sent from the country to London'[84] suggests that valentines were being used by migrants to sustain affairs with girls left behind in their home villages.

The decline of the valentine was as rapid as its rise, but less easy to explain. By the time Flora Thompson was growing up in the early 1880s, the 'daintily printed and lace bedecked valentines' had been superseded by 'crude coloured prints on flimsy paper representing hideous forms and faces intended to be more or less applicable to the recipient',[85] and these in turn had disappeared by 1914. Whether the vulgarisation of the form was a symptom or a cause of its fall from fashion remains unclear; however, it was quickly replaced by a more generalised and eventually more prolific expression of sentiment, the Christmas card.

The first modern card appeared in 1843, designed by Henry Cole, Rowland Hill's chief assistant in the introduction of the Penny Post. Early versions were patterned closely on the valentine, and it was not until the 1860s that the genre began to achieve an identity of its own. The development of cheap colour printing enabled firms to publish increasing numbers of attractive cards at prices from a penny upwards. The consequent growth in seasonal mail first became apparent at Christmas 1877, when the Postmaster General reported that an extra four and a half million letters had passed through the Inland Branch.[86] Within two years the London Post Office was dealing with a rush of nine million items and the public was being asked to relieve pressure by posting early.[87] As with the valentines, the new custom appears to have embraced the entire social spectrum. At the top end of the market were expensive novelties and picturesque depictions of the children of the poor; at the bottom were millions of mass-produced cards produced by firms such as Raphael Tuck and offered for sale not only in stationers but tobacconists and toy shops.[88] From the beginning, secular themes predominated. The exchange of cards celebrated less the Nativity and more family and friendship.

The third major innovation of the period was the picture postcard. The halfpenny postcard had been an immediate success on its introduction in 1870, but until 1894 customers were forced to use official pre-paid cards.[89] The removal of this restriction, followed by the relaxation of regulations over the size of the card in 1899, led the way to the inclusion of photographic views. By the year ending March 1901, over 350 million cards were being delivered in England and Wales, about fifty for each household.[90] In 1902 permission was given to write the message on the same side as the address, leaving the reverse for the picture alone, and the subsequent craze for sending and collecting postcards was only brought to an end by the outbreak of war.[91]

All classes of society could participate. The rich could display their life-style by the size of their cards and the proof they gave of the distance which had been travelled; the poor could celebrate their growing opportunities to visit the seaside. At last Rowland Hill's original hope that mobility would promote correspondence was being realised on a mass scale. However, the writers were travelling in search of pleasure rather than work. The enlarged use of the post was a consequence of an increasing standard of living, cheaper transport and a shorter working week. To a certain extent it was also a consequence of the rise in literacy rates, which had passed 90 per cent by the time the picture postcard came into being. But as with the valentine and the Christmas card, the essence of the success of this genre was the minimal demand it made of the skills of both correspondent and recipient. There was little that could be written and little that needed to be read on one half of one side of a card.

A final indication of the dynamics of correspondence in this period may be gained by setting the postal rates in the context of European development as a whole. Column 1 in table 2.2 demonstrates that half a century after the introduction of the Penny Post, the United Kingdom had much the heaviest flow of mail. The rest of Europe, indeed the rest of the World save the United States, which was to gain the lead in the 1890s, struggled in our wake. This in itself was a cause of much national pride. 'If asked for a true index of the degree of civilisation attained in a given country', wrote Henniker Heaton at Queen Victoria's Golden Jubilee, 'I should suggest the number of letters forwarded and received by its inhabitants.'[92] As early as 1858 the Postmaster General had drawn attention to the fact that as many letters were being delivered in Manchester alone as in the whole of Russia, and the subsequent work of the Universal Postal Union confirmed Britain's success.[93]

Table 2.2. *European postal flows and comparative development in 1890*

	1	2	3	4	5	6
Per capita	Postal deliveries	Elementary school attendance	Pig iron (kilos)	Railway (metres)	Railway passengers	Literacy
UK	68	13.0	240.0	0.84	21.6	93
Belgium	47	10.1	200.0	0.74	13.5	74
Switzerland	41	16.1		1.12	11.1	97
France	40	14.6	50.0	0.87	6.3	87
Netherlands	39	14.3		0.59	4.3	
Germany	34	15.9	80.0	0.87	8.6	90
Denmark	22	15.2		0.91	4.4	
Austria	19	13.2	30.0	0.64	3.1	71
Italy	14	8.0	0.5	0.45	1.7	62
Sweden	12	14.4	30.0	1.67	2.6	90
Norway	12	13.3	0.5	0.78	2.0	
Portugal	11	5.1		0.45	1.3	
Spain	9		15.0	0.57	1.5	39
Hungary	8	11.0	20.0		1.7	
Serbia	5	3.0		0.25	0.1	
Finland	4	2.3	10.0	0.80	1.0	
Romania	3	3.8		0.50	0.6	
Russia	2		8.0	0.26	0.4	28

Source: UPU, *Statistique générale 1890*, p. 2; B. R. Mitchell, *Abstract of European Historical Statistics* (2nd edn, London, 1981), pp. 412–15, 629–35, 786–806; Graff, *Legacies*, pp. 302–12; Cipolla, *Literacy*, table 30. The literacy figure for Spain is for 1887; for France and Italy, 1901.

The extent to which correspondence might be seen as an epitome of civilisation depended in part on the value attached to the use of literacy, and in part on the relationship between postal flows and other more conventional criteria of progress. Columns 2 to 5 of table 2.2 present comparative data on education in the form of elementary school attendance, industrialisation in the form of pig iron production, and transport in the form of the railway. In general terms the columns conform to the expected pattern, with the centre of development in the North-West, and countries becoming less advanced towards the southern and eastern borders of Europe. There are, however, significant variations in the degree of association between the separate indices.

The most obvious candidates for a strong correlation are columns 1, the use of literacy, and 2, the machinery for its provision, but in the event the two sets of variables are only loosely connected. The United Kingdom is ninth in the table of elementary school attendance, two places behind Norway, which has less than a fifth of its postal flow. Only towards the bottom of the table does the effort to spread the skills of literacy appear to match the demand for their employment. Whilst it is not possible to compile a complete set of European literacy rates for 1890, column 6 suggests again that whereas low standards inevitably inhibited correspondence, high scores did not in themselves guarantee equally high postal flows. Spain's nine letters a head and Russia's two may be explained by their illiteracy rates of 61% and 72% respectively,[94] but elsewhere Sweden, half-way down the league of correspondence with twelve letters a head, was about as literate as the United Kingdom at the top.[95]

It is evident from column 3 that there is also no simple association between industrialisation and the use of literacy. Whilst the United Kingdom and Belgium are at the head of the league of both correspondence and per capita pig iron production, Switzerland, the Netherlands and Denmark manage to achieve respectable rates of postage with no heavy industry at all. In the middle of the table Sweden and Norway display exactly the same propensity to write letters in spite of a wide divergence in their respective levels of industrial development. At the bottom, Finland's forty-year history of manufacturing iron had made little or no impact on its use of the post.

The one index of progress to demonstrate any consistent relationship with the postal service is the other major form of inland communication in the nineteenth century, the railway. In one sense the connection is obvious. The railway and postal systems were created alongside each other throughout Europe, and from the beginning were dependent on each other's development. Without the introduction of a rapid and reliable means of transport, the postal reformers could not have realised their ambitions, and conversely the fledgling railway companies derived immense benefit from the revenue generated by carrying mail. Rowland Hill in fact attributed part of the fall in profits following the introduction of the Penny Post to the exploitation by the railway companies of their position as monopoly carriers on important routes.[96] He was, however, successful in persuading the Brighton Railway Company, of which he became chairman, to carry letters free of charge, on the grounds that 'residence in Brighton, and therefore custom to the railway, would be increased by every addition to postal facilities between that town and the metropolis'.[97]

Throughout the remainder of the century, the success of one form of communication stimulated the expansion of the other, but even so the correlation between use of literacy and use of the railway displayed in the table is remarkably close. With a few minor adjustments the parallel rankings are maintained from top to bottom. Even the proportions between the returns in each column are broadly similar. At almost every point the postal flows predict the weight of railway passenger traffic and vice versa. As the contrast between columns 4 and 5 makes clear, the key factor was the work of the railway and not its length of track. By 1890 most countries had completed their rail networks, and those with a small population scattered over a wide area, such as Norway or Finland, had achieved per capita distances as high as the United Kingdom. Just as the post represented the employment rather than merely the possession of literacy, so its mirror image was to be found in the business rather than the existence of the railway.

The financial interdependence of the two forms of communication only partly explains their affinity. Of greater importance were the common features in the pattern of demand for each service. Like the post, the early growth of the railway was largely dependent on middle-class patronage. And whereas the needs of business and businessmen generated much of the custom, there was from the beginning an unexpectedly high volume of recreational use by those with the time and money to exploit the new opportunities.[98] Working-class people by contrast continued to walk to work, or in search of work, and confined their recreational activity to the vicinity of the home. The penny a mile 'Parliamentary Train' was introduced only four years after the Penny Post, but for the labouring poor a railway journey remained an even more special occurrence than the receipt of a letter. The most immediate impact of the railway on this section of the community, as was the case with the Post Office, was in the provision not of a new service but of a new form of employment. It took a long time for the working class to begin to make large-scale use of the new means of transport, and with the exception of a limited amount of commuting to work in the biggest cities, the journeys were made not by individuals but by families. Communication was for pleasure. It was both a consequence and a celebration of a marginal increase in prosperity. Literally and symbolically the railway and the post came together at the seaside. The working-class family left home on the excursion train, and returned through the picture postcard.

Conclusion

In his *Early Recollections*, Moses Horler, an 82-year-old mason who had spent all his days in the Somerset village of Radstock, looked back to the operation of the postal services in the early 1830s. Letters were delivered to the families in the community by an old woman called Shukey Cottle, whose chief attributes were her fondness for snuff and her complete illiteracy. Each time the mail coach left an item at the Bell Inn, the landlord would give her verbal instructions about where to take it. When, eventually, she found the right house, the addressee was often equally illiterate, and so the letter 'had to be taken round to some cottage or other where somebody lived who was more learned, who would kindly read it for them'.[99] The skill of reading, like every other skill the village needed for its daily affairs, was at once a personal and a collective possession. No matter how simple the way of life, there was inevitably a degree of specialisation in the acquisition of knowledge and expertise. A combination of aptitude, opportunity and necessity would cause an individual to develop particular skills of use to the family or the wider community. Some were so difficult to master that those who possessed them might expect payment if called upon to exercise them. Others were more commonplace and could be exchanged on the basis of mutual obligation. Into the former category came the shoeing of horses and perhaps the delivery of babies; into the latter came brewing or mending furniture or reading and writing, everyday skills that might be distributed within the household as well as across the village or neighbourhood. As with so many tools, an essential quality of literacy was that it could be borrowed when it was needed, by other members of the family or other families in the locality.[100] In this sense the variegated patterns of marks and signatures created by the weddings were a means of binding rather than dividing the community. They were one more element in the complex structure of reciprocity which enabled the working class to make the most effective use of its meagre resources.

As the occasion to make use of literacy increased, so families took steps to increase their access to it, but the continuing presence of those unable to make effective use of such education as they had received guaranteed that the need to share the skills continued throughout the period. In the 1880s we find Flora Thompson composing letters for itinerant farm labourers, while her mother was entrusted with the task of writing to the soldier son of a neighbour who could read but had forgotten how to use a pen. Incoming mail was often read aloud at cottage doors.[101] In only two respects is it possible, in this context, to detect ways in which the increasing presence of literacy was creating new lines of demarcation.

Firstly the inter-generational inequalities of attainment created by the rapid spread of literacy during the second two thirds of the century introduced a distinct bias in the exchange of services. The old sought the help of the young more often than children required the assistance of their parents and grandparents. On the eve of the First World War, Kathleeen Dayus, growing up in a Birmingham slum, discovered that her elementary schooling was reversing the direction of dependency. When her mother, one of the illiterates who survived well beyond the official triumph of nominal literacy, went on a large shopping expedition, she had to get her daughter to write out a list,[102] and when her parents applied for free school clothing, they were helpless when Kathleen came home with a form to fill in: 'I always read the leaflet to Mum and Dad and explained what it was all about because Mum couldn't read or write, and although Dad could write, he could only manage to read the newspaper.'[103]

More generally, it had been hoped that the spread of literacy, and its application for purposes such as letter writing, would connect families across the boundaries of their communities. The 'one dead level of isolated communes',[104] separated from each other and from educated society by their reliance on the spoken word, was to be replaced by a network of communicating individuals. The privacy of the working-class neighbourhood would be broken down, and the private realm of the working-class family extended by means of epistolary intercourse. Whilst outside observers under-stated the ability of the labouring poor to get in touch with each other over long distances in times of domestic crisis, the experiment of postal reform nearly foundered on the disinclination of the mass of the population to make use of the new facilities. However, at the very end of the period there was some evidence that families were beginning to use correspondence to maintain relationships beyond the immediate locality. Following the seasonal success of first the valentine and then the Christmas card, the postcard made easy contact possible at all times of the year. Edith Hall, the daughter of a foundry worker in Hayes, vividly remembered this long-delayed impact of Rowland Hill's reform:

> Just prior to the Great War of 1914 when I was about six years old, postcards with the then half-penny postage were sent between my relations each day. My grandmother would send us a card *each evening* which we received by first delivery the next morning. She would then receive our reply card the *same evening*. If one lived in the same town as one's correspondent, an early morning posted card would be delivered at twelve mid-day the same day and a reply card, if sent immediately, would be received the same afternoon. I still have many of these postcards proving what a wonderful service it was; *all in one day* – and that families like our own could keep in daily touch if they so wished.[105]

When the family travelled by train to see her grandmother, postcards would be sent to relations living along the route, 'and an aunt and cousin would be on the platform at Grantham and another aunt at Peterborough. We would chat and exchange gifts through the lowered window of the carriage door, then continue on our journey.'[106]

Mass communication was beginning to transform the perception of family. Hitherto the limits of effective day-to-day relationships had been co-terminous with the neighbourhood. Only in an emergency had distant relatives possessed a function, and their willingness or capacity to respond to calls for help was always uncertain. Now almost the same level of intercourse could be maintained with an aunt in the next county as an uncle in the next street. News, gossip, small services, tokens of affection, could be exchanged with little effort and less expense. The subsequent arrival of the telephone and cheap road transport merely completed the transition which was set in motion not by the Penny Post but by the halfpenny postcard.

3

EDUCATION

From the beginning, the rates of literacy derived from the marriage registers were seen as an index of the progress of the nation's schools. In his second annual report the Registrar General explained why he had decided to extend the analysis of births, deaths and marriages to include some of the ancillary information collected at the weddings: 'I have found', he wrote, 'the Registers of Marriages calculated to throw much light upon the state of education with respect to writing, among the adult population of England and Wales.'[1] On the face of it, the tables which appeared in the subsequent reports bore witness to a striking achievement. Whereas the New Poor Law did little more than keep pauperism in check, and the public health legislation was for decades ineffective, the field of elementary education could be regarded as an outstanding example of successful co-operation between private philanthropy and public intervention. We now know that during the eighty years between Hardwick's Marriage Act and the beginning of state involvement in education, male illiteracy had been almost stable at 40 per cent and female illiteracy had fallen only ten points from an initial level of over 60 per cent.[2] During the succeeding eighty years, as public expenditure on education rose from £50,000 to £19.5 million,[3] the level of illiteracy fell with gathering momentum. In the report for 1879 the Registrar General contrasted the annual rate of decrease of 1.34 per cent for the 1845–50 period with the rate of 5.37 per cent for 1875–9, and concluded that 'these figures bear indisputable testimony to the increasingly rapid spread of elementary education in comparatively recent years'.[4] In the following three and a half decades the consolidation of a compulsory school system bore fruit in what appeared to be the final abolition of nominal illiteracy.[5]

There is, however, another way of reading these statistics. At the outset the levels of literacy during the first half of the period were an indication of how much could be achieved without the presence of the state or even of a widespread system of church education. The patchy efforts of the charity schools do not explain how three men in five could sign their names in the 1750s. By the time the State began to make a token contribution to the pioneering efforts of the National and the British and Foreign School

Societies in 1833, the final drive towards full literacy was already under way, despite the difficulties caused by a rapidly growing population. As the mean age of marriage was some fifteen years beyond the latest time a child was likely to be at school, it is necessary to look forward to measure the impact of educational developments. Such a calculation reveals that the average for brides and grooms had passed 60 per cent before the State spent a farthing on education, and had reached almost 90 per cent before it entered the field in its own right following Forster's Education Act of 1870.[6] The full consequences of compulsion were not apparent until the mid 1890s, by which time less than 5 per cent of the task remained.

The Registrar General's tables in fact draw as much attention to the consumers as to the suppliers of education.[7] They suggest that the foundation for the eventual victory was laid not in the schoolroom but in the working-class family. During the first half of the period the comparatively high levels of marriage register signatures were sustained by teaching which took place in the home or in schools largely supported by the fees of their pupils.[8] During the second half the increasingly elaborate efforts of the churches and the State were, until almost the end, dependent on whether working-class parents were prepared to send their children to school. Whilst parents and children were subject to an ever more complex range of pressures, for the most part they retained freedom of choice. The defeat of illiteracy was in the last resort the responsibility of the illiterates themselves.

In the broadest sense, every parent was a teacher. The tools of written communication were only one element of an intricate body of skills, values and information which had to be transmitted in and around the home. The experience of formal education has to be set in the context of the general learning process which took place in each generation. It will be argued in this chapter that the role of the classroom in teaching literacy throughout this period was dependent upon and in turn deeply influenced the wider relationship between school and home. Reading and writing came to be the principal currency of exchange in the long-running negotiation between parents and teachers. The outcome of the debate determined the part to be played by the acquisition of literacy in the overall intellectual development of the children who were growing up in the period.

The domestic curriculum

For most of those born into the families of the labouring poor, childhood was a period of compromise and conflict. Parents struggled to reconcile their responsibilities to nurture their children with the need to exploit their earning potential in order to keep the family economy afloat.[9] From an early age the child was both a dependant and a contributor, ill protected by its family and ill used by the labour market. Yet however harsh and brief the experience, childhood was always a time of learning. It is possible to identify four components of the *cursus honorum*. Firstly the child had to master the essential skills for living and working. Secondly an elaborate body of information concerning the identity of the child and its community had to be acquired. Thirdly the child had to discover and develop its imaginative faculties. Finally a set of moral values had to be absorbed. The content of the curriculum varied according to when, where and how the child was brought up. It was rarely completed, but it was as inescapable as formal schooling was to become in the last quarter of the nineteenth century.

In the beginning there was walking and talking. Physical and cultural deprivation might cause delay, but by school age substantial progress would have been made in the development of muscular co-ordination and speech. Little is known about the early stages of acquiring either skill. The future naturalist Edmund Gosse could remember what it felt like to see and think before he could act or speak,[10] but for most adults the first steps towards participation in the family's affairs were taken out of reach of memory. We must rely on modern child psychology for accounts of the learning process in infancy. The transition from crawling to walking represents a major achievement, and it is now accepted that sophisticated cognitive skills are employed as the power of communication is extended from simple words to what is likely to be a wide range of sentence structures by the age of four or five.[11]

It was not until the child had gained some independence around the home that the period of conscious learning began. Through encouragement and ambition, imitation and trial, faculties were enlarged and capacities were discovered. Growing up near Oundle in the middle of the nineteenth century, the stonemason's son Alfred Ireson gained his first lessons whilst at play: 'Child life in the village is full of romance. The free open country provides fun and mischief for boys and girls alike. It was here where I first learned to swim and fight. These things formed a great part of a boy's life.'[12] Later he could set himself the more specialised task of mastering the fife and playing in the town band, but by this time his parents were directing his attention to more practical skills: 'Our dear mother taught us all to net. This became a financial advantage. I spent my time in making potato nets. Potatoes were then boiled in nets, which I sold for 2d each.'[13] Other jobs were tried before his real occupational training began at the age of about fourteen: 'my father having charge of building new schools at Warmington decided that I should go with him to learn the stone-mason's trade'.[14]

Whether in recreation or work, this education was as continuous as it was varied. Milestones were reached – one day a particular tree was climbed, another, something was made for the first time that could be sold – but always a new challenge was waiting. In this context, the task of gaining command over the tools of written communication was merely one amongst many. It was far from being the most difficult. A bright child could pick up a basic command of literacy at an age when it was incapable of performing any but the most limited manual tasks. 'I learned to read, they said, almost without instruction', recalled Thomas Cooper, the son of a widow, 'and at three years old I used to be set on a stool in Dame Brown's school, to teach one Master Bodley, who was seven years old, his letters.'[15] Master Bodley might be a more representative member of his generation, yet in the nineteenth century teachers expected to finish with their pupils by the time they were nine or ten and often younger, in spite of the assumed cultural poverty of the home background and persistent irregularity of attendance. The evidence of the marriage registers confirms that at the most basic level of achievement, their ambitions were not misplaced. In the sphere of work training, on the other hand, the requirements of an artisan trade were traditionally held to be so demanding that a boy was not considered capable of even beginning to acquire them until he was fourteen. An apprenticeship ended at about the same age as a modern university education, and whilst the preservation of the institution owed much to custom and its role in strengthening the position of the artisan in the labour market, recent research suggests that at the end of the century many workers still faced a substantial course of learning if they were to function effectively in the modern industrial processes.[16] The craftsman had a far wider range of skills and information to impart to his apprentice than the schoolteacher had to his pupil. It is likely that Alfred Ireson learned a great deal more building schools than attending them.

Whereas some form of work training was inescapable, reading and writing could be excluded from the world of learning altogether. 'The ploughman learns to plough', observed William Cobbett,

> the gardener to dig, the shepherd's boy how to feed and fold the sheep, the carpenter and the bricklayer how to build houses, the shoe-maker how to make shoes; these and many other things, people may learn to do without the aid of books; and great numbers of people are very clever at their different trades, and earn a great deal of money, and bring up their families very well, without even knowing how to read.[17]

Although literacy became a more common element in the overall curriculum as the nineteenth century progressed, it always had to compete for the child's limited time with a wide range of skills which had equal or greater priority. Only occasionally did it serve as the key to other forms of learning. Ireson was able to use the education he had patched together from two day schools and a Wesleyan Sunday school when he bought a 'sixpenny tutor' to help him play the fife, but the rest of his complicated learning process relied on imitation, experiment and verbal instruction.

The acquisition of skills depended upon and in turn widened the child's body of knowledge. 'In Great Britain and Ireland', wrote the founder of the National Schools Society, 'at least 1,750,000 of the population of the country at an age to be instructed, grow up to an adult state without any instruction at all, in the grossest ignorance.'[18] In reality, the ever-increasing number of children of school age spent all their time finding out about the world into which they had been born. By adulthood they would be in possession of an immense variety of information about the people, places and events which constituted their community. In most cases, the perspective of the knowledge stretched back beyond the child's birth. Those who came to write about themselves could usually manage to begin their narratives by outlining their family background. Thus, for instance, the waggon-way wright Anthony Errington established where he had come from: 'My farther, Robert Errington, was Sun of William Errington of Nither Witten, Northumberland, Farmer at the Langlee, who removed from their to Kiblesworth, near Lamsly, in Durham, wheare they farmed.'[19] However limited, there was a tradition to inherit, and as the child grew up, an environment to discover. Overcrowded houses, non-existent gardens and distant parental supervision encouraged the exploration of every street or field, every lamp-post or tree, every pond or stream which could be reached in the course of a day's play. Each child was its own cartographer, compiling in its head a traveller's guide to all the sources of pleasure and danger in the neighbourhood. In this way Joseph Gutteridge, the son of a Coventry weaver, gradually extended his horizons:

> whenever an opportunity occurred, either in the early morning or after school hours, we were in the fields and lanes of the neighbourhood collecting bird eggs, insects, and flowers ... By this time I became well acquainted with the locality in which we lived and for miles around, and also knew the common names and habits of the birds that frequented the neighbourhood.[20]

Other forms of knowledge were more abstract and often more painful. Poverty was experienced from birth, but deprivation had to be learned. The discovery was delayed until the child was capable of seeing and thinking for itself. 'It was when I was about 10 or 11 years of age', recalled the cab driver's son Ernest Robinson, 'that I came to realise how poor my parents were indeed the whole of the people round about.'[21] However it occurred, whether through a chance encounter with some form of privilege, or through a sudden insight into what had always been visible,

'First knowledge of disadvantage',[22] as Charles Shaw described it, was never forgotten. Philip Inman's mother had to take in washing and go cleaning to keep her four children: 'We always knew, and it seemed as if we always had known, the struggle my mother was having to bring us up. We accepted the fact that life was harder than for other families. It was only the first time that it came home to me with vivid force that it hurt.'[23] It was a lesson which split childhood in two. Once the existence of inequality was grasped, once the child realised where its family stood in the social and economic hierarchy, every fragment of information about its world was brought into focus.

The teachers for the course of study which permeated every moment of work and play were both personal and impersonal. Much was learned through what Francis Place called 'the education of circumstances',[24] much else from the tales and reminiscences of those who were further ahead in the curriculum. Literacy and schooling played at best a subordinate role. 'My education was very meagre', wrote the 'Chartist Rebel'; 'I learnt more in Newgate than at my Sunday school'.[25] In assessing the value of an instructor, the child paid little attention to his or her educational qualifications. 'William Bowyer', the son of a Battersea ironmonger, had a proper respect for his grandfather, who was then in his late eighties:

> In a small boy's eyes he was a man of immense learning, with an astonishing memory and a vast fund of information on every subject I could mention, and I do not doubt that actually he was a well-informed man, of penetrating and balanced judgment, though he had had no opportunity whatever of formal education.[26]

No schoolteacher could hope to compete at this level, and no text book could match so rich a vein of knowledge.

Reading and writing could perform just two functions here. Firstly they might supplement the traditional means of storing and transmitting information. A particular example was the use of the Bible as a record of family history. John Clare spent long hours in his childhood in the company of an old shepherd, who used to read aloud

> from an old fragment of a Bible which he carried in his pocket for the day a family relic which possesd on its covers and title pages in rude scrawls geneoligys of the third and fourth Generations when aunts uncles and grandmothers dyd and when cousins etc were marri/e/d and brothers and sisters born occupying all the blank leaves in the book and title pages bhorders which leaves

were pres/r/ved with a sacred veneration tho half the contents had been sufferd to drop out and be lost.[27]

Secondly they could extend the limits of the knowable world. Whilst the details of the community's past and present were virtually inexhaustible, always there lay periods and places beyond its collective knowledge and experience. If the child reached the boundaries before its curiosity was satisfied, the only recourse was to books. The facts proffered by the schoolmaster often seemed irrelevant, boring or merely confusing. The young Joseph Ashby and his companions found it difficult to reconcile private and public learning:

> the boys had a whole body of knowledge, much of which was special to themselves, or shared only with a few men in whose retentive memories boyhood lived and from whom they learned the old names. Until the reading-books in school and the puzzled looks of strangers made the names seem odd, the spotted wood-pecker was a hickwall, the hedge-sparrow Betty bumbarrel, and the heron Mollyhern.[28]

There is, however, no doubt that the extracts from scientific, historical and geographical studies which began to appear in the better school textbooks during the last quarter of the nineteenth century did meet a real need. Travellers' tales in particular had always been eagerly welcomed by those who came across a battered copy on a bookstall or in a free library. With Captain Cook at the helm, the child could voyage beyond the streets and fields which bounded its reality.

At this point, the distinction between fact and fantasy begins to blur. The South Sea Islands appealed primarily to the reader's sense of the fabulous. 'To a child', wrote Robert Blatchford, 'the boundaries of fact and fiction are ambiguous; old King Cole is as real as King George, and a mermaid no more remarkable than a policeman.'[29] Few children could change their circumstances or their prospects, but each was free to create and people a private mental world. The faculty of imagination was the birthright of the poorest and hungriest child; material possessions might aid its development, but their absence could never prevent its expression.

The principal arena for discovering and enlarging the imagination was play. 'The love of it is so natural in youth', wrote the Cornish fisherman's son and future Chartist William Lovett, 'that the more it is sought to be restrained, the more it is craved after, and the buoyancy of feeling at times breaks through all restraints, especially when great temptation presents itself.'[30] No upbringing was more deprived than that of the Yorkshire collier George Marsh. His father died when he was four, leaving his mother to bring up a family of eleven children. He was in and out of the workhouse and begging on the streets for bread before he was six, thereafter dragging tubs underground to help feed himself and his siblings. Yet still he found the opportunity to be a child: 'My playmates and I used to play football bare footed. We punched the ball up a bank and it rolled back again to us. We also in the frosty weather went to slide on Peck's pond.'[31] The pattern of recreation was infinitely varied yet always familiar, each game an intricate combination of invention and convention, whether the playground was a field or a river bank or the cobbles of an industrial town. 'Our street games were simple and traditional', recalled the Bolton mill-hand's daughter Alice Foley, 'but we found them wholly captivating. They came around with the seasons . . .'[32]

Children fed off each other's imaginations, and at the same time were nourished by the story-telling of parents and grandparents. John Harris, the Cornish tin-miner and poet, attributed his creative powers to the stimulus he received in early childhood:

> And how often my gentle mother charmed me in the light of the spluttering furze-brand, as we clustered around her knees in the dear old kitchen, and she told us tales of long-ago, when men loved virtue more than gold, and simpleness and truth were unalloyed gems. Sitting by the old hearth-stone where my grandfather had sat before me, and another generation had mused and passed away, I listened to her loving stories with wondering joy . . . And as I listened my young heart beat, and imagination bore me away on her dazzling wings.[33]

As John Harris was growing up in the 1820s, polite culture was finally losing contact altogether with this practice. Writing in 1843, 'Felix Summerley' (Henry Cole) lamented the apparent loss: 'The many tales sung or said from time immemorial, which appealed to the other and certainly not less important elements of a child's mind, its fancy, imagination, sympathies, affections, are almost all gone out of memory, and are scarcely to be obtained.'[34] The broader question of the fate of the oral tradition in imaginative discourse will be discussed in chapter 6, but in this context there is little evidence that working-class parents were ceasing to tell stories to their children when the need and opportunity arose. Like Harris, the future radical journalist Robert Blatchford discovered an alternative world at the knee of his mother, who 'used to sing and read to us and tell us stories',[35] and Alice Foley could turn from her street games to her father, who when sober 'could quickly capture my imagination by his store of Irish folklore'.[36]

Neither the games nor the stories required the acquisition or employment of the skills of literacy. In their own powers of invention, and in the memories of the older generation, the children of the labouring poor possessed rich resources which could be tapped without the aid of education. Jack Lawson's mental development owed a great deal to his father, who was a merchant seaman: 'Although he was almost illiterate, he told wonderful stories in choice English – never using a word of dialect . . . All unconsciously he was playing the schoolmaster to me, for he was quickening the mind and touching the imagination.'[37] School itself was scarcely the natural ally of such entertainment. 'Like most children, when very young', admitted William Lovett, 'my love of play was far greater than that of learning.'[38] Those who subsequently wrote of their childhood rarely associated their time in the classroom with the development or expression of their creative powers. However, it can be argued that of all the categories of the learning process, the discovery and enhancement of the imagination had long been the most deeply influenced by literary artefacts. Directly or indirectly, few children failed to gain some benefit from what they or others in their family or community had read.

As it developed from John Newbery onwards, the genre of 'children's literature' remained largely out of reach of working-class families.[39] Prices were too high for outright purchase, and whilst occasional second-hand copies might be bought, begged or borrowed, it was almost impossible to gain controlled access to new books until the public libraries began to follow the example set by Manchester, which opened a special children's department in 1862.[40] Instead the staple fare comprised works which at one time had been read by all ages in all sections of society. Samuel Bamford's 'assiduous quest after the wonderful' was transformed when his parents moved to Manchester to manage a workhouse, and he discovered a bookshop in whose window 'were exhibited numerous songs, ballads, tales and other publications, with horrid and awful-looking woodcuts at the head'.[41] He had by now received just enough education to exploit this opportunity:

> Every farthing I could scrape together was now spent in purchasing histories of 'Jack the Giant Killer', 'Saint George and the Dragon', 'Tom Hickathrift', 'Jack and the Beanstalk', 'The Seven Champions of Christendom', the tale of 'Fair Rosamond', 'History of Friar Bacon', 'Account of the Lancashire Witches', 'The Witches of the Woodlands', and such like romances, whilst my metrical collections embraced but a few pieces besides 'Robin Hood's songs' and 'The Ballad of Chevy Chase'. Of all these tales and ballads I was soon master, and they formed the subjects of many a wonder-creating story for my acquaintaince both at the workhouse and elsewhere.[42]

The heady brew of drama, fantasy and morality was several hundred years old by the time Bamford encountered it. 'Tom Hickathrift' and 'The

Seven Champions of Christendom' had been in the packs of chapmen as they walked from village to village in the early seventeenth century.[43] Such works were at once ephemeral and ageless. They were as flimsy in their construction as they were in their sensations, yet they survived from generation to generation, connecting the old with the young, the country with the city. Far away in the village of Helpston on the edge of the Lincolnshire fens, Bamford's contemporary John Clare was absorbed in a similar list of '6py Pamphlets that are in the possession of every door calling hawker and found on every bookstall at fairs and markets whose titles are as familiar with every one as his own name'.[44] In his reading he shared the experience of both the children in the industrial centres to the north and his own almost illiterate father, who 'could read a little in a bible or testament and was very fond of the supersti/ti/ous tales that are hawked about a sheet for a penny, such as old Nixons Prophecies, Mother Bunches Fairey Tales, and Mother Shiptons Legacy etc.'.[45] Here, the distance between the Bible and Mother Shipton need not be large. The New and in particular the Old Testament contained much to encourage 'the quest after the wonderful', as did *Pilgrim's Progress*, which survived in popular culture alongside the contemporary chapbooks. 'This book it was', wrote the Kettering weaver and poet J. A. Leatherland, 'that early awakened my imaginative powers.'[46]

Reading is a solitary activity, and as literacy spread and it became possible to get hold of a wider range of books, tensions were set up within the traditional pattern of recreation which will be examined later. In terms of the child's imaginative development, however, there was no necessary conflict between oral and literary sources of inspiration. The stories told to the children may have started life in print and then been passed down through memory, and in turn those who had the opportunity to read recounted their findings to those who had not. Books reinforced and extended play. Bamford and Clare both encountered Robinson Crusoe, 'that ever exciting day-dream of boys',[47] and thereafter became shipwrecked mariners resourcefully combating the perils of a desert island. If the growing towns isolated more and more children from the woods and ponds which could become jungles and oceans, some compensation could be found in the wider range of fiction which appeared in the second half of the nineteenth century. Mark Grossek, the son of a Bermondsey tailor, had little difficulty in transcending the limitations of the streets through which he roamed with his companions:

> We did all these things, and in doing them, we quaffed the heady cup of make-believe to the dregs. Make-believe which was the product of mixed literary influences, but largely Conan Doyle, Ballantyne, Guy Boothby, and Talbot Baines Read. Make-

believe, which was amply eked out by the peculiar features of South-East London itself.[48]

By contrast, the final category of the learning process, the moral education of the growing child, was essentially a matter of people rather than books, precepts rather than formal instruction. Concerned as they were to discuss their moral as well as their intellectual development, many of the autobiographers devoted attention to the influences on their character during the formative years of their life. In most cases the principal role was attributed to their parents. At a general level there was the example set by their fathers and in particular by their mothers as they struggled to raise their children. No matter how early they were forced to send sons and daughters out to work, no matter how little attention they were able to devote to the needs of an individual child, all who made any attempt at parenthood were faced with a life of toil and sacrifice on behalf of their family. Complaints about the age at which labour commenced abound in these accounts, but the only occasion on which blame was attached to parents was where a drunken or neglectful father wilfully undermined the family's limited resources. Children knew, sometimes because they were told, more often because they came to see for themselves as they grew older, the reality which lay behind the choices which had to be made on their behalf. Whilst material pressures constantly threatened the destruction of the family, it was the resistance to them which bound it together. Philip Inman described his home as a

> frail little ship, for ever driven through heavy seas, any of which, at any moment, might swamp it. There was a kind of joy and triumph because of this, in all our life together. We were keeping going, because of the devotion of the crew, but above all because of the unflinching courage of the crew.[49]

From their experience, children were capable of distilling abstract values. Lessons were taught by action and attitude. James Saunders, the son of a butcher, was able to trace his own principles back to their source:

> I believe my mother was one of the most absolutely unselfish women who ever breathed, but at the same time I never met any one with a more clear and emphatic sense of right or wrong, or with so accurate and instantaneous an insight into character ... She instilled into my mind a firm belief in the certain victory of integrity and perseverance.[50]

This was a basic practical morality, exemplified by conduct and transmitted through the day-to-day relationships of members of the family. 'My mother', recalled the shoemaker's son David Barr, 'was a woman of beautiful, exemplary and heroic character, whose influence did much to mould my life and has followed me through the intervening years.'[51] It was not necessarily spiritual, although it was difficult to avoid religious language when it came to writing about it, as when the trade unionist and MP George Edwards looked back to his poverty stricken childhood: 'I owe all I am and have to my saintly father and mother. It was they who taught me the first principles of righteousness.'[52] Edwards' parents were totally illiterate, and their son remained so until his marriage. Yet it is clear that they had been most effective teachers. The key to success was character rather than learning. 'My mother was unable to read or write', recalled Henry Snell, 'but I have never known, or heard of, anyone who excelled her in forethought and matronly concern for those dependent upon her.[53]

Literacy only became relevant where religion was a recognised component of the moral training. The particular references to Christianity might amount to little more than an extension or reinforcement of some general precepts, as in the framework Errington's father gave to his children: 'his Law was to us all to be honest, to be Charatable, to shun bad Company, and to keep the Comandmants in a Christin life And to love each other was the Charge from our parents'.[54] But in some cases it took the form of a systematic teaching which formed the basis of an active faith in later life. Detailed surveys carried out during the late 1830s and early 1840s revealed that both in the countryside and the towns books could be found in at least three-quarters of the homes of the labouring poor.[55] These cottage libraries were very small and their contents frequently unread, but almost always they contained some religious literature – a bible, or a prayer book, or a few old tracts or sermons. If a parent wished to turn to the Scriptures to assist a lesson, he or she would not have had far to go to find a text. For its part the child could begin its own spiritual explorations, once the basic skills and knowledge had been acquired. Recuperating in bed after a severe illness, the seven-year-old farm labourer's son James Bowd asked for

> My Books. My father and Mother never tryed to keep the Books from me as I was so fond of Reading. I Remember One Day having a Bible to read I was Looking in the book of Psalms and I Read the twenty third psalm The Lord is My Shepherd I shall not want the words never wholy Left me from that day to this and Blessed be god I have lived to prove the truth of them words I can truthfully say that I never have known wants to this day.[56]

Insofar as schooling, particularly as provided by the Church societies until the middle decades of the nineteenth century, was heavily dependent on the Bible both as a primer and a prime source of moral instruction, it could serve as a natural extension of this aspect of domestic teaching. It is perhaps surprising, therefore, how infrequently formal education was attributed a positive role in this process. For most children, morality seems to have been a family concern, and where their classroom experience did play a part, the key factor was not the curriculum but the personality of the schoolmaster acting *in loco parentis*. Not all parents matched the standards set by those of George Edwards, and conversely not all teachers were either incompetent amateurs looking for an undemanding alternative to manual labour or half-trained professionals attempting to apply an ill-conceived method to enormous classes of bored children.

From time to time the child encountered an individual with a real gift for teaching who was capable of taking an effective interest in the welfare of his or her pupils. A committed Sunday school teacher, a talented proprietor of a private day school able to build upon the assets of a small class and a shared cultural background, a Church or Board school teacher whose sense of vocation survived the system in which he or she worked, could have a major impact in circumstances where the child's parents were losing the struggle to protect their family from the pressures of the outside world. Charles Shaw had to begin his working life at the age of seven, and when his father, a painter and gilder, was blacklisted for leading a strike, the entire family was forced into the workhouse, where he was permitted to see his mother for just one hour a week. When he re-emerged it was back to work, but he was able to return to a Sunday school, where he entered the class taught by George Kirkham: 'I cannot tell all this "saintly" young man was to me . . . but in his hands I was a plant carefully tended, nurtured and watered.'[57] The influence of such teachers was often in inverse proportion to their level of professional training. The farm-labourer's son Henry Snell owed much to the staff of his Sunday school:

> These instructors of village youth had no claim to learning in the subjects they taught, nor had they knowledge of the problems of the wider world which existed beyond the boundaries of their own parish; but from their example and the homely wisdom of their teaching I learned a portion of the alphabet of duty and personal responsibility.[58]

In the rare instances where a teacher possessed both the personal qualities and the opportunity to exercise such care, it was not forgotten. In most children's lives there were too few adults able or willing to treat them as children.

It is of course possible that schooling exerted an influence on the child's moral development of which it was unaware, either at the time or later when an account came to be written. This is a matter which will be examined later in the chapter when the ambitions of the various categories of educators in the period will be discussed in more detail. The hours in the classroom, however brief, are likely to have made some impression, but it is important to put the experience into its proper context. Every child had received, alongside and beyond whatever formal education might be available, profound lessons in conduct, in the application of right and wrong to situations which it would later face as an adult and parent. It may be that the passage of time increased the tendency of sons and daughters to canonise a mother or father who had struggled against poverty to bring up a family. There were instances enough of parents who had failed to meet the challenge. Continuous privation cauterised the emotions and drove some to drink or desertion, blighting the lives of those around them. Such defeats were later recounted with a combination of pity, pain and sometimes contempt. But where the family survived, the interdependence which held it together provided the basis for whatever moral sense the child would acquire as it grew up.

The pattern of learning which took place in childhood, the acquisition of skills, knowledge, imaginative powers and moral values, constituted what is loosely called 'socialisation':[59] the induction of a new generation into the ways of thinking and behaving established by its predecessors. In a sense it was a conservative process. Parents passed on what they knew, and children had little enough time to find out about their inheritance before they joined the adult world of labour. Yet all learning involved discovery; for the child, everything was new. The education was both a means of establishing the complex ways in which the child was part of the community, and of defining its separate, unique identity. In that literacy was a means of both recording information and of creating new knowledge, it had a natural and slowly growing place in this process. It was one amongst the many skills which might be mastered, and as a tool it could be used in the remaining areas of curriculum which was gradually becoming more elaborate. At the same time its role remained marginal, with perhaps its most valuable application, in the enlargement of the imagination, lying furthest from the essential business of living and working. In a child's eyes, an adult could be learned, wise and endlessly entertaining yet quite illiterate, and in turn a child could graduate with honours from its course of learning without once encountering the written word.

Becoming literate

The sense in which literacy was an optional but far from alien presence in the traditional pattern of child-rearing is reinforced when we turn our attention to the established methods of acquisition. By the end of the nineteenth century, attendance at school was bidding to override all other priorities in the working-class family. Every concern and activity had to give way to lessons in reading and writing in the classroom. However, if we take a view of the period as a whole, a rather different perspective emerges. In essence, literacy was merely one amongst a range of goods and services which parents might obtain on behalf of themselves or their family. It was a more or less desirable commodity which had to compete with many others for the available resources of time and money.

The life of the labouring poor was full of luxuries. Very few things could be counted as absolute necessities. Food and drink could not be dispensed with altogether, but nearly every item in the diet save perhaps bread could be deleted or substituted. The replacement of clothing and furniture could be postponed virtually indefinitely, as could all forms of recreation. Even for a prosperous artisan, controlled access to a commodity over a period of time was extremely difficult to obtain. Almost any purchase was an indulgence, almost any diversion from the daily round of work and sleep a privilege, and in this sense the provision of literacy, whether or not in the context of formal schooling, was no different in kind from the addition of meat to the dinner table, or a new shirt to the wardrobe. As with any form of consumption, the strategy of acquisition was founded in improvisation and adjustment. Both the source and the timing of the training in the skills of reading and writing had to be as flexible as possible.

The most striking characteristic of the procedures adopted to teach children their letters up to the imposition of universal and compulsory elementary education between 1870 and 1880 was their sheer variety. No form of schooling, or formal schooling itself, had a monopoly. Parents who conceived the ambition of educating a child had at their disposal a wide range of possible courses of action. The first option was that the instruction could be conducted by the parents themselves. 'As soon as I could run about', recalled the tanner's son William Heaton, 'I was taught the alphabet by my beloved and much respected mother.'[60] Such teaching depended on a number of circumstances. Like every other domestic activity, it required some stability in the family unit. The milkwoman and poetess Mary Collier was the daughter of 'poor but honest parrents, by whom I was taught to read when very young, and took delight in it; but my Mother dying, I lost my education, never being put to school'.[61] It required some spare time together, which was never easy to find. Nathaniel Dale's father, a smallholder, instructed his son 'on Sunday and winter evenings'.[62] Those who laboured in domestic workshops could instruct children as they worked, like John Nicholson's father, who taught his son as he sat at the 'wool-sorting board'.[63]

Some progress could be made by verbal instruction alone, but sooner or later reading matter would be required. As has been suggested, most homes would contain literature of some sort, especially if one or both parents were literate. For the most part it would be a question of adapting books, tracts or newspapers written initially for adults, but there are indications that by the early nineteenth century primers and spelling books were being used in working-class homes. In 1805 Darton and Harvey, a leading publisher and distributor of children's literature, listed a wide range of teaching aids for parents, including twelve separate types of spelling books at prices from 6d to 1s 6d, 'Alphabet Cards with Picture, 6d per pack coloured', and 'Battledores for Children 1d, 2d, 3d each'.[64] William Cobbett's *A Grammar of the English Language in a Series of Letters. Intended for the use of Schools and of Young Persons in General, but more especially for the use of Soldiers, Sailors, Apprentices and Plough Boys*, first published in 1818, had sold 100,000 copies by 1834,[65] by which time it had been joined by his *Spelling Book with Appropriate Lessons in Reading*.[66] Many of the primers were originally intended for a middle-class market, which began to expand rapidly in the middle decades of the eighteenth century, but they were so cheap and published in such numbers that it was not difficult for a working-class parent to get hold of something like William Mavor's *English Spelling Book*, which was into its 322nd edition by 1826.[67]

Finally, and most obviously, lessons at home required a literate parent, grandparent or older sibling. The greater the dependence on domestic instruction, the more limited were the prospects of overall improvement in literacy. In the absence of a major expansion in formal schooling, each generation was constrained by the standard attained its predecessor, which may help to explain the inertia of the rates during the first half of the period. However, if they failed to register a significant increase, the levels in general remained remarkably resilient in the face of substantial population increase and economic dislocation, which in turn reflected two important characteristics of the transmission of literacy within the family.

Firstly, as we saw in the previous chapter, the aggregate rates for males and females culled from the marriage registers always understated the presence of literacy in the families created by the ceremonies. The incidence of those who could not write marrying those who could significantly increased the chances of the next generation finding someone in their household who could offer basic instruction.

Secondly, it is evident that those parents who wished to educate their children were not inhibited by the inadequacy of their own command of literacy. By the end of the nineteenth century it was becoming difficult to dissociate reading and writing from qualification and examination. Teachers had to be trained; pupils had to achieve rigidly defined standards. In the broader domestic curriculum, however, the lines of demarcation had never been so clearly drawn. Across the wide range of skills and information which could be transmitted, the notion of learning was purely relative. Those who knew a little passed it on to those who knew less. Absolute illiteracy would prevent a start being made, but once a parent could make out a few words or sign a name, lessons might take place. 'My father being able to read and write a little, taught me all he knew',[68] recalled the handloom weaver's son John Wood. For the child it was a matter of picking up whatever was available. Joseph Mayett was taught his letters by his barely literate mother, and was then presented with a testament by his grandmother, 'but mother not being able to read the first chapter of St. Matthew's Gospel, I began the second and read it through as well as she could teach me'.[69] Lack of reading matter and competent instruction constantly held him back, yet between them, Mayett and his mother were able to consolidate their meagre achievement: 'I made very little progress in learning until the year 1794, only my mother borrowed the Pilgrim's Progress and Doctor Watt's hymns for me and told me the meaning of them as well as she could which kept me from going back but I could not advance because I had no one to teach me.'[70]

In this context, formal schooling was merely an additional resource. Just as an item of food or clothing might be home produced or purchased according to the circumstances of the family and state of the market, so the services of a specialised teacher extended the range of domestic instruction. The efforts of Mayett's mother and Wood's father were eked out by brief spells at Sunday schools, and others who had begun at home were sent on to day schools when the opportunity arose. The transition was facilitated by the character of the schooling which could be purchased. At the beginning of the period covered by this study, about one pupil in four attended schools run by either religious or secular public bodies.[71] By 1833 the National and the British and Foreign Schools Societies had begun to make some inroads in the market for elementary schooling, but still only two pupils in five received an education under the control of outside organisations.[72] Although the proportion had been reversed by 1851, progress remained uncertain; the Newcastle Commission was alarmed to discover that in some areas the percentage of private scholars had actually risen during the 1850s.[73] As late as 1870 there were 44,000 children in private day schools in London,[74] and it was not until the passage of Lord Sandon's Act in 1876 that Church and State began to realise their long-cherished ambition of driving the unqualified, unsupervised independent school-teacher from the field. As an alternative or addition to day schooling, three-quarters of working-class children were attending Sunday schools by 1851, receiving instruction from teachers drawn largely from their own community.[75]

The education which could be bought in the dame and private schools varied extensively in its quality, but above all it was familiar. Where the home in which the bulk of the child's training took place was noisy and

overcrowded, dark and cold in winter, hot and stuffy in summer, so was
the room in which it was taught its letters. Where a mother fitted spells of
instruction into her daily round of labour, so the woman in the neighbourhood to whom she might send her children drew little distinction between
her private and professional duties. Edward Davis, whose childhood in
the Birmingham of the 1830s was blighted by a drunken father, was at one
point sent out to a dame school: 'The short time I spent at this school was
divided between wading through a few words in a much-thumbed primer
and playing with coloured pieces of paper, while my respected governess
attended to her domestic duties.'[76] Where a father's only qualification as a
teacher had been gained in the workplace, so those who launched the
usually ephemeral day schools had come from and would often return to
the harsher life of manual labour. 'My only school education was
obtained at the village school', recalled Passmore Edwards, the son of a
Cornish carpenter,

> which was conducted by Mr. James Blackeney, who became
> schoolmaster after he had injured his health by working under-
> ground as a miner. He commenced his school and carried it on for
> a year or two in a room about nine feet square, and afterwards in
> a little schoolroom built for the purpose. He taught reading,
> writing and arithmetic, and a smattering of grammar and geo-
> graphy; and once a week he treated his scholars with a good dose
> of catechism, when he read both questions and answers.[77]

Where the domestic instruction occupied the interstices in the working
lives of parents and children, so attendance at private day schools was
determined from day to day, from month to month, by the fluctuating
needs of the family economy.

During the first three quarters of the nineteenth century, the more alien
systems of the Church and eventually the Board schools were an increasing presence in the market place, but until the late arrival of compulsion,
parents retained their traditional right to determine whether, when and in
what form their children were educated. They were free not to send their
children to school, except in certain factories after 1833 and in workhouses after 1834, and if they did decide to seek outside assistance for one
element of the domestic curriculum, they were free to pick and choose
between the available institutions and teachers.

Once they entered the market, parents seem to have been willing to
make full use of such purchasing power as they possessed, shopping
around and transferring their patronage from one establishment to
another. Two sets of criteria influenced their strategy of acquisition, both
of which were identified by Joseph Lancaster in his survey of education in
1803. In the first instance, education was just one more item in the cycle of

expenditure and debt through which every working-class family progressed. As Lancaster observed, even relatively prosperous artificers and
mechanics experienced regular periods of low pay or unemployment, and
as a consequence, 'Debts are often contracted that do not exceed a few
shillings, then the parents remove their children from school, and never
pay it: the smallness of the sum proving an effectual bar to its recovery.'[78]
If better times returned before the parents had given up trying to provide a
formal education for their children, they would have to find a school
where they could begin again with a clean slate.[79] In turn the teacher, faced
with unpaid bills himself, might have to join the ranks of the unemployed,
causing further children to interrupt or terminate their schooling.[80] From
the child's point of view, the sequence could be quite bewildering. Isaac
Anderson, one of ten children of a farm labourer, born in the Essex village
of Prittlewell, found himself sent to a 'Free School' costing a penny a
week, then to a 'private school' at the expense of a farmer who had taken
an interest in the family, and then, still only seven, was forced to conclude
his formal education in a workhouse school when his father was unable to
find work in the hard winter of 1840.[81] There was a wider choice in the
towns, and with the continual short-term mobility of families, more
likelihood of change,[82] but it is surprising how often alternative forms of
schooling could be found even in communities as small as Anderson's
home village.[83]

Alongside such material considerations, parents could exercise their
judgment about the quality of a school or a teacher. If for any reason they
disliked what was offered, action could be taken. 'The poor parent often
becomes sensible that something is amiss', wrote Lancaster, '... and
induced by this motive, hurries his child from one school to another.'[84] To
the outside observer, the pattern of change and withdrawal often seemed
merely capricious,[85] but there was a logic in the strategy adopted by
parents who entered the market. At the outset it was in their interests to
keep to a minimum the loss of control which the use of a professional
teacher entailed. Preference would be given to the system which permitted
the greatest flexibility of attendance. Faced with the unpalatable fact that
as late as 1872 private schools were still proving attractive, the Committee
of Council of Education explained that parents, 'for their own conve-
nience, like to have the privilege of sending their children late to school, or
to have them come home before the usual time, and no questions asked;
this can not be done at inspected schools'.[86]

The reaction to the teaching the child received was conditioned by the
character of the individual master or mistress. Few day schools, inside or
outside the public sector, possessed more than one adult teacher, and the
calibre of the instruction was heavily dependent on the personality of the
individual concerned. For the parents it was a matter of seeking out

competence where it could be found. Joseph Blackett, one of twelve children of a day labourer in the village of Tunstall in Yorkshire, was sent to the only local school, and then, 'another school being opened, by a man who my parents thought better able to instruct, I was placed by them under its tuition'.[87] In this context, competence consisted in the ability to provide the most cost-effective education. For any working-class parent, formal schooling represented trouble and expense. It disrupted the intricate relationship between learning and practice within the household, prevented a child from contributing to the family economy or looking after younger siblings while parents worked, and caused the diversion of always scarce resources into not only fees until the Fees Act of 1891 began the process of their abolition, but ancillary items such as presentable clothing or contributions to the heating of classrooms. It was essential, therefore, that if it was decided to supplement home instruction, as little effort was wasted as possible. From the school was required efficient teaching in the one element of the domestic curriculum which parents might lack either the time or the competence to undertake themselves. In 1851, as the competition between the private and Church schools was, reaching its height, the HMI for Cheshire, Staffordshire and Shropshire, the Rev. J. Norris, conducted an inquiry into the sort of education parents desired: 'all would agree', he found, 'in mentioning reading the Bible, writing a good hand and casting accounts'.[88]

The impact on the education system of this instrumental approach will be discussed later in this chapter. Its consequence for the child was to limit the significance of formal schooling and to emphasise the makeshift nature of the entire learning process. Developing a command of formal communication was a subordinate component of the home curriculum, and expenditure on outside teachers was a luxury difficult to justify and easy to suspend. Until the final quarter of the nineteenth century it is almost a contradiction in terms to refer to a pattern in learning to read and write. As had always been the case with every aspect of domestic activity and consumption, the skills were mastered when and how circumstances permitted. The acquisition of literacy was rarely continuous and infrequently from a single source. Writing of the 1880s, Flora Thompson contrasted the now systematic and inescapable process of learning to read and write at the elementary school with the way in which the literate older members of the community had gone about their education: 'They would have to pick up what learning they could like chickens picking for grain – a little at school, more from books, and some by dipping into the store of others.'[89] The image is appropriate. At the centre of the growth in literacy rates throughout much of the nineteenth century were generations of children scratching in the farmyard for whatever they could gain.

Official schooling

The long journey towards the imposition of compulsory elementary education commenced with a sweeping rejection of the value of domestic instruction. Those who campaigned for intervention, firstly by the Churches and then by the State during the late eighteenth and early nineteenth centuries, based their appeal on a denunciation of the training provided in the homes of the labouring poor. As Sarah Trimmer wrote in *The Oeconomy of Charity* in 1801,

> Whoever seriously considers the present manners of the lower order of people must surely see the necessity of vigilant attention towards the rising generation; since no less than the safety of the nation probably depends upon the education of those children, who are now growing up to maturity, whose parents are not only incapable of giving them proper instruction, but are likely, it is to be feared, to lead them astray by their own bad example.[90]

'The education of the children of the poor', she concluded, 'therefore should not be left to their ignorant and corrupted parents; it is a public concern, and should be regarded as public business.'[91] The more the public accepted its responsibilities, the more inadequate the parents of the rising generation appeared. 'Shall we forget', lamented Samuel Wilderspin, the pioneer of infant schools, 'the immoral language, the improper sentiments, the domestic discord, which the child frequently hears or sees at home? Shocking it is to think that the breath of a mother or a father should be the first to contaminate the minds of their children; yet such is the mournful truth.'[92] The task of the schoolmaster was to rescue children from the influence of the domestic environment. 'The child properly taught', continued Wilderspin, 'neither sees, hears, or attends, to much that is going on at home.'[93] Those whom the State appointed to oversee the education of such children accepted that, as one HMI put it, 'It is indeed a sad and evil necessity, if the first lesson which they learn at school is to beware of their own parents and to look with disgust, if not horror at the filthiness and abominations of their own homes.'[94]

The elementary school was to supplant rather than supplement the work of the home. It was the responsibility of the 'Christian Schoolmaster', wrote the author of a widely used eighteenth-century manual for teachers, to give 'such fatherly Instruction and Admonitions as would otherwise be incumbent upon the *Parents* themselves, if their Capacity and Attendance on the necessary Affairs of Life would permit. So that their whole Duty, with Regard to the Education of these Children, is devolved upon the Master.'[95] The teachers strove to become parents to their pupils, and hoped that in turn the pupils would become parents to their own mothers and fathers. 'Many instances have occurred to my knowledge', claimed the joint secretary of the National Society's Normal School, 'where the order of nature has been inverted, by the children becoming the teachers of their parents; and I know of instances, to which I can speak personally, where the children have been the means of bringing the parents to church, who have never been in the habit of going to church at all.'[96]

It was a large ambition. From the beginning the content and objectives of elementary education were conceived in the widest terms. If the teacher were to act *in loco parentis*, he or she would have to take responsibility for every aspect of the child's development. Church attendance might reinforce the spiritual content of the curriculum, but essentially the school itself was to replace every aspect of the training the child would otherwise receive at home and in the community. Joseph Fletcher, writing in 1846, summarised the view of those who had recognised the challenge:

> Education in this, its highest sense (embracing physical, intellectual, industrial, moral and religious education), they are well aware is not the work of the school only, but likewise of the church, the Sunday-school, the home, the playground, the street, the workshop, the field, the mine, the tavern, and the court-house. They are equally aware that no sane individual, in any conceivable state of society, can escape education in every branch, either to truth or error, to good or evil; that the choice to be made for them is not between 'education' or 'no education', but between 'good' and 'bad' education. Distrusting, and with reason, the education which is given to the poor by the 'world' – by the unregulated influences which bear upon them in the scenes of their daily life – their conception of a school for the children of the poor, is, that it should be a little artificial world of virtuous exertion.[97]

In this little artificial world, literacy was accorded a low priority. Talbot's *The Christian School-Master or the Duty of Those who are Employed in the Public Instruction of Children: Especially in Charity Schools*, first published in 1707 and still in print in 1811, devoted just six of its 176 pages to the teaching of reading, and as to writing, 'the particular Methods ... are so well known by everyone who professeth that Art, that it will be needless to say any Thing more in this Place'.[98] Prospective teachers were left in no doubt about the nature of the task which lay ahead: 'it must be the first Care of every Teacher in these Schools to imprint the Minds and Memory of Children committed to his Instruction, the fundamental Doctrines and Duties of our Holy Religion'.[99] New pupils were to be taught to say the Lord's Prayer and the Creed before their first reading lesson, and thereafter the teaching of literacy was only important insofar as it provided a medium for instruction in religion and moral duties.[100] In this context, reading was obviously more useful than writing. Although there were instances, which have attracted much historical attention, of writing being excluded from the curriculum altogether,[101] the prevailing attitude was one of indifference rather than hostility. 'Rewards should be occasionally bestowed upon children in Charity Schools', wrote Mrs Trimmer, 'for such actions as are truly commendable, but not for excelling in penmanship or reading, which are very inferior things in comparison with upright conduct.'[102]

The replacement of the charity schools by the more extensive and systematic endeavours of the National and British and Foreign Schools Societies during the early decades of the nineteenth century initially made little impression on this philosophy of education. Writing was now to be taught concurrently with reading, but only because the processes of acquiring each skill were thought to be mutually reinforcing. Mere 'learning' remained a secondary concern. 'The first great and leading principle of the British system', explained its manual in 1831, 'is that it is the teacher's duty to pay more regard to the formation of the character of his scholars than to the success in any, or all of the branches of learning professedly taught.'[103] 'Character', in turn, was still conceived in spiritual terms; 'our endeavour', emphasised the secretary of the rival National Society, 'is to produce a religious frame of mind.'[104]

When the State began to supervise the work of the Church Societies in 1839, it was anxious not to lose sight of the wider objectives of elementary education. On the key question of training teachers for the expanding system, the Home Secretary, Lord John Russell, instructed the Lord President of the Council that 'In any Normal or Model School to be established by the Board, four principal objects should be kept in view: namely, religious instruction, general instruction, moral training, and habits of industry.'[105] Although reformers were beginning to entertain the prospect of universal literacy, such an objective remained as a means to an end rather than an end in itself. In the face of the corrupting influence of the home and the workplace, it was essential that the precepts of the teacher were reinforced by the higher authority of the Bible and other religious literature; for that reason it was impossible to dissociate moral instruction from literacy, but the latter remained firmly subordinated to the former. Reading and writing bore no relation to the other skills for living or to the enlargement of the child's imagination or stock of knowledge. The Church schools were founded on a notion of cognitive development which could not have been broader or more limited. As the *Manual of the System of teaching Reading, Writing, Arithmetick, and Needle-Work in the Elementary-Schools of The British and Foreign Schools*

Society put it, 'The cultivation of the mind bestowed in these elementary schools, opens and expands the faculties of the children, gives them clear notions of the moral and social duties, prepares them for the reception of religious instruction, forms them to habits of virtue, and habituates them to subordination and control.'[106]

However, if the status of literacy remained little changed since the founding of the charity schools, it was no longer possible to take so relaxed an approach to the way that it was taught. '*The method of conveying instruction* is peculiarly important in an Elementary School', wrote Kay-Shuttleworth, 'because the scholars receive no learning and little judicious training at home, and are therefore dependent for their education on the very limited period of their attendance at school.'[107] Pressures generated by increasing numbers of children who needed to be educated and teachers who needed to be trained forced attention on the techniques of acquiring the skills of reading and writing on which the wider ambitions of the elementary schools depended. The subsequent elaboration of pedagogic theory can best be understood by considering the concept of system which informed the structure of teaching, the concept of language which constituted the medium of instruction, and the concept of intelligence which brought into focus the purpose of learning to read and write.

The method of teaching children their letters inherited by the early-nineteenth-century Church Societies was older than printing.[108] A medie-val schoolmaster would not have found himself out of place in the early-nineteenth-century classroom. Long-established techniques were even-tually formulated in the first primer published in 1538. Subsequent versions became increasingly elaborate until by the early eighteenth century they had arrived at a formula which was to remain unchanged until the 1840s and 1850s.[109] The consistency with which authors laid claim to originality was matched only by the underlying similarity of their works. There was no difference in substance between the primers of Thomas Dyche[110] and William Markham[111] written for the early charity schools and those of Henry Innes[112] or Cuthbert Johnson[113] which formed the staple fare of the schools visited by the first HMIs. After learning the alphabet the child was faced with lists of disconnected syllables, 'ba be bi bo bu' in lesson one in Dyche's primer of 1710, 'ba ab ca ac' in the first lesson of Innes' 'Plain, Pleasing, Progressive System' of 1835, followed by columns of monosyllabic words which might then be grouped into sentences of a relentlessly spiritual or moral quality. Once these had been mastered, the procedure was repeated with words of two syllables, and so the child progressed until, in the case of the more ambitious primers, it was capable of reading lists of seven-syllable words.[114]

The process of decomposing language into what was thought to be its constituent elements perfectly suited the enterprise of Bell and Lancaster, who were seeking to remodel elementary education along the lines of factory production. The organisation of instruction in the classroom could be based on the sequence of rebuilding words in the primers. The early schools of the British and Foreign Schools Society, for instance, were divided into eight classes. The first read and wrote the alphabet; the second, third and fourth dealt with words and syllables of two, three and four letters. The fifth and sixth graduated to sentences of one- and two-syllable words, and finally the child encountered sustained prose in the form of the New Testament and then the Bible as a whole, together with 'a selection of the best readers'.[115] The parallel classification of language and pupils lay at the heart of the new method. The carefully graduated pattern of instruction permitted the use of monitors and demanded their supervision by trained teachers. Parents and amateur teachers in the private day schools could not hope to understand, let alone administer, the artificial and complex structure. Neither could they afford the complete sets of primers upon which the work of the Church schools now depended. The provision of teachers, books and schoolrooms large enough to accommodate the hierarchy of classes in turn required the creation of educational bureaucracies with their own rules and regulations.

Subsequent developments in pedagogic theory served only to widen the gap between professional and untrained teachers. By the late 1830s the use of monitors and the reliance on rote-learning were coming under attack. Official support was now given to the 'synthetic method', which combined the approach of the traditional primers with associationist psychology to produce a theory which could be applied to all parts of the curriculum. It rested on a strict division of labour. The teacher was responsible for the analysis and classification of the subject matter, and the pupil for the synthesis.[116] The more active participation by the class was to be matched by more thorough preparations by the teacher and the authors of the manuals and textbooks upon which, increasingly, he or she relied. Writing, which hitherto had involved little more than copying, together with guidance on how to hold a pen,[117] was elevated to a similar level of sophistication with the introduction of the 'Mulhauser method'. Each letter was decomposed by the teacher into its four 'elements' of lines, curves, loops and crotchets, and then recomposed by the pupil in specially prepared grids of rhomboids.[118]

Whilst attempts to introduce a single State education system were fiercely resisted, within the Church schools every effort was made to standardise the curriculum and the method by which it was conveyed. The process was furthered by the appointment of an inspectorate under a Committee of the Privy Council in 1839, which gave full support to the introduction of a 'rational basis' for instruction in writing: 'Formerly . . .

the method of teaching to write, from the absence of any acknowledged system, was necessarily abandoned to the inventive powers of the master.'[119] Improvisation was the mark of the amateur. The existence of an elaborate system, with the structure of textbooks, trained teachers and educational administrators which it implied, became the touchstone by which the validity of an education could be judged.[120] Its absence condemned not only domestic instruction, but the entire body of 'Common Day Schools', whose characteristics were summarised in a report of the Manchester Statistical Society:

> There are very few schools in which the sexes are entirely divided, – almost every boys' school containing some girls, and every girls' school a few boys. They are chiefly the children of mechanics, warehousemen, or small shopkeepers, and learn reading, writing, and arithmetic, and in a few of the better description of schools, a little grammar and geography. In a great majority of these schools there seems to be a great want of orderly system. The confusion arising from this defect, added to the very low qualifications of the master, the number of scholars under the superintendance of one teacher, the irregularity of the attendance, the great deficiency of books, and the injudicious plan of instruction, or, rather, the want of any plan, render them inefficient for any purposes of real education.[121]

The approach to the language through which literacy was acquired initially stemmed, like the systematic curriculum, from the form of the early primers. The deconstructed words and sentences which faced the child as it began to read and write bore no relation to the linguistic skills which had been mastered in infancy and early childhood. At no stage in the domestic learning process had the child spoken in disconnected syllables, or been expected to memorise columns of words which had in common only their length. The steady elaboration of primers for use in charity schools accentuated the difficulty. Where once they had served only as a preface to work on continuous prose, they were increasingly designed to stand as complete courses of learning in their own right. Mrs Trimmer's 162-page *Charity School Spelling Book* of 1805, for instance, took the child all the way from the alphabet and basic syllables to encounters with the most arcane regions of the English language. Learning to read now involved doing battle with sentences such as 'and the names of Joktan's sons were Almodad, Sheleph, Hazarmareth, Jerah, Hadoram, Uzal, Diklah, Obal, Abimael, Sheba, Ophir, Havilah, and Johab'.[122]

By the early 1830s it was coming to be recognised that the tables of syllables and 'unmeaning combinations'[123] presented an unnecessary obstacle to young pupils, but little could be done about the more advanced lessons. The logic of the synthetic method demanded a relentless escalation of complexity until six- and seven-syllable tongue-twisters such as 'antitrinitarian' were reached, and the requirement to prepare the class for reading the Bible made inevitable the lists of words which began 'Abel, Achar, Achim ...'.[124] As late as 1867 W. B. Hodgson found that in inspected schools

> The letters are taught by their names, not by their sounds, in the arbitrary order of the alphabet, instead of the natural order of the organs by which they were pronounced. Spelling is still taught by means of columns of long, hard, unconnected words, selected for their very difficulty and rarity, to be learned by rote, or, as is said with unconscious irony, 'by heart'.[125]

A second attack on the child's acquired language was generated by the manner in which lessons were conducted. From the early days of the charity schools to the Board schools of the 1870s and beyond, both teaching and learning were predominantly oral. At the outset, the form of instruction was derived from the experience the Church had gained over the centuries in transmitting the tenets of Christianity to illiterate and semi-literate parishioners. The pedagogic method of the charity schools was founded on the Catechism. Reading was taught in the same way as religion. The subject matter of the lesson was committed to memory by repetition and tested by means of question and answer. Pupils were catechised in their letters and as they became proficient were set to memorise the Catechism itself.

From the beginning to the end of the school day the classroom was filled with the sound of the human voice. The complexity of the verbal exchange was intensified by the development of the monitorial system in the early nineteenth century. Words were read out to the monitors, who spelt them aloud as they wrote them down, and then each monitor repeated the words to its class, who in turn pronounced as they inscribed slates or sand trays. The subsequent revisions of the 1830s merely shifted emphasis from repetition to interrogation. In an effort to reduce the dependency on rote learning, every pupil had to give an account of the words and sentences it was asked to read, spell and write. 'We never allow them to do anything', stated the secretary of the BFSS, 'without asking how they do it and why they do it.'[126] Teaching was slightly less mechanical but it was no quieter. School libraries began to be provided for more advanced pupils, but the books were not for use in the classroom.[127] The introduction of systematic oral examination under the Revised Code prevented any drift to private study. Each child had to be prepared for the random questions of the school inspector. F. H. Spencer, who commenced his education in 1878, recalled that 'we read nothing silently in school, for amusement or information'.[128]

The sheer volume of noise the pupil encountered throughout the period helped to reduce the unfamiliarity of the school experience, but at the same time it focused attention on the issue of pronunciation. If reading was learned through talking, how the child articulated language became the legitimate concern of the schoolmaster. Talbot's manual for charity school teachers insisted that 'great Care must be taken from the Beginning, that each Syllable and every word may be pronounced very plainly, distinctly and audibly'.[129] By this time the notion of 'plain speech' embodied an increasingly rigid value judgment. The development of a system of elementary education coincided with the final stages of the creation of standard English. The publication in 1755 of Johnson's *Dictionary* had set the seal on a long process of codification. Henceforth it was possible to determine the correct meaning and spelling of words, and this security provided the basis for enforcing correct speech. By the end of the eighteenth century it was accepted that in theory pronunciation should where possible follow spelling, which in practice meant that the language of the London merchant class became the touchstone by which all the dialects of popular culture were judged and found wanting.[130] The subsequent construction of the public school system served to bind the ruling class into a single speech community, whilst the elementary schools of the Church Societies set about imposing linguistic discipline on the lower orders.[131] Their ambitions were frankly stated in *The Rhetorical Class Book* of 1834:

> It is equally important that there be a common consent and established custom, to regulate and fix the sounds used in speech, that these may have a definite character and signification, and become the current expression of thought. Hence the necessity that individuals conform in their habits of speech to the rules prescribed by general usage, or, more properly speaking, to the custom of the educated and intellectual classes of society, which is by courtesy generally acknowledged as the law of pronunciation.[132]

The status of the law was reinforced by its identification with written language. It was assumed that proper prose was composed in standard English, and could only be read in an equivalent tone. John Gill of Cheltenham Normal School explained in his *Introductory Text-Book to School Management* that the source of 'improper accentuation'

> is to be sought in the difference between the language of books and that of the common people. Much of the language is strange

to the ear, and hence is so to their intelligence. Its pronunciation is often picked up, not from correct speakers or readers, but from others as ignorant as themselves; or with nothing but analogy to guide them, is as often fixed by themselves.[133]

The remedy for the tendency of pupils to import or invent their own rules lay in the 'phonic method', which followed the principles of decomposition and synthesis already being used for teaching reading and writing. The child first learned the correct sounds of individual syllables, and through a process of combination gradually acquired the ability to speak complete words and sentences.

The transition from oral to written communication was bound to place a strain on the child's use of language. Under any circumstances, learning to read and write presented a challenge to the modes of expression practised in the home and in daily life outside the classroom.[134] William Cobbett began his best-selling *Grammar of the English Language* by insisting that the acquisition of book knowledge demanded the development of more sophisticated skills:

> In the immense field of this kind of knowledge, innumerable are the paths, and GRAMMAR is the gate of entrance to them all. And if grammar is so useful in attaining of knowledge, it is absolutely necessary in order to enable the possessor to communicate, by writing, that knowledge to others without which communication the possession must be comparatively useless to himself in many cases, and in almost all cases to the rest of mankind.[135]

Reading and writing were specialised instruments, and their use had to be learned like any other: 'Soldiers, Sailors, Apprentices, Ploughboys all have to know the names of parts of guns, ropes, tools, implements. Thus with grammar.'[136] Together with the authors of the increasing number of grammars written for schools and self-taught adults, Cobbett was building on the work of Lindley Murray, who had freed the study of its reliance on Latin. It was now possible to teach and learn Grammar without a knowledge of the Classics, and by 1851 a third of schools visited by HMIs included the subject in the curriculum.[137]

Cobbett himself was careful to stress that learning how language worked need not involve an attack on the speech skills the child already possessed:

> Children will pronounce as their fathers and mothers pronounce; and if, in common conversation, or in speeches, the matter be good and judiciously arranged, the facts clearly stated, the arguments conclusive, the words well chosen and properly placed, hearers whose approbation is worth having will pay very little

attention to the accent. In short, it is sense, and not sound, which is the object of your pursuit; and, therefore, I have said enough about Prosody.[138]

Elsewhere, the anglicisation of grammar served only to complete the transformation of written English into a foreign language. Where Cobbett had gleefully shown how sentence analysis could be used to expose 'Errors and Nonsense in a King's Speech',[139] grammars written for elementary schools reinforced the attempt to impose upon the lower orders the language of their social superiors. Rather than extending the child's linguistic skills, the lessons in reading and writing sought to dismantle those which had already been acquired. Now pupils were taught that not only were they illiterate, but they could not even speak properly. The natural tendency to think of words as part of larger units was replaced by an approach which treated them as isolated entities. Children were faced with an unfamiliar vocabulary and unrecognisable syllables which they were expected to pronounce in an alien fashion. Teachers who had been instructed to distance themselves from the speech communities from which their pupils came were equipped with schoolbooks which, as the Newcastle Commission found, were written in a language 'utterly unlike their vernacular dialect, both in its vocabulary and construction'.[140] For those who passed through the elementary schools of the period, the encounter with literacy was a strange and threatening experience.

One of the main arguments in favour of extending the study of grammar was its relevance to the cognitive powers of the child. 'A person who does not understand Grammar', claimed one of the early schoolbooks, 'can scarce think correctly.'[141] From the inception of the school inspectorate onwards, increasing emphasis was placed on the 'intelligence' of the elementary school pupil. This quality was seen as both the immediate objective of the school curriculum and the principal criterion for measuring the success of the reading and writing lessons. In report after report teachers were castigated for their failure to train their classes to read with intelligence. It was no longer enough to spell out words and reconstruct sentences. The pupils had to show evidence of an underlying mental activity. A typical verdict was given on a school in 1851: 'The character of the instruction is in many respects fair; the intelligence of the children however is not sufficiently called forth, and they find great difficulty in answering any questions which are not put exactly in the usual forms.'[142]

In recent times, the definition and measurement of intelligence have become issues of intense controversy, but in the 1840s and 1850s, the term seemed quite unambiguous. By intelligence was meant the capacity to understand established knowledge. It was seen increasingly as a principal objective of teaching literacy. The move away from rote learning the elements of language stemmed from the assumption that the lessons would be more effective if the pupils actively responded to the process of decomposition and recomposition of words and sentences. 'Once thoroughly understood', explained the Minutes of 1840/1, 'the new object of study fully satisfies the intelligence, and becomes as it were a part of it.'[143] The experience of building up the skills of literacy would rescue the pupil's mind from the mental inertia of the domestic environment. Whereas 'the house is not furnished with objects which awaken intelligence',[144] the course of instruction in the classroom could have an irreversible impact on the capacity to grasp the meaning of whatever forms of knowledge were subsequently encountered. The synthetic method of learning to read and write would endow the pupil with habits of intellectual inquiry and self-discipline which would counteract the sensual tendencies engendered by its upbringing and lay the foundation for a rational and moral approach to life outside the school.

At the completion of an elementary education it was hoped that the working man's child would be in possession of both the tools for imbibing knowledge of its duties and responsibilities and the capacity to use them. The character and function of the cognitive skills which the schools sought to inculcate were summarised in the *Explanations of the Intentions of Her Majesty's Government* of 1839, a peak year of Chartist activity:

> The sole effectual means of preventing the tremendous evils with which the anarchical spirit of the manufacturing population threatens the country is, by giving the working people a good secular education, to enable them to understand the true causes which determine their physical condition and regulate the distribution of wealth among the several classes of society. Sufficient intelligence and information to appreciate these causes might be diffused by an education which could easily be brought within the reach of the entire population.[145]

There was, however, no sense in which this newly gained intelligence was to be used critically or creatively. Neither was the child encouraged to relate the information to the knowledge it already possessed. The persistent complaints of pupils' failure to read 'intelligently' was a reflection of their inability or refusal to assimilate lessons to their own experience. The cognitive processes they were expected to master seemed to bear no connection to the skills that had been acquired before school and that would be required beyond it. Rather than developing qualities of intellect which would enable the child to communicate more effectively,[146] the pattern of decontextualised learning appeared to be producing generations of children unable to communicate at all.

The method of teaching literacy which was developed during the first half of the nineteenth century owed much of its character to the initial rejection of the domestic curriculum. The construction of an elaborate system of instruction, the dismantling of oral language and the promotion of a mechanistic concept of intelligence were justified by a dismissal of the value of all that might be learned in and around the home. Yet by the 1850s there were increasing signs that the Church schools were failing to overcome the influence of the parents of working-class children, and that further progress was impossible unless greater respect was paid to the attainments and needs of the community from which they sought to recruit their pupils. Very gradually, and with much controversy, the inspected schools began to turn their sails to catch the interest of the children who seemed to be gaining so little from their efforts.

The pressure for change was registered at three levels. In the first instance, the constant round of inspection and the writing and rewriting of textbooks and teachers' guides began to force attention on the evident shortcomings of the analytical method of teaching basic literacy. Doubts were raised about the principle of disregarding the linguistic abilities the child had acquired before ever it encountered the written word. The outcome was the emergence of the 'Look and Say' method, which was under discussion in the late 1840s and received official sanction in the 1852 *Minutes.*[147] Instead of commencing with disconnected syllables, the pupil was to be introduced to complete, monosyllabic words, preferably in the context of short sentences. The way in which the words were constructed would be taught after, not before, the pupil had learned to recognise them.[148]

In practice, the inspectors advised that teachers adopt a mixture of Look and Say and the now traditional alphabet–syllable approach, and it is difficult to be certain how far and how fast the new method spread. However, its appearance marked an important change in outlook. It demanded that the teacher should make a positive response to the knowledge and skills that pupils brought into school. Where a young child learned to talk by imitation, only later understanding the rules which controlled spoken language, now for the first time it was permitted to use guesswork as it began to read. And where the oral vocabulary had been discounted, it was now recommended that 'The first lessons should consist entirely of words with which the ear of children is familiar.'[149] Like every innovation, the work of the teacher was increased rather than diminished, and the gap between professional and amateur widened still further. The utmost care had to be exercised in selecting the words the pupil was to encounter. But when the teacher planned the curriculum, the point of departure was to be the language the class already possessed. As J. S. Laurie insisted in his *First Steps to Reading* of 1862, in the lessons which introduced 'the learner by easy stages to the phonic and orthographic difficulties of language', 'it is most important that they should also contain matters which shall be interesting to him, and that the words that occur in them should be within the compass of his vocabulary'.[150]

The move towards Look and Say was accompanied by a more general secularisation of the curriculum. This was partly caused by the growing specialisation of teaching methods, which rendered the Bible increasingly unsatisfactory as a medium of instruction, but it was also the delayed consequence of a contradiction inherent in the original conception of the Church-based elementary schools. At one level, the work of the National and British Societies reflected the renewed confidence and ambition of the Churches, which appeared to have found an immensely powerful means of reaching the hearts and minds of the lower orders. But as Bernard Mandeville had pointed out when the SPCK was launched in the early eighteenth century, the use of elementary schools for religious instruction represented an abdication of responsibility by the clergy.[151] The more effort that was channelled into education, the greater the threat to the proper role of the Church. By the 1830s, the British Society was instructing its staff to 'teach everything with eternity in view',[152] yet at the same time implicitly denying organised religion a significant part in the task of reforming society: 'Whatever others may think, the teacher must be satisfied, that any great moral change in the community, will be mainly effected by the instrumentality of schools.'[153]

The turning point came in 1838, when, with Chartism gaining momentum, the Central Society of Education carried out an influential inquiry into the bloodiest single episode in the history of English popular protest, the 'Battle of Bossenden Wood', in which a wine merchant turned messiah led a group of desperate but, as it transpired, mostly educated farm labourers in an onslaught on a party of militia.[154] The CSE concluded that the cause of the disaster was cultural rather than political or economic, and that the problem was not illiteracy or the absence of schooling, but rather the limitations of the traditional curriculum. The success of the new 'messiah' had been founded on the vulnerability of a church-educated community to a stranger adept at citing inflammatory Biblical texts. 'It may be doubted', observed the CSE investigator, 'if a course of exclusive religious reading, has not a tendency to narrow the mind, and instill fallacious ideas.'[155] Henceforth serious attention began to be paid to the demands of teachers that the religious content of instruction be leavened by secular knowledge which would broaden the outlook and anchor the judgment of the newly literate. Although the decision to introduce a new generation of readers was taken shortly afterwards, it was not until the early 1850s that their presence began to be felt in the inspected schools.[156] The Bible was displaced from the centre of the curriculum in an effort to bring the moral instruction, which remained the principal concern of education, closer to the real world of the pupils and their parents.[157] The development extended the horizon of the professional teacher, who could now entertain the prospect of engaging with all aspects of the child's body of knowledge, but it also represented the final defeat of the time-honoured hope that the moral education of the entire community could be contained within an accepted framework of religious doctrine. Now the content and the boundary of the curriculum could only be determined by debate and negotiation.

Such a debate was not long in coming. The immediate cause of the third and much the most significant shift in the relationship between the learning processes of the school and the home was the rapid escalation in the State subsidy to the church societies. With expenditure rising at a rate of £100,000 a year by the mid 1850s, increasing attention was paid to the question of value in education.[158] The definition of value, as the subsequent Newcastle Commission came to realise, was ultimately a matter of perspective. A key passage of its report of 1861 set out for the first time the conflicting objectives of the suppliers and consumers of elementary education:

> The general principle upon which almost every one who for the last half century has endeavoured to promote popular education has proceeded, has been that a large portion of the poorer classes of the population were in a condition injurious to their own interests, and dangerous and discreditable to the rest of the community; that it was the duty and the interest of the nation at large to raise them to a higher level, and that religious education was the most powerful instrument for the promotion of this object. The parents, on the other hand, cannot be expected to entertain the same view of the moral and social condition of their own class, or to have its general elevation in view. They act individually for the advantage of their respective children; and though they wish them to be imbued with religious principles, and taught to behave well, they perhaps attach a higher importance than the promoters and managers of schools to the specific knowledge which will be profitable to the child in life. It is of some importance in estimating the conduct of the parents to keep this difference of sentiment in view.[159]

This grudging acceptance that there might be some rationality in the attitude of parents to the education of their children and that future policy should take account of it stemmed from the analysis of demand undertaken by the Assistant Commissioners who were charged with examining the progress of schooling in different parts of the country. A quarter of a century of State subsidy provided ample evidence of the behaviour of the working-class community in what was, for the most part, a free market. As we saw earlier in the chapter, the parents of the children the Church societies sought to attract had always adopted an instrumental approach to institutional education. Their limited objectives were met when and in what form the broader concerns of the domestic curriculum and the family economy permitted. What forced the Commission to give formal recognition to a truth well enough known to many teachers was the realisation that unless the system responded to the demands of those who would otherwise patronise private adventure schools or no schools at all, it would be impossible to achieve the objectives which would justify the ever-increasing cost. The most urgent question, therefore, was what sort of education working-class parents thought advantageous to their children, and to this Mr Cumin, one of the busiest and most able of the Commissioners, had a clear answer:

> I have been asked whether the poor have a preference for one system of education over another, whether they neglect the education of their children because of religious indifference, and whether in short there is anything in the present schools which indisposes parents to send their children to school. I made the most diligent inquiry into these matters, and found no difference of opinion. Schoolmasters, clergymen, ministers, city missionaries, all told me that the poor in selecting a school, looked entirely to whether the school supplied good reading, writing and arithmetic.[160]

The Revised Code of 1862 was a direct result of this discovery. Where the teaching of basic literacy had been the subordinate concern of the schoolmaster, a means to a much larger and more important end, it was now placed at the centre of the curriculum. The Bishops protested at the acceleration in the decline of religious instruction, and the professional educationalists were appalled at the reversal of the trend towards a wider range of secular subjects. 'The reclamation of these children from barbarism is a good', thundered Kay-Shuttleworth, 'greater far than mere technical instruction in the three lowest elements.'[161] But both contemporary and most later critics missed the crucial element of compromise in the new system. A major justification of the reform was the inescapable fact that working-class parents were only interested in 'mere technical instruction in the three lowest elements'.[162] The concession to the demands of the consumers was the sole means of realising the increasingly urgent goal of universal elementary education without incurring on the one hand unmanageable costs and on the other unmanageable hostility from the working-class community. Those who thought compulsion inevitable saw in the shift of emphasis a way of minimising the prospective conflict with recalcitrant parents; those who hoped to postpone compulsion indefinitely grasped the last hope of encouraging voluntary attendance. In the midst of the contraction and rigidity of the Revised Code was to be found the first real attempt to negotiate with the domestic curriculum. Where the subordinate status of reading and writing in the early Church schools had reflected the more general dismissal of home instruction, so the prominence now given to literacy was a consequence of the respect which the Government had been forced to pay to the requirements of the working-class family. Henceforth inspected schools would do more to extend than dismember the learning which took place in the home. If the retreat aroused bitter resentment in some quarters, it represented a victory, however Pyrrhic, for those hitherto consigned to barbarism.

At first sight, the implementation of the Revised Code confounded the expectations of proponents and critics alike. Where all had agreed that the enforced emphasis on teaching basic literacy marked a radical departure from past practice, there was a strong sense of continuity in the comments of the inspectors on the operation of the new scheme. Report after report rehearsed the familiar complaints about unimaginative rote-learning leading to performance devoid of intelligence and expression. After a quarter of a century of payment by results, the Cross Commission found that 'Reading ... does not receive sufficient attention in the matter of fluency and intonation; its chief fault is that it is too mechanical and unintelligent.'[163] Little seemed to have changed: 'I should say', concluded one witness, 'that the criticisms that were passed upon Reading by the earlier Commission of 1861 might be applied to the same subject now'.[164]

It can be argued, however, that in several important ways this sense of stasis was misleading. There was no doubt that the reform induced an element of anxiety in the process of teaching literacy which delayed the move away from rote-learning. In the early years of the new system, the annual examination was based on a single reader. The consequence, reported the inspectors, was that the pupils' encounter with the written word began and ended with a set of paragraphs in which they were drilled every week until they were capable of 'reading' the text upside down yet unable to answer the most basic questions about its meaning. At the same time the increased attention that was now paid to the performance of each schoolchild in the three Rs produced gains in practice and eventually new insights into the problems of transmitting literacy in the classrooms.

In the field of reading, the newly defined standards brought forth a generation of textbooks which represented a clear advance over their predecessors.[165] J. S. Laurie's Graduated Series of Reading Lesson Books, for instance, which first appeared in 1866, consolidated the innovations of the final years of the old system, and looked forward to the more ambitious enterprises of the 1870s and 1880s. In the reader for Standard

V, the child progressed straight from the alphabet to complete sentences and would meet self-contained passages of prose before moving up to the next Standard. The concern to promote moral values remained, but these tended to be both generalised and secular; *Aesop's Fables* replaced the Bible as the most common source of precept. For the first time material was included for no other purpose than the entertainment of the pupil. 'I am going to tell you a very funny story about two very nice clever cats',[166] began one of the Standard II pieces. Alongside extracts from *Pilgrim's Progress* were traditional tales such as 'The Billy Goats Gruff', retold without a trace of improving sentiment. The children who lasted as far as Standard V would find their vocabularies and imaginations stretched by encounters with Macaulay, Spenser, Milton and Byron.[167] The pattern was extended by later series, most notably Nelson's Royal Readers, which first appeared in 1872. Here the more advanced pupil was presented with a cornucopia of prose, poetry and drama, interspersed with travellers' tales and natural history. 'There was plenty there to enthral any child', recalled Flora Thompson: "The Skater Chased by Wolves"; "The Siege of Torquilstone", from *Ivanhoe*; Fenimore Cooper's *Prairie on Fire*; and Washington Irving's *Capture of Wild Horses*.'[168]

In the first Revised Code, 'writing' still meant no more than a combination of penmanship and spelling. The summit of a school's ambition was to turn out children capable of setting down to the inspector's satisfaction a 'short ordinary paragraph in a newspaper, or other modern narrative, slowly dictated once by a few words at a time'. However, there had already been some experiments in going beyond reproduction,[169] and when the Code was modified in 1871, composition at last entered the curriculum. Pupils who reached a redefined Standard VI were to be taught how to write a 'short theme or letter or an easy paraphrase'. Three decades after its introduction, the children of the labouring poor were to learn how to make use of the Penny Post. The subject was strictly functional – there was no sense of linking writing to the imagination – but at least there was now a recognition that it could be an active and not merely a passive skill.

On its own terms, the Revised Code seemed to be working. Costs were held down, and there was a marked increase in the sheer volume of lessons in basic literacy. By the end of the first decade of the new system, two-thirds of a million children were being examined annually in one of the six Standards; ten years later, with attendance now compulsory in all elementary schools, the figure had passed two million.[170] Given the variations in ages of schooling and marriage, it is difficult to give an accurate measure of the impact of classroom experience on the literacy rates, but if we take the most illiterate group, the unskilled labourers, we find that their performance in the sample increased from 48.5 per cent to

70.7 per cent in the twenty years before and after the introduction of the scheme.[171]

The system of examination by Standards made it possible to display the progress of the schools, but it also enabled suppliers and consumers alike to form a clearer picture of the remaining shortcomings of the methods of teaching reading and writing. In place of the occasional attempts to distinguish between pupils able to read 'imperfectly' or 'decently', there was now available a precise statement of the levels of competence which had been achieved. Although the rubrics of the separate Standards were frequently revised over the period of the Code's operation, a definite pattern emerges. The children who crowded into the inspected elementary schools in such unprecedented numbers could be divided into three groups: those whose attendance was so limited that they were unable to take the annual examination, those who succeeded in grasping the rudiments of reading, spelling and forming words, which were measured by the first four Standards, and those who began to demonstrate some mastery of reading and made an attempt at composition. In these terms, the bare figures are sobering. In the year ending August 1882, for instance, with the Code in its maturity, the Board schools well established and compulsion universal, there were just over three and a half million children present at the annual inspection, but of these, only 47 per cent entered and passed one of the first four Standards in reading and 43 per cent in writing. At the top a mere 1.9 per cent proved their capacity to 'read a passage from one of Shakespeare's historical plays, or from some other standard author, or from a history of England' as demanded by Standard VI, and 1.7 per cent had taken the first steps towards using a pen to make up their own sentences.[172] The following year, fewer than one child in six hundred even attempted the newly introduced Standard VII.[173]

In spite of the care that was devoted to drawing up the higher standards and providing suitable teaching material, most schools were content to inculcate an acquaintance with literacy rather than an effective command. By Standard IV a child knew what reading and writing were, in the same way that it might know of the existence of Australia or the kangaroo, but it was no more capable of reading whatever literature it encountered outside the classroom, or of writing for business or pleasure, than it was of making its own voyage of discovery to the Antipodes. After Mundella's Act of 1880, most school authorities accepted the reality of the situation by permitting children between ten and thirteen to terminate their education once they had reached Standard IV. Some combination of natural ability and supportive or prosperous parents might enable a pupil to venture into the higher reaches of the Code, but the classes were rarely large enough to justify the teaching which they required. In the 1880s there were on average no more than four Standard VI passes a year in each inspected institution, and only in the larger centres of population did it become possible to collect the advanced pupils into separate higher-grade schools. The system of 'Standards' was itself an impediment to the future application of such skills as had been acquired, as it encouraged the child to put a full stop to its intellectual life once the requisite level had been reached. 'The modern system of education', observed the *Quarterly Review* in 1890,

> is admirably adapted to prevent the youth of the period from troubling itself greatly about literature in any form. The son of the working man, who leaves school as soon after he has passed the age of thirteen as possible, has no love for books, having 'passed his standard', and not unnaturally thinks he has practically done with the whole apparatus of learning for the rest of his life.[174]

The inspectors' continuing dissatisfaction with this state of affairs was focused, as before, on the assertion that schools were failing to develop the 'intelligence' of their pupils. However, their employment of this key concept was undergoing a subtle but profoundly important evolution. The association with comprehension remained, and indeed it was a formal requirement of the Code that children answer questions on the meaning of the text they had read, but the cognitive process involved was being construed in an increasingly active sense. Where previously the concern had been with the capacity to receive a set body of information, the emphasis was shifting to the pupil's ability to make its own connections. Thus, for instance, the Rev. J. G. C. Fussell, inspector for Finsbury, defined the problem with reading: 'This failure in intelligence does not, I am convinced, arise from want of previous hard work on the part of the teacher – on the contrary hard work is often too painfully evident – but rather from the want of a more intelligent system of training the children to observe and think for themselves.'[175] The task was to convince the pupils that written language was not an enclosed body of signs, an artificial game played to amuse the teacher; rather, 'they should be made to understand that these words mean something, so that when they read "dog", "pig", "mat", &c. they should know that these words really stand for things – things with which they are familiar'.[176]

Some observers began to realise that the central problem was the quality of the relationship between bodies of knowledge. The child displayed intelligence in its capacity to connect what it knew with what there was to know, and to communicate what it knew to an audience. In this process of communication literacy was an invaluable tool, but a level of intellectual control was required to make effective use of it. At the time, the function of this insight was largely critical, but at least the nature of the issue was becoming clearer. Although the value of oral communication was still too readily dismissed, the old assumption that children were entirely ignorant was gradually being replaced by a realisation that they had yet to be sufficiently equipped with the means of enlarging and transmitting the knowledge they possessed. 'The truth is', observed one inspector, 'that the intelligence of the children is but little developed, and they have but little power of expressing in language or on paper what they actually know. They have words without ideas, and ideas without words.'[177]

Conclusion

In the context of the hopes which had been entertained by the founders of the Church Societies, the situation at the end of the nineteenth century represented a striking combination of near total success and almost complete failure. There was much to celebrate. All working-class parents were now forced to yield control of their children's education for at least five years, and the private day schools had been driven from the field. In spite of a three-fold increase in the population, there had been a dramatic rise in the literacy rates, and it would only be a matter of a few years before the Registrar General's return of marriage partners signing with a mark fell below 1 per cent. Yet at the outset, reading, and still more so writing, had been subordinate concerns of the Christian schoolmaster, the means to a much larger and more important end. The Church schools had set out with the ambition of dismantling the process of cultural transmission which took place in the homes of the labouring poor, and replacing it with a self-sufficient body of values, information and cognitive skills. Over the decades a series of modifications to the content and method of teaching, many implemented in the name of expanding the work of the schools, had diminished and eventually almost destroyed this enterprise.

The pattern of victory and defeat was set by the Revised Code. The concession to the demands of working-class parents for greater emphasis on the three Rs made possible the eventual achievement of mass literacy and at the same time marked the abandonment of the attempt to supply through the schools alone a coherent, hierarchical culture held together by the literature and doctrines of Christianity. The subsequent success of the new curriculum, reinforced by the Acts of 1870 and 1880, served only to expose the fragmentary quality of the education the pupils were now receiving. Although some attempt was being made to respond to the linguistic skills the child brought into the classroom, there was little sense that the lessons in reading and writing represented a natural extension of the learning process which took place outside the school. And in spite of the introduction of 'specific' and 'class' subjects,[178] the teaching of literacy remained too mechanical and too limited to act as the basis for an exploration of wider areas of abstract knowledge.

By the end of the century it was evident to some educational writers than no further progress could be made without a wholesale re-examination of the relationship between the school and the domestic curriculum. In 1900 George Collar and Charles W. Crook, respectively the principal of a training college and a headmaster, published a teaching manual which represented an almost complete reversal of the principles upon which the elementary schools had been founded. The first chapter was devoted exclusively to 'School and Home', and began with an attack on the notion 'that school and home are distinct phases of the child's education, and that one was inimical to the other'.[179] Observing that HMIs now appeared uncertain as to the proper role of the pupil's family, they set about redefining the responsibilities of parents and teachers. They recognised that instruction in 'truthfulness, obedience and cleanliness' began in infancy, and as the child grew up these matters remained the concern of the mother and father: 'While the mental training is largely the work of the school, the moral training is the work of the home.'[180] There was still a profound mistrust of the mores of the wider working-class community, and Collar and Crook sought to achieve 'a more complete union of school and home life' in opposition to the 'evil influences of the streets'.[181] Inside the classroom, the success of the instruction rested on the creation of 'greater sympathy and cordiality between parent and teacher', which in practical terms meant building upon rather than neglecting or dismissing the work of the domestic curriculum: 'the natural way of teaching reading is to start with what the children already know: – to base our teaching on the vocabulary and powers of expression the children have when they first come to school'.[182] This was best achieved by a combination of Look and Say and alphabetic methods, reinforced by carefully organised homework. There should be less emphasis on reading aloud,[183] and the catechism mode was to be replaced by conversation in which the child could ask as well as answer questions. Throughout the curriculum more attention should be paid to developing the pupils' ability to employ their skills, with lessons in composition beginning as early as Standard III.

The impact of this attempt to forge an alliance between the school and the family in opposition to the culture of the streets would not be felt until after the War. For the children who passed through the elementary education system towards the end of the period covered by this study, the major problem remained one of grasping the relevance of their labours in the classroom to the intricate body of skills, information, values and imagination they continued to absorb in and around the home. For most of those who successfully completed the basic standards, the mental tricks they had been taught appeared artificial and remote from everyday existence. 'Their interest', observed Flora Thompson, 'was not in books, but in life, and especially the life that lay immediately about them.'[184] This was a grief to the teacher, and it was also a loss to the pupils, who now spent long years of their childhood acquiring but failing to learn how to use tools which could have extended the scope of a domestic curriculum less able than once it was to introduce them to the intellectual product of their society. In only one respect was there a natural empathy between the two courses of learning. The witness to the shortcomings of an Oxfordshire village school was also the participant entranced by the stories and poems she found within the covers of the Royal Readers. After so long a struggle to rescue the minds of working-class children from the corrupting influence of the home background, it was ironic that the most effective point of contact should be in the realm of fantasy.

4

WORK

In his diary, A. J. Munby records a series of encounters with a young woman called Sarah Tanner. He knew her first as a 'maid of all work to a tradesman in Oxford', and then met her a year or so later in Regent Street, 'arrayed in gorgeous apparel':

> How is this? said I. Why, she had got tired of service, wanted to see life and be independent; & so she had become a prostitute, of her own accord & without being seduced. She saw no harm in it; enjoyed it very much, thought it might raise her & perhaps be profitable. She had taken it up as a profession, & that with much energy: she had read books, and was taking lessons in writing and other accomplishments, in order to fit herself to be a companion of gentlemen.[1]

Several years later he came across her again, now soberly dressed, the respectable proprietor of a coffee house she had bought with her savings from a three-year career on the streets. In the field of work, reading and writing rarely had so straightforward and so successful an application. Even amongst her own kind, Sarah Tanner's attainments were unusual. Only 3 per cent of London prostitutes could read and write fluently, and 54 per cent were wholly illiterate.[2]

Neither the association of specific occupations with the skills of literacy nor the long-term interaction between the technologies of production and communication can be reduced to simple generalisations. In recent years a substantial body of research has challenged the assumption that the connection between education and economic growth was mutually beneficial. It has been argued that the comparatively high level of literacy attained in England by the middle of the eighteenth century was a victim rather than a cause of the world's first industrial revolution.[3] Insofar as the nineteenth-century economy eventually demanded an educated workforce, the impact of mass schooling was confined to the inculcation of attitudes of discipline and deference. Throughout the period, it is suggested, the actual skills of reading and writing were either irrelevant to the performance of occupational tasks, or served only to reinforce existing inequalities of opportunity and power.[4] At times, the process of revision has threatened to replace one over-simplification with another, and in order to achieve a more balanced view, it is necessary to make a closer examination of both the mechanics of the relationship between literacy and occupation and the uses of reading and writing in the workplace. The first section of this chapter will consider the evidence yielded by the marriage registers, and the remainder will investigate the function of the skills in the three principal areas of occupational activity: learning how to work, finding and undertaking work, and conducting labour relations.

Occupational literacy

The point of departure for an understanding of literacy rates amongst the labouring population is the range of performance within and between the separate occupational sectors. Each group of workers pursued their own path to the summit: some made steady progress though still trailing stragglers in their wake until late in the nineteenth century; others started later, experienced setbacks, and then had to climb much faster to catch up. An indication of the complexity of the process of change underlying the smooth graph of improvement which can be derived from the aggregate returns of the Registrar General is provided by table 4.1. Here the five-fold census classification[5] has been modified by dividing the large social class 3, the skilled manual workers, into six categories; traditional handicraft trades (H); trades in which some degree of literacy was not just highly desirable but an actual or de facto condition of entry (L); and then four trades in the vanguard of the Industrial Revolution – textile workers (T), potters (P), metal workers (Met) and miners (M). The sample of ten registration districts is grouped into decades to display the profile of the separate categories between 1839 and 1914.

Setting aside the special case of the 'literate' occupations (printers, railway employees and postal workers),[6] there was a range of sixty-six points across social class 3 in 1839. At the top, the handicraft trades, though carrying a solid minority of illiterates, had more in common with the clerks and officials than with the groups directly exposed to industrialisation. At the bottom the miners, four-fifths of whom were unable to sign their names, were less literate than even the unskilled labourers.[7] As late as the 1870s the traditional artisans were twice as literate as the miners, and if allowance is made for the bias towards youth to be found in any sample based on marriage registers,[8] it is evident that for the working population as a whole, substantial differentials were a reality throughout the nineteenth century.[9]

For all the working-class groups, there appears to have been a general stagnation if not a recession in the 1840s, but thereafter the chronology of

Table 4.1. *Occupational literacy of grooms, 1839–1914*

Social Class	1	2	3						4	5
			H	L	T	P	Met	M		
1839	100	90	87	100	63	58	53	21	58	27
1844/9	96	91	83	89	58	50	60	20	62	31
1854/9	96	91	85	93	70	56	61	30	66	41
1864/9	100	90	85	100	85	61	79	47	71	51
1874/9	100	96	90	100	84	78	75	47	79	56
1884/9	100	96	94	98	93	88	88	70	92	71
1894/9	100	98	99	100	86	100	95	88	97	86
1904/9	100	100	99	100	100	97	100	97	99	97
1914	100	100	98	100	100	100	100	99	99	99
Number	178	1,390	1,347	242	358	293	982	1,057	1,630	2,574

growth varied considerably. Apart from the handicraft trades, which had the least distance to travel, most sections experienced periods of both relative stasis and rapid progress. On the whole, the lower the threshold, the longer a group had to wait for take-off. The textile workers made large strides in the fifties, the metal workers in the sixties, the potters, after slipping back, in the seventies, and the last three categories in the eighties. For the semi-skilled labourers, whose largest constituent were workers in non-mechanised transport, the jump of fifteen points in this decade finally brought them into line with the artisans, but the miners and labourers still had some way to go. In terms of a basic command of reading and writing, it was these two categories alone of the workers in the sample which displayed the results of the introduction of comprehensive and compulsory elementary education.[10] If we allow the notional fifteen years for pupils to grow into marriage partners, the impact of the Acts of 1870 and 1880 is dramatically revealed in the figures for 1884/9 onwards. In the space of a single generation the miners leapt fifty points and labourers forty-one.

Taken together, the performance of the textile workers, potters, metal workers and miners in the early part of the sample period is scarcely impressive, but the returns do not in themselves resolve the issue of the impact of industrialisation on the literacy rates. As Laqueur and West pointed out in response to Sanderson's original article, if allowance is made for the time-lag between childhood and marriage, the decline to which he drew attention was largely a phenomenon of the late eighteenth rather than the nineteenth century.[11] The subsequent debate has been greatly hampered by the absence of evidence of the rates of separate groups of workers in the period before the recording of the groom's occupation became compulsory in 1837. It is difficult to draw general conclusions from the scattering of case studies of local publications unless

Table 4.2. *Occupational literacy in industrial districts, 1754-1914*

	1754–69	1774–89	1794–1809	1814–29	1834–49	1854–69	1874–89	1894–1909	1914	n.
Stoke										
All grooms	56	54	52	58	56	62	74	95	100	3,071
H	67	69	68	76	77	71	94	100	100	593
P	46	53	43	45	55	56	82	99	100	786
M	32	24	17	19	—	45	60	96	100	286
L	10	28	24	47	—	52	50	87	100	262
Macclesfield										
All grooms	60	65	66	66	64	79	93	98	100	2,715
H	68	74	79	84	82	89	92	96	100	560
T	50	61	59	61	59	76	95	92	100	645
L	45	45	48	51	44	47	82	95	100	398
Dudley										
All grooms	59	47	40	32	35	45	64	94	98	1,137*
H					74	60	65	100	100	103
Met					30	55	76	97	100	295
M					17	25	35	86	89	256
L					15	36	48	89	100	176

* 1839–1914

the underlying mechanism of change can be identified. Few of the registers contain this information, and the twenty-three located by Schofield for his occupational analysis were predominantly rural. However, it transpires that in the principal parishes of two of the industrialising districts selected for my sample, Stoke and Macclesfield, the vicars had been in the habit of entering the occupation of the groom alongside his marital status throughout almost the whole of the period back to 1754.[12] Thus it is possible for the first time to examine in detail what was happening inside the communities faced with the arrival of new forms of production.

Table 4.2[13] displays the evolution of the literacy of the major occupational groups in Stoke and Macclesfield for a century and a half, together with Dudley from 1839, where the aggregate figures from 1754 to 1837 have been the subject of a separate study by Jacky Grayson.[14] Each of the districts encountered different facets of the early Industrial Revolution. The expansion of the pottery industry in Stoke was under way by 1750, leading to both the proliferation of small enterprises and the introduction of major innovations in the organisation of production, most notably in the Wedgwood factory at Etruria, founded in 1769.[15]

In Dudley, the developments in metal manufacture, especially nail making, resulted in a similar intensification of small workshops, which were increasingly challenged by factories from the 1830s.[16] Macclesfield, one of the principal centres of the silk industry, acquired its first water-driven factory as early as 1737, and by the 1790s a growing number of weavers were at work alongside the well-established spinners.[17] The

Potteries and the Black Country also experienced a concomitant expansion of the mining industry. In all three areas there was a gradual increase in the population during the second half of the eighteenth century followed by a much more rapid rise in the first half of the nineteenth.

However, if the three communities can all be subsumed under the headings of industrialisation and urbanisation, the performance of their literacy rates varied sharply. Stoke went into a shallow decline during the second half of the eighteenth century and revived and then stagnated in the second quarter of the nineteenth, before taking off in the 1860s. Dudley suffered a steep and continuing decline which did not bottom out until the 1830s and 1840s, and although matters then began to improve, the rate in the 1870s was still below that of the 1750s. Macclesfield, by contrast, was relatively stable throughout a period of substantial growth in both its population and its main industry. Other studies of manufacturing centres have yielded equally uneven returns. Despite his pessimistic conclusion, the data advanced by Sanderson for the Lancashire cotton towns conforms to no single chronology or scale of change,[18] and the most interesting essay in Stephens' volume has to explain the radically different profiles of the neighbouring towns of Hyde and Ashton.[19]

In order to bring the picture into focus, it is necessary to consider more carefully how the literacy levels were determined in an urban area in this period. If the rates for the separate occupational groups are examined in detail, it is evident that at any point the record of a given community represented a balance between upward and downward forces. Different sectors of the workforce, each with their own traditions of educational attainment, expanded at different rates, altering the occupational profile of a town and thus its overall literacy rate. The handicraft trades in Stoke and Macclesfield were buoyant throughout, gradually improving their returns and always running ahead of the towns as a whole. The numbers in social classes 1 and 2 in the area samples were too small to be analysed, but it may be assumed that they too were pushing the rates ahead; this certainly was the case with the farmers in the countryside around Macclesfield, who returned an average of 89 per cent between 1764 and 1834. Working in the opposite direction were the major manufacturing groups, the potters in Stoke, the textile workers in Macclesfield, and, to judge from the situation in the 1830s and 1840s, the metal workers in Dudley, brought up in the rear by the miners, who in Stoke, as elsewhere, found it difficult to rise above 20 per cent. The impact of industrialisation was not to depress the rates of any given group, or to force down the rates of all of a given population, but rather to shift the balance between the absolute numbers in the separate categories. In Macclesfield, the stability was the fortuitous outcome of the substantial and gradually improving handicraft sector, set against the proliferating textile workers. In Stoke the traditional trades, though still numerous, were gradually outweighed by the potters, with the presence of the miners ensuring that an overall improvement would be long in coming. We can only speculate about the cause of Dudley's decline before 1839, but the relative proportions of the major groups after that date would suggest that the influence of the handicraft trades was overwhelmed by the very much larger number of nailers and miners.

The issue of the relationship between early industrialisation and literacy rates thus needs to be reformulated. It is quite evident that the workforce engaged in the areas of innovation in the century following 1750 was less literate than the skilled trades, though, with the exception of miners, more so than general labourers. That does not mean, however, that a transition from workshops to factories of itself pushed down the rates of groups of workers. Partly this is because many of the trades caught up in the Industrial Revolution – nailers, miners and many potters being obvious examples – worked in ever larger numbers in established types of production. The problems in Dudley were a consequence of a proliferation of workshops with mechanisation not appearing until the trough of the depression had been reached. And partly this is because where there was a sharp cleavage between domestic and factory production, the process of change was far from straightforward. The available evidence argues against a simple movement of home workers into the mills.[20] Rather it is likely that a new workforce, recruited at least in part from less literate farm labourers, displaced the domestic spinners and weavers. The recording of occupations in the pre-1837 registers was too imprecise to distinguish between silk workers in workshops and factories in Macclesfield, but the maintenance of the literacy levels of the textile workers in the town at a time when the mills were expanding lends no support to a pessimistic view.

The key factor was the balance of pressures in the new urban communities.[21] Given the great variations in the rate and timing of growth in the new occupations in the late eighteenth century, and the range of patterns which could be formed with existing groups of workers, the absence of a dominant mode in the movement of literacy rates becomes more comprehensible. It was possible for disasters to occur, but equally conflicting forces could cancel each other out. Whilst economic change created persistent downward pressure, it also generated countervailing currents. Many of the handicraft trades were no mere survivals, but were themselves the product of increased activity in other sectors of the economy. The final drive towards full literacy would begin either when an expanding artisan sector managed to overcome resistance from below, or, as in the case of Stoke and Dudley, a dominant manufacturing sector at last began to put its own house in order.

There remains the question of education. If the emphasis is to be placed on the communities as a whole, the impact of a rapidly growing population on the provision of schools must be taken into account. In this context, the problem of evidence is particularly acute. There is no reliable source of information on the precise extent of elementary education in the latter part of the eighteenth century, particularly that provided and paid for by the working class, nor, as was argued in chapter 3, are there any grounds for assuming that formal schooling was exclusively responsible for the transmission of basic literacy. At this stage, we can make just three general points. Firstly there is no reason to suppose that education was exempt from the general dislocation of services in the expanding towns,[22] and conversely, it might be expected that the local initiatives to repair the damage, such as took place in Ashton, or more widely, in the Sunday school movement, might bear some fruit. But secondly, if there was damage, it seems not to have affected those in the skilled trades, who, perhaps through reliance on their own efforts, managed to maintain their levels through thick and thin.[23] Finally, if schooling was critically disrupted, it is remarkable how quickly the recovery began. Subtracting the elapse of time from school to marriage, the decline was in most cases over by the end of the Napoleonic Wars, and thereafter the transmission of literacy at least held its own in the face of continuing population growth. Although the industrial areas still lagged behind the national average, they were no longer going backwards. By contrast, other indices of urban dislocation, such as death rates, were still worsening in the 1830s and 1840s. The attention focused on elementary education in the debate over the Condition of England Question was a function of rising expectations rather than a continuing decline in performance.

Behind the grooms, the brides displayed an equally smooth graph of improvement during the second two thirds of the nineteenth century. However, chapter 2 has already drawn attention to significant variations in the performance of women in different parts of the country, and it is now possible to look more closely at the mechanism which enabled the supposedly backward section of the population to overtake their husbands in an increasing number of counties as the century wore on. Table 4.3 indicates that as with the grooms, levels of literacy were deeply affected by occupational status. The handicraft trades were once more at the top of the working-class league in 1839, with a rate five times higher than the miners, who could barely reach double figures. At the same time a closer comparison with table 4.1 reveals interesting variations in the relative performance of the occupational groups. Set against the grooms, the most striking feature of the brides' figures was the poor performance of all the sectors in the skilled working class. Most began the period around thirty points behind their male counterparts, and only caught up in the last

Table 4.3. *Literacy of brides by occupation of father, 1839–1914*

Social class	1	2	H	L	T	P	Met	M	4	5
					3				**4**	**5**
1839	93	79	56	50	21	29	36	11	48	29
1844/9	100	77	57	67	23	37	35	15	48	33
1854/9	97	82	65	71	35	47	42	21	52	48
1864/9	100	89	73	70	56	43	49	27	66	61
1874/9	95	91	74	92	69	44	65	43	73	69
1884/9	100	92	79	94	83	81	82	66	87	82
1894/9	100	99	93	100	86	93	89	92	93	95
1904/9	100	99	98	95	96	93	98	98	97	97
1914	100	98	99	96	100	100	98	99	98	97
Number	216	1,695	1,394	144	419	262	876	791	1,165	2,738

Table 4.4. *Literacy of grooms by occupation, of sons by occupation of father, of daughters by occupation of father, 1839–1914*

Social class		1	2	H	L	T	P	Met	M	4	5	Number
						3				**4**	**5**	**Number**
	G	97	91	83	87	63	52	59	23	60	32	2,804
1839–54	GF	98	83	74	75	67	67	53	30	57	37	2,739
	BF	97	78	54	57	27	36	37	15	50	34	2,720
	G	98	91	85	92	78	61	73	41	74	49	2,445
1859–74	GF	94	91	79	90	74	69	67	46	76	53	2,382
	BF	98	88	73	75	49	43	48	30	65	60	2,361
	G	100	96	95	98	87	90	84	78	90	71	2,346
1879–94	GF	98	95	92	100	86	91	85	75	89	76	2,244
	BF	100	95	82	97	77	83	81	70	86	81	2,244
	G	100	100	99	100	96	98	100	95	99	95	2,421
1899–1914	GF	100	98	99	100	98	96	99	96	99	96	2,389
	BF	100	99	97	96	94	94	96	98	98	97	2,366

G – Groom GF – Groom's father BF – Bride's father

decades of the century. By contrast, the unskilled labourers alone of the ten groups actually ran ahead of the grooms until both sexes reached the upper nineties. As a consequence, it made much less difference whether a bride came from industrial or non-industrial trades, or indeed from the skilled or the unskilled.

The absence of information on the occupation of the brides themselves prevents a direct correlation between the marriage partners. However, the returns of both fathers in the ceremony displayed in table 4.4 indicate that

Table 4.5. *Occupational literacy by groom and bride's father for selected districts, 1839–1914*

Social class		Stoke		Bethnal Green		Cleobury Mortimer		Samford		Woking-ham		Maccles-field	
		%L	%P	%L	%P	%L	%P	%L	%P	%L	%P	%L	%P
1 & 2	G	94	10	83	12	93	23	99	14	98	17	96	23
	BF	84	14	76	13	95	30	95	18	96	22	88	28
H	G	84	13	89	35	89	12	96	13	94	19	92	16
	BF	69	16	72	38	78	12	87	11	85	16	70	18
Ind	G	70	53	73	11	76	16	9	5	86	4	77	26
	BF	60	46	56	16	73	12	92	3	77	3	68	27
4	G	76	14	89	24	76	9	84	19	92	19	88	20
	BF	62	12	77	19	76	7	90	15	92	12	72	12
5	G	51	10	69	18	46	40	56	49	52	41	70	15
	BF	55	12	63	16	55	38	74	57	70	47	58	15
All	G	75		83		70		76		78		85	
	BF	65		70		74		82		81		73	
Number	G	927		913		1,079		929		1,120		958	
	BF	911		860		1.035		943		1,094		903	

L – Literacy, P – Population, G – Groom, BF – Bride's father

gender rather than generation was responsible for the marked degree of equality in the literacy of working-class women. In every category of the skilled working class, daughters were much less likely to become literate than sons. Amongst the unskilled, on the other hand, daughters pulled away from both sons and grooms in the second and third quarters of the sample period.

The suggestion that the reversal of the traditional hierarchy of the sexes was the achievement of those at the bottom of the social scale is confirmed if attention is paid to the profiles of the individual communities. Of the ten registration districts in the sample, those of Samford, Wokingham and Cleobury Mortimer, all predominantly rural areas, produced returns in which brides out-performed grooms over the period as a whole. In table 4.5 their major occupational groups are set against those in the industrial centres of Macclesfield and Stoke, and the traditional urban district of Bethnal Green.[24]

It is evident that the key factor in determining the relative standing of the sexes was the size and literacy of the unskilled sector. In each of the rural communities, between a third and half of the brides had agricultural labourers for fathers, and it was here that the grooms were left behind, in the case of Samford by as much as eighteen points. There was a rough parity amongst the semi-skilled, but elsewhere in these districts the menfolk retained their superiority. In the manufacturing centres on the other hand, the size of the handicraft and industrial sectors, where the daughters fared so much worse than the grooms, ensured that even if women were ahead amongst the unskilled, as in Stoke, they would end up in second place.

The pattern of differentiation also helps to explain the variations in performance which were a feature of all the counties. In Suffolk, for instance, the three districts in 1864 not following Samford's example were the county's only large towns, Ipswich and Bury St Edmunds, together with Mildenhall, where the figures were almost level.[25] In Staffordshire, whose women had the distinction of being the most illiterate in England at this time, brides were only marginally behind the grooms in Lichfield, which contained a large area of countryside within its boundaries, and were actually ahead in the predominantly rural district of Tamworth.[26] The causes of the increase in female literacy are partly obscured by the absence of data on the occupational identity of the bride. However, as W. B. Stephens has recently argued, the explanation may lie in the combination of a falling demand for the labour of school-age girls and a rising demand for functionally literate domestic servants.[27] It may also have been a product of a reduction in the gap between the possession of the ability to read and the acquisition of the skill of writing. The contrasting fortunes of the sons of the labouring poor require a further examination of the perceived relevance of literacy to the male workforce, which will be the concern of the remainder of the chapter.

Occupational learning

In the realm of labour, as elsewhere in popular culture, the function of literacy was more complicated than might at first appear. The most obvious purpose of learning to read and write was the enhancement of career prospects, but in the event both the educators and the educated invested the issue with much wider significance. Those who taught reading and writing in the Church and later in the Board schools were consciously attempting to create new types of intelligence for new modes of production. The worker was not to be educated merely to enrich himself, still less to escape from his class, although this prospect might be held out to a fortunate few. Rather the goal of the teacher was to produce young men able to approach the task of earning a living, whether in an established trade or in an industrialising sector, in an entirely new frame of mind. The task of deconstructing and reconstructing language on the basis of its inherent rules was to be replicated as the pupil entered the workplace. Both the acquisition and the practice of occupational skills were to be reduced to a framework of ordered, written rules which could form the basis of a complex yet rational, hierarchical, and above all stable economic order. As enterprises became more capital intensive and grew beyond the simple unit of the master and a handful of artisans, so their efficiency would increasingly depend on the bureaucratisation of the workplace, the development and application of impersonal, formal regulations of production, devised by the management and observed by their employees.[28] The increasing verbal support given by manufacturers for public education suggested that they and the teachers were engaged in a common cause. Whether this was in practice the case will be a central concern of the remaining sections of this chapter.

For the workforce itself, mass literacy was an ambiguous prospect. As we have seen, no section of the labouring population was wholly illiterate, and as will become evident, the skills of literacy and many of the structures of thought educators associated with them had long been used in a wide variety of employments. In some contexts, the working class as a whole, or particular groups within it, had much to gain from an extension and formalisation of rules in the workplace. In others, the attempt to translate existing modes of absorbing and applying occupational techniques into a written code threatened an irreversible loss of status and power. At every point the issue of the existence of rules, who defined and enforced them, and whether they were recorded and transmitted orally or in writing, raised questions of authority and independence.

The most obvious application of the schoolmaster's endeavours was in the field of learning to work. On the one hand the rising generation was being equipped with the tools thought necessary to acquire information; on the other, the accelerating pace of innovation demanded workers capable as never before of mastering new techniques and processes. To some it appeared a simple matter of the workshop becoming a classroom. William Cooper, author of the *Crown Glass Cutter and Glaziers Manual* of 1835, was convinced that this had already happened: 'The general diffusion of knowledge, and the improvements in the modes of its dissemination which have occurred within these few years, have made literature as familiar in the workshop of the artisan as in the closet of the student.'[29] Such optimism was misplaced. It was far from clear what such literature should encompass, or how the artisan could be persuaded to read it. The attempt to bring together the separate forms of learning turned out to be fraught with difficulty. Whilst it could be doubted if a child received any valid moral or intellectual training outside a school, it clearly underwent a course of occupational education, whatever the status of its future employment. The basic problem was how to conceptualise this activity in such a way that the skills gained in the classroom could be applied to it.

The solution was proffered by the nature of the event which made the issue so important. Just as the Industrial Revolution was founded on an increasing division of labour, of a separation of the work process into its constituent parts, so the business of gaining expertise could be thought of in the same way. The division between the manual and mental elements of labour came to rest on the notion of discrete rules. On the one side was a body of unwritten, irrational, non-analytical practices, handed down from generation to generation; on the other were scientifically deduced principles which underpinned every branch of production. These could be separately learned and then combined to form a working man capable of responding to the next stage in the course of innovation. The contrast was vigorously drawn in one of the earliest trade manuals, *The Taylor's Complete Guide or a Comprehensive Analysis of Beauty and Elegance in Dress Containing Rules for cutting out Garments of Every Kind*, published in 1796. In the absence of 'science' or 'theory', its authors explained, 'The Taylor, whose sprightly walk in life is to give grace to drapery, sits down upon the folorn hope of struggling through without ever enquiring farther than the maxims of his father, or what his master always did before him.' 'It is not to be wondered at', they concluded, 'that so many mistakes happen among Taylors who have no rule or criterion to go by, but leave everything to blind chance, or what is almost as bad, following the maxims of ill informed masters without ever consulting either their reason or nature whether such practice was within the pale of likelihood to succeed.'[30]

Until about the middle of the nineteenth century, the struggle to exploit literacy in the context of training took place outside the schoolroom. The charity schools had originally attempted to combine moral and manual teaching, but the experiment foundered in the face of problems which were to recur throughout the period. It had been hoped that pupils could simultaneously learn a trade and earn sufficient sums to offset the cost of the teaching, but in practice it proved impossible to devise tasks from which such young children could derive any benefit, financial or otherwise. Given the desire to distance the schools from both the domestic curriculum and classes run by unqualified working men and women, there was little resistance to the victory of the moral and literary side of the curriculum.[31] The subsequent development of the National and British Schools Societies served merely to consolidate the exclusion of work training. As their staff sought professional status, they were naturally reluctant to acquire or display an ability to teach manual skills. Neither their own training nor the pedagogic theory upon which it was based allowed room for the integration of the schoolroom and the workshop. The most that could be attempted was the instruction of the girls in basic domestic tasks such as knitting and sewing. The only way in which the curriculum could respond to the continuing demand for relevance to the practical needs of the workforce was through an adaptation of some element of the three Rs. The most obvious candidate was arithmetic, and in particular geometry. Here, it was hoped, was a subject which could be applied to all categories of manual labour. 'The use of the scale and compasses in drawing', explained the Minutes of 1851–2, 'is a useful acquirement for workmen in almost every handicraft;– to the blacksmith, the carpenter, and the mason, for instance, in making plans and sections of their work, and to the gardener or the agricultural labourer in laying out a plot of ground to a scale, or planning a shed or a cottage, or the drainage of a field.'[32]

The main engagement with the problem during the first phase of the Industrial Revolution centred on the fate of apprenticeship. The legal protection of the institution was removed in 1814, and an effort was made to replace its work training function with a combination of work manuals and mechanics' institutes. The justification for the attempted reform and the defence of the existing method of transmitting occupational skills rested on the meaning and relevance of a key phrase of the artisan's vocabulary. When he signed his articles and paid his premium, every apprentice expected to be taught the 'Art and Mystery' of his trade. These two words encapsulated much of what it meant to be a skilled working man, and much of what was held to be outmoded about his way of life.

The phrase signified first of all an activity which demanded more than mere physical strength. 'As in other trades', explained James Devlin's guide to shoemaking,

> the boy of the shoemaker is mostly bound for the term of seven years, to learn the 'art and mystery' of the business – the term *art* and *mystery*, or *mystery* and *craft*, implying a trade that requires, as the Act of the 5th Eliz. says, 'skill and experience', as distinguished from the operations of the mere labourer, such as digging.[33]

Head and hand combined in a way which was disciplined yet creative. By 'art' was meant a process which was at once structured and unfinished. The true artisan, like the true artist, never stopped learning, never repeated himself, never exhausted the possibilities of his material. The rules of a trade were too extensive ever to be fully encompassed, their application too diverse to be wholly predictable. 'Is the business of a carpenter, a business requiring considerable skill and long servitude to acquire a proficiency in it?' enquired the 1812 Committee on Apprentice Laws. 'I have been at it 19 years', replied John Watts, 'and am not a proficient myself. There is something almost every day fresh.'[34] The unenclosed quality of the artisan's knowledge was a cause of both humility and pride. 'A mason can never be said to have learned his job', wrote Fred Bower, 'for he might be fifty years at the trade and then get a piece of stone to hew into a shape, and a way, he has never seen before.'[35] By 'mystery' was meant a corpus of knowledge which could not be codified, which was the property of the trade and therefore private, and which within the trade belonged to no individual but to the body of craftsmen past, present and future. Serving members were no more than guardians of a tradition which they inherited from one generation, refined still further and then passed on to the next.[36] Writing might be used in the practice of the mystery, and formal regulations might be employed to protect it, particularly in the Statute of Artificers, but in essence the concept was fundamentally alien to the publicly accessible, privately owned, transparent world of the printed word. Apprenticeship embodied a sense of knowledge which belonged to the pre-Caxton era.

For the proponents of mass literacy, however, the tide of change was flowing against the inherited structure of occupational learning. The educational reformer J. A. St John observed, 'It is the tendency of civilisation to destroy all crafts and mysteries.'[37] By the beginning of the nineteenth century, the market for educating children both at home and in the classroom had already been opened up by enterprising publishers, and as the reading public continued to expand, it was inevitable that attention should be turned to what was, for the bulk of the population, the next phase in the learning process. A trickle of guides to various trades broadened into a flood of publications by 1850. As a genre, the work manuals were diverse in their contents and ambitions.[38] Some of the early texts were written by tradesmen partly to profit from and partly to celebrate their specialised knowledge. 'Of the various branches of manufacture which this country is so highly distinguished for, none are less understood than Hat-making', observed *Lloyd's Treatise on Hats*. Most of the population were wholly ignorant of the techniques of constructing so common an item of dress and thus incapable of appreciating the quality of workmanship: 'to form a correct judgment of the external material, when manufactured, whether it be hair, wool, or beaver, although many pretend, none are really competent but those *experienced* in the *trade*'.[39] Some artisans went further and began to explore how print might be used as a tool in particular trades. M. Cook, a working tailor, defended the appearance of his *Sure Guide Against Waste in Dress* in 1787:

> Many to whom the idea has been communicated, with a degree of resentment have put the question: What! Sir, do you presume to teach the trade? To those he begs leave to reply, that without such presumption, he submits to their use, a set of Tables, warranted by experience, which will save them much time in calculation; since it is allowed by every one impossible to recollect from memory alone with certainty, what quantity of different widths of cloth is required for various garments.[40]

Other surveys were compiled to meet a growing demand from middle-class readers for facts and figures to confirm the unprecedented growth of the economy. 'It is not until we have glanced steadily in all these directions', explained *The Textile Manufactures of Great Britain*, 'that we shall be in a condition to appreciate the enormous amount of population, of capital, of skill, of mechanical ingenuity, of energy, of patience, involved in the production of clothing in this country.'[41] However, the manuals reveal as much about the dilemmas as the triumphs of progress. Beneath the rhetoric of the tourist guide was a deep conflict over the means of acquiring the skills upon which the expansion of manufacture was based. The spread of capitalism in both the handicraft and industrial sectors raised two fundamental problems about the transmission and improvement of occupational knowledge. Firstly, the move towards greater specialisation and the introduction of more specific techniques threatened to break down the totality of the artisan's skill. Secondly, the demand by employers for greater flexibility within and between processes collided with the barriers erected by the concept of the mystery of each trade. In each case the appearance of a new literary genre was the other face of the attack on apprenticeship through the law.

The division of labour provided the point of departure for many of the manuals. On the one hand it undermined the argument that a traditional apprenticeship was the only means of producing the complete craftsman. 'Formerly, indeed', observed James Devlin, 'there might have been those who, to use the trade phrase, could "box the *craft* round", though at present or óf late years I neither know nor have ever known one, such a high excellence is required . . .'[42] On the other, it pointed the way forward. 'These wonderful effects', wrote Thomas Carter of advances in printing, 'are produced by a perfect division of labour, in which there is activity without hurry, and in which the superintending mind is the moving and regulating power of a human machine, composed of many parts, but all working in harmony to the same end.'[43] This new type of 'superintending mind' was to be found not just in the industrialising occupations such as textiles or engineering, but right across the traditional trades. Thus, for instance, Thomas Tredgold defended the existence of his 1820 *Elementary Principles of Carpentry*: 'In the course of the last century several treatises on Carpentry have appeared; but in none of them is to be found anything on the mechanical principles of the art, except it be a few rules for calculating the strength of timber; and these are founded upon erroneous views of the subject, and therefore not to be relied upon.'[44] All species of the artisan's art could be reduced to such principles if the correct approach were adopted. Once the separate rules were identified, both the practice and the acquisition of skills would be transformed. Devlin was able to provide a remedy for the increasing inability of the shoemaker's apprenticeship to produce the all-round craftsman: armed with his manual, a youth would gain

> a clear idea of the connexion and proportion of those parts, which will render more perfect his judgment of the whole; and will accelerate his learning with greater facility, by his mind being brought to think of those dependencies; so that he will sooner gain that expertness which is the result of the mind having a clear and mechanical knowledge of the combination of those parts.[45]

Where most of the manuals were a response to the increasing specialisation within occupations, some reflected the growth of firms in which a variety of skills were combined under one roof. A particular example was the building industry, which led the way towards the creation of enterprises whose masters could not gain a working knowledge of all the trades at their command through the established channels of occupational education. The consequence was the genre of Builder's Price Books, which listed the cost of labour and materials in the numerous trades required for the construction of the simplest of dwellings. They first appeared in the eighteenth century, written by and largely for the combined architect/builder,[46] but it was the gradual emergence of the larger contractor during the first half of the nineteenth century[47] which consolidated their place in lists of the work manual publishers. To take one example, *The Builder's and Contractor's Price-Book* of the largest firm in this field, John Weale, presented 5,391 entries on twenty-seven different trades ranging from 'Asphalte and Lava Work' to 'Zinc Work'.[48] The contractor costing his project could discover, for instance, that a yard of plaster, one coat only, rough on brick, would cost $2\frac{3}{4}$d for labour and 6d with materials if straight, $3\frac{1}{4}$d and 7d if curved. As prices varied by area and, crucially, according to the fluctuating power of the appropriate trade society, only average figures could be presented, but at the same time the publishers hoped that their lists could come to play a part in the arbitration of labour disputes.[49]

By 1854 Weale's list contained over 1,400 entries, with 105 items in a recently launched Series of Rudimentary Works for the Use of Beginners.[50] At first sight it appeared as if the entire world of manual labour had been translated into print for the purpose of recording and codifying its knowledge. However, a closer examination reveals an important division of labour in the production and consumption of these works. Many reformers in this period, including in particular Henry Brougham, a leading sponsor of the Society for the Diffusion of Useful Knowledge and the mechanics' institutes, had hoped that the identification of the rules inherent in trade practices would pave the way towards a mutually beneficial integration of manual skills and scientific inquiry. In the event, the publications of the SDUK reached only a fraction of their intended audience, and the lectures of the mechanics' institutes were boycotted by artisans unwilling to accept middle-class patronage and unable to bridge the gap between their elementary education and more advanced scientific theory.[51] So far from serving as a means of uniting art and abstract knowledge, the manuals came to exemplify the growing divide between manual and mental labour. In the early handbooks for the building industry, design and execution overlapped extensively. William Pain, author of an influential series on house construction in the third quarter of the eighteenth century,[52] described himself as an 'Architect and Joiner'. Fifty years later, such an individual was almost extinct. The architects, together with the civil engineers, led the way towards the separation of the professional from the skilled labourer. The Institute of Civil Engineers was incorporated in 1818, and the Royal Institute of British Architects received its charter in 1837.[53] A distinguishing mark of the new professions was their reliance on book knowledge. Where artisans learned principally by oral transmission, architects and engineers read and then took exams, with the practical element of their training rigorously enclosed in a framework of theory. They, rather than the joiners and masons, came to form the chief market for the manuals, and inevitably, became mainly responsible for compiling them. *A Rudimentary Treatise on Masonry and Stonecutting*, for instance, published by John Weale in 1849, was the work of Edward Dobson, 'Assoc. I.C.E., M.R.I.B.A.'.[54] Despite the early ventures into trades such as tailoring and shoemaking, the bulk of handbooks on sale by mid century fell within the fields covered by engineering and building. Those with letters after their names wrote for those who wished to acquire them.

The attempt to break down the secrecy of occupational knowledge arose from a deep concern about its effect on the continuing cycle of technical innovation. The problem was forcefully stated by Charles Tomlinson in his *Cyclopaedia of Useful Arts*:

> A large number of manufacturing processes have preceded scientific theory; they were discovered after repeated trials and failures of other processes: a slow and costly method necessarily standing in the way of improvement. Moreover, the processes thus discovered were kept secret and formed the *mystery* of the trade, gradually revealed to the young mechanic in the course of his apprenticeship. Nor could the master pretend to do more than teach the processes in their prescribed order: the reasons for them, and for one particular order rather than another, he could not teach, and hence the *art* and *mystery* gradually assumed a

fixed and consolidated character apparently incapable of improvement.[55]

If the light of science was to disperse the darkness of mystery, a way had to be found of undermining the artisans' instinctive secrecy. The most obvious solution was to publish their knowledge. Thus Thomas Carter welcomed Cooper's early treatise on glazing:

> We mention Mr. Cooper's book, as an honourable exception of that narrow jealousy which fears to divulge the processes by which a trade or manufacture is carried on. We would beg to impress on the mind of a youth about to enter upon this, or any other business, that an intelligent and liberal tone of mind is perfectly compatible with success in business.[56]

It was not, however, compatible with the artisans' defence of what they regarded as their property. If a youth could learn how to make shoes in the same way that he learned how to read and write, not only would craftsmen lose their status and pride, but their capacity to protect wages and conditions of employment would be fatally undermined. Their bargaining power was founded on an ability to restrict entry to a trade, which in turn was dependent on a denial of access to its corporate knowledge. This was why Cook's early attempt to codify aspects of tailoring met with 'a degree of resentment'. Only a thin line divided the useful table of calculations and measures from the fatal exposure of what were claimed to be the rules of practice of a complete process, and as the system of apprenticeship came under increasing pressure in the early decades of the nineteenth century, artisans were less and less willing to risk crossing it.

Taken together, the ambitions of the new professions and fears of the old crafts had the effect of polarising rather than integrating oral and literary modes of acquiring occupational knowledge. The pressures generated by the increasing division of labour prevented any effective exploitation of the opportunities it offered. The artisan was deeply conscious that his skill incorporated an ordered body of knowledge. It was the essential discipline of his practice which separated him from the 'operations of the mere labourer'.[57] As such, there was no reason why manuals could not be used by both apprentice and working journeyman. There had long been a place for ready reckoners such as *Hutton's Mensuration*,[58] and many craftsmen could benefit from making contact through the printed word with developments elsewhere, whether practical or scientific. Instead the interaction between the expansion of publishing and the attack on the traditional apprenticeship raised the prospect that rather than embodying the rules of his skill in his practical judgment, the artisan would be reduced to a mere extension of the abstracted, codified, 'mechanical principles' of his increasingly sub-divided trade. This led to an unnecessary divide between books and occupational learning, and, by extension, between rational inquiry and working practice. The extreme statement of this outlook was presented in Sturt's classic account of the traditional crafts-man. 'A good wheelwright', he wrote, 'knew by art but not by reasoning, the proportions to keep between spokes and the felloes; and so too a good smith knew how tight a two-and-a-half inch tyre should be made for a five-foot wheel and how tight for a four-foot, and so on. He felt it in his bones.'[59] Such skills were esentially oral: 'The nature of this knowledge should be noted. It was set out in no book. It was not scientific.'[60] These dualities of art and reason, skill and science, were a product of the times; the early-nineteenth-century craftsman would not have recognised the conflict.

During the middle decades of the nineteenth century, the problem of occupational training took on a new form. The focus of attention shifted from the obstacles created by the domestic artisans to the threats posed by overseas competitors. Doubts raised amidst the success of the 1851 Exhibition[61] were confirmed by the Paris International Exhibition of 1867, which, according to a report to the Schools Inquiry Commission of that year, afforded clear evidence 'of the inferior rate of progress recently made in manufacturing and mechanical industry compared with that made in other European countries. It has been stated to us that this alleged inferiority is due in great measure to the want of technical education.'[62] France, Prussia, Austria, Belgium and Switzerland all now possessed a system of training managers and workers, claimed the leading advocate of reform Lyon Playfair, whereas Britain had nothing and was beginning to reap the consequences.[63] As it was now evident that neither commercial publishers[64] nor voluntary agencies could meet the deficiency, a major reorganisation of the entire process of developing work skills was required. The problem, as before, was partly conceptual and partly practical. What was meant by the new phrase 'technical education',[65] and how was it to be acquired? A witness to the subsequent Royal Commission on Technical Instruction was asked, 'How do you propose to arrange for the union of the mechanical knowledge, which can only be gained in the shop, with the theoretical knowledge, which can only be gained in the school?'[66] It was to prove far from easy to find an answer.

If concern over the future of production provoked the demand for reform, the characteristics of its growth in the second half of the century generated the major obstacles. There were two related difficulties. Firstly, the extremely uneven development of the economy, with advances in factory production and scientific techniques accompanied by a continuing expansion of handicraft trades and unskilled manual labour, made it virtually impossible to conceive a single structure of technical education which would complement the emerging national system of elementary education.[67] This problem was compounded by the now entrenched ideology of laissez-faire, which might countenance State activity on the fringe of the economy but was resistant to its invasion of the workplace. Secondly, the increasing division of labour and the creation of specialised tasks, which remained the major argument for the replacement of the traditional apprenticeship, produced contradictory requirements. On the one hand there appeared a need to intellectualise manual labour in response to the theoretical content of advanced processes, on the other, a need to empty it of the last vestiges of art and mystery to accommodate the demands of mechanised production.

In the light of the failure to infuse apprenticeship training with abstract rules, the advocates of technical education were now anxious to keep the two modes of learning apart. 'The impression on many people's minds', explained Mundella,

> is, that those who advocate technical education want to instruct apprentices in their trades instead of teaching them in their workshops, while, what we want is, simply to teach them the technical principles of chemistry, mechanics, of geometry, in order that when they get into the workshop they may know the rationale of their work, and apply it to practice in their business.[68]

Thus the evening classes subsidised by the Department of Science and Art from 1853 onwards could teach the elements of science without trespassing on the prerogatives of either manufacturers or artisans. However, from the outset the project was beset by problems. It was not just that the limited funds available and the use of payment by results restricted the scope of the Department's work. In 1867 scientific instruction in Leeds amounted to just one chemistry class of thirty pupils whose teacher received an annual grant of just £11.[69] The real problem was continuing doubts about the relevance and practicality of making this form of instruction available to artisans.

The emphasis on 'principles' raised as many difficulties as it resolved. Its inherent ambiguity was exposed by the machine-tool maker Whitworth:

> The thorough knowledge of first principles, and the steady pursuit of them, lies at the heart of every branch of production, but especially of mechanics. To make things as simple as possible, and then to introduce system so as to get the immense economical advantages of repetition in manufacture, are the grand objects to which our efforts should be directed.[70]

But those whose efforts were concentrated on mass production saw no point in wasting time and money on theoretical knowledge for those whose labour, as a Manchester chemical manufacturer put it, 'is so much a matter of routine and mechanism'. 'The subdivision of labour by which we obtain our economical results', he continued, 'is carried out so far where it can be, that I do not think, being scientifically trained, would make a man a better workman, apart from the higher moral training which might, or might not, accompany it.'[71]

There was some argument that if all workmen possessed a theoretical knowledge of what they were doing, there would be less waste in increasingly expensive processes and a greater willingness to implement new ones, but the dreams of the founders of the mechanics' institutes that working artisans could themselves make a contribution to the cycle of invention had faded. There was a case to be made for at least giving foremen more extensive training, but as they were recruited exclusively from the shop-floor, on the basis of their 'natural aptitude, steadiness and industry',[72] it was not easy to see how they could receive separate instruction during or instead of their apprenticeship. There was unquestionably a need for schools of art to meet the enormous demand for new designs in the textile and pottery industries in particular, and these expanded rapidly, but the relevance of a wider education to those who applied the patterns remained in question. 'A man makes plates all his lifetime from Monday morning to Saturday midday', commented one of the Wedgwoods, 'simply taking it off again when dry enough to fettle. I do not see why any scientific enquiry can be of service to him.'[73] The campaign for new forms of instruction was less a solution to the problems created by 'the division and sub-division of labour under capitalistic employers', as the Secretary of the House Painters put it, and more a symptom of the crisis:

> The deficiency of skilled workmen has no doubt induced employers to make a general demand for 'technical education', as if that, or more properly speaking 'scientific instruction', could ever take the place of handicraft skill. It is yet to be learned whether the technical instruction as now given is calculated to improve the character of work done, or simply to increase the man's power of production.[74]

Some efforts were made to resolve the dilemma, particularly the technological examinations sponsored by the City and Guilds from 1879, which also founded its own colleges in South Kensington and Finsbury, and there were occasional attempts to organise classes within factories, most notably by the engineers William Mather at Salford,[75] but until the last decade of the century, the distance between learning the skills of literacy in the classroom and the skills of work outside it remained enormous. Even when the employers and artisans could agree on the need for some form of book-based training, the poor quality of the tools of reading and writing acquired in the schools made progress very difficult. A. J. Mundella, a hosiery manufacturer with a special interest in this field, carried out an extensive survey in 1867, and found that 'the ability to read a very simple paragraph is not possessed by nearly 50 per cent of the people employed in our large establishments in Nottingham and the immediate neighbourhood, in the lace factories, in the hosiery factories, in the bleaching works, and in the dye works; in the brick yards it is an utter failure, the people cannot read at all'.[76] Although the mechanics in the district were 'clever men', even they lacked 'sufficient primary education to avail themselves of technical education'.[77] Whilst the Revised Code made a marked impression on the numbers signing the marriage registers, with all the manual groups in our sample save the miners and unskilled labourers near or beyond 90 per cent by the 1880s (see table 4.1 above), it did little to bring school and work together. As we have seen, the mode of instruction did not encourage pupils to apply the tools of literacy to other forms of learning, and initially the new curriculum marked a retreat from the teaching of subjects other than the three Rs. In response to criticism, elementary science returned as a 'specific subject', and successive modifications to the Code extended the scope of the lessons, but the instruction was pitched at too abstract a level, and there was a shortage of both qualified teachers and interested pupils.[78] According to a school inspector's survey of Lambeth in the early 1880s, of 43,243 pupils in the district, only 5,377 were taking Grade IV and above, and of these, 336 were taking botany, 29 mechanics and 21 mathematics, as against 3,590 studying English literature.[79]

Until 1890, Parliament had largely confined its involvement to debate and inquiry; however, in that year two initiatives were taken to bring a semblance of order to the field of work education. A century and a half after the charity schools had abandoned the attempt to teach boys how to use their hands as well as their heads, manual skills re-entered the curriculum in the form of woodwork. The subject was meant to constitute much more than a temporary respite from the serious intellectual work of the classroom. Gaining dexterity with tools would connect with the three Rs through an insistence that the practical aspect was based on technical drawing, and more generally through the hope that a proper teaching of carpentry would form an extension of the cognitive skills gained in other lessons. This ambition rested on a more sophisticated attempt to forge a link between the two phases of learning which faced every working-class child. As Philip Magnus, the guiding force behind City and Guilds, wrote of the innovation,

> The training obtained from the use of tools refers more particularly to the senses – the muscular sense, the sense of sight and

touch; but so intimately connected with intellectual operations is the development of one sense, that working with wood serves not only to train the hand and eye, but also to quicken our perceptions, to stimulate the faculty of observation, and to create in us habits of accuracy, self-reliance, and truth.[80]

Having set their face against the prospect for so long, the teachers were slow to respond to the reform. In 1898 the subject was being taught in only 295 schools to 18,390 pupils, but thereafter there was a rapid expansion and ten years later just over two hundred thousand boys (not girls, who were proceeding from knitting to domestic economy) were learning how to use a saw and a plane.[81]

Outside the schools, the work of the City and Guilds, which had long suffered from an absence of State funds, was supplemented by the Local Taxation Act, which made over to local authorities the so-called 'Whisky Money', the proceeds of an extra 6d a gallon on spirits levied in that year's Budget.[82] The funds were to be used to expand the network of evening classes, which remained the principal location of post-school technical teaching. In the following two decades, something like a national system was created, and by 1912–13, 180,000 men over the age of sixteen were studying science subjects after work.[83] By the end of the period, day classes in vocational subjects were also available in the major cities in 'Central' and 'Junior Technical' schools.[84] At the same time, some attempt was made to shift the emphasis away from pure theory. 'Technical Education' became 'Technical Instruction', with the implied expectation that the scientific problems encountered in the evening classes 'should be made more relevant to the practical problems which would be met on the return to the workshop.

When measured against the provision of work education at mid century, much had been achieved, but there was a striking continuity with both the theory and the practice of the earlier phase of the Industrial Revolution. In spite of the hopes held out for the extended curriculum, woodwork became a ghetto subject, enjoying a low status in the schools and disregarded by both employers and skilled workers outside. And up to the very end of the period, the efforts to develop the science teaching begun in the classroom were hampered by the mechanical grasp of literacy with which the pupils had been equipped.[85] It remained the case that by far the bulk of the teaching of occupational knowledge in what was still one of the world's leading industrial economies was undertaken by working men in the context of formal or informal apprenticeships.[86] A century after the abolition of the Statute of Artificers, there were more than a third of a million apprentices in any one year,[87] together with a large number of 'learners' who acquired their training by moving from process to process within a given industry, working alongside and under the supervision of older skilled men.

In some respects, the skilled workers could regard the outcome of the long struggle to invade the art and mystery of their trades with considerable satisfaction. Learning how to work remained embedded in the structure of orally transmitted knowledge and practice which lay at the heart of the artisans' sense of independence and pride. Their success was less a consequence of trade union pressure, and more of a tacit compromise between masters and men. If the continuation of the pre-industrial system diminished the threat to the privileges and authority of the skilled worker, it also suited the short-term interests of the employers, whose resistance to change was the despair of advocates of reform, most of whom came from outside industry. Training conducted on the job was cheap, and, notwithstanding the prophecies of decline which had been made for half a century, capable of turning out efficient and productive workers.[88] The concern expressed by the 1884 Royal Commission on Technical Education was tempered by the observation that Britain was still 'at the head of the industrial world',[89] and despite the increasing challenge of Germany in particular, large profits were available to firms which invested little or nothing in teaching their workforce.

In the event, few trades replicated the model established by textiles in the early phase of the Industrial Revolution. They either remained unaffected by machinery altogether, with the tendency towards larger enterprises merely transferring the responsibility for teaching from masters to journeymen, or they embraced new processes without reducing the demand for a level of manual dexterity which could only be acquired by long years of practice. Industries at the forefront of innovation were still largely dependent on what a bricklayer once described as the 'trade "knack" which all the language of literature would never be able to explain'.[90] The division of labour which took place in this period was sufficient to encourage a jealous defence of their traditions by skilled workers, but never extensive enough to force employers and the State to grasp the nettle of the wholesale reorganisation of work training. In engineering, where the continuing reliance on short runs of diversified products required a flexible and well-trained workforce, any shortcomings in the old apprenticeship system were made good by the practice of migration and recourse to evening schools for some lessons in technical theory where the youths struggled to stay awake at the end of their long working day.[91] Rather than stimulating a wholesale revision of the relationship between manual and mental labour, the efforts of City and Guilds, the Department of Science and Art and the local authorities were in the end confined to meeting the limited demands of a handful of advanced industries, gas and electricity, for instance, alongside engineering, for specific items of scientific knowledge.

In one sense, therefore, the threatened divorce between conception and execution, which Marx had located at the heart of the division of labour, never fully materialised.[92] Comparatively few workers were reduced to learning codified rules of production to meet the impersonal demands of machinery. The particular balance of mind and hand embodied in the concept of art and mystery remained a reality throughout the period. However, there was a price to be paid for success in confining the 'language of literature' to the margins of occupational training. The pace of technical innovation meant that implicitly or explicitly, a new relationship between manual 'skill' and abstract 'knowledge' would have to be forged.[93] The more the traditional concept of art and mystery was kept in isolation, the greater the danger that professional teachers and the professions themselves would monopolise the possession of book knowledge, and the status and power which accompanied it.[94] The failure seriously to integrate oral and literary forms of occupational learning could only widen the gulf between those who worked with their 'heads' and those who worked with their 'hands'. The *OED* lists an emergent late-nineteenth-century meaning of 'manual': 'New esp. of (physical) labour, an occupation, etc., as opposed to mental, theoretical'.[95] This in turn increased the fragmentation of the learning process which every working man had to undergo in childhood and youth. The tools of written communication acquired in the long years of elementary schooling had only marginal relevance to the next phase of the curriculum, and where they were called upon, they were usually too blunt to be of much use. 'When he leaves school', wrote N. B. Dearle of the London child in 1914,

> he reaches a point at which the earning of wages first takes a definite place in his life, and learning, even in the case of an apprentice to a highly skilled trade, occupies at most only a part of his mind . . . A lad's attitude often is that having left school he is finished with bookwork and henceforth his business is to earn wages.[96]

Occupational recruitment

One of the issues embedded in the problem of work training was the relationship between literacy and occupational recruitment. If work education was transferred from the workplace to the school, then the process of determining a child's eligibility for a job would begin and end in the classroom. If, on the other hand, training was not to commence until after a place had been found, and was to involve little or no use of books, then the relevance of the lessons in reading and writing to the subsequent entry into the labour market was called into question. It was a matter of establishing new criteria of worth. From the founding of the British and National School Societies onwards, teachers had been engaged in the classification of children on the basis of their performance in reading and writing, and later in arithmetic. The intention was to establish formal rules of achievement which would serve both as a model for the progress the child should achieve in life and a guide for employers to the relative merits of potential recruits. The monitorial system and then the Revised Code with its clearly defined Standards were associated with the move towards an exam-based meritocracy in the middle class. In both cases the paper qualifications were designed to erode the pervasive influence of birth and family connections in the sphere of occupation. Just as the professional and Civil Service exams were to replace nepotism and patronage, so the structured curriculum, as we saw in the previous chapter, was at the centre of the attack on the power of the working-class family. The hierarchy of attainment in the schools would challenge the scale of values in the home, and the evidence of ability represented by a completed education would substitute for the recommendation of a parent or a relation to an employer.

At the 1867 Select Committee on Scientific Instruction, James Platt, MP for Oldham and an engineer employing between five and seven thousand men, was asked about his recruitment policy: 'You employ a very large number of people? – Yes. When they come to you to be engaged, do you inquire into the education they have received? – No.'[97] Such indifference to the applicant's school career might be expected of a small employer in a local community, or of the master of an artisan workshop, but not of the head of what was claimed to be the largest machine engineer in the world. Whilst Platt, like so many contemporary manufacturers, had hitherto relied on the traditional apprenticeship system for training his employees, he was convinced that the time had come 'when it is necessary that workmen should be acquainted with the science of mechanics, as well as its practical use,'[98] and with so large an annual intake of beginners, he appeared to have everything to gain from establishing formal rules of entry. His dismissal of the evidence available from the schools, in which the Revised Code was now well established, draws attention to a major inconsistency in prevailing estimates of the value of the home background of working-class children.

There is no reason to suppose that Platt was alone in his approach. The same committee asked Mundella: 'before employing young people, do manufacturers inquire much into the state of their education when they come to them at first, whether as full-timers or as half-timers?' 'I should say', he replied, 'as a rule, it is a question never asked; what employers look at is their capacity for work.'[99] The most obvious way to test this 'capacity to work' was some form of post-entry trial. Let a youth work alongside skilled men for a few months, and his aptitude for the job would soon be revealed. The tendency to move from formal to informal apprenticeships in this period made it easier for employers to rectify mistakes in recruitment by such a method, but it was a wasteful procedure for all concerned. It remained necessary to operate some pre-entry criteria of selection, and with few exceptions these were supplied not by teachers but by parents.[100]

There were a number of reasons for carrying into industry the dependence of kinship which had characterised recruitment in the handicraft trades. Firstly, it was cheap. Devising and administering an impersonal, paper-based system of selection would have forced a company to set up and maintain a substantial bureaucracy. Most firms in the period were reluctant to commit themselves to this form of expenditure, particularly when, as was the case here, the workforce would perform the task for nothing.

Secondly, it was a means generating loyalty and enforcing discipline amongst existing employees. Permitting workers to treat the workplace as an extension of the family reinforced the paternalism which employers were attempting to foster. The threat to personal identity and authority posed by large concerns was diminished by giving employees a significant role in determining who should work in them and by allowing their responsibilities as fathers or elder relatives to be exercised inside as well as outside the factory gates. The other side of this coin was that workers who courted dismissal knew that they risked destroying not only their own employment prospects but also those of their sons and possibly their relatives' children as well. The system performed a similar function for the recruits themselves, who were less likely to feel they were joining a faceless organisation if they had been introduced by and were to work in the company of a relative, and were less likely to misbehave if their employer's sanctions were reinforced by those of their family.[101]

Finally, the dependence on the valuation of kin was the most likely means of identifying the attributes which employers were looking for. The key quality was the 'character' of the youth in question. By this was meant first and foremost an approach to work – a sense of self-control, of moral probity, and of pride in workmanship. The more specific requirements of the worker, dexterity with tools, the ability to learn and remember new techniques, even the capacity to read and write, were seen as subordinate to and dependent upon the larger matter of attitude. The skills of communication taught in the schools were at best only an adjunct to the creation of the new workforce. Industries varied in their employment of the printed word. Larger firms in advanced sectors such as engineering gradually developed bodies of written regulations concerning time-keeping and conduct within the factory, but no manager ever supposed that discipline and efficiency could be reduced to producing lists of rules and ensuring employers were able to read them.[102] And whilst it was hoped that teachers, acting in conjunction with or in place of the clergy, would strive to instil new habits of deference and obedience, when it came to the point of selecting entrants, employers found themselves forced back on the working-class family. This was partly because for much of the period the experience of schooling remained too slight to eradicate the influence of parents, and partly because, unlike the teachers, employers were capable of investing the domestic curriculum with a positive value. Had they accepted the ideology of the elementary schools, that the home background was at best neutral and at worst utterly corrupting, and that success in the classroom was the only valid measure of the worth of the child, morally as well as intellectually, they could never have risked delegating their recruitment policy in such a fashion. In practice they believed in the force of heredity. A good worker was likely to be the son and the father, the nephew and the uncle, of a good worker.

This is not to say that larger firms in the second half of the century expected to recruit wholly illiterate employees. It might be assumed that as part of his duties, a responsible parent would ensure that his child received a basic education. In addition, the half-time system, which was established in textile factories in 1844 and later extended to other mills, workshops and mines, ensured that recruits would have some teaching in reading and writing, either before or after entry, and the consolidation of compulsion in 1880 offered a further guarantee that the beginner had at least made the acquaintance of the written word. But that was all. In spite of the manifest shortcomings in attendance and teaching in all forms of schooling throughout the period, few employers made a consistent attempt to check whether or how far a supposedly educated youth was capable of using his skills outside the classroom.

The major exception was the industry most directly associated with the spread of written communication, the Post Office, whose workforce increased from around 20,000 at the introduction of the Penny Post to a quarter of a million by 1914, making it the largest single employer of labour in the country.[103] A report in 1854 recommended that in place of the dependency on patronage, the 'Postmaster General should lay down strict rules for the examination of all Candidates for admission, either into the class of Clerks, or into that of Sorters and Letter Carriers, in order to test their capacity'.[104] In 1855 such a system was instituted at headquarters, and to obtain confirmation of appointments outside London, town postmasters were required to make a written report on the candidate, 'accompanied by a specimen of his writing and power of calculation'.[105] The Post Office was unique in the scale of its reliance on the skills of reading and writing, and in its early use of large numbers of clerks. The one other large employer of working men to institute a literacy test in this period was the police force. Here recruits were specifically required to write as well as read,[106] but even so much greater weight was attached to the background of the individual, and some constabularies were prepared to give post-entry education to semi-literate but otherwise suitable candidates.[107] Elsewhere, formality was present in the recruitment of manual labour only where the pervasive concern for moral worth was embodied in a demand for a 'character' written on behalf of the applicant by a reputable member of the community. These were rarely required in manufacturing industry, but were an essential precondition for entry into the railways, domestic service and other occupations, including the Post Office, where the trustworthiness of an employee was thought to be of particular importance.[108] Such documents might make reference to schooling or literacy, but principally as indicators of the possession of more abstract virtues. Time in the classroom could add to the reliability of a worker, and make him a more attractive candidate, but it was not a sufficient guarantee of probity. However much employers welcomed the extension of elementary education as an aid to the creation of a disciplined workforce, it is striking that only at the very end of the period did they begin to turn as a matter of course to schoolmasters to nominate suitable candidates and provide testimonials.[109]

The relationship between kinship, regulation and recruitment was nowhere better illustrated than on the railways. This was one of the first large-scale bureaucratised industries, and both literacy and numeracy were de facto requirements of its workforce, if not to drive the engines and punch the tickets, then to master the complex written rules of conduct with which every employee was issued. Yet the companies relied on family connection, backed up by references, rather than examination.[110] In the mid 1840s, David Barr, the son of a Warwickshire country shoemaker, became disenchanted with the prospect of following in his father's footsteps, and began to look around for an alternative career. As it happened, he had an elder sister employed as a servant to the son-in-law of the vice-chairman of Midland Railways. This was enough. Contacts were made, and within a few weeks, a two-fold nepotism had secured him a job at Staveley railway station.[111]

Throughout the period, very few working men ever had to write anything down when seeking employment. The situation was in stark contrast to a recent survey of Nottingham, which found that 'Roughly only one half of 1 per cent of the 17,000 jobs covered were effectively available to adults unable to complete the application forms.'[112] In the nineteenth century, it was not industry but the trade unions which led the way to the formalisation of entry procedures. If Platts the machine engineers relied on verbal recommendation, a workman requiring admission to the Amalgamated Society of Engineers had to pass through the following procedures:

> Every candidate on being admitted into this society, shall be furnished with an entrance card, on which shall be inserted all sums paid as entrance money. Every person, before being admitted, shall express his concurrence with the rules furnished to him, and shall sign a form of proposition, which will, on application, be given to his proposer by the secretary, containing all necessary particulars bearing upon his fitness to become a member; these forms, together with the registry of birth, medical certificates, and all other documents relating to his admission, to be sent to the general office to facilitate the keeping of the registration book.[113]

Within the unions, the increasing complexity of collective bargaining (see below) led to the introduction of formal examinations for union officials. The first generation of full-time union officials, whose careers were surveyed by the *Bee-Hive* in a series of profiles in 1873 and 1874, displayed a pattern of variegated, interrupted and limited schooling characteristic of the working class as a whole.[114] The paper for the post of General Secretary of the Bolton Operative Cotton-Spinners in 1895 included arithmetic, and a 1,200-word essay for which 'the points taken into consideration will be handwriting, spelling, composition, and the clear concise marshalling of whatever facts or arguments are adduced'.[115] The officials at the negotiating table could frequently boast better qualifications for the task than the employers who faced them. The system of houses of call and tramping which constituted the only organised structure of job-finding until the creation of Labour Exchanges in 1909 was also heavily dependent on documentation.[116] In early-nineteenth-century London, a register of unemployed artisans in a particular trade would be kept in a public house, and when vacancies were notified by masters, men would be sent out in the order in which their names 'stood in the book'.[117] A journeyman who had to leave the area in search of work needed good paperwork as much as stout shoes. Henry Broadhurst described the routine in his trade in the 1860s: 'When a mason on tramp enters a town, he finds his way to the relieving officer and presents his card. On this card is written the applicant's name and last permanent address. In addition he carries a printed ticket bearing the stamp of the last lodge at which the traveller received relief. He was entitled to receive a relief allowance of one shilling for twenty miles and threepence for every additional ten miles traversed since his last receipt of relief money.'[118] The cards, or in some cases small books, were known as blanks, and were evidence not only of identity but of standing in the trade. The London brushmakers had a rule that 'no member be allowed his blank without first showing a certificate signed by his employer, or one of his shopmates certifying that such a member has finished his work at the shop where last employed'.[119] Through this elaborate system, standards were maintained, abuse by unqualified men was curtailed, and unemployment kept to a minimum. An artisan was as dependent on his 'passport', as one hatter termed it,[120] as a traveller in a foreign country.

The outcome of the infrequency of formal literacy tests in recruitment is reflected in the returns of the marriage registers. In the survey period as a whole, there were substantial numbers of grooms unable to sign their name at all occupation levels below social class 1, which featured just one maverick 'gentleman', the son of a soldier, who married an equallly illiterate printer's daughter in Bethnal Green in 1849. In class 2, it was still possible to find in the second and third quarters of the nineteenth century individuals who were managing to engage in commerce or production without the slightest ability to use a pen. This world bore little relation to the modern economy where, as one recent observer has put it, 'The citizen who cannot read or write is an economic liability to himself and his society.'[121] In the sample, one in thirteen describing themselves as farmers and one in fifteen shopkeepers signed the register with a mark. Amongst the skilled working class, one shoemaker in six and one mason in eight were plying their trade despite the absence of a command of the written word. As Graff found in North America, illiteracy, at least as measured by signatures, was not an absolute bar to relative success in the economy.[122] The inability to engage in formal communication did not condemn an individual to the lowest ranks of the labouring poor. Conversely, a basic education was evidently no guarantee of any degree of occupational advance. In the first quarter of the sample period, a third of the unskilled labourers had acquired sufficient education inside or outside school to inscribe a usually fluent signature, yet they remained at the bottom of the social hierarchy.[123] The surveys of prisoners undertaken to highlight the shortcomings in elementary education nonetheless demonstrated that of those reduced to mostly petty crimes to supplement usually little or no regular income, over half could make some attempt at reading and writing, and a further one in ten were fully literate.[124]

That literacy was not a sufficient protection against poverty or disgrace should come as no surprise. In the world of the labouring poor, no amount of occupational endeavour and no degree of learning were proof against unemployment, ill-health or alcohol. The most prosperous artisan could do no more than adopt a strategy of living which reduced but never abolished the chances of disaster.[125] Absolute security demanded either a substantial inheritance or entry into a profession. Teaching and journalism, the principal escape routes for an educated working man, guaranteed neither prosperity nor status. In this context it is ironic that the railways, which pioneered the concept of the lifetime career for manual workers, continually threatened the livelihood of their employees by the application of the elaborate rule book, with its draconian punishments for the most trivial infringements of conduct.

Of greater interest is the success of the illiterate. It is difficult to be certain just how those who could not sign their name survived in business. The occupational descriptions in the registers are too imprecise to identify the size of the farms or shops in question, nor do we know about the reading abilities of this disparate group. But by the same measure, many of their colleagues who could write their names may have been unable to cope with more complex demands on their skills, and it was evidently possible to find ways of compensating for such shortcomings. In the first instance, most commercial transactions outside the larger manufacturing concerns or official bureaucracies were still conducted on an informal basis. In agriculture, for instance, although greater use was being made of written accounts and aides-mémoire, it was still uncommon for a farmer to attempt to calculate his profit and loss for the year, and many of his dealings at market or with his workforce were kept on a verbal basis. Shopkeepers and artisan tradesmen were often engaged in a more complex range of dealings with a larger number of customers, but they could get by with a less than complete command of written English. *The London Saturday Journal* of August 1839 devoted an article to the functional semi-literacy of the typical shoemaker, giving the following account as an example:

	£ s. d.
To hailing and souling your Bots	3 10
To too peaces on your Shos	1 3
To pare Shos for the childde	2 0
To pare bots for yorself	1 10 0
To sowling pare Shoos	2 6[126]

However wayward the spelling and cramped the writing, the figures were always accurate. Finally, as was argued in chapter 2, literacy was a tool which could be borrowed when the need arose. Seventy-two per cent of illiterate shopkeepers and innkeepers and 47 per cent of illiterate farmers had literate wives to help them out, as had 35 per cent of illiterate skilled artisans. Others may have depended on educated children, assistants or fellow journeymen.

Beyond acquiring and retaining a job, there remained the question of betterment, rising through or out of the ranks of manual labour. At school, children had been taught that if they learned the rules of formal communication, they would ascend a structured hierarchy of classes in the monitorial system or Grades under the Revised Code. In the outside world it remained to be seen whether the model of attainment would be reproduced in the form of a clearly defined ladder of promotion, and how far the skills of literacy could be used to climb it. For those who performed outstandingly well at their lessons, the introduction of the pupil teacher scheme in 1846 provided an immediate extension of the system of examination and advance. Through a combination of practice and further testing, bright children could move directly into the nascent teaching profession, with the most successful eligible for Queen's Scholarships and another two years at a training college. Otherwise the only careers which bore any resemblance to the progression of the schoolroom were again those created by the growth of mass communication.

Both the Post Office and the railway companies sought to maintain order and discipline in their increasingly extensive workforces by instituting elaborate systems of grades, each bearing rigid differentials of income and status. By 1891 a London postman who entered the service at the age of twenty-one would take thirty years to reach the top of his scale, and beyond lay the rank of sorter with its own ladder.[127] The railways categorised their employees with much the same precision as the army, from which many of their early administrators were drawn. The road from engine cleaner to fireman to driver was long and slow, and each grade was further broken down by a procedure known as 'classification'.[128] In neither industry, however, was there a clear association of formal qualification and progress. Promotion was at the discretion of superiors on the basis of an unpublished range of criteria which included length of service, performance and general merit. On the railways, described by Frank McKenna as 'the first paper-dominated industry',[129] mastery of the rule book was a necessary but not a sufficient condition of upward mobility. 'It is superfluous to say', commented Alfred Williams, 'that the cleverest man is not usually the one advanced.'[130] So far from enhancing the individual's control over his career, the long ladder of promotion left him at the mercy of his employer and embittered labour relations throughout the period.

In other advanced sectors of the economy, performance was evaluated on a largely traditional basis. The summit of ambition for textile and metal workers was to become a foreman, a key figure in the industrialised processes.[131] In deciding who should rise from the ranks, employers paid next to no attention to educational qualifications or functional literacy. 'Are the foremen in the machine shops of the midland counties good draughtsmen?' A. J. Mundella was asked. 'Such a thing is almost unknown; some of our longest foremen can hardly sign their own name.'[132] It was not that foremen were especially illiterate, but rather that they displayed the same range of standards as the rest of the workforce from which they were selected. 'You begin with a workman', explained Platt, 'and if he is superior in the manipulation of what he is doing, and shows general intelligence, he is then promoted to the position of foreman; but although he is so, he is very little better instructed than the workman who is placed under him in scientific matters.'[133] Thomas Wright, indeed, believed that many workers were actually better educated than their foremen.[134] Managers applied a more advanced version of the criteria which controlled the initial recruitment of the labour force. 'The first qualification for these places', wrote W. A. Abram of overlookers in the textile industry, 'is not superior education or exceptional intelligence, but a rough force of character and activity of habit, which enable the man to keep in check the heterogeneous and at times mutinous mass of a mill population.'[135] As with the would-be apprentice, the aspiring foreman was, as a chemical manufacturer put it in 1882, 'more often dependent upon his character than his previous education'.[136] Whilst there might be a similar assumption that those who could display higher moral qualities would have been sent to school by their parents, the judgment was made on the basis of performance in the factory rather than the classroom, a state of affairs which persisted until at least 1945.[137] For their part, the workers made no attempt to encourage any imitation of the regulated progression within the Post Office and the railways. As the Webbs commented, 'The very conception of seniority, as constituting a claim to advancement, is foreign to Trade Unionism.'[138]

By the end of the century efforts were being made to enhance the formal qualifications of the elite of the industrial workforce, but those from a working-class background who attended the proliferating evening schools tended to have their sights fixed on escaping from the shop-floor altogether and entering white-collar supervisory grades.[139] Little is yet known about the precise extent of social mobility during the Industrial Revolution or of the relevance to it of education. Sanderson's research suggests that in the early decades of the century, the growth of the factory system and the destruction of the remnants of the old grammar schools severely curtailed what chances there were of a working-class child climbing an educational ladder to the class above. The consequences of the subsequent spread of both industry and elementary schools for the prospects of ambitious parents and hard-working children have yet to be examined in any detail, and here the marriage register sample which has generated the literacy data for this study may perform an additional function. The requirement of the 1837 Registration Act to enter the trades of both the groom and his father ensured that the marriage registers would thereafter provide a snapshot of intergenerational occupational mobility. All but 3 per cent of the grooms were at least into their twenties at their weddings

Table 4.6. *Social mobility, groom's father to groom, 1839–1914*

	Groom's father	1	2	3	4	5
Groom	1	42.7	2.7	0.5	0.6	0.1
	2	29.3	49.0	6.7	7.4	2.5
	3	19.1	27.3	72.8	35.8	22.4
	4	4.9	11.9	10.1	43.2	14.3
	5	4.0	9.1	9.8	13.0	60.6
	Number	225	1,656	4,356	1,182	2,764

Table 4.7. *Social mobility, groom at same, higher or lower class than father, by period*

	1839–54	1859–74	1879–94	1899–1914	All periods	Number
Same	67	65	60	54	62	6,266
Higher	16	19	20	23	19	1,964
Lower	17	17	20	23	19	1,951

and had therefore found their adult jobs, and as most vicars recorded the father's occupation whether or not he was still alive, it is possible to take a measure of how often a son's upbringing had placed his feet on a higher or a lower rung than his father had occupied at the completion of his career.

The relationship between the generations across the whole sample is displayed in table 4.6. The clustering of figures across the diagonal indicates a comparatively stable society, but there are sufficiently large movements at all points in the scale to suggest that it was far from automatic for sons to follow their fathers, even in the broad terms of social class. Only in the large categories of the skilled and unskilled working class do the proportions exceed 50 per cent, and always there are a handful of individuals who have travelled a long distance from their family background by the time of their marriage. The pattern of occupational movements which underlies these figures is very complex, and is now the subject of a separate study at the University of Keele.[140] Here it is only possible to draw attention to the general profile as it evolved over the period.

In table 4.7, the mass of transitions from father to son have been compressed to a simple question of stasis or movement up or down the scale. The figures clearly indicate a gradual increase in mobility across the second two thirds of the nineteenth century and into the first decade of the twentieth. If there was a reduction in the chances of a son departing from

Table 4.8. *Literacy and mobility of sons of working-class fathers, 1839–1914*

	1839–54	1859–74	1879–94	1899–1914	All periods	Number
Up	4.2	5.6	6.3	7.4	5.8	482
% literate	88.0	87.0	94.0	99.0	93.0	
Same	95.8	94.4	93.7	92.6	94.2	7,818
% literate	50.0	63.0	83.0	98.0	72.0	
Mobility of all literate sons	7.1	7.6	7.1	7.5	7.3	6,108

Up – Groom's father 3–5, groom 1–2
Same – Groom's father and groom 3–5

the class of his father in the early years of the Industrial Revolution, the trend was reversed as the economy continued to expand. The incidence of stasis declined from two-thirds to little more than a half, whilst the frequencies of upward and downward change showed parallel increases from a sixth to almost a quarter. Much of the movement took place inside the working class, but table 4.8 demonstrates that the key area of transition from manual to non-manual status was subject to a similar evolution.[141] From the first to the last quarter of the period the proportion of sons making it to what were usually the lower reaches of the middle class increased by 76 per cent. The figures lend some support to the argument that a more open society was emerging, although it was not necessarily those most exposed to mechanisation who gained the most. In the sample, 9.6 per cent of the sons of handicraft workers rose to the middle class, compared to 7.1 per cent of sons whose fathers were employed in the industrialising processes of metal, textile and pottery manufacture. And in general, the opportunities for advancement remained severely limited. In the early years of the twentieth century, with the industrial economy firmly established, over 90 per cent of the sons of labouring men were themselves working with their hands at the time of their marriage.

The minority who did succeed in rising from their background were, as table 4.8 also shows, substantially more literate than those who failed to do so. In the first quarter of the sample period, there was a gap of thirty-eight points in the literacy of static and mobile sons, with only half those still in the working class having been taught to sign their names, as against almost four-fifths of those whose upbringing had launched them into the ranks of the white-collar occupations. Confirmation of the association of literacy rates with mobility is provided by table 4.9, which examines the destinations of literate and illiterate sons in the two largest occupational groups in the sample, unskilled labourers and miners. In both cases, those

Table 4.9. *Literacy and mobility of sons of unskilled labourers and miners, 1839–1914*

Social class	1	2	3						4	5	Number
			H	L	T	P	Met	M			
(i) Unskilled Labourers											
Literate	0.1	3.6	8.0	2.4	1.7	0.8	3.8	7.0	19.0	53.7	1,593
Illiterate sons	0	1.5	1.9	0.1	1.2	0.4	2.4	6.6	8.7	77.1	1,063
(ii) Miners											
Literate sons	0.2	3.0	4.4	1.8	1.0	2.2	5.4	67.5	5.6	8.8	498
Illiterate sons	0	1.5	1.8	0	0.7	1.8	3.3	76.8	4.4	9.6	271

who could sign their names were more likely to have moved away from their father's occupation than those who could not. The contrast is most striking amongst the labourers, where only just over half the literate sons were still following in their father's footsteps, compared with more than three-quarters of those making a mark.[142] The majority of those who got away travelled no further than the ranks of the semi-skilled or the industrialising trades, but they were five times more likely than their illiterate peers to have reached handicraft or 'literate' occupations, and more than twice as likely to have climbed out of the working class altogether. The miners were the most illiterate and least mobile group in the sample, but even here it made a difference whether the sons had learned to sign their names, with more of them appearing in every non-mining sector except the unskilled at the bottom of the scale.

There was clearly a connection between learning to read and write and escaping from the parents' economic background, but the precise nature of the intersection between literacy, mobility and occupational change requires further consideration. Firstly it is necessary to ask whether the increasing rates of mobility were a consequence of rising literacy, or of an expansion in the number of jobs in which literacy was necessary. If the latter was the case, the incidence of upward mobility of literate sons of working-class fathers would rise across the period. Table 4.8 indicates that this did not happpen. Between the first and second quarters there was a small rise from 7.1 to 7.6 per cent in the mobility rates of literate sons, which suggests that the openings in the middle-class occupations were expanding slightly faster than the literacy levels. However, in the third quarter, the jump of almost twenty points in the signatures actually reduced the prospects of educated children finding their way into bourgeois employment. Only in the final quarter, as literacy levels began to reach their ceiling, did the openings in the middle class begin to outstrip the expansion in qualified applicants. What seems to have happened across the period as a whole is that the labour of the schoolmasters more or less kept pace with the creation of new posts in the non-manual sector.[143] Whilst the literacy scores of the sons of working-class fathers were rising from 52 per cent to 98 per cent, the sectors of the economy directly dependent on the use of literacy expanded much more rapidly than the occupied population as a whole. Those identified by Crossick as 'white collar workers' grew from 2.5 per cent to 7.1 per cent of occupied males between 1851 and 1911, their absolute numbers climbing from 144,035 to 918,186, with the most dramatic progress shown by commercial clerks and travellers.[144] The career of a man like Joseph Keating, born in 1871, who left school to become a door-boy at a colliery but later became a salesman, telegram clerk, reporter, rent-collector, shorthand clerk and private secretary, belonged very much to the end of the nineteenth century.[145] The old middle class was too small to meet the demand for new staff; in the sample, 56 per cent of the clerks were drawn from working-class backgrounds, with 70 per cent of the transitions displayed in the registers from 1879 onwards.

At the same time, the growth of opportunity in literacy-based occupations did not necessarily imply a move to another class. As we have seen, the related industries of the railway and the Post Office, most of whose employees were functionally literate manual workers, grew even more rapidly than the white-collar class, as did the sector which was the most direct consequence of the spread of literacy in the nineteenth century, the paper, printing and publishing trades, whose workforce leapt from 44,000 in 1841 to 253,000 in 1911. Even at the margins of the economy, reading was creating employment, as delivering newspapers became a familiar rite of passage for working-class children who could use their education to find work which compulsory schooling otherwise forbade.[146] By contrast, occupations such as agricultural labouring, where the demand for and possession of the skills of reading and writing were traditionally low, were in relative and eventually absolute decline.

Secondly, it needs to be emphasised that the acquisition or use of the skills of reading and writing were not necessarily the determining factors in all instances of ascent into the middle class. In the sample, only 29 per cent of those who rose from the working class entered occupations where fluency with the pen was an absolute condition of recruitment or practice (see table 4.10). Those who became clerks, who comprised much the largest proportion of this group, teachers,[147] bureaucrats or members of the professions, were amongst the very few working-class children in this period who could view success at school as a precondition for success in after-life. 'William Bowyer', for instance, an ironmonger's son born in 1889, stayed on at his Board school until he had reached Standard VI, and then took an examination for 'Temporary Boy Clerkships' in the Civil

Table 4.10. *Destinations of upwardly mobile sons of work-ing-class fathers (%)*

Farmers	14
Shopkeepers	31
Salesmen, agents	5
Managers, business proprietors	8
Hotel managers, innkeepers	7
Professionals	3
Bureaucrats	1
Clerks	21
Teachers	4
Others	5
Number	482

Service before choosing instead what seemed like a more secure job as a Post Office clerk.[148] The remainder crossed the often ill-defined boundary between labouring and farming, or between manual and white-collar jobs in the retail, manufacturing or service industries. Given the absence of information on acreage, the scale of movement on the land is impossible to measure, and equally the distance between shop assistants and shop-keepers, between artisan masters and small manufacturers, and between hawkers and commercial travellers could vary extensively. In these instances, however, literacy was so far from being a sufficient condition of success, it was not even necessary; almost all the handful of illiterate grooms who fetched up in the middle class were shopkeepers or farmers. Some combination of hard labour, natural aptitude, business sense and plain good fortune, perhaps in the form of a small inheritance, lay behind much of the achievement documented in the marriage registers. For those who aspired to the status of shopkeeper, which was the most common destination of upwardly mobile working-class children, functional numeracy was probably more important than functional literacy.

Thirdly, it should be stressed that the increases in literacy and mobility did nothing to diminish family involvement in the future of children. As has been argued in this and the previous chapter, parents bore a heavy responsibility both for the education their child received and for arranging its entry into the labour market. Although some of the marriage partners may have learned to sign their names after they had left home, most will have acquired or failed to acquire this skill as part of the domestic curriculum, and in the same way, most will have been dependent on the initiative of their father or other relatives for the crucial processes of training and initial job-finding. Whilst the imposition of compulsory schooling eventually deprived families of a final authority in one aspect of child-rearing, for much of the period the expansion in the range of occupations within and outside the working class, together with the growing though still limited use that could be made of literacy, tended to enhance the influence parents could exercise over the prospects of their offspring.

Finally, there remains the possibility, as some modern studies have suggested, that learning to read and write, or the more general experience of schooling, created a more mobile personality, an individual better disposed to seek a different or more prosperous occupation.[149] However, it has to be noted that the greater tendency for literate grooms to seek pastures new was purely relative. The literate sons of unskilled labourers and miners in table 4.9 were still more likely to follow their fathers' footsteps than to go elsewhere in the working class, let alone climb out of it. Equally almost a quarter of those unable to sign their names were able to seek out alternative ways of earning a living. Ironically, it would seem that for the upwardly mobile, the success of those entering sectors demanding extensive use of their literacy was more often achieved early in their working lives, when family influence was paramount, whilst those who attained advancement later in life, when they were dependent on their own skills and attitudes, more often entered the areas where reading and writing were of less relevance. A much higher proportion of those rising to be clerks were under thirty in the registers than those achieving the status of farmers, innkeepers or managers.[150] It was the preponderance of destinations in the retail, service and agricultural sectors which accounted for the fact that those aged thirty and above in the sample were one and a half times more upwardly mobile than those in their teens and twenties. A start had been made in connecting the rules of progress in the classroom with the ladder of success outside it, but the ideology of achievement preached in schools was difficult to recognise in the world beyond. 'In regard to this especial theory of the educated working man necessarily rising above the uneducated one', observed Thomas Wright, 'the working classes see that this is practically false.'[151] For the great majority of the children of manual workers, occupational change or advancement was still dependent on the quality of family support at one end of their careers and the traditional combination of toil and good fortune at the other.

Labour relations

For most of their lives, the principal concern of labouring men was not acquiring training or new employment, but just working, executing particular tasks in return for sufficient income to support themselves and their families. It was here that the relevance of literacy was most critical. Up to the point at which a youth became, for instance, an indentured journeyman in an artisan workshop, he may have made negligible use of the skills of reading and writing which his section of the working class had possessed for generations. He could take his place amongst the elite of his class, where he might out-earn not only the unskilled but also many clerks and teachers, with the period of schooling he had once endured having played little or no part in his progression. Henceforth his prosperity and his satisfaction in his work were dependent partly on his aptitude for the particular process, partly on extrinsic factors such as his health or the well-being of his wife and children, and partly on the relations of production into which he entered. Income, status and conditions of employment in the market economy were conditioned by the distribution of power within the separate categories of labour, which in turn rested on the structures and tactics of the contending forces.[152] A system of labour relations is a system of rules.[153] The history of attempts to defend or promote interests in the economy can be viewed in terms of how far, in what manner and by whom these rules were formally recorded and enforced.

The workplace of the early-nineteenth-century artisan was as much a judicial as an economic entity. 'Most well regulated shops', observed the *Mechanics' Magazine*, 'are governed internally by a particular code of laws.'[154] Knowledge of the code was, as Thomas Wright observed, 'as essential to the comfort of those whose lot is cast amongst them, as technical proficiency is necessary to obtaining or retaining employment. To these unwritten, but perfectly understood and all-powerful laws of workshop life, all working men whatever may be their private opinion – must in some degree bow.'[155] The function of the laws was to protect the trade, or the 'town', or the 'republic', from outsiders seeking to exploit market forces for personal gain. Membership was defined and in turn policed by legality. 'What we mean by legal', explained a shoemaker to the Artisans and Machinery Committee, 'is, that it is legal for any man belonging to our shop meetings to work for it.'[156] Every moment of the working day was pervaded by a sense of justice; courts were convened to try those who transgressed the laws, and masters who disregarded them were denounced as tyrants.

In their language and rituals, workshops and trade societies would deliberately imitate the official courts, but in codifying their rules, the distinction between common and statute law, between oral and written forms of embodying practice over time, was much more flexible. What in other contexts were mutually exclusive categories were now interchangeable. R. Lloyd's survey of the rules of his trade was entitled *The Laws and Customs of Journeymen Hatters*, the phrase applying equally to all the rules governing apprenticeship, tramping, work routines and relations with masters, as well as the complex system of three separate courts which dealt with infringements.[157] Here, more clearly than in any other aspect of popular culture, literacy was employed not for its status or its intrinsic authority, but simply as a tool, capable of serving particular purposes in particular circumstances.

There were, at the outset, powerful reasons why the great majority of the laws and customs should be stored and transmitted orally. Firstly, the sheer scope and complexity of the conventions which had grown up over the centuries in the separate trades defied any attempt to reduce them to print. 'To enter fully', began Lloyd, 'into the various regulations and forms that the "trade" have, from time to time, instituted and acted upon, would of itself fill a volume.'[158] A written record could only be an imperfect translation of the intricate pattern of accepted practices which stretched all the way from trivial habits of behaviour in individual workshops to fundamental bulwarks of artisan strength such as the number of apprentices a master was permitted to take.

Secondly, the essentially collective nature of orality reflected the sense of mutual interest which gave rise to the rules. The artisan trades had laws but no law-givers. The codes of behaviour grew out of the experience of working together and existed to enforce the will of the group over the wishes of the individual. 'Every artisan', explained the Operative Society of Masons, 'has an interest, in common with all those similarly engaged, in forming rules by which the particular trade should be regulated.'[159] Neither the artisan nor the regulation could have an existence outside the face-to-face relationships of the workplace.

Thirdly, the capacity of trades to sustain large bodies of rules over long periods of time without recourse to print complemented the continuity of practice which lay at the heart of their identity as workers. Tradition put their status and privileges beyond the reach of prevailing market forces. 'Established custom' for the masons, as for any trade society of the time, both defined and defended their authority over recalcitrant journeymen and masters.[160]

Finally, the privacy of the oral tradition reinforced the artisans' sense of property in the rules governing the workplace. Word-of-mouth communication belonged exclusively to the speaker and his audience. The customs and laws thus transmitted were regarded as the possession of the journeymen and not the masters, however much conflict and negotiation might have determined their effective limits. 'The society lays down certain rules that we know we have to go by', explained the masons; 'the employers know that these are our terms, and we perfectly understand each other on the matter.'[161] The tendency to protect the property by restricting access to its content was reinforced by the increasing bitterness of labour relations, and in particular by the period of persecution under the Combination Laws. Just as the mystery of the apprenticeship had to be emphasised in the face of attempts to destroy it, so the opacity of the regulations had to be increased in response to Government intimidation.[162] Printed rules were evidence of illegal organisation; written communications between groups of workers were intercepted and used to mount prosecutions.[163] Whilst the Laws were repealed in 1824, the Seditious Practices Act of 1817, which forbade on pain of seven years' transportation correspondence between or within societies, remained in force.[164]

However, as in every area of working-class life, the spoken word was becoming increasingly inadequate as a means of recording and transmitting the information thought necessary for survival. The rules which governed workshop activity assumed conflict. They recognised that in a market economy, self-interest continually threatened group interest, and that spontaneous fellowship could never be a sufficient safeguard against backsliding artisans or aggrandising masters. And in spite of the continuing reliance on oral communication, as soon as any structure developed within a trade, writing was inescapable. The earliest document Raymond Postgate could find for his classic *Builders' History* was this entry in the Preston Joiners' Cashbook for 1807:

		s	d
1807, Feb. 9	By 1 Quire of paper	1	6
	By Ale 4 Glasses		8
	By 2 books		8
Feb. 25	By Expenses of Com^e Meeting	8	8
Feb. 27	By 8 Glasses of Ale	1	4 [165]

By the beginning of the nineteenth century, paper was as much a part of the artisan's world as beer.

At the root of the move towards writing was money. As soon as a workshop began to co-operate with another to pool resources for assisting journeymen in distress or for conducting a dispute with a master, financial transactions were involved, and as soon as that happened, records had to be kept. Although the incidental needs of a sick or injured workmate might be met by an ad hoc collection, once it was decided to seek the advantages of a more reliable and extensive system of mutual aid, some form of book-keeping was inescapable. In the beginning it might be no more than a note of the cash locked away in the club's 'box' at the end of each week's gathering at a local public house, but as the contributions became more regular and the disbursements more systematic, the collective memory of the group would no longer be able to cope with the detail of the proceedings. One of their number had to start making entries of, as Kiddier wrote of the Brushmakers' Book of General Account, 'monies paid by poor men to poor men', and thus bureaucracy entered the life of the artisan.[166]

The concern was to prevent error and fraud, for the sake both of the individual and of the club as a whole. Bankruptcy was as immediate a threat to the early trade societies as it was to the businesses in which their members were employed. On the insurance side, the problems, although real, were comparatively straightforward. Balancing the books depended on elementary actuarial skill, competent management and much good fortune, but where a society sought to engage in collective bargaining, the challenge was more complex. Strikes were a trial of strength between the financial resilience of the contending parties. To stand any chance of success, a society had to ensure that all those liable contributed to the struggle, and only those eligible received benefits. In either case this meant that every 'legal' man in the society's sphere of influence had to be named and his role identified. Throughout the conflict the society's funds had to be carefully monitored, and if, as frequently happened, they threatened to run out, other societies in the trade or in the town would be approached for a gift or a loan. This in turn required correspondence and a record-making of the debts incurred. Amongst the smaller clubs, survival might be ensured by the transfer of a few tens of pounds, but as early as 1810 Manchester textile workers were contributing from £1,000 to £1,500 a week in support of members of their General Union engaged in an ultimately unsuccessful four-month strike.[167]

The basic requirement of solvency generated the more specialised applications of the written word. The first of these was communication. Alongside the consumption of alcohol, the exchange of information had always been the principal activity of every gathering of artisans. Amidst the anecdotes and gossip was vital information about the state of trade and the whereabouts of jobs. Incoming tramps were interrogated about conditions in other towns, and throughout the period would be welcomed in houses of call for the knowledge they had gleaned on their travels. 'Thus wandering they became wiser', wrote the 'Rolling Stonemason' of his contemporaries in the 1890s: 'They would be able to talk of other places. They acted as itinerant news agents. They would become carriers of folk-lore, tellers of tales and of no small account in those days.'[168] However, talk of other places had long since ceased to be an adequate channel of information for even the smallest of trade societies. In spite of the cost of the unreformed postal system, every secretary of an early-nineteenth-century club would find himself writing and receiving letters. John Alexander, who had served in this capacity for the City of London journeymen boot and shoemakers in the 1810s explained his responsibilities: 'I corresponded, I think, when I was in office, as nearly as I can say, with between seventy and eighty societies in our trade.'[169] As with the private letters of the labouring poor,[170] the society officials only put pen to paper when faced with an urgent financial problem. 'What object have you in corresponding with them?', Alexander was asked, 'We borrow and lend money according as we need.' 'For what purpose do you borrow or lend?' 'To support, in case of strikes, the towns that want it.'[171]

The requests for assistance rested on an acceptance of mutual obligation, but prudence dictated that each one was judged on its own merits. No society would risk its meagre funds unless it was certain that the dispute in question could and should be won. Thus every demand had to be accompanied by a full account of the circumstances, which would include not only details of the grievance, but the current strength of the society and in particular the state of trade in the area. However just the cause, supporting a strike in a falling market was a waste of money. The more organised and ambitious societies became, the more conscious they were of the barriers that separated them. 'We have every wish to ascertain what they are doing in Barnstaple and Tiverton', complained the framework-knitters' leader Gravener Henson, 'and other places that are in the lace branch; but we are as entirely ignorant as if they were in the centre of America.'[172] In terms of the exchange of information, adjacent communities were foreign countries: 'We frequently know no more of what is going on in Leicester and Leicester knows no more of what is going on in Nottingham, than people residing in different states.'[173]

The use of the post was made easier by the reform of 1840, and still more necessary by the emergence of permanent union bureaucracies. In 1869 the miners' leader Alexander Macdonald calculated that he had written 17,000 letters over the preceding seven years,[174] and postage bills became a regular item in union accounts. But the thirst for information was too great to be satisfied by such labour-intensive means. As trade societies began to establish more formal structures of reciprocal support, they adopted the device of the regular circular. The Operative Stonemasons had instituted a hand-written 'Fortnightly Return' by 1834, which took the form of a public letter to the Society's lodges. The hard-working though often misspelling National Secretary Angus M'Gregor found the task of copying out the document increasingly onerous, and in 1836 he proposed a move to a more advanced technology of communication: 'The price of printing one hundred copies of these letters is ten shillings and sixpence, and the advantages of such a mode is evident; it gives all lodges the same information, and enables district Secretaries at once to forward to the out Lodges the information, and gives the grand Secretary a fair chance of giving explicit information.'[175] With an annual income of around £3,000 the Society could well afford the expense, and henceforth the Return served as a unifying force in an organisation still struggling to maintain its existence in the face of frequent defeats and defections amongst its branches. Every fortnight it circulated appeals for help from embattled lodges, news of the state of trade in the localities, lists of new or blacklisted members, celebrations of victories, correspondence from members and notifications of proposed or agreed rule revisions, together with details of the Society's finances and administration. Although the masons held back from the growing practice of launching a union newspaper,[176] they remained convinced of the central importance of this sphere of activity: 'Experience has proved to us, that proper information and regular communication have been chiefly instrumental in raising our society to its present prosperity; and that whatever improvements can be effected in these points, will be attended with proportionate benefit.'[177]

Most of the communication was concerned with actual or potential conflict. The Fortnightly Returns served not only to concentrate resources in disputes with masters but also as a channel of authority within the organisation. The accounts left by artisan autobiographers describe a world full of arguments and allegations of rule-breaking. Some arose from no more than minor personality clashes, but others involved serious infringements of established laws or basic disagreements about recognised customs, especially those relating to the consumption of alcohol.[178] Every shop had its own means of ensuring conformity, ranging from verbal intimidation to specially convened tribunals. Charles Manby Smith, working in a London printshop in 1834, found himself at odds with his fellow compositors for working too fast, and was finally goaded into knocking down one of his tormentors: 'For this I was "chapelled" on the spot – that is, I was tried by a general jury of the whole room for a breach of the peace, and fined five shillings by sentence of the "father" of the chapel for striking a comrade.'[179] In this case, the fine was paid and drunk on the spot, but in the mobile existence of the journeyman craftsman, there was always a danger of a disgraced shopmate evading punishment by moving on to another job. Withholding tramping documents was a deterrent, but could not prevent the individual making his own way to the next town. A major attraction of a federated union was that it offered for the first time the prospect of enforcing discipline throughout the trade, thus extending the jurisdiction of the separate workshops, and, crucially, diminishing the threat of blacklegs by exposing illegal workers wherever they might appear. Here, print was indispensable. From the beginning, the masons' Fortnightly Return carried requests from lodges to 'publish' men who had left the area after failing to pay fines or working on blacked jobs. The next step was to collect the names into a regularly updated blacklist, which could be kept for reference by each lodge. By the early 1850s this had become a publication of extraordinary size and complexity. The Revised Black List of April 1853 contained 2,302 names of men who had fines outstanding for contravening every aspect of the union's laws, ranging from strike-breaking to 'Acts of Indecency at Lodge Houses', in every corner of the country since it began keeping records two decades earlier.[180] The document constituted a roll-call of all the battles the Society had fought, as well as a monument to its unforgiving memory. It is difficult to think of any other bureaucracy of the time, public or private, which could attempt to keep track of the activities of so many working men over so long a period.

Although the choice between print and the spoken word was important in matters of communication and discipline, its greatest significance was in the embodiment of rules of collective action. As they sought to establish a permanent presence in the expanding economy, the craft unions were heavily dependent on the discretionary use of alternative means of recording the regulations which controlled their internal and external relations. The initial pressure for a formal representation of accepted practice stemmed from the mutual assistance functions of the early trade clubs. Just as the collective memory was an unreliable witness to the growing volume of financial transactions, so the rights and obligations which underpinned them required a more authoritative statement. Printed regulations were a necessary concomitant of a system of benefits and contributions, and from 1855 organisations depositing their rule books with the Registrar of Friendly Societies could gain legal protection for their funds. Much greater flexibility was demanded, however, in the case of collective bargaining. No two unions followed exactly the same practice, but in general the strategy was to draw a clear distinction between published laws and usually unpublished bye-laws or workshop rules. The former tended to be restricted to the bureaucratic procedures of the union; the latter dealt with the substantive issues of pay and conditions of work. It was left to the branches to define the bye-laws, which could take the form of written or printed agreements, but for the most part existed as a set of enforceable customs and rights.

For outsiders, the stark contrast between the meticulous detail of the publicly visible laws specifying, for instance, the conduct of committee meetings or the auditing of accounts, and the submerged body of regulations referring to hours of work or permitted numbers of apprentices, was deliberately confusing. It enabled the unions to draw maximum attention to the acceptable side of their affairs, the sober, responsible, professional administration of business, whilst keeping at arm's length the more controversial objectives, such as opposing new machinery or limiting work-rates, and the less defensible methods, such as picketing, rattening, sending to Coventry or occasional acts of violence. Leaders who proudly displayed their elaborate machinery for curbing strikes could become studiously vague when the actual conduct of collective bargaining was raised. Within the unions, however, there was a clear rationale in the selective recording of rules.

Firstly it was ι response to the problem of maintaining nation-wide organisations in industries where there were still significant variations in working practices and rates of pay. If the structure was too loose, the advantages of federation were lost; if it was too rigid, local interests and pride would create unmanageable tensions. In 1844, for instance, an attempt was made to unite the printers of England, Scotland and Ireland into the National Typographical Association: 'However, the differences of feeling, and the different modes of payment and customs of the provinces as compared with London soon broke that up, it did not last above three years.'[181] The solution was to standardise the bureaucracy wherever the writ of a union ran, whilst leaving the creation of uniform conditions as a distant destination to which individual lodges could make their own way in their own time. Thus William Allen of the Engineers was able to boast that 'one code of rules governs the whole of the members'[182] – even the lodges in Australia followed exactly the same procedures – but in fact the union had not immediately found the correct balance between printed and unprinted regulations. Initially the rule book contained specific laws referring to overtime, piece-work and apprentices, but after the bitterly fought and near fatal national lock-out of 1851–2, these were deleted to enable the union to conduct a more flexible campaign on their behalf.[183]

Secondly it was a response to the need to extend the authority of a union beyond its paid-up membership. Recruitment varied extensively from trade to trade from year to year, but apart from the engineers, none of the 'New Model Unions' attracted more than a third of eligible skilled workers, and some were unable to manage one in ten.[184] To attract new members and protect those who had made regular contributions, the system of benefits had to be rigorously defined, but if working rules were to be enforced outside the lodge, it was often better that they remained implicit rather than explicit. Unions had to temper ambition with caution. The only consequence of demanding conformity to formally defined practices would be the exposure of the organisation's weakness. The 1869 Royal Commission interrogated the masons' leader Thomas Conally on the prevalence of 'chasing' – requiring all those engaged on a given job not to exceed an agreed work-rate: 'Is this custom which you have spoken of acknowledged by non-union men, that is to say, where masons not members of the society are at work?' 'Tacitly' was the eloquent reply.[185] What was expected was not obedience but the absence of disobedience. Quiet observance of working customs ensured membership of the trade, if not the trade union, and exempted the non-paying artisan from any sanctions. 'It is a practice of the trade then', continued the Commission, 'whether men are members of the society or not? – Yes.' 'But if a non-union man working with union men were to disregard your rules and work as fast as he chose, the union men would not work with him? – Precisely.'[186] Once the rules were broken, the journeyman was relegated to the ranks of the unskilled, and treated with unremitting hostility. It was an unheroic but effective strategy, which ensured that the fledgling federated unions cast much longer shadows than their size justified.

Finally, the controlled use of print was a means of balancing the conflicting requirements of spontaneity at the periphery with caution at the centre. The key issue was expenditure on strike action. Federation and its accompanying centralisation were becoming increasingly necessary as employers gained in strength and confidence and began to explore the possibilities of concerted action against workers' customary rights.[187] A larger and more integrated union offered the benefits of enhanced resources, but threatened in return the loss of local autonomy. The dilemma was a further manifestation of what the Webbs called 'the long and inarticulate struggle of unlettered men to solve the problem of how to combine administrative efficiency with popular control'.[188] As the craft unions grew in size, new solutions had to be found. In most cases, expansion was accompanied by an elaboration of the regulations sanctioning a withdrawal of labour. Rule 20, Section 2 of the 1863 laws of the Friendly Society of Operative Carpenters stated that

> When application is made to the general secretary by any lodge or lodges for leave to strike for a new privilege, the government committee shall, within seven days from the date of the application, instruct one of the adjacent lodges to appoint a deputation, consisting of two members, to investigate their affairs as regards the state of trade, and the probability of such strike being successful or otherwise; the report of the deputation to be printed with the minutes of the executive committee, and submitted to the union for decision.[189]

Members were allowed twenty-eight days to vote, and if the application was supported, the employers in question had to be given three months' notice of impending strike action, during which time three officials of neighbouring lodges would endeavour to negotiate an 'amicable arrangement' between the contending parties. Furthermore, applications could only be made twice a year, in November and March, by lodges which had been in the union for at least twelve months and had submitted no previous requests during that time, and leave would be refused automatically if more than one in sixty members were already on strike.

Offensive industrial action had to be planned as carefully as the invasion of a foreign country, with every avenue of diplomacy explored first, and the commitment of troops dependent on the most favourable conjunction of circumstances. However, to prevent the deliberately cumbersome system exposing lodges to sudden attack by employers, a sharp distinction was drawn between aggression and defence. The freedom enjoyed by localities to establish working rules and rates of pay was extended to the right to call a strike immediately these were challenged. Like the carpenters, the masons insisted on full consultation before granting funds, except where 'any employer attempt to reduce the current rate of wage at any period of the year or attempt to introduce piecework where it has been abolished, or to increase the hours of labour, or infringe upon the established meal hours, or to introduce individuals not of the trade'.[190] In such circumstances, it was the content of the largely unwritten bye-laws rather than the detail of the union's procedural rules which determined expenditure on strike activity.

The complex balance between formality and informality which characterised the growth of union structures during the first two thirds of the nineteenth century represented a compromise between the strengths and weaknesses of both the artisans and their employers. The trade clubs were heavily dependent upon the pen and the printing press as they sought to evolve into stable, federated societies, but their inability to achieve comprehensive membership or standardised conditions of employment dictated a continuing reliance on oral forms of communication in defining relations of production. The maintenance of the craftsman's authority in the workplace demanded both the elaboration and the strict limitation of the jurisdiction of the rule book. For their part, employers found it more practical to use union regulation than statute law to curb workplace militancy, but more desirable to leave working rules unwritten in order to preserve their right to manage. The continuing small scale of manufacture inhibited the creation of permanent alliances which could negotiate on equal terms with the federated unions and encouraged the acceptance of a distinction between codified procedural structures and uncodified substantive practices, where masters were free to attack the workers' claims to independent control.

The discretionary use of writing and print left a two-fold legacy to collective bargaining as the industrial economy continued to expand during the remainder of the period. In the first instance, it led to a relentless escalation in the sheer volume of paper attached to any union activity, so much so, indeed, that some observers doubted whether working men would ever be able to cope with the administrative problems of running a national organisation.[191] By the middle of the nineteenth century the OSM had come a long way from the tin box with its handful of documents. The standard issue from headquarters to lodges comprised the following items: 'Green cheques, sick lists, trade fund cards, surgeon's certificates, account sheets, shop steward books, white cheques, yellow cheques, black lists, initiation forms, laws, sick fund cards, summonses, secretary's book, treasurer's sheets, treasurer's book, contribution book'.[192] The bureaucracy was as intricate as it was inescapable. The increasing use of the pre-printed regulations, forms and returns was the only way of dealing with the instability of branch organisations and the rapid turnover of local officials. If a newly elected lodge secretary, who perhaps had handled nothing finer than a chisel since leaving school, was to cope with the regular business of the union together with the constant correspondence, it was imperative that procedures be standardised as far as possible.

The pressures transcended the divisions between the established craft societies and the 'new unions' which burst into life in 1889. The founder of the first of these, the National Union of Gas Workers and General Labourers, was a 31-year-old brickmaker's son, Will Thorne, who at his wedding ten years earlier had been unable to sign the marriage register.[193] In the intervening period he had taken lessons in reading and writing from, amongst others, Eleanor Marx, but even so was quite unprepared for the consequences of the decision reached on 31 March 1889 to form a provisional committee 'to draft a set of rules' for the proposed union.[194] Mass membership created mass paperwork. After six months of rapid growth he was in danger of drowning in the sea of documents generated by 20,000 members in over forty branches:

> I had a multitude of correspondence, vouchers, bills, etc., which were simply strewn everywhere about the office. There was no regular system of filing of any kind ... There were bills of every imagineable shape and size, written on all kinds of paper, in pencil and ink, a large proportion of them almost undecipherable. Our office was just one small room, with meagre and primitive furniture, where the whole of our work had to be done, including the holding of committee meetings. I shall never forget the sight of this room, simply covered as it was in all directions with those papers.[195]

However, as was so often the case when the uneducated suddenly had to use the tools of literacy, it was possible to borrow and improvise. John Burns of the ASE might call by and criticise the handwriting, grammar and composition of the letters received and written by Thorne,[196] but at least the correspondence took place. More constructive advice came from the union's first treasurer, Will Byford, who had gained invaluable administrative experience as secretary of the Yorkshire Glass Bottle Workers' Association. And after working day and night to clear up the backlog, Thorne arranged for permanent clerical assistance to take care of the union's routine business.

Secondly, the momentum established during the 1860s raised increasingly difficult questions about the relationship between rule-making and the market economy. The problems centred on the issue of conciliation and arbitration, which in various forms rapidly spread across wide areas of the union movement. By 1875, standing joint committees of employers and workmen with provision for arbitration, and ad hoc practices of using third parties to settle disputes, could be found in most sectors of the economy where trade societies had been established. Although a number of liberal manufacturers, MPs, and lawyers, particularly A. J. Mundella and Sir Rupert Kettle,[197] played a key role in launching the movement, it was sustained by the initial enthusiasm of the unions themselves.[198] To their leaders, the new negotiating structures offered a real prospect of extending the authority of formalised rules to every employer in a given industry.[199] In the Potteries, for instance, all the major sectors of the workforce campaigned for the introduction of conciliation. For those seeking to consolidate the local branch of the Amalgamated Association of Miners, it was argued that

> The past has proved how advantageous it has been to the trade that organisation among the miners has brought about regulation and discipline. The men have now a right to ask that the employers should have more discipline in their own ranks ... North Staffordshire would be enormously benefited as a district by the establishment of a mining tribunal that would prevent the mad race of reduction, would regulate reckless competition, and seek to do justice to all interested in these industries.[200]

Since the eighteenth century trade societies had been struggling to protect their notions of justice in relations of production from increasingly hostile competitive forces, and now it seemed as if the tide might be turning in their favour.

The arrival of conciliation and arbitration was a reflection of the strength of organised labour in the early seventies, a time of economic growth and the achievement of legal recognition, and throughout the remainder of the period up to 1914, the development of regulated bargaining accompanied an uneven but eventually substantial growth in the size, scope and power of the trade union movement. However, the new procedures placed severe strains on the complex balance between formality and informality which characterised the existing strategies of collective action and exposed the unions to the threat that instead of subjugating the market to the rule book, the reverse would happen. The tensions were revealed in three areas. Firstly, the use of arbitration to determine wages, which was most common in industrialised processes where unions were still struggling to establish themselves, brought into the open a latent contradiction over the criteria for determining settlements. Trade societies traditionally had always maintained that matters as basic as pay belonged to the realm of justice, codified and recorded as custom, rather than market forces. At the same time it was recognised that when the state of trade was adverse, conditions of employment would come under pressure, and conversely that in times of growth, the boundaries of custom might be pushed forward.[201] This in turn implied a recognition, which was gradually becoming more widespread during the third quarter of the century, that the employer's rate of return on capital had some part to play in the bargaining process.

For their part, the middle-class advocates of arbitration, as Sir Rupert Kettle made clear, did not accept that unions had any right to challenge 'the great fundamental principle – as inevitable in its action as gravitation – that "a fair day's wage for a fair day's labour" is determined by the proportion which the supply in the market bears to the demand'.[202] Whilst the negotiations remained informal, even if they occasionally resulted in printed wage or price lists, both sides could claim that their principles remained intact, but this was impossible once the matter was put before an arbitrator, who would demand written submissions and publish his findings. A major factor in the unions' subsequent loss of confidence in arbitration was, as the Webbs put it, 'their feeling of uncertainty as to the fundamental assumptions upon which the arbitrator will base his award'.[203]

As a case history we may cite the bitter experience of the pottery unions. In the boom years of the early seventies they managed to gain advances of around 10 per cent on the 'Green Book', a list of piece-rates which had remained unchanged since 1836. In 1876, with prices falling, they went to arbitration to defend their gains. In the face of an appeal by the masters to market conditions, the union representative argued that 'reducing wages when trade is depressed would introduce a new feature and custom in connection with the pottery trade. I believe our wages cannot be governed by the rise and fall of the markets.'[204] On this occasion the umpire, a stipendiary magistrate, agreed: 'it seems to me that the great strength of the workmen's cases consisted in the contrast between the inevitable vicissitudes of selling prices and seller's profits, and the permanent character of wages'.[205] However, the potters were now committed to the arbitration machinery, and two years later a hearing under Lord Hatherton rejected the criteria of custom and the cost of living, and awarded a penny in the shilling wage-cut on the basis of the state of national and international trade.[206] When both the decision and its grounds were confirmed the following year by the Liberal MP Thomas Brassey, the unions withdrew from the machinery, and tried to recoup their losses in a disastrous six-week strike.[207] In 1885, in a weakened state, they rejoined a conciliation and arbitration system, but fared no better, their efforts to win back the gains of the early seventies being finally defeated in a hearing under another Liberal MP, H. T. Hinckes, in 1891.[208] Other industries suffered similar problems, particularly mining, where it was even more difficult to appeal to custom in pay bargaining. After a series of unsatisfactory ad hoc arbitrations in the mid seventies, most districts conceded the principle of basing wages on trade conditions in return for participation in determining the relationship between the two factors. Whilst the ensuing sliding scales rested on verifiable data and discouraged aggression by militant employers, they subordinated negotiations to market forces in a way which proved increasingly unacceptable as union strength grew once more in the 1890s.[209]

The next area of difficulty concerned the extension of formal rules governing relations within the trade unions. A central attraction of conciliation and arbitration to the larger employers had been the prospect of the emergence of a corporate economy, with power shared between a handful of individuals at the head of the major institutions in each sector. Lindsay Wood, President of the Durham Coal Owners' association, explained to the 1892 Royal Commission why increased bureaucratic control was now necessary: 'I think we are coming now to having large bodies of industries managed by two bodies of executives composed probably of a very small numbers of men, their decisions are extremely important for the welfare of large masses of the population and therefore there ought to be some very strict rules to carry out the decisions.'[210] The unions were vulnerable to this proposition partly because the discipline was supposed to be reciprocal, with the employers' associations curbing member companies who broke agreements, and partly because the issue of restricting workplace spontaneity was, as we have seen, as old as organised labour itself, and was becoming more critical as the growth in units of production increased the stakes in industrial disputes. The federated craft societies had themselves invented the devices for delaying strike action and referring local disputes to non-participants; the new mechanisms merely deprived them of sole rights in arbitrating between the masters and their own members.

It was not so much that rules existed where before there were none, but rather that participation in structured collective bargaining made it less easy to resolve long-standing tensions by tactical shifts from formal to tacit regulation. If there was to be regular discourse with groups of employers, the authority of the union executive had to be clarified. It was in this context that an ambitious young stonemason called Henry Broadhurst became a full-time official in 1872 and immediately set about introducing a 'Central Committee' to exercise 'executive powers', and, in a move of practical and symbolic importance, ended the peripatetic existence of headquarters by establishing a permanent base in London.[211] As the scope and observance of agreements became more sensitive, so the often hazy distinction between being 'in the trade' and 'in the union' had to be sharpened. This tendency became particularly marked in the aftermath of the outburst of 'New Unionism' in 1889, when all the established trade societies embarked on recruitment campaigns, using the additional dues to employ more full-time staff, who in turn had to deal with a greater volume of paperwork. In 1892, for instance, the ASE took a dual decision to expand its membership and increase its permanent officials from four to seventeen.

However, the accretion of authority to union bureaucracies stopped a long way short of the vision held out by Lindsay Wood. There were practical difficulties. The persistence of regional variations in conditions of employment made it impossible to set up national bargaining systems before 1914, and within the area conciliation boards, the sheer volume of disputes over the mass of unwritten customs and practices continually threatened to overwhelm the machinery.[212] But above all there was opposition from below. As much as the union executives had long experience of curtailing workplace militancy, so the local branches had equally long traditions of resistance, and could now often obtain the support of the new full-time regional officials in their conflicts with the centre. The creation of negotiating structures was greeted with suspicion, which easily turned into outright hostility once the boards attempted to impose cuts in pay and conditions after the end of the boom in the mid seventies. Employers constantly complained of the inability of unions to enforce decisions on their members, and sooner or later every one of the schemes of which so much had been expected collapsed, usually as a consequence of withdrawal by the workers, who frequently were then able to drive their leadership into strike action. The habits of plant-bargaining remained remarkably resilient, surviving, in the case of the engineers, not only the chequered history of conciliation and arbitration, but even the apparently successful employers' lock-out of 1897–8, which was designed to put an end to workplace control over matters such as the recruitment of apprentices and overtime. Rather than causing an irreversible shift from informality to formality, the developments made it less easy to reconcile the two modes of governing behaviour, the growth in membership accompanying an increasing instability within the union structures which was to culminate in the unprecedented disorders of the 1910–14 period.

The final problem was in relations between unions, particularly their leadership, and the employers. Individual officials and manufacturers came together to devise rules and then met regularly to administer the system they had created. For many of the masters it was an enlightening experience. J. Peate of the Leeds Chamber of Commerce recalled his service on a weavers' board of conciliation: 'During that time it was my pleasure, I may say, to come in contact with the leaders of the working men of the Union. I was extremely surprised by their reasonableness, by their sense of justice, and by their good sense all round.'[213] Increasingly the union bureaucrats had opportunities to impress in related spheres. Men whose working lives had been outside the law until the reforms of 1871 and 1875 now found themselves appointed magistrates by reason of their office. Their role as community leaders was confirmed by their election as MPs,[214] councillors, poor law guardians and school board members, and their capacity as professional administrators was recognised by their recruitment to posts created by the formation of trade boards, labour exchanges and national insurance schemes under the pre-war Liberal Government. An epoch separated the account of blacklisting, poverty and endless defeats in Edward Allen Rymer's *The Martyrdom of the Mine, or, 60 Year Struggle for Life*, published in 1898, and *Henry Broadhurst, M.P., the Story of His Life from a Stonemason's Bench to the Treasury Bench*, which appeared just three years later.

There was a danger that a competence in rule-making was becoming the passport away from industrial conflict rather than the means of giving coherence and force to workplace militancy. Participation in regulated collective bargaining threatened to separate leaders from their members and subordinate them to the employers' version of rational behaviour. For all the missionary zeal of Mundella and Kettle, the outlook of the middle-class members of the boards remained patronising. It was assumed that those who spoke for manual workers, particularly if they were to return to the workshop at the end the hearing, were amateurs in the world of management. The potters' claim for the restoration of wage cuts in 1880 was finally dismissed by the arbitrator Thomas Brassey with the observation that 'The rudeness of the tests by which the operatives have endeavoured to check the estimate of the employers presents an illustration of the difficulty they experience in estimating prices and profits.'[215]

As we have seen, however, the potters' leaders rejected this judgment and organised a strike, and the reality of the union officials' situation was rather more complex than complacent outside observers assumed. So far from borrowing skills and language from their enlightened employers, they displayed techniques of negotiation and compromise at the conciliation boards which had been the common possession of generations of union organisers as they sought to balance the conflicting requirements of procedural formality and substantive informality within their own organisations. J. Peate's surprise at the 'sense of justice' of the Leeds weavers indicates that it was the masters rather than the unionists whose outlook was changing most in this period. The employers had a greater distance to travel towards the formalisation of collective bargaining, and remained uncertain about its procedures. Their complaints about union indiscipline were fully reciprocated, and they were even more prone to violent reversals of tactics, particularly in textiles and engineering where, in the 1890s, compromise was temporarily abandoned for all-out conflict.

In practice, rather than simply divorcing the entire leadership from the workforce, the developments in formal collective bargaining, together with the growth in union bureaucracies and the creation of opportunities outside the movement, increased the already intense pressure on the individual leaders. How they responded depended partly on temperament and partly on the traditions and prospects of their own organisations. The journey through literacy to rule-making could lead to quite different destinations. If Will Thorne's lessons in reading and writing made possible his translation from workshop militant to union bureaucrat, they also permitted his transition, through wide reading, from unfocused malcontent to committed socialist. Unless he was one of the fortunate few who found a berth as a £1,000 a year Board of Trade inspector, the labour leader at the end of the period still found himself working day and night for no better wages than a skilled worker could take home for a fifty-hour week.[216] And if craft union officials now enjoyed some occupational security, this privilege was not extended to those seeking to organise the unskilled sectors. Like Will Thorne, the Norfolk farm workers' leader George Edwards learned to read and write after his marriage, and he used his literacy to create bureaucratic structures, take part in conciliation boards, serve on national insurance committees, and become an MP, yet his life as a trade unionist was as full of physical toil and deprivation as those of the labourers he sought to represent.[217]

Conciliation and arbitration had been promoted in the 1860s and early 1870s by middle-class reformers convinced that the twin forces of rising living standards and spreading education were transforming the texture of popular culture. The workforce, and in particular its leadership, were becoming more rational, self-controlled and responsible, creating the possibility of a new era of stable, rule-based industrial relations. In the event, they misread both the strength of the economy and the consequences of mass literacy. The buoyancy of markets up to the mid seventies enhanced the confidence of organised labour and encouraged employers to offer accommodation rather than confrontation, but thereafter fluctuations in the trade cycle subjected the new negotiating structures to frequently unbearable strains. And whilst sympathetic observers were right to detect the dependence of trade unions on the printed word, they persistently misunderstood the complex nature of its employment.

The final drive against illiteracy had its most direct impact in areas in which there was little or no stable union activity at the beginning of the last third of the century. The spread of organisation to groups outside the ranks of the artisans took place in the context of dramatic surges in their literacy rates, as displayed in the marriage register sample. Between the 1870s and the 1890s, the scores of miners leapt from 43 per cent to 92 per cent, potters from 44 per cent to 93 per cent and unskilled labourers (predominantly agricultural) from 69 per cent to 95 per cent (see table 4.3 above). Given the propensity of the labouring poor to borrow and improvise when confronted with a sudden requirement to read or write, it is difficult to argue that unions amongst, say, the farm workers or the gas workers would have been wholly impossible without these gains, but the careers of men like Thorne and Edwards demonstrate how shallow were the educational foundations of their bureaucracies.

Once formed, however, these unions faced many of the same difficulties of their older counterparts. At issue was not a transition from non-rational to rational strategies, or a displacement of autonomous by centralised control,[218] but rather an increasing strain on the intricate balance between written and oral modes of governing behaviour. On the surface the traditional approach of the unions to labour relations survived remarkably unscathed as their strength doubled and redoubled during the last three decades of the period. Despite the hopes of the employers, the negotiating structures proved too brittle to survive prolonged attempts to force down wages or increase the authority of managers, and despite attempts to subject unwritten workshop practices to formal definition, these remained largely uncodified in most industries on the eve of the First World War. The most that happened was that changes agreed through conciliation often survived as additions to the every changing body of customs once tne board in question had collapsed. This was a consequence in part of the refusal of the State to go further than establishing a legislative framework for formal bargaining. It made no attempt to enforce conciliation[219] or to control the substance of negotiation, and offered little encouragement to the occasional attempts by groups of employers to imitate German and American anti-union practices. In part it was a function of the limited and inconstant ambitions of the employers. Notwithstanding their protestations, they mistrusted, often with good reason, the willingness and ability of organised labour to maintain regulated collective bargaining, but lacked the unity and the strength of purpose either to pursue the implications of establishing a corporate economy or to engage in full-scale industrial warfare. And in part it was the result of the experience and traditions of the unions themselves. For all the temptations with which they were faced, union leaders had no need to step outside their own values and skills to engage in the making and administration of procedural rules, and for all the pressures bearing down on them, the workplace groups retained the capacity to resist permanent encroachments on their independence.

The outcome of this success was the peculiar combination of continuity and profound instability which characterised labour relations in the period from 1910 to the outbreak of the War. As recession turned to boom, union leaders lost control of their members, who forced them to abandon conciliation for strike action in favour of basic rights which would transcend market forces.[220] The emptiness of the employers' dream of achieving a pliant workforce in the era of mass education was exposed at just the moment when full nominal literacy was attained. Those union officials who had hoped that the increasing size and complexity of their negotiating machinery would finally resolve the problem of local autonomy faced a serious reverse. It appeared as if the era of day-to-day adjustment between the centre and the periphery had merely been replaced by a cycle of containment and rebellion. At the same time, workplace militancy proved limited in its ambitions. In this respect, as in others, oral means of recording and enforcing rules of behaviour were inherently conservative. In attack, most shop-floor activists looked no further than minor adjustments to the accumulated body of custom and practice. As such they proved generally unsatisfactory material for the early syndicalists, and offered their union leadership little long-term alternative to a return to conciliation practices, with all the difficulties they contained, once the wave of strikes was over.

Conclusion

In 1842, the Children's Employment Commission interviewed a nineteen-year-old iron-moulder named Thomas Delay on his educational attainments. 'I can read and write a little', he replied; 'I cannot cipher much; I am more for work.'[221] Up to the end of the period the relevance of reading and writing to employment was often difficult to discern. As Robert Roberts observed of pre-war Salford, 'Most men struggling for a living knew well enough that for them literacy brought no bread.'[222] Just as the smoothly rising graph of marriage register signatures dissolved into an irregular landscape of plateaus, declivities and sudden ascents when correlated with occupation, so there was no unilinear development in the function of literacy in the industrialising economy. The attempt to translate the formal, rule-based world of the classroom into the workshops and factories involved at every turn issues of control and autonomy. The parallel between the divisions of language and pupils in the schools and the separation of the processes and employees in manufacture ensured that the application of literacy would become embedded in the conflict between capital and labour, with the outcome dependent on an intricate and continuing series of negotiations.

Given that the Industrial Revolution had commenced with a workforce substantially more literate than the minimum now held to be necessary for economic take-off, and that by the end of the period the school system was at last producing cohorts of new workers who could all display some command of the written word, the progress made by employers towards the bureaucratisation of the labour process was strikingly incomplete. The sheer inconsistency of the use being made of formal regulation in even the most advanced and well-organised sectors of the economy is nowhere better illustrated than by the procedures at Crewe railway works in the early 1900s. On the one hand, the structures of discipline had become so elaborate that employees wishing to relieve themselves had to deposit their work-check with an attendant stationed outside the lavatory who recorded in a book the length and frequency of the visits; if either were deemed excessive, the offender had to write a letter of explanation to the manager. At the same time, recruitment to this elite sector of the workforce was largely based on heredity or personal contact, with the principal qualification for entry being the presence of a close relative in the factory, and the apprenticeships in what were amongst the most sophisticated technologies of the day were still conducted largely on the basis of imitation and practice. The only concession to the labour of the schoolmasters was the insistence that those qualified by birth had also to pass Standard VII, and that some apprentices could obtain release for technical training on a Friday afternoon.[223]

The development of the first industrial economy was in the end too uneven and on too small a scale to overcome the obstacles to the wholesale exploitation of the opportunities presented by one of the first fully literate workforces. The example set by the creation of systematic procedures for appointment, promotion and management in the industry most directly dependent on the growth of mass literacy, the Post Office, was rarely followed elsewhere. In large areas of manufacture, the most efficient solution to the problem of reconciling the increasing size of firms and the limited skills and resources of their owners was to continue to rely on precisely the traditional forms of learning and authority which the schoolmasters had for so long attacked.[224] Labour was still so plentiful, production runs were still so limited, and bureaucracy was going to be so expensive, that it still made sense to sub-contract teaching, recruitment and discipline to a workforce whose command of literacy was rarely checked. It was partly that employers lacked confidence in their own strength, and – when it came to it – in the transforming power of schooling, despite the lip service they paid to it, and partly that the patchwork of innovation and continuity which had evolved by the First World War was producing good profits, notwithstanding the forebodings of the educational reformers.

Throughout the period, those who were increasingly coming to be categorised as 'manual' workers had displayed both resilience and opportunism in their relationship with the printed word. Where their independence was threatened, craftsmen had delayed the introduction of formal rules of practice and achievement, but where their resistance to market forces could be enhanced, they, and later other sectors of the workforce, had often demonstrated a more sophisticated grasp of the possibilities of bureaucratised action than their employers. The sections of the workforce who from the beginning had needed the tools of reading and writing to build their institutions and more generally to maintain their status as rational and self-disciplined craftsmen had sustained high levels of literacy amidst the turmoil of urban growth and economic change. Elsewhere, occupational groups had responded to the appeals and initiatives of Church and State only as fast as the costs of remaining illiterate increased. Compulsion directly affected the rates of just the miners and labourers, and it is impossible to know how rapidly the rates would subsequently have risen had parents retained the freedom to react to the increasing possibilities of mobility and union organisation.

In several senses, therefore, the labouring population conducted its encounter with literacy very much on its own terms, but there were costs. The largely defensive attitude to the invasion by the printed word of occupational training and recruitment and areas of collective bargaining tended to reinforce inequalities within the working class and failed to control growing inequalities between the classes. The reliance on tradition and heredity in transmitting skills and allocating posts meant that education failed to provide the children of the poor with significant opportunities of mobility within the ranks of labour, let alone out of them.[225] The system of labour relations which had developed was at once conservative and unstable, with the potential for disruption as much a threat to the union leadership as to the employers. And perhaps most seriously, a sector of the community which at least in its upper ranks had been as accustomed to using print as consuming alcohol, which particularly in the course of the nineteenth century developed bureaucracies at least the equal of those of the State or industry, was becoming excluded, at the moment of universal literacy, from the status of mental labour.[226]

5

THE NATURAL WORLD

The tenth of Joseph Lawson's *Letters to the Young on Progress in Pudsey* was entitled 'Superstition the Child of Ignorance'. 'In proportion as people are deprived of knowledge and are ignorant of the causes of what they constantly see and hear', he began, 'their imagination is let loose and their reason being weak, they become a prey to every false rumour or popular prejudice and delusion.'[1] The dichotomy between knowledge and superstition has been at the heart of movements for mass education from the late eighteenth century to the present day. In 1980 Unesco set out the objective of a mass literacy campaign: 'The knowledge which should be created here is first of all self-knowledge. In practice it is self emancipation which includes emancipation from superstition, apathy and fatalism. It is the creation of a man who understands his physical environment correctly and is willing to conquer and develop it.'[2] A command of the tools of communication would lead to a command of the natural world. The double absence of control was at once a measure and a cause of the divide between advanced and backward countries, and between polite and popular cultures within societies. The early folklorists claimed to be the first to discover the true state of mind of the uneducated. 'Those who mix much amongst the lower orders', wrote the mid-nineteenth-century collector William Henderson, 'and have opportunities of enquiring closely into their beliefs, customs and usages, will find in these remote places,– nay, even in our towns and larger villages,– a vast mass of superstition holding its ground most tenaciously.'[3] The problem was that over the centuries, whole sections of the community had been excluded from a knowledge of how their environment functioned. 'This universal ignorance of the laws of nature', he concluded, 'goes far to account for the widespread superstition which for ages pervaded all Europe.'[4]

All those who sought to assess the impact of literacy in this period leaned heavily on the notion of superstition. Its extent justified the work of the schoolmaster, and its decline measured his success. Yet the confidence with which the term was applied was matched only by the absence of agreement about its definition. In essence the word is merely a pejorative description of any belief with which the user disagrees. During the eighteenth century it generally referred to a false religious belief, usually Catholic, but it also came to be employed by those rejecting more extreme forms of Protestantism,[5] by secularists dismissing all species of revealed religion, by radicals attacking the pretensions of the middle-class press,[6] and even, as in W. H. Mallock's *Studies of Contemporary Superstition*, by Christians attacking supposedly scientific philosophies such as Fabian socialism.[7] In practice the deployment of the term revealed as much about the belief system of the writer as of his subject, throwing light not only on the nature of change but its meaning for those who witnessed it at first or second hand.

Underlying the shifts and conflicts in emphasis were three basic assumptions about the relationship between literacy and the natural world which will be the concern of the separate sections of this chapter. Firstly, sets of beliefs sustained and perpetuated by an enclosed oral tradition were inherently irrational, giving those who held them a false perspective on their world. There was much that divided the educated and often leisured folklore collectors and the working-class autobiographers looking back on the mental environment of their childhood and youth, but they were united in their conviction that merely by writing about superstitions they stood on the other side of a divide from those who still accepted them. Modern communications, principally the printed word but also the associated forces of new transport systems and gas and electricity, were literally and metaphorically lightening the darkness of those hitherto isolated from their influence. The study of superstitions, wrote W. C. Hazlitt, 'would render it more possible for us to judge the amount and degree of progress in knowledge and culture, which has been attained in the intervening time, and of which we are in actual enjoyment'.[8] Whether the change was regarded with relief, nostalgia or celebration, it could not and should not be reversed. However colourful and diverting they might be, the orally transmitted folk traditions embodied a fundamental failure of comprehension. Charlotte Burne, an influential late-nineteenth-century folklorist, advised her readers on the best approach to the central question raised by popular beliefs:

> *How* such a vast growth of superstitions and customs arose out of (comparatively speaking) a few simple myths, will perhaps never be fully understood, but the best way to arrive at this end is, to my mind, to study the modes of thought of uneducated people at the present day, and to observe what extraordinary mistakes they make about things they do not understand.[9]

Secondly it was assumed that the overthrow of superstition involved the displacement of established forms of authority within the culture of the uneducated.[10] Palpably false beliefs were accepted not because of their intrinsic likelihood, but because credence was attached to their source. In the first instance, this was a matter of the status of the older generation in the eyes of the younger. Children learned from their parents, who were not above reinforcing their control by manipulation of the more frightening elements of traditional lore. Like many children, Joseph Barker suffered more from psychological than from physical punishment. After one misdemeanour, he recalled, he was 'put into a dark cellar, and told that the *boggard* would have me. This was the most terrible affair of all.'[11] Behind the senior members of the community stood tradition itself, derived from the era brought to an end by the twin events of the Reformation and the invention of printing. 'As to the Opinions they hold', explained the first major study of popular beliefs in England, 'they are almost all superstitious, being generally either the Produce of Heathenism; or the Invention of indolent *Monks*.'[12] The mutually reinforcing dominion of older generations and ancient religions could only be challenged by an alliance between literacy and Protestantism. 'It has been handed down to us', wrote William Hone of one practice,

> from the bewildering ceremonies of the Romish church, and may easily be discountenanced into disuse by opportune and mild persuasion. If the children of ignorant persons be properly taught, they will perceive in adult years the gross follies of their parentage, and so instruct their own offspring, that not a hand or voice shall be lifted or heard from the sons of labour, in support of a superstition that darkened and dismayed man, until the printing press and the reformation ensured his final enlightenment and emancipation.[13]

The Protestant Churches could break the chain of transmission partly through the presence in every community of their educated representatives, and partly through their promotion of mass education as a means of reorganising the domestic curriculum.

The third assumption was that the fate of superstition was associated with a fundamental change in the relationship between popular culture and time. Its decline marked the invasion of the circular, immutable rhythms of nature by the progressive, man-made movement of an historically conscious society. Folklorists, especially those influenced by the new science of anthropology in the last quarter of the nineteenth century, were motivated by the conviction that the beliefs they were hurrying to record had remained unchanged for centuries or even millennia, and were therefore capable of yielding unique insights into the consciousness of primitive societies. Those observing from within popular culture saw in the erosion of superstition an index of the transformation of their world during their own lifetimes. 'In looking backward', wrote the

Cornish miner Thomas Oliver in 1914, 'I have seen many changes these last seventy years. Seventy years ago there was scarcely a village or town that had not its haunted house, and every old Manor house would be sure to be haunted with ghosts.'[14] A new sense of history arose from both the mode and the substance of change. As the channels of oral transmission began to break down, new means of storing the past and communicating it to the future had to be found. And as the supernatural beings lost their hold on the imagination, so the mutually dependent structure of popular beliefs and the cycles of nature began to decay.

Commentators in this period were much less concerned about the distinction between the separate categories of their subject matter than modern anthropologists might wish. The celebrated 1846 article in the *Athenaeum* which introduced the term 'Folklore' to the English language, described its field of study as 'the manners, customs, observances, superstitions, ballads, proverbs &c., of the olden times'.[15] The common denominators of these artefacts and practices were their orality, their confinement to the culture of the uneducated, and their connection with natural time. William Hone's anthologies of the late 1820s and early 1830s gathered together the work of the pioneer collectors and provided a storehouse for those working on the subject during the remainder of the century. The title page of the first of these, published in 1826, indicated the organising principle of his enterprise: 'The every-Day Book and Table Book or Everlasting Calendar of Popular Amusements, Sports, Pastimes, Ceremonies, Manners, Customs and Events incident to Each of the Three Hundred and Sixty-five Days in Past and Present Times; Forming a Complete History of the Year, Months and Seasons and a Perpetual Key to the Almanack'. Each belief and activity belonged to a part of the calendar, and each would be repeated as the year was renewed. It was a world at once dominated by and outside time, alien to the directional and directed cycles of educated society.

Knowledge

Those who set out to communicate to a more enlightened age the character of supernatural beliefs had first to establish the sheer scope of the phenomenon. 'The people were soaked in superstition', wrote the 'Suffolk Farm Labourer' of his youth. 'Fifty years ago three fourths of them were firm believers in witchcraft.'[16] It was not only that there were relations and neighbours on every hand to confirm and embroider the tales that were told, but that once the existence of paranormal powers was accepted, their influence pervaded every activity, and every feature of the landscape in which it took place. In this world the bizarre was commonplace and daily life suffused with the extraordinary. Magic took form in conversation, and it often appeared as if little else were talked about. In John Sykes' industrial village in the 1860s,

> Frequent discussions were everyday gossip about the powers possessed by some of the neighbours who had an 'evil eye' and who could produce bad luck among others by simply wishing it to occur. Bad omens were plentiful and too serious to go unnoticed. If a big 'humble-bee' bumped against the window, or if the first row of potatoes was slow in coming forward, or if a girl mended her clothes upon her back or if anything occurred out of the ordinary way, all had a meaning for the good or the bad which was sure to follow upon such warnings as they had had.[17]

No event was too trivial to be immune from forces which lay beyond rational explanation, but at the same time no supernatural agency was too remote to be beyond human intervention. In exchange for final control over the circumstances of existence, magic offered limitless opportunities for accounting for past trials and reducing the likelihood of future tribulations.[18] Insights into why a love affair had gone wrong, a cow had died, an illness had been contracted, could assuage the pain and offer the prospect, however illusory, of avoiding a repetition; foreknowledge of misfortune might allow a change of course, or at the very least prepare the mind for the inevitable.

Nothing could have been less passive than the acceptance of the sovereignty of the fates. The belief system demanded an extreme sensitivity to all forms of individual and social conduct, and to all manifestations of animate and inanimate nature. Indeed it was the capacity of the supernatural to invest every tree and field, every bird and animal, with enhanced significance which both repelled the newly literate and pointed the way forward. On the one hand it appeared to dramatise the vulnerability of the ignorant, and particularly their children. The stories told to Henry Snell as he grew up in Nottinghamshire in the 1860s and 1870s turned his neighbourhood into a waking nightmare once the sun had set: 'The slightest noise of unseen bird or beast in those dark lanes filled me with terror, and I imagined that every tree or dark corner sheltered distressed and prowling creatures of the spirit world.'[19] On the other hand it drew attention to the real body of knowledge which lay at the doorstep of the poorest working man. The crime of Snell's upbringing was that he was simultaneously immersed in and repelled from nature: 'I knew every yard of those quiet and beautiful lanes, and I have never forgiven the superstition which made me fear them.'[20]

Now the printed word offered the prospect of establishing a more constructive relationship with the countryside. We have already come across the weaver's son Joseph Gutteridge getting to know the commons around his native Coventry.[21] As a child he was free to wander as far as his legs would carry him, his explorations confined only by the boundaries of the available oral knowledge: 'At the outset of my endeavours to become acquainted with nature, I was beset with difficulties in regard to the common and the technical names of plants and animals. They were beyond me and foreign to my former experiences.'[22] He could not afford the books he wanted, but the gift from his father of an ancient *Culpeper* extended his grasp of the traditional terms for the specimens he collected from the hedgerows and woods, and eventually, during a period of unemployment just after his marriage, he made the breakthrough to the Linnean classification via one of the first attempts to popularise the system in this country:

> Scarcity of work afforded opportunities for pursuing botanical studies. I lived near Hearsall Common, the scene of my child-hood's delightful rambles amongst the wild flowers. Many a stroll I had over it in leisure hours, of which unfortunately there were too many. By this time I had got a smattering of botany, and began after a fashion, as best I could without a tutor, to arrange specimens of flowers by the aid of an original copy of Dr. Withering's work, published in 1776, obtained from an old bookstall.[23]

For Gutteridge, as for the thousands of self-educated artisans who formed botanical and geological societies in the middle decades of the century, the attraction of nature was its new-found order. Where once increased knowledge meant increased caution when dealing with natural phenomena, now, the more they read, the greater the prospect of intellectual control. They could walk out from the workshops and factories in what were still compact industrial towns, and on Summer evenings or on Sundays find themselves in a laboratory whose materials they could never exhaust.[24] The combination of a little book learning and a lot of exercise enabled them to engage in genuine scientific inquiry into their environment. Gutteridge himself went one step further and applied his craftsman's skills to the construction of a small microscope: 'It would be almost impossible to describe the intense pleasure or the valuable instruction received from these examinations of the structure and func-tions of plant life. The wonders unfolded by this instrument enabled me to form more rational conclusions as to cause and effect.'[25]

Such pursuits were the cause of private satisfaction, but they also had an impact on the communities in which these naturalists resided. The possibility that new and more powerful secrets of nature were being revealed soon attracted the attention of neighbours whose need for assistance outweighed any suspicions they might have of modern science.

Once his expertise as a botanist became known, Gutteridge found himself cast in the role of unofficial, and in his case, unpaid doctor:

> It became a necessity therefore, especially in regard to the mixture of powerful and active substances used in medicine, to keep a fair supply of books of reference upon these subjects. I did not feel at liberty to use this knowledge as a means of profit, though great demands were made upon it by sufferers amongst our friends and neighbours. It was a source of pleasure to be able, by relieving pain and suffering, and sometimes even curing deep-rooted diseases, to earn the gratitude of those benefited.[26]

Pain and suffering were never far from the door of any working-class household. At every moment the fragile balance of the family economy was threatened by the prospect of the illness of a parent or a child. Here the forces of nature were at their most malign and unpredictable. Whilst the practices gathered together by the folklorists under the heading of superstitions covered all the uncertainties of existence, those purporting to avoid, relieve or explain ill-health were the most numerous and widely held. 'We were intensely superstitious', recalled the seaman's daughter Rose Gamble, 'and it is hardly surprising that much of the nonsense in which we unquestionably believed was concerned with sickness, dying, death, misfortune and downright disaster.'[27] The cures associated, with, for instance, whooping cough, one of the major diseases of childhood throughout the period, included passing the afflicted child three times before breakfast under a forked blackberry bush, or nine times under the belly and over the back of a three year-old donkey, or under a piebald horse, dipping it nine times in a south-running stream, carrying it through the smoke of a brick kiln, along a different road every day, or into a field where the sheep had been lying, asking the advice of the rider of a piebald horse, giving the child porridge made over a south-running stream, bread baked by a woman who had retained her surname at marriage, or a drop of communion wine from a Romish priest, putting the head of a frog, a toad, or a live trout in the sufferer's mouth, and having the child wear a necklace of elder twigs, a string with nine knots, a caterpillar in a bag, a spider in a nutshell, an amulet of hair from the cross on a donkey's back, a godmother's stay lace, or a godfather's garter, or three yards of black ribbon which had been passed three times through the body of a live frog.[28]

Everything was attempted, and in the case of whooping cough as in many others, nothing can have worked. The afflicted and those who cared for them were trapped between the hope that at least some of the tales of successful cures in circulation were true and the knowledge that nothing was certain to be effective. The more a disease resisted a remedy, the more desperate became the search for alternatives, some of which only came to light at inquests into those whose families had refused to give up trying. 'One was a girl in Somersetshire', reported an article on 'Popular Superstitions' in 1851, 'who was taken out in the last stages of consumption on a moonlight night, and passed three times over the back of a donkey at a point when four roads meet. She died on the way back.'[29] To outsiders, such credulity was at best an obstacle to proper health care, and at worst directly responsible for the relentlessly high infant and adult mortality rates. This was the view of the adult educator James Hole: 'Want of better objects of pursuit, and utter ignorance of themselves and of the natural laws – these are the causes which above all others produce the mass of disease and demoralisation witnessed in our large towns.'[30] In the event, however, the encounter between mass literacy and the 'natural laws' of ill-health was to prove more complex and less satisfactory than had been anticipated.

At the outset there was a limit on how much could be achieved by the self-educated naturalists. In the northern industrial towns the isolated initiatives of men like Gutteridge were for a time transformed into a network of medical botanists who formed societies to encourage the pursuit and application of herbal remedies. They sought to use the new possibilities of mutual learning to reinforce the old traditions of mutual caring. Through empirical inquiry they could prevent the mystification of the economy of nature by either inherited superstition or the manufactured obscurantism of the medical profession.[31] In the words of *The Working Man's Model Family Botanic Guide*, the most rational approach was to assist 'nature to overcome diseases by giving the remedies which act in harmony with the eternal laws'.[32] It was now possible, claimed A. I. Coffin's *Botanic Guide to Health*, for everyone to 'become acquainted with the nature of his own constitution', but instead, 'in the midst of these advantages, selfishness steps in and proclaims abroad that none – save the DIPLOMATED – are competent to cure the sick, or administer to the afflicted, when every day's history proves the folly of such a vain and egotistical policy'.[33]

Yet in the 1860s, the movement was losing its momentum. Where it had derived its strength from the freedom of working people to explore their locality, so further progress was impeded by local discrimination against the acquisition and use of knowledge. Inadequate schooling made it extremely difficult to proceed beyond elementary levels of inquiry. Once the old grammar schools had closed their doors to the gifted sons of the local labouring population, the chances of a poor man's child gaining a knowledge of Latin upon which new systems of botanical classification were based were remote. The sense of isolation was compounded by the behaviour of the proliferating societies of middle-class enthusiasts, who kept their distance from those who had to return to the plough or the factory bench after a field-trip.[34] Behind and beyond the discrimination lay the basic obstacle of poverty. Gutteridge, ironically, had to sell his entire collection of specimens at one stage because of the expenses and loss of earnings caused by the illness and subsequent death of his wife.[35] Although collective endeavour could help to reduce the problems caused by the constant shortage of time and money, it remained extremely difficult to build a coherent body of medical knowledge on the foundations of chance purchases from second-hand bookstalls and intermittent forays into the surrounding countryside.

For those whom the medical botanists sought to treat, there was now the alternative of the medical profession itself, whose identity and power was transformed in this period. Although the development of the institutional status of doctors has been well documented,[36] we still know much too little about the actual impact of the new race of general practitioners on the daily lives of the mass of the population. There were three routes which a doctor might take to the door of a working-class household. From the mid eighteenth century, parishes had begun to employ medical officers to attend to the needs of the indigent sick,[37] and in 1834 these uncoordinated but often effective initiatives were translated into a country-wide system in which the new Poor Law Unions were divided into districts for the purpose of hiring a doctor to work under the direction of the relieving officer.[38] As elsewhere in the New Poor Law, bureaucratic order was gained in exchange for the quality of assistance. The range of services the doctors could provide was narrowed, they had too many patients spread over too large an area, they were under-paid and resented lay control, and those they treated in hospitals were until 1885 disenfranchised as paupers.[39] However, they were at least a presence in every district, if not in every home, their numbers rising from 2,300 in 1842 to 5,000 in the mid 1880s, and their acquisition in 1840 of the responsibility for administering smallpox vaccinations, which became compulsory in 1853, ensured that few families can have escaped contact with a doctor at some stage in their cycle.[40]

Alongside and in reaction to the New Poor Law, the more prosperous sections of the working class made their own arrangements for medical assistance. During the second half of the nineteenth century, the services of the 'club doctor' became a standard benefit of the friendly societies.[41] Again there were frequent tensions between the practitioners and those who employed them, with the patients in the form of society members much more likely than the paupers to complain about shortcomings in treatment.[42] At its best, however, the system could make a major impact on the availability of health care, as was the case with Henry Snell's lodge of the Ancient Order of Foresters:

the benefits of 'the club', even though small in amount, gave real consolation, for the services of the doctor with ten shillings per week during sickness together with the assurance that in the case of death there would be ten pounds available for expenses, gave to the labourer and his wife some touch of that peace that passeth bourgeois understanding ... The doctor was the neighbour and friend of everybody; he called every man by his Christian name and enjoying the full confidence of his patients, he served them with skill and cheerful devotion.[43]

By the end of the period about half the country's doctors were engaged in some form of contract medicine.[44] The accessibility of private treatment is more difficult to measure; however, the evidence of those who left accounts of ill-health suggests that it could extend to the less prosperous sections of the community. Such doctors were often remote, both socially and geographically, and expensive, with fees for poor patients settling down to 2/6d to 5s a visit in the second half of the nineteenth century, to which had to be added the cost of medicine, which could far exceed the initial diagnosis, and the associated dislocation of the family economy. Nonetheless parents, for instance, desperate that this time a child should not die, would contemplate the sacrifice. James Bowd, the son of a Cambridgeshire farm labourer, owed his introduction to literature to the gift of a

> new Halfpenney or Penney Book as a distraction from the application of leeches by a doctor who was treating him for scarlet fever and swellings in his throat and on his knee. The leeches proved a failure, 'And now my Father's and Mother's patience with the Doctor had come to an end and they have to seek advice Somewere Els. My father was working for Mr Dodson Gentleman of Swavesey he kindly lent my father a horse and cart. My father and Mother took me to Cambridge to a Doctor Zachery and when he saw me he said they must not set their Affections on this Child. He ordred me to be put in a hot Bath morning and night and I was to take my Medicine while I was in the Bath.'[45]

Bowd was fortunate in his parents, as his father was fortunate in his employer, but it is of interest that as early as 1830, such a family would know where to find not one but two doctors, and have the confidence to dismiss the first and look for a better. By mid century the doctor was becoming as familiar an element in the community's stock of resources as the schoolmaster,[46] but whereas the trained teachers were soon to drive their unqualified competitors from the field, the medical profession was to face a longer and less conclusive campaign against its rivals. At the heart of their difficulty was the basic fact that apart from smallpox, doctors were still incapable of curing or specifically preventing the major diseases, and with few exceptions were to remain so until the First World War.[47] It was only the strength of Bowd's constitution that enabled him to survive not just his afflictions but also lancing, leeches and a medicine so fierce that it burnt a hole in his shirt when some was spilled. Scarlet fever was still killing 4,000 children a year in the 1890s; an antitoxic serum against diphtheria was introduced in 1894,[48] but there was no proven remedy for whooping cough, measles, tuberculosis or sexually transmitted diseases. The major scientific advances were largely confined to diagnosis, relief of symptoms and isolation of victims. Instead of dispelling the mists of ignorance, the rise of the medical profession added one more layer to the mass of claim and counter-claim which had always faced the sick and their relatives.

In such conditions, the consequences of mass literacy were fraught with ambiguity. It was not just that confining ever larger numbers of children for ever longer periods of their lives created reservoirs of infection, putting health and education in direct conflict in times of local epidemics.[49] Rather the basic functions of reading and writing, the codification of information and its transmission over time and distance, were at least as attractive to the supposed enemies of scientific medicine as to its increasingly self-confident proponents. By the mid eighteenth century, the production of proprietary medicines had become one of the most advanced and profit-able sectors of the burgeoning market economy. It depended upon enterprising capitalists, the development of standardised, large-scale manufacture, and, above all, on the growth of mass communication. If the inventor of a new cure was to compete successfully with orally transmitted remedies for a particular ailment, he had first to establish a more authoritative claim for the validity of his preparation, then he had to find a means of extending his market beyond the local speech community, and finally he had to create a system of distribution. None of this was possible without advertisements, and without the newspapers and periodicals which carried them.[50] Paragraphs extolling the virtues of branded medi-cines and giving instructions on how to obtain them were as much a part of the eighteenth-century press as the supposedly factual information it published.[51] Neither inherited wisdom nor medical science could establish a basis for contradicting the ever-more elaborate and strident claims of the advertisers, who from the beginning made extensive use of testimonials from satisfied customers. And as the metropolitan and provincial news-papers expanded into their hinterland, the medicines went with them, opening up regional or even national markets. In turn the publishers not only reaped the benefit of the advertising revenue but themselves engaged directly in the trade, handling the distribution and often the manufacture as well.

During the eighteenth century there was no clear division between doctors and medical entrepreneurs. All operated in a market place in which public confidence rather than paper qualification was the controlling force.[52] Although reputable practitioners waged war on the more obvious frauds in their trade, they were quite prepared to exploit the latest commercial techniques to promote themselves and any therapeutic discoveries they claimed to have made.[53] However, the further elaboration of the print culture during the remainder of the period created new lines of demarcation. The doctors sought to achieve the security and status of a profession on the basis of a written examination of book learning. The Medical Registration Act of 1858 was designed to create an impermeable barrier between the trained, certificated, disinterested practitioner and the self-taught amateur wise-woman or the self-promoting vendor of unproven remedies.[54] Those not on the register of the General Medical Council who still claimed that they could cure the sick were now isolated from the professional doctor,[55] although the Act stopped short of sanctioning their prosecution. At the same time the manufacturers of proprietary medicines seized with both hands the opportunities created by the dramatic increase in the channels of communication. The flood of national and provincial newspapers, and of periodicals associated with every cause and interest, bore along and was in turn sustained by advertisements from a new generation of entrepreneurs.[56] As early as the 1850s, 'Professor' Holloway, who was to make a million out of his pills, was spending £30,000 a year on his products: 'it does indeed seem incredible', observed the *Quarterly Review*, 'that one house should expend upon the advertising of quack pills and ointment a sum equal to the entire revenue of many a German principality'.[57]

The 1875 Sale of Food and Drugs Act gave a further boost to the larger capitalists in the trade by exempting from its provisions those who could gain a patent for their preparations, and by the end of the period it was calculated that the cost of promoting proprietary cures was running at two million pounds a year.[58] Many of the advertisements relied upon the facilities of the Penny Post, whose potential had been exploited from its inception. Mail order was used on an increasing scale, particularly after the introduction of the sample post in 1863, with stamps used as currency for purchases. 'Love Lozenges', ran an advertisement in *Reynolds' News*, 'certain in effect. Post free. 10 stamps. Extra strong 15 stamps.'[59] An official inquiry in 1910 found that the unlicensed rivals of the professional doctors were just as dependent on the use of paper: 'unqualified practice increases in large centres of population, attracting dwellers in the smaller urban and the rural districts. This is assisted by the ready means of access to the towns which now exist, by the extensive advertising in newspapers and magazines which brings quackery of all kinds under the direct notice of all classes; and by the facilities, extensively used, of obtaining advice and medicine through the post.'[60] Mailing lists were bought and sold, with those for consumptives fetching the highest price, testimonials were garnered or invented, doctors were bombarded with leaflets and invited to participate in 'trials' for new products, sufferers were sent 'free' books, leaflets and 'symptom forms' which all advocated the purchase of expensive products, and at the bottom end of the market, fears about the abuse of the secrecy of postal communication were realised by the sellers of abortifacients and cures for venereal diseases who followed up replies to advertisements with blackmailing letters.[61]

This dual exploitation of the printed word constantly threatened the assumed dichotomy between educated and folk responses to physical disorders. In the free medical market of the eighteenth century, fashionable medications enjoyed the patronage of the highest levels of society, and the subsequent development of scientific medicine and the growing institutional opposition failed to overcome the appeal to those who should know better of every sort of preparation for every sort of ailment. Faced on the one hand by increasingly sophisticated marketing and packaging, and on the other by pain and fear of death which no amount of professionalisation could yet answer, those who had long ago emancipated themselves from magic turned to cures which defied rational explanation.[62] Even the less chronically sick remained, in the view of the BMA, distressingly gullible:

> It is not, however, only the poorer classes of the community who have a weakness for secret remedies and the ministration of quacks; the well-to-do and the highly-placed will often, when not very ill, take a curious pleasure in experimenting with mysterious compounds. In them it is perhaps to be traced to a hankering to break safely with orthodoxy; they scrupulously obey the law and the Church and Mrs. Grundy, but will have their fling against medicine.[63]

The doctors themselves had to bear some responsibility for their failure to make more headway against their opponents. Committed to instilling an instinctive deference amongst their 'patients', they found the sick displaying a similar disinclination to interrogate the advertisers. Engaged in the process of classifying ill-health and establishing more intricate connections between symptoms and diseases, they played straight into the hands of the entrepreneurs whose trade had long thrived on inventing fresh ailments and associating new fears with old complaints. Employed in dividing the profession into specialisms, they found their unqualified rivals equally prepared to give themselves new titles, such as 'Pile Specialist', 'Sight Specialist', 'Disease Specialist', or even, when invention failed completely, just 'Specialist'.[64] But above all, the separation between commerce and service proved easier to prescribe than sustain. Their campaign against 'quack medicines' reached its climax with the publication in 1909 of *Secret Remedies*, in which a variety of preparations were subjected to chemical analysis and found to range from the ineffectual to the lethal.[65] However, the purity of the BMA's cause was compromised at the subsequent Select Committee on Patent Medicines when it was pointed out that the *British Medical Journal* was still advertising some of the concoctions it had exposed, that many testimonials for proprietary cures had been solicited from doctors, sometimes for a fee, and that qualified practitioners were still prescribing on a large scale branded drugs of whose constituents they were entirely ignorant.[66] It was all very well for the doctors to respond that their training enabled them to make a privileged reading of the contents of medical advertisements and the labels on the bottles of pills; in the event they lacked sufficient ethical and scientific certainty to insulate them from the capitalists and quacks.

If there was confusion amongst the educated, those who lacked the benefit of any learning beyond the three Rs could not be expected to reconcile the conflicts. Where once they had read and earned too little to be reached by the advertisements, now they were exposed to the full force of commercial medicine. The newspapers they read, which often had difficulty in attracting revenue from reputable manufacturers, could ill afford to discriminate between those who were prepared to buy space in their pages.[67] To judge from the advertisements in the *Northern Star*, Chartists were as much concerned with alternative medicine as radical politics, and the Sunday papers, which became the principal source of news for the next generation, were packed with insertions from the vendors of every type of preparation, as were the penny almanacs and the covers of penny fiction.[68] By 1912 it was estimated that over thirty-one million items of the cheapest patent medicines, in addition to those which evaded excise, were being sold annually.[69] Already under increasing pressure from the medical profession, transmitted wisdom stood little chance in the face of such competition.[70] 'Domestic remedies', observed the *British Medical Journal* in 1911, 'are ... being driven out of the home by the array of advertised remedies.'[71] Parents of children with whooping cough could now buy Crosby's Balsamic Cough Elixir, Dr B. Assman's Whooping Cough Remedy, Tussothym, Veno's Lightning Cough Cure, or the Carbolic Smoke Ball. Attractively packaged, offering certain and speedy cures, bearing testimonials, in the case of the Carbolic Smoke Ball, from both a clergyman and a doctor,[72] they outbid at every level the opaque, laboured, outworn remedies handed down from generation to generation.

The consequence was the displacement of one form of incoherence by another. The traditional responses to ill-health had lacked nothing in variety. The stock-in-trade of the 'King of the Norfolk Poachers" grandmother, who was 'a bit of a quack Doctor ... the People used to come to her with all there ills', ranged from possibly effective herbal recipes to harmless devices such as wearing the toe of a pig as a charm against rheumatism, to gruesome rituals such as placing the hand of a corpse on a bleeding tumour in the hope that both would wither together.[73] But rather than building on the potentially therapeutic elements of folk medicine, whether physiological or psychological,[74] and discarding the remainder, the new print culture destroyed confidence in the entire structure. 'There was a lot more sense in some of my old Grandmother's cures', observed the poacher, 'but of corse people dont hold by them in the same way as they did now they have lerned the ways of the World and got more Education.'[75]

The newly literate were faced with a fresh species of medical pluralism, in which they moved back and forth between trained but often ineffective doctors and enticing but frequently useless proprietary drugs. They had even less basis than before for making a secure judgment between the various alternatives, certain only that ill-health was a constant threat to which no agency or institution could provide an adequate response. Where once they could engage with unofficial practitioners in their midst as social equals, if often distant and intimidating, now they faced the professional doctors and the capitalist pill-makers in an essentially subordinate role. The Enquiry of 1910 found that in 'the Rural Districts', 'old women, who are sometimes known as "wise women", still do a certain amount of medical and surgical practice', but concluded that 'This class of practice appears to be diminishing in quantity.'[76] In the towns the herbalists who in some respects were the heirs of the medical botanists were now as dependent as the vendors of abortifacients and venereal disease cures on the use of advertisements and mail order.[77] Their work was now a branch of commercial rather than democratic epistemology. Only the impressive if limited venture of the club doctors, which was fatally undermined by the 1911 National Insurance Act, offered the prospect of creating a health service at least nominally under the control of the patients.

Elsewhere the intensely interventionist world of 'superstitious' cures found a mocking echo in the consumer's notional freedom to pick and choose amongst the endlessly over-sold proprietary remedies. 'Beecham's Pills' were indeed 'Magic'. Those which were merely commercialised versions of genuine prescriptions may have done some good, and others may have exercised a temporary placebo effect, but in general they offered false hopes in return for real cash. Every prospect of relief, however bogus, was matched by newly manufactured fears, as commonplace ailments of manual labourers such as backache were connected through spurious science to serious diseases such as kidney failure. Almost all the genuine improvements in working-class health in this period can be attributed to marginal shifts in prosperity, leading to better diet, clothing and housing.[78] As far as getting 'more Education' was concerned, it may well be that by the end of the period, as a direct result of mass literacy, more of the emotional and financial resources of the poor were being diverted into ineffective remedies for sickness than ever before.

Authority

The future temperance advocate Thomas Whittaker grew up in a succession of northern mill towns, but his parents had originally worked on the land, and still retained much of the oral tradition of their background. He well remembered whilst living in Preston in the late 1820s how the family would sit 'around the cheerful hearth', 'while my mother, as was her wont, would be rehearsing to us some of her early histories, and relating those thrilling stories of Lancashire witches in which she was a strong believer'.[79] Both the sources and the substance of this knowledge were personal. The information was derived from and validated by individual members of the older generation, and the supernatural forces it described were embodied in identifiable figures in specific neighbourhoods.[80] As elsewhere in the working-class community, there was a specialisation of function when it came to magic. Parents knew more than children and less than grandparents, and whilst everyone was capable of making some effort to exploit or ward off its influence, there were those who claimed or were attributed particular powers in this field.

Witches had been officially deleted from the belief system of polite society by the abolition in 1736 of the crime of 'Witchcraft, Sorcery, Inchantment or Conjuration'.[81] Thereafter it was not the witches but their supposed victims who were assumed to be guilty of irrational behaviour, and the law intervened only when ill-feeling escalated into assault or even murder. The women thus slandered or mistreated were observed with sympathetic distaste by the magistrates, clergymen and folklore collectors who came upon them. 'A WITCH', explained Francis Grose, 'is almost universally a poor, decrepit, superannuated, old woman.'[82] However, if this attitude was increasingly shared by the self-consciously progressive elements amongst the labouring population, there is evidence that the phenomenon retained a hold late into the nineteenth century. The old and the eccentric remained obvious targets for resentment at misfortunes which were themselves genuine enough. 'People in these times have no idea of the superstition then prevailing, even amongst the better-class villagers', wrote George Sanger of the third quarter of the century:

> Witches and warlocks were very real beings to many of them, and Satan was supposed to take an active personal interest in the business of blighting crops, spoiling the brews of beer or cider, turning milk sour, laming and killing cattle, and various other misdeeds credited to unfortunate persons whose outward marks of evil were all too often only age, poverty, and lonely wretchedness.[83]

It is possible that some of these 'unfortunate persons' may have incited trouble by trading on the propensity to personalise the causes of disease and disaster, but for the most part they suffered as a consequence of the continuing shortcomings of medical and veterinary science and the endless capacity for neighbourly animosities in the still confined rural communities.[84]

Lacking the support of the law, or of the Church, which had no wish to give implicit endorsement to the existence of witchcraft by acting against it, those in fear of the malevolent possessors of magical powers had recourse only to the more benign carriers in the form of 'wise' or 'cunning' men and women. These figures, however, were more than merely the mirror image of the increasingly marginalised practitioners of the black arts.[85] They exercised a broader range of functions, and the more successful could translate the demand for their services into a decent livelihood. The occasional prosecution for fraud served only to highlight the scale of their activities, as in this trial in Kent in about 1850:

> The defendant, who had the appearance of an agricultural labourer, resided at Rolvenden, where he enjoyed the reputation of being 'a cunning man', able to cure diseases, to explain dreams, to foretell events, to tell fortunes, and to recover lost property. He was resorted to as a wizard by the people for miles around, principally by the ignorant, but also by parties who might have been expected to know better; and for many years had made a good harvest from their credulity.[86]

'Dr Cotton', as he was known, was nothing if not cunning in his willingness to bridge gaps in explanation and knowledge across so wide a field of experience. Such practitioners were by turn astrologers, exorcists, matchmakers, herbalists, psychiatrists, detectives and marriage guidance counsellors, operating wherever science and religion would not or could not provide an answer to an urgent problem.[87] Whereas witchcraft could survive only in isolated neighbourhoods, wise men and women flourished in much larger constituencies, and were not restricted to backward rural areas. 'There is scarcely a town of any magnitude in Lancashire', observed Harland and Wilkinson in 1882, 'or in one or two adjacent counties, which does not possess its local "fortune-teller" or pretender to a knowledge of astrology, and to a power of predicting the future events of life, under the talismanic name of "fortune", to a large and credulous number of applicants.'[88]

As individuals, the witches and wise men and women excited varying degrees of compassion, curiosity and contempt amongst outside observers. The real problem was the state of mind of those prepared to persecute or patronise uneducated members of their community who were believed to be in touch with supernatural forces. Their persistent 'credulity' presented a double challenge to enlightened authority. The traditional deference to the older generation and their oral wisdom had to be broken, and then replaced by a respect for those who through their training and commitment had a proper grasp of the possibilities and limitations of controlling natural forces. Whilst all those who came into contact with the labouring population might play a part in this process, the Churches clearly had a pre-eminent responsibility. It was not just that revealed religion was the only sure guide to metaphysical belief, but also that its potential for organisational endeavour far outstripped any other private or official agency. At the outset the ingrained propensity of the uneducated to derive knowledge from personal rather than abstract sources had to be met on its own terms. Working from opposite doctrinal positions, the Evangelicals and the Oxford Movement combined in the 1830s to launch a belated but energetic response to the remorselessly increasing population, the numbers of clergy rising from 14,613 in 1841 to 19,336 in 1861 and reaching 25,363 by the end of the century.[89] In relation to their predecessors, these men were younger, better trained, more likely to be found working in parishes, and more committed to bringing the gospel into the homes of their flock. On either side, the Catholic and Nonconformist Churches kept pace, and as late as 1881 there was on average one paid minister of religion for every 146 households in England and Wales.[90]

However, personal contact was no longer enough. It was now realised that the process of cultural transmission was too complex and began too early to be controlled by a weekly sermon and an occasional home visit, always supposing the family came to church and let the minister into the house. More than any other organisation in the period, the Churches seized upon mass literacy as a means of realising their objectives. As we saw in chapter 3, the provision of elementary education was seen as the most powerful device for reshaping the domestic curriculum which formed the knowledge and the values of the rising generation. With the bureaucracies of the National and the British and Foreign Schools

Societies behind them, the newly recruited ministers forged a weapon for intervening in the family on an unprecedented scale. In and beyond the classroom, the labouring population needed assistance in the practice of their skills. 'In order that the ability to read may prove an unquestionable privilege', stated the Religious Tract Society at its foundation in 1799, 'we must not fail to inculcate upon all who share it the importance of selecting good materials; we must *provide* materials by bringing into view those which exist, and by stirring up the ingenious to produce more.'[91] Print is a commodity, and like shirts or nails or tea cups, those who could concentrate the most capital on its production and establish the most efficient channels for distribution were best placed to exploit the growth in demand.

The Churches had a long and successful history of mass marketing in the field of literature. An indication of the cumulative effort of the SPCK and other bodies during the eighteenth and early nineteenth centuries is to be found in the surveys of book ownership carried out by various statistical societies during the growth of Chartism.[92] Not only was possession surprisingly widespread given the prevailing levels of literacy, with usually at least 70 per cent of households, whether urban or rural, containing some literature, but a high proportion of this material was spiritual. In Bristol, scene of the worst riots in the recent Reform Bill crisis, 57 per cent of 5,981 families had religious books; in West Bromwich 85 per cent of 2,193 families owned bibles; in Hull 75 per cent of 5,000 homes had bibles or testaments; in the parish of St George's Hanover Square, London, of 1,465 families crammed into 690 houses, 89 per cent had either a bible, testament or prayer book and 68 per cent had all three; only twelve out of 209 families of the agricultural parish of Eversholt in Bedfordshire lacked a religious book of any sort.[93] But the rising tide of political unrest indicated that merely ensuring that the bulk of the population had access to the central texts was not sufficient, as the study of the 1838 Battle of Bossenden Wood concluded.[94] 'But though the judgment is thus rendered inactive', explained the investigator, 'the imagination in such cases is often morbidly alive to impressions from every unusual object. Hence a people so circumstanced are more open to superstition than others.'[95] To combat the 'credulous ignorance', which sustained equally an extensive belief in witchcraft and 'envious' and 'vindictive' feelings towards the rich,[96] the scope and the volume of the literature aimed at the poor had to be broadened, and its language simplified. In response to the Reform Bill crisis, the SPCK had instituted a General Literature Committee in 1832 and a Tract Committee in 1834,[97] and together with the Religious Tract Society now engaged in a programme of publication which in its scale and its variety was matched only by the great broadside and penny dreadful entrepreneurs like Catnach and

Lloyd,[98] whose techniques the Societies deliberately sought to imitate.[99] Between 1840 and 1850 the RTS issued 23,290,301 publications in the British Isles, and by 1850, the SPCK was distributing about four million items a year.[100] The machinery of mass communication could provide a means of extending the authority of the minister far beyond the pulpit. 'In 1852', reported a survey of 'the Literature of the Working Classes',

> a penny miscellany, with one or more superior wood engravings containing sixteen well-filled pages of letter-press, giving valuable information to all, but especially the working classes, in language correct, refined and lucid, was issued by the Religious Tract Society, entitled the *Leisure Hour*. Truly 'wisdom crieth without; she uttereth her voice in the streets'.[101]

The primer and the pamphlet now replaced the shepherd's crook as the most appropriate symbols of the pastor's care of his flock. Yet in the realm of the supernatural, the men of God had no monopoly of the tools of literacy. Those whom mass education was supposed to put out of business proved adept at exploiting the opportunities created by the schoolmasters. As communications improved, wise men and women were able to extend the scope of their operations, and where their reputation extended beyond an easy walking distance, they, like so many other entrepreneurs of the period, could make use of the Penny Post. When the cunning man of Rolvenden was arrested, 'Letters were found upon him, soliciting his magical aid.'[102] And as in other situations, those who could not write sought the help of those who could. In 1875 a 'public official' of Oakengates was asked to assist an old man whose wife and grand-daughters were ill: 'he believed they were suffering from some witchcraft, and he wanted a letter written to a Mrs P— of Wellington, who was a wise and good woman, to ask her to put a stop to it. He said he had a pig, and he was afraid that would also be bewitched.'[103]

Such personal services could be generalised by the use of print. As in France,[104] there was an established chapbook genre of fortune-tellers and dream-books, which constituted a do-it-yourself resource for those anxious to gain insights into or control over the future. Some of these, such as the numerous versions of *The History of Mother Bunch*, which purported to distil the wisdom of an old wise woman, had been the stock-in-trade of chapmen for centuries; others, such as *Napoleon's Book of Fate*, which circulated widely in the north of England during the middle decades of the nineteenth century,[105] were evidently of more recent derivation. These texts, which were available in the towns as well as the countryside, provided explanations of dreams, ready reckoners controlled by magic cyphers for telling the future, lists of omens and unpropitious dates in the calendar, and instructions for undertaking a variety of important tasks, such as naming a future spouse, and even, as in the case of a Glasgow edition of Napoleon's guide, assessing the veracity of love letters brought by the postman.[106]

The written word not only stored and transmitted knowledge about the supernatural, but was itself an integral element of a wide variety of charms and rituals. *Mother Bunch's Golden Fortune-Teller* recommended that the girl anxious to discover whom she would marry should write the names of three candidates on pieces of paper and 'death' on a fourth, and after she had worn them in her bosom, shaken them in her left shoe, gone to bed backwards and thrown away three without looking, the remaining name would be that of her husband, or if 'death' was left, none of her suitors would succeed.[107] There were alternative formulae involving other wording and different actions, but sooner or later those determined to know the future and who could at least read would have recourse to the most authoritative text in the family's possession, the Bible. Below the level of the educated classes, religion and magic had long been enmeshed in a complex, pluralistic structure of observations and practices.[108] The Devil was too active a presence to be left to a Church which except in the case of the more extreme Protestant sects no longer saw his hand in every moment of the daily round; at the same time he was too strong to be fought without the aid of the rituals and formularies of Christianity.

Religion was seen here not as a solace but as a source of power which irradiated every manifestation of its existence. The buildings were an aid to foretelling the future in the practice of watching the church porch on St Mark's Eve, when apparitions of those who were to marry or be buried in the coming year would be seen; holy water and 'sacrament shillings', and even rainwater collected on Holy Thursday, were efficacious for various diseases, as was ground up stone from a statue fallen from Exeter Cathedral.[109] However, it was appropriate that in a nominally Protestant society, the literature of Christianity was the most commonly exploited for magical purposes.[110] Although it is possible to find accounts of weighing a supposed witch against the big church bible in the early nineteenth century,[111] the texts in general use were those which, as we have seen, had been so successfully distributed to the homes of the labouring poor during the previous century. Everyone owned or could borrow a testament and then subject it to one of the commonest methods of bridging gaps in knowledge, especially in respect of identifying marriage partners or thieves, namely divination by bible and key, in which a bible was suspended by the house key (or sometimes a large pin) inserted at an appropriate chapter, while a succession of names was pronounced, each accompanied by a verse from the chapter, until the bible fell to the ground and the individual was revealed.[112]

Although the passages chosen for these purposes sometimes had a loose relevance to the object of the exercise, it is evident that their power resided in their general association with religion as a source of supernatural authority, or more vaguely still, with print as a force which transcended human agency. As long as some text was intoned, it did not much matter where in the Bible it came from, or on occasions, whether it derived from a religious source at all. Charlotte Burne recorded an instance of the old chapbook *The Life of Guy Earl of Warwick* being substituted for a testament in a bible and key ceremony designed to locate a missing husband.[113] So far from constituting a natural antibody to the pathology of superstition, books were themselves a form of magic, and as such, an uncertain ally to those who wished to eradicate irrational beliefs from the minds of the uneducated. Whilst the middle decades of the nineteenth century appeared to represent the apogee of Protestantism in England, with more clergymen ordained than at any time since the Reformation, with more literature at their disposal since the invention of the printing press, in the event the means adopted to extend the personal control of ministers of religion proved impossible to control.

At the outset there was the threat to theological discipline inherent in the encouragement given to the most humble members of the community to acquire and make active use of the skills of reading and writing. This was a problem experienced most acutely by those sects which relied upon the participation of self-educated lay preachers to disseminate their message. Wesley had sought to reconcile the contradictory forces of intellectual exploration and doctrinal conformity by himself organising the publication of an ever more extensive body of reading matter for his movement. After his death, schisms within Methodism and the continued growth in the transmission and employment of literacy enhanced the prospects of conflict between individual readers and the societies to which they belonged. Participation in Sunday schools, Bible classes and finally the preaching circuit would rest upon and in turn encourage pleasure and confidence in deploying the tools of literacy until the point was reached when the young man began to encounter books and entertain speculations which crossed the often narrow boundaries of his sect's theology. George Edwards, for instance, was in the early 1870s given a post as an 'exhorter' in the local Primitive Methodist circuit whilst still illiterate. However, grasping for the first time the value of the printed word, he persuaded his wife to teach him his letters, and threw himself into the world of books, reading voraciously and becoming an energetic lay preacher until, almost inevitably, he found himself in the front of the Quarterly Meeting of his circuit, charged with heterodox beliefs.[114]

Edwards eventually made his peace with his more cautious brethren, but the prospect that free thought would turn the Christian reader into a freethinker was a real one. Few movements of the period were more heavily dependent on the printed word than the infidels.[115] An initial encounter with the widely circulated classics of deism, such as Paine's *Age of Reason* or Volney's *Ruins of Empires*, was a crucial step in undermining the hegemony of Christian faith, and any subsequent involvement in a secularist organisation would be dominated by reading, writing and debating pamphlets, periodicals and books on or about Christianity and its alternatives. It was by no means inevitable an autodidact would become an unbeliever, but for those who made the journey, it seemed the natural and most complete expression of their commitment to book learning. Henry Snell studied his way out of both the superstitions and the Methodism of his upbringing, and eventually enrolled in the Nottingham branch of the National Secular Society, where he 'read greedily everything that appeared in Bradlaugh's weekly journal, the *National Reformer*, and all the pamphlets, magazines, or books dealing with the modern interpretations of religion I could find'.[116]

Although attempts to limit the reading of those they had educated could cause great disruption to individual congregations, on the whole the tensions were contained, and the fully committed secularists remained a numerically small, if vocal, minority. In the long run the most serious problem was that having taken the decision to utter her voice on the streets, organised religion was at the mercy of the forces which were encountered there. As early as 1861 Mayhew noted that the heyday of the religious tract sellers was passing. There were now about fifty in London, 'but they were at one time far more numerous. When penny books were few and very small, religious tracts were by far the cheapest things in print.'[117] Once the initial advantage of publishing experience and access to capital had been exhausted, the tract societies simply could not keep pace with their commercial rivals. 'The total (annual) issue of immoral publications' was estimated in 1850 at 'twenty-nine millions, being more than the total issues of the Society for Promoting Christian Knowledge, the Religious Tract Society, the British and Foreign Bible Society, the Scottish Bible Society, the Trinitarian Bible Society, and some seventy religious magazines'.[118] The Religious Tract Society reckoned that the publication of 'infidel and licentious works' in London alone was about fifteen times the circulation of all its material in England, and the situation could only worsen.[119] Lacking a genuine market for their material, the operations of the societies were restricted by the gifts and bequests they could attract and the time and goodwill of their largely amateur distributors, whereas the metropolitan and provincial publishers of cheap fiction and, from the mid 1840s onwards, penny Sunday newspapers, were able to take full advantage of the demand created by the elementary schools which the denominations had done so much to sponsor. The new literature threatened to undermine all that had been achieved. 'If the

Sunday newspaper be substituted for the Sunday sermon', complained 'Clericus Londinensis' in 1846, 'what else can we expect, than that the people of England should become a nation of irreligious infidels, or, at best, superstitious Papists?'[120]

The Church organisations fought hard, with the SPCK, for instance, increasing its annual output from 4.5 million in 1857 to 12.5 million by 1897, but it was a losing battle.[121] Not only was the daily reading of the newly literate dominated by cheap fiction, but the Churches' long campaign to defend Sundays from commercial distraction was fatally undermined by the weapons which they had themselves forged. *Reynolds' News*, the *News of the World*, and *Lloyd's Weekly News* ensured that the products of an increasingly universal education system had a vibrant, topical and sensational alternative to the testaments and prayer books of the Sunday services. A survey in 1886 of 'What the Working Classes Read' drew attention to the outcome:

> Years ago, had one walked into almost any poor but respectable man's room in the kingdom, one would probably have found two books at least – the Bible and the *Pilgrim's Progress*. Both were held in extreme veneration. Now it is to be feared that very few working men and women read the *Pilgrim's Progress* and the Bible is far from being what it was – *the* book of the home. For this the propagation of Sunday newspapers is largely to blame. The weary toiler now spends his Sunday afternoons smoking his pipe and digesting the week's record of criminalities.[122]

Whether the spread of Sunday papers was a cause or merely a symptom of the Churches' failure to monopolise the attention of the labouring poor is open to debate. What is clear is that the printed word was compounding rather than resolving the difficulties facing those who wished to extend or preserve the dominion or organised religion. As late as 1901 a standard manual for clergymen was insisting that 'The first thought of every parish priest will turn to his schools ... the work of God cannot really go on without them',[123] yet the increasing secularisation of both the school curriculum and the teaching profession which was traced in chapter 3, together with the use that was likely to be made of the skills taught in the classroom, meant that mass literacy was at the very least generalising and dispersing the influence of the parish priest[124] and, with the possible exceptions of the sects which worked through lay preachers, his Nonconformist counterpart. And inasmuch as the alternative sources of information about the supernatural had also attempted to exploit new means of communication, so they too suffered a displacement by their own literary props. The mass production of penny do-it-yourself fortune tellers and the assumption by the magazines and newspapers of the role of problem solvers to their readers[125] saved the newly literate from the embarrassment and expense of laying their difficulties before the familiar but strange figures of the wise men and women. The most commonplace concern about the future, the weather, was answered by the appearance of scientific forecasts in the Sunday papers of the 1880s, and in the 1890s *Reynolds' News* began to respond to one of the deepest anxieties of the labouring poor by running a 'Missing relatives and friends' column. Rather than shifting the balance of power from the traditional sources of knowledge in the oral tradition – the old and the wise – to the representatives of the revived and restaffed churches, universal literacy had the long-term effect of depersonalising both forms of authority. Although, as the examination of schooling indicated, parents retained far more influence over their children's upbringing and future than had once seemed likely, there had been a loss, especially by mothers and by older women generally.[126] As John Demos has argued, belief in witches reflected a deep respect for the power of women, and the decline in persecution was in part a consequence of the general loss of status of the female sex in the print culture.[127] It is perhaps no accident that the only Nonconformist sect seriously to entertain the reality of witches in the early nineteenth century, the Primitive Methodists, was also the only one to give genuine responsibility to its women members, and as witchcraft was later expelled from its theology, so the ranks of lay preachers became a predominantly male preserve.[128] Increasingly individuals were respected not because of their privileged access to information whose ultimate forms were oral – in the beginning was The Word, or the words of earlier generations – but because of their access to wider bodies of printed secular knowledge.[129] Whilst traditional modes of storing and transmitting collective wisdom such as proverbs survived long after their expulsion from polite culture, they and those who remembered them were losing their ascendancy.[130] Those who declined to read themselves were turning to a growing variety of individuals who did. These might include a clergyman or a schoolteacher, but they were in competition with trade unionists, doctors, local councillors, magistrates, shopkeepers and autodidacts of every sort, any of whom might find themselves asked for advice on subjects only distantly related to their nominal specialism. No one person, no representative of a single institution, could any longer be expected to command a monopoly of wisdom.

Time

The challenge to established forms of wisdom about natural and supernatural forces raised at every point questions about the use of time by the labouring poor. The cultural function of time is contingent upon the way in which it is measured and recorded. In the absence of the widespread use of literacy, the passage of the seasons and of the years was specific to the life of the community, and only loosely connected to the progressive chronology of educated society. The oral mode of preserving information about the past required no dates, and no agency external to those to whom the past belonged. Time was given shape and substance through the essentially social processes of conversation, ritual and festival, and in turn individual experiences were linked to each other and to those of earlier generations through participation in the events of the calendar. 'Before writing was deeply interiorized by print', W. J. Ong argues, 'people did not feel themselves situated every moment of their lives in abstract computed time of any sort.'[131] At the heart of the attack on superstitious modes of thinking and behaving was the desire to generate a far more precise and disciplined atttitude towards time. The minutes and hours of the day were to be saved and used to greater advantage, and the cycles of the year were to be placed in the context of a more ordered, formal and public notation of history.[132]

John Clare was one of the very few collectors of ballads and customs of the period who still lived in the world to which his material belonged.[133] His was a view from the inside; the crisis of the oral tradition was for him no antiquarian curiosity, but central to his identity as a labouring man and as a poet. He responded to the transformation of his culture partly by making a formal record of the songs and practices which were threatened with extinction, and partly by attempting to measure the scale and consequences of change through his own poetry. His deep sense of the interconnection between work, time and the oral tradition found its most complete form in *The Shepherd's Calendar*, first published in 1827, in which he traced the annual round not just of the shepherd but of an entire labouring community. It was a way of life in which time was essentially local. The working day moved to a rhythm controlled partly by the organisation of labour, partly by the forms of production appropriate to the Peterborough fens, and partly by the seasons and the weather. Time was integrated with rather than imposed upon work. Just as the daily tasks were adjusted to the cycle of agriculture in the area, so too the measurement of time was private to the parish. Clare's survey took in the parish clerk, whose responsibilities included the church clock:

> And the knowing parish clerk
> Feign to do his jobs ere dark
> Hath timd the church clock to the sun
> And wound it up for night and done.[134]

In the 1820s this was still the only means of establishing official time in Helpston or in any other locality. For the farmers and their labourers it was neither desirable nor possible to subordinate their time to a national standard. However, those engaged in the growing system of mass communication were already at odds with the sun, and within a few decades the twin forces of transport and the post were to bring to an end this most accurate yet most unscientific mode of setting the clock.

The revolution had been set in motion in 1784 with the introduction of the post coaches which ran at measured speeds to a published timetable, and to reduce the problems caused by local time, especially when travelling on an east–west axis, carried their own locked clocks.[135] Much more was required, however, by the mutually supportive innovations of the railways and the Penny Post. The ever more elaborate timetables, and the ever more complex system of collecting and distributing mail, were threatened with chaos by the absence of a single time-band. The introduction in 1837 of the electric telegraph, whereby the exact minute could be transmitted over long distance, enabled the railway companies and the General Post Office to launch a programme of standardisation. By 1847 most of the railway network had been converted to Greenwich Mean Time,[136] and every post office was synchronising its clocks ten years later.[137] The eventual passage in 1880 of the Definition of Time Act[138] merely recognised an accomplished fact. Every parish possessing either a station, which included Helpston, now bisected by the main line to the North-East, or a regular collection and distribution of letters, and almost all were inside the system by 1864,[139] now had to keep step with the clock at Greenwich. Communication over distance could not tolerate private time.

Whilst the transition from local to national time implied the breakdown of barriers between communities, in another sense it foreshadowed new divisions. The more formal notation threatened to widen the distance between the present and the past of the labouring poor, and between the separate categories of activity in the daily round. The first prospect surfaced in a concern that with the erosion of oral means of measuring the passage of time, the central mechanism for connecting one generation with another would become increasingly unreliable. 'One used to hear it seriously argued', recalled W. E. Adams, who as a compositor and journalist had devoted his working life to the new technology of communication, 'that people who were not educated had better memories ... than those who were.'[140] Men and women who relied not on conversation but on reading for establishing the dimensions of the world into which they had been born would gradually lose the art of retaining in their heads extensive bodies of knowledge. They would come to rely on the crutch of print, and would be helpless without it. Clare was acutely conscious of the problem as he collected songs and stories from his neighbours, 'whose memorys never faild',[141] and translated them into prose and poetry which all too often was never read. He confronted the issue in his 'Essay on Popularity in Authorship' of 1825: 'Superstition lives longer than books; it is engrafted on the human mind till it becomes part of its existence; and is carried from generation to generation on the streams of eternity, with the proudest of fames, untroubled with the insect encroachments of oblivion which books are infested with.'[142]

The claim for the natural superiority of oral modes of recall has itself survived over time, and become the subject of extensive research which has concluded that there is no inherent difference in the capacity for recollection displayed by literate and illiterate.[143] Rather there takes place a shift from formulaic to verbatim memorisation, which alters both the process of storing information and the criteria for measuring the accuracy of reproduction. Thus in nineteenth-century England, the seemingly limitless memories of those who did not possess or never used the tools of literacy can be contrasted with the feats of men like the shoemaker Thomas Cooper, who in the same year that Clare wrote down his fears was embarking in Gainsborough on a course of self-education which entailed committing to memory 'the entire Paradise Lost and seven of the best plays of Shakspeare'.[144] Where the old created their mental archive without thinking, the literate did so as a conscious act, but the memories of the latter were neither less capacious nor more accurate than the former. If the depths of knowledge held by the uneducated could never be plumbed, so the scope of the material which the readers might absorb could never be measured. Whilst information reproduced by recitation could be checked against the printed text, that retrieved through conversation would be validated by reference to collective wisdom. At one level the oral tradition appeared a more secure conduit of knowledge over time because it belonged exclusively to those to whom it related. Text-based forms of storage were vulnerable to interference from those outside popular culture and to diminishing relevance to the lives of those within it. Yet as Clare well knew, the beliefs and practices subsumed under the heading of 'Superstition' were themselves threatened with oblivion by the insect encroachments of literacy and the more general disruption of established social and economic relationships. As elsewhere in assessing the impact of mass literacy, the question of gain or loss resolved itself into issues of control and context.

Much of the material which appeared in the proliferating folklore compilations related to collective forms of measuring the passage of the working year. Time had never been neutral in relations of production. For as long as they could insist that past structures of behaviour were replicated in current practice, groups of workers could maintain some defence against the encroaching authority of their employers. If continuity was embodied in ritual, it was beyond the reach of the contemporary pursuit of profit. Conversely, it was in the interests of those who owned or managed farms, workshops or factories to transfer attention from the seasonal cycle to the daily clock. For those who witnessed the decline in the traditional celebrations, the balance of power seemed to have shifted irrevocably. In the life of orally transmitted custom, the society Clare described in *The Shepherd's Calendar* had already reached winter, the practices he delineated now little more than 'green ivy when the trees are bare'.[145] The frost which had caused the damage was the deterioration in the relations of production. Events associated with milestones in the working year, from Plough Monday to Harvest Home, embodied a structure of reciprocal rights and obligations which was coming under increasing strain. The gradual withdrawal of the landowners and then the farmers from the local customary calendar was part of a broader transformation in the tenure and use of land. Just as those without documentary proof of ownership suffered through enclosure, which had a particularly devastating effect on Clare's Helpston, so the observances and festivals which had no substance outside communal memory were proving vulnerable:

> As proud distinction makes a wider space
> Between the genteel and the vulgar race
> Then must they fade as pride oer custom showers
> Its blighting mildew on her feeble flowers.[146]

Here print was performing a posthumous function. The appearance of a calendar ritual in an antiquarian collection or, less often, in the poetry or memoirs of a working man was the equivalent of an obituary, or at least the last rites. In the oral tradition, observance and memory were mutually dependent; only in literature could they be separated. Clare wrote in response to the breakdown of a mode of transmission which had simultaneously given form and legitimacy to the activities. 'And soon the poets song will be', he wrote of the inherited practices, 'The only refuge they can find.'[147] Alongside the poetry, he sent lists of customs to Hone, who incorporated them in collections pervaded by a sense of accelerating loss: 'Such observances have rapidly disappeared', he wrote of material in *The Year Book*, 'and the few that remain are still more rapidly disappearing.'[148]

However, it was possible to use the written word and the institutions associated with it to make a more active response to the decline. Either the use of custom to keep one generation in touch with another could be given new form, or alternative means of establishing links between the present and the past could be found. In the first case the Churches were particularly active in applying the new tools of communication to perceived deficiencies in popular culture. The harvest supper, the 'grand event of the year', as the 'Suffolk Farm Labourer' described it,[149] was commuted to cash payments and then reappeared in the 1860s as the newly invented 'harvest festival'. Where individual farmers and their labourers had once sat down together in a joint celebration of gathering in the crops, vicars mounted a simulated display of communal rejoicing, in which the assembled workforce were expected to give thanks for the benevolence of the Almighty and the generosity of their employers.[150] The sermons and the speeches which accompanied the proceedings reminded the men and their families who had toiled in the fields throughout the year of their obligations to those who were responsible for their continuing well-being.[151] Three months later, Christmas was given a new dimension with the aid of the Post Office.

Thus as other traditional customs disappeared altogether, organised religion was able to introduce a new calendar of observances based on its educational endeavours. From the late eighteenth century onwards, the focal point of the year in every Sunday school was its anniversary sermon, feast or procession, in which children, parents and teachers would be brought together in an affirmation of the value of Christian teaching.[152] 'By this method', recalled the miner's son George Parkinson, 'the annual children's day became a most powerful agent in stamping on the memory and understanding facts, principles, and doctrines of the utmost importance and of permanent value.'[153] Whitsun was the most popular occasion for these events,[154] although in particular localities church leaders were not above timing their festival to compete with a profane survival in the traditional calendar of recreation. With the expansion of the railways in the 1840s, the bigger Sunday schools and the professionally organised day schools were increasingly able to use their resources to exploit the new opportunities for travel.[155] At a time when journeys for pleasure were still beyond the majority of the population, the annual school excursions to the seaside or rural beauty spots could become, as Louise Jermy recalled, 'the chief event of the year',[156] eagerly anticipated and long remembered in the life of the community. Week in and week out the classes were taught the values of order and punctuality, and once a year displayed the rewards available to those who embraced the new attitude towards time.

The extent to which these new rituals were imposed on or grew out of the culture of the labouring poor depended to a large extent on the degree of their control over the institutions which sponsored them. Where the Sunday or day school was administered by parents or by teachers risen from the ranks of their pupils, the outings and anniversaries were a genuine addition to the collective forms of celebrating mutual endeavour over time. Increasingly the key to survival or reinvention was the capacity to organise. Informal structures were no longer adequate vehicles in the face of the pressures bearing down on orally embodied tradition from employers and elsewhere. Only those who through a combination of prosperity and literacy could work together in educational projects, friendly societies or trade unions could now afford the luxury of customs. In part this power was used defensively. As we saw in the previous chapter, a central function of the increasingly bureaucratised trade unions was the maintenance of customary means of connecting work with the passage of time. Most of the folklore collectors of the period carefully excluded the contentious topic of workplace ritual from their field of interest. Only William Hone retained sufficient sympathy and personal contact with the urban artisans to obtain and publish details of practices which were as much part of the oral tradition of the labouring poor as the maypole dances and well dressings which were the staple fare of the antiquarian compilations.[157] Whilst the trade clubs did not encourage the recording of their customs, they sought with some success to employ the tools of formal communication to protect them from erosion by market forces. At the same time, it was possible to use the collective strength of the unions and the friendly societies to develop new rituals which at once displayed and reinforced their capacity to maintain elaborate patterns of behaviour over time.

From the perspective of the promoters of mass education, the new traditions, though valuable in themselves, were an insubstantial defence against the increasing dangers of a dehistoricised labouring population. The French Revolution had provided a dreadful warning of what happened when the accumulated wisdom of previous generations was disregarded, and as the nineteenth century progressed, the older forms of maintaining continuity decayed or were deliberately destroyed in the interests of economic growth, the need for remedial action became more urgent. 'Our main safeguard against a revolution', wrote the *School Board Chronicle* in 1872, 'was the patriotic love of one's country arising from a knowledge of the past, leading men to see how much preferable a gradual reform was to violent changes . . .'[158] Mass literacy itself might breach the isolation of the uneducated community and make possible an enhanced consciousness of the national culture, but it would not automatically instil a knowledge of the country's institutions and dominant values. Although textbooks were available for school use from as early as 1812, as with other secular subjects history remained on the margin of the inspected curriculum until mid-century, and suffered further discouragement with the introduction of the Revised Code.[159] Not until 1867 was it given official status as a 'specific subject', and educational publishers then began to respond to a growing demand for juvenile versions of the standard histories. These sought to present a version of the past which denied the significance of conflict within it or the possibility of argument about it. Chartism, for instance, the most overt and sustained incident of class hostility of the century, was presented as a temporary aberration caused by unprincipled demagogues who had led astray otherwise well-meaning working men.[160]

Whilst the lessons to be drawn from history were clear, the impact of the teaching remains open to doubt. The 'specific subjects' of 1867 were confined to the minority of pupils studying Standard IV and above, and although its translation into a 'class subject' in 1875 was intended to make history available throughout the curriculum, a further revision of the Code in 1882 once more restricted its study to the sparsely populated upper reaches of the elementary school. In 1884 grammar was being taught as a 'class subject' in 19,080 schools, and history in just 382.[161] Greater priority was attached to promoting communication amongst the present generation than with those in the past. Only after 1890 could the subject be taught to all pupils, but as late as 1895 there were still twice as many schools offering needlework as history. Over the period as a whole it is likely that the bulk of the study of written history was undertaken in their own time by self-educated adults. When the more serious readers began to build up their own libraries of usually second-hand books they had bought, borrowed or begged, volumes dealing with the past featured more prominently than those commenting on contemporary issues. This was partly because newly published works were beyond their pocket, at least until the expansion of the public libraries in the second half of the nineteenth century, but it also reflected a marked taste for historical writings of every sort. However dense and fascinating they might be, the memories of elderly relatives and neighbours were ultimately confined by place and period. To the listeners who now had the chance to become readers, the chief attraction of written history was its sheer otherness. They read not so much to connect the nineteenth century to the eighteenth and seventeenth centuries, though occasional copies of Hume of Macaulay were to be found in their reading lists, but rather to establish the specificity of the present by contrasting it to the wholly unfamiliar worlds of the more distant past. Books such as Robertson's *History of Ancient Greece*, Rollin's *Ancient History*, Ramsay's *The Travels of Cyrus*, even Gibbon's *Decline and Fall* exercised an abiding appeal to those reared on the larger than life events which filled the chapbooks and old wives' tales.[162] The rise and fall of great dynasties and empires met their predilection for the dramatic whilst at the same time putting into perspective the ever more strident celebration of Britain's industrial and military power.

At the same time, those who gained the confidence to wield a pen had the opportunity to become producers as well as consumers of history. The need to intervene in the written record grew increasingly urgent as working men became ever more dependent on formal means of communication to assert their right to a place in the historical development of their country. Movements which had been based on correspondence, leaflets, addresses, agendas and minutes, journals and newspapers, could not be preserved over time by an oral tradition alone.[163] Just as, for instance, the Chartists struggled against the constant misrepresentation of their cause in the contemporary middle-class press, there was a real danger that its historical significance would be appropriated by writers who based their accounts on a partial reading of the surviving evidence.[164] Memory was too fragile and too private to perpetuate so large and so public an event. Thus in the half-century which followed the failure of the Third Petition in 1848, at least seventy autobiographical accounts were written to revive what by 1883 seemed to the author of *Chartist Recollections* to be 'an almost forgotten past'.[165] They varied extensively in the scope and quality of their coverage, but all sought to create a permanent and accurate statement for those who came after them. Yet as the children reached by the school text-books remained limited in number, so the readership of the alternative accounts was, with a few notable exceptions, confined to the author's locality or a small-circulation periodical. On the one side was a coherent body of history belatedly taught in a handful of classrooms, on the other a fragmentary corpus of writing which reflected a continuing debate about earlier political struggles, but fell far short of constituting a separate tradition of written history. However inadequate the individual and collective memory was becoming, it remained for the bulk of the newly educated by far the most important link with the past they had helped to make.

If the schools moved only very slowly towards the construction of new links with the past, they attached much greater urgency to the task of reorganising the consumption of present time. From the outset the Church societies had recognised that the success of their endeavours depended on and could in turn be measured by a major change in the way the passing hours were divided and filled. 'In education', wrote Joseph Lancaster at the beginning of the drive to mass literacy, 'nothing can be more important than economy of time.'[166] Unless the children, and by extension their parents, learned new habits of regularity, attendance could not be maintained; unless the teachers learned new techniques of conducting the school day, the increasingly complex curriculum could not be covered; and unless the pupils took from their education a new sense of responsibility in their use of time, their lessons would have been in vain. Although the requirement for discipline and the means for enforcing it were partly a function of the school as an institution, the teaching of literacy was itself central to the process. Just as learning to read and write demanded the decomposition of language and its reconstruction on a systematic, progressive basis, so the future employment of the skills would encourage and sustain a more structured and purposeful management of temporal resources.[167] Above all, the newly literate generation would be prepared for the increasing divorce between work and leisure in the industrial society.[168] Not only would it understand the rules of punctuality and continuous labour imposed by the factories, but, perhaps more importantly, it would be able to exploit the newly enclosed free time in a rational and improving fashion.

Expelling the traditional cycle of recreation from the working week was difficult enough, with Saint Monday persisting well into the 1860s,[169] but even when victory was in sight, there remained the problem of filling the evenings, Sundays and gradually Saturday afternoons, which were now emptied of toil. As the adult educator James Hole recognised, every attention had to be paid to 'the leisure hour': 'what portion of life is of more importance, and what more liable to abuse?'[170] The inspected schools had always been sharply conscious that the tools with which they were equipping their pupils would be of particular value in helping them to fill the dangerously formless hours which stretched from the end of one working day to the beginning of the next. In the 1841 *Minutes of the Committee of Council on Education* James Kay-Shuttleworth outlined the benefits to the labouring poor of elementary education:

> By increasing and elevating their domestic affections it may invest their homes with an undecaying charm: by inspiring them with a thirst for knowledge it may provide rational and ennobling amusement for the hours of leisure; and by both these additions to their spiritual existence may rescue some from spending their evenings idly in their chimney corner in mere vacuity of thought; and others, from resorting to the public-house for the pleasure of talking obscenity and scandal, if not sedition amidst the fumes of gin and the roar of drunken associates.[171]

There was good reason to suppose that the skills acquired in the classroom could play a central role in the modern demarcation of leisure. Although more serious self-educators would walk out into the fields on light evenings or summer weekends to escape the noise and confined space of their overcrowded living rooms, reading was essentially a domestic activity. Unlike the public, collective pastimes of the customary calendar, it was both private and malleable.[172] Whilst books, like beer, could still be smuggled into the workplace and consumed out of sight of the super-visor,[173] their use could readily be confined to the home, where they might be picked up and put down as time and circumstance permitted. Family ties would be strengthened as the lure of the public house was weakened, and the newly literate sat by the fireside reading to those too old or too young to have benefited from the expansion of education. Where the reader was led away from home in search of company or more literature, this would be found in the form of well-ordered self-improvement societies or penny readings, or in the silent, rule-bound world of the public library.

In practice, however, the expectation that literacy would ensure that time would be both divided and used in a more responsible fashion was faced with two major problems. In the first instance, the skills of reading and writing were to have their greatest application not in the various categories of 'rational and ennobling amusement' which in the event had limited popular appeal, but in rather more impassioned and questionable fields of activity. The forces of commercial and professional recreation which finally cemented the divide between work and play were as much dependent on the elementary schools as the public libraries and the publishers of improving literature. Football, and in particular, gambling on racing, which became the great passions of the male urban working class during the last quarter of the nineteenth century, were quintessential products of the era of mass communication. As Seebohm Rowntree was forced to admit, the rise of the betting industry was a direct consequence of the work of the schoolteachers: 'By teaching the children to read we make it easy for them to follow the betting news in newspapers and to keep their betting-books.'[174] From the 1880s football and horse-racing exploited and in turn sustained popular sporting journalism in the form of supplements to Saturday papers, extensive coverage in the cheap Sundays, and nationally circulating weeklies.[175] The new sports needed the speedy dissemination of their time-tables and results, and the press required the rapidly improving transport and telegraph systems. What brought them together was the enlarged reading public, attuned to the discipline and regularity of organised sport, and prepared to participate in it through the medium of the printed word.

Secondly, as a recreational activity, reading was intrinsically neither structured nor purposeful. When outside observers began to pay serious attention to the ways in which the labouring poor occupied themselves between work and sleep, they were as much concerned with the formless consumption of the hours of rest in private as with the collective modes of dissipation in the public house and elsewhere. The survey of Kentish labourers in 1838 found that the majority passed their evenings 'at home, in the house, doing sometimes one thing, sometimes another; most times, going early to bed'.[176] It appeared they made too little use of the tiny libraries of religious works which most possessed. However, when late in the century investigators returned to the subject, they discovered that the dramatic increase in both the level of literacy and the availability of literature had done little to improve the situation. In essence, reading belonged to the category of leisure which encompassed fishing, gardening, strolling through the fields, and gossiping on front door-steps, types of activity which if they were increasingly confined to certain periods of the day and the week, themselves neither required nor imposed a time-table. Only at the boundaries did the encounter with literature demand a heightened sense of the passing minute. In this sense the self-educated artisan setting out for the regular meeting of his debating society and the semi-literate labourer awaiting the first edition of the sporting paper to plan his next betting coup had something in common, and indeed might encounter each other in the periodicals section of the public library.[177]

Between the poles of improvement and immorality, however, lay a featureless plain of inconsequential leisure which was the natural habitat of the newly educated reader. It was not even necessary to get out of bed or get dressed to enjoy the fruits of the schoolmaster's labours. This was especially true of the Sabbath, where the development of mass journalism in the second half of the nineteenth century reinforced rather than eroded traditional methods, at least for the menfolk, of recovering from the week's toil. The vendors of cheap literature had always been at their busiest as the church services took place,[178] and the growth of the Sunday papers, whose circulation amongst the lower orders far outweighed the dailies until after the Second World War,[179] merely confirmed established patterns of behaviour. 'What Do the Masses Read?' asked the *Economic Review* in 1904, and its correspondent found men on Sunday mornings sitting 'akimbo on their door-steps, clad mostly in their shirt sleeves', catching up on the week's news.[180] The practice was particularly galling to the religious leaders. Charles Booth reported the bitter observation of a Congregational deacon: 'They get up at nine or ten, and as he passes to his chapel he sees them sitting at breakfast half-dressed or lounging in the window reading *Lloyd's Weekly Newspaper.*'[181] It was a poor reward for expending so much effort in the classroom attempting to instil a new sense of self-discipline amongst the labouring poor.

The implications of mass literacy for a new sense of time were thus far from straightforward. It was clear that major changes had been set in motion. There was a decisive shift from local to national time, ways of connecting the past to the present in the oral tradition became increasingly attenuated, and the schools did much to consolidate the growing divide between work and recreation. Yet there was no unilinear, uniform move to clock time.[182] At every point there was resistance or appropriation. Least able to respond were the women in the neighbourhood. They had played a crucial role in the transmission of information between generations, and taken a full part in measuring and celebrating the passage of the years. Now they were reduced to silent witnesses of their loss of function and respect. It was the men who formed the organisations that defended or remade custom, who wrote most of the autobiographies which became the principal formal link with the past,[183] who took their ease with the paper on Sunday mornings while their dinner was cooked for them. 'Nearly all women of the working classes', observed Lady Bell, 'have a feeling that it is wrong to sit down with a book.'[184] Even so, the wives and mothers remained members of the communities which were constantly seeking ways of evading or exploiting the drive towards a rationalised and rational consumption of time. Perhaps the best example of the scope and the limitations of the opportunities which remained to the newly literate is to be found in what for centuries had been the main printed survey of time present, past and future.

The almanac described a familiar trajectory through the layers of public taste in this period. By the middle of the eighteenth century, the Company of Stationers, which possessed a legal monopoly in the field, was struggling to maintain its position in what had been a large and fashionable market place. It was threatened on the one hand by increasing scepticism amongst polite society about the astrological claims of the almanacs and on the other, by attempts to open up the trade to growing demand from below.[185] For the remainder of the century it managed to retain the patronage of the newly rational by providing genuine scientific information alongside the astrology, and resisted the consequences of the abolition of its monopoly in 1775 with the aid of a heavy stamp duty which kept the price of legitimate almanacs out of reach of the mass of the population. However, when the duty was repealed in 1834, the market was finally exposed to full commercial exploitation. This took two sharply contrasting forms. The immediate beneficiaries were the firms seeking to use the new forms of communication to develop a mass market for their goods and services. The free distribution of almanacs which combined vestigial calendars and summaries of useful information with advertisements and price lists became one of the major categories of the dramatic expansion of business mail following the introduction of the Penny Post in 1840.[186] Items such as L. Hyam's *Tailoring, Fashionable Ready Made Clothing and Outfitting Almanack for 1846* were brought to post offices by the sackful and found their way on to the walls of shops, offices and farmhouses throughout the country.

There was a concern that the invasion of the market by either gratuitous commercial or cheap improving almanacs would drive the previously illegitimate sector out of business, in the same way that the reduction of the newspaper stamp spelled the end for the unstamped press, but in the event, the popular form survived and flourished. In 1828 the Society for the Diffusion of Useful Knowledge had launched the *British Almanack* in an attempt finally to displace the 'mixture of ignorance and imposture' found in those 'used chiefly by the people'[187] by a more factual treatment of time. However, the newly literate were unlikely to be attracted by 'full and correct lists of the Royal Family, Houses of Parliament, and other public functionaries', or to be moved by such 'Advice to the Poor' as 'The great mass of mankind are destined inevitably to live by labour . . . the rich are as justly entitled to their large possessions, as the cottager to his hearth.'[188] In the event, what little prospect the venture had of success was overwhelmed by the rapid and diverse growth of the penny trade after 1834.[189]

The most striking feature of the swarm of new works was their confident and irreverent appropriation of the traditional components of the almanac. The struggling provincial publisher was able to exploit the opportunity provided by a product which could be recycled annually with only minor alterations to develop a close rapport with a local market. In the North in particular there emerged a genre of dialect almanacs which at once parodied and rejuvenated *Old Moore*.[190] Compilers experimenting with ways of integrating speech with print gleefully set upon the Latin-based vocabulary of the annual calendar. 'Jenewerry Hez XXXI Days', began Tom Treddlehoyle's *The Bairnsla Foakes Annual an Pogmoor Olmenac for 1850*.[191] There was nothing sacred about the Church festivals, with 'Bill O' Jacks'' *T'Bishop Blaize Olmenac for 1857*[192] rendering into Bradford dialect 'Hesh Weddanzda' and 'Kwinkwajesema'. The lurid, apocalyptic prophesying, which was still to be found in the plentiful penny version of *Old Moore*,[193] was brought down to earth: 'Ah look nah for great convulsions', warned Treddlehoyle's 'Voice at the Stars, December', 'but whether it be e all Europe, or Ruth Ruddleputty's youngest bairn, it izant clearly depicktad; haivver, it al be wisdom to be prepared for awthur.' More importantly, the cycles and chronology of specific communities displaced the dates of law terms and quarter sessions and the lists of kings and queens and great battles which filled the Stationers' almanacs and their imitators. Local fairs and festivals which had survived the attack on the customary calendar were catalogued, and the new recreational rituals of the urban working class were anticipated or remembered. The June entry of Arthur W. Bickerdike's *The Beacon Almanack, for 1873*[194] discussed the excitement of the annual Sunday school outing; the month of July gave John Hartley's *The Halifax Original Illuminated Clock Almanack, 1869, In the Yorkshire Dialect*,[195] the opportunity to celebrate a day's outing to Blackpool. Time past was particular to place, the incidents recorded ranging from notable accidents, freak weather and deaths of local characters to major events in the political history of the readership, such as the 1842 Plug Plot riots, which were featured in 'Bill at Hoylus End's' *Howarth, Gowenhead an Boythorn 1873 Almenac*.[196]

Conclusion

To those engaged in the struggle to emancipate the minds of the uneducated from the hold of superstition, progress could be hard to detect. In 1867, Charles Knight reviewed with dismay the continuing success of the cheap, prophesying almanacs: 'The people of England are essentially as ignorant now as they were in the palmy days of Francis Moore. Undoubtedly a larger number can read and write; but this is not education.'[197] In a number of ways, his pessimism was misplaced. The increasing use of the printed word was causing or furthering major changes in the ways in which the labouring poor responded to natural forces. Their environment was gradually becoming less magical, and lessening its capacity to instil terror in the hearts of children and constant apprehension in the minds of their parents. As the newly literate turned from folk cures to those conveyed and endorsed by print or by practitioners whose authority was derived from paper qualifications, many of the useless and sometimes gruesome or humiliating remedies against misfortune fell into disuse. There was an increasing tendency to break out of the confines of the local body of oral wisdom and seek information about the workings of their world from more extensive and less personal sources. Customary modes of consuming time which blurred the distinction between the present and the past and between work and leisure were being recorded for posterity as they lost their meaning for contemporaries. That the outcome of the transitions was so often proving unsatisfactory was the consequence of two related factors. Firstly the control over natural forces which the new means of communication proffered to the newly educated was at best partial and frequently wholly illusory. Secondly those who had been equipped with the tools of literacy continually sought to use them through collective action or in the market place to find their own solutions to their continuing needs.

The contours of the new landscape are best displayed by the phenomenon of working-class gambling, which at the end of the nineteenth century was causing increasing alarm amongst both religious and secular observers. In one sense it was, as we have seen, wholly dependent on the labours of the schools;[198] in another it appeared to represent as complete an abdication of a rational response to the world as the traditional evil of alcohol. The practice of regularly betting on races on the basis of information supplied by the sporting press represented an almost perfect parody of the intentions of those who had sought the overthrow of the superstitious mind. The gamblers who were depleting their family's meagre resources by guessing the future were men who had emancipated themselves from a belief in the animistic universe of rural folk beliefs; they had broken out of the enclosed oral community to exploit impersonal bodies of formal knowledge which transcended distance; they were embracing the opportunities of defined and more extensive leisure; they were acutely conscious of clock time, and their capacity to manipulate complex bodies of print-derived information held in their memories could win the grudging admiration of the fiercest critic of the use they were making of it.[199]

At issue, as so often, were alternative perspectives on rationality. In the face of the mindless toil of the working week, and the practical impossibility of breaking out of the circle of credit and debt through saving or upward economic mobility, the regular expenditure of small sums of money on the outcome of races combined entertainment, mental exercise and the real prospect of at least the occasional intermission of the cycle of deprivation. It made sense, but the pleasure of the pursuit rested on an underlying pessimism. Few of those eagerly searching the pages of *The Winning Post* would dissent from the verdict of the 'King of the Norfolk Poachers' on the erosion of the belief in magic by modern communications: 'Still the world is wiser than what it was in the olden time, but I think weaker.'[200]

6

IMAGINATION

The accounts left to us by working men and women who gained sufficient mastery of the tools of literacy to write about themselves tended to be extremely reticent where strong feelings might be involved. For reasons of literary convention and authorial intention the narratives were oblique and generalised on sexual and domestic relations.[1] However, when it became necessary to describe the impact of reading on the imagination, a complete thesaurus of emotional language was deployed. Literature ranging from chapbooks to Shakespeare evoked 'rapture', 'wonder', 'joy', 'desire', 'delight' and 'pleasure'.[2] To those making their first encounter with books, it mattered little whether they were designed merely to entertain or had some higher purpose. 'The story was the great thing', recalled the plasterer's son William Adams – 'the trials of Christian, the troubles of Gulliver, the adventures of Aladdin.'[3] Even where subsequent intellectual pursuits were confined to the factual or the spiritual, it was admitted that the simple, all-consuming enjoyment of fiction had played a crucial role in translating the barely literate schoolchild into the fully fledged reader.[4] Most never lost their taste for the fabulous in all its forms, as outside observers were continually discovering as they monitored the progress towards universal literacy. 'The general results, then, of our enquiry', concluded the *Fortnightly Review* in 1889, 'are first, that there is an enormous demand for works of fiction, to the comparative neglect of other forms of literature, and, secondly, that there is a decided preference for books of a highly sensational character.'[5] Some deplored the use to which the skills so laboriously and expensively taught in the classroom were being put: 'It is humiliating', protested the *Quarterly Review* in 1867, 'in the midst of all the schools and teaching of the present day, to find such rubbish continually poured forth, and eagerly read';[6] others argued for tolerance of the need to relax after a day's labour.[7] Eventually the schools bowed to the demands of their customers, and as we have seen, began to introduce selections from standard authors and poets which, fragmented though they were, proved capable of enthralling hitherto bored and alienated pupils.[8]

Of all the possible functions of literacy in this period, the development and feeding of the imagination was much the most intensive. Instead of the usual patchwork of exploitation, indifference and resistance, we are faced with an early and continually expanding application of the written word by producers and consumers alike. No other category of popular culture covered by this study was so easily and completely invaded by print. If newly educated readers made the slightest attempt to employ for their own benefit their uncertain skills it would be to glance at a broadside or some later form of cheap fiction, and if newly equipped printers wanted to enter the popular market, fantasy rather than fact offered the most certain return on their investment. From as early as the mid seventeenth century, when the warehouses of wholesale chapbook merchants could contain as many as ninety thousand items,[9] the publishers of fiction for the common people had been pioneers in the mass production of standardised articles for large-scale distribution, and in the nineteenth century men like Catnach, Pitts, Reynolds and Lloyd could rightfully taken their places in the pantheon of industrial entrepreneurs. With the State increasingly confined to the role of spectator, and voluntary bodies overwhelmed by less idealistic competitiors, the field of the imagination presented the most direct engagement between capitalism and the use of literacy.

There is a tempting consonance between the polarities of the oral and the literate, and the workshop and the factory. In each case as the article becomes a commodity, producer and consumer become separated from each other, the relation between them increasingly mechanical and barren.[10] David Buchan's *The Ballad and the Folk*, for instance, draws an explicit parallel between the way in which the 'agrarian and industrial revolutions had broken up the old communities' and the process by which the printed word had destroyed the ballad's capacity to 'tell stories that express a community's outlook on life'.[11] Where work and imagination had grown out of collective experience, both were now fragmented. In the songs and tales, form and content had been contained within a single aesthetic pattern which was under the joint control of performer and audience. But by the end of the nineteenth century, he concludes, 'Literacy had not only ensured the atrophy of the old balladry, but also greatly reduced the possibilities for the folk's creative participation in the new balladry. Inevitably the songs of the folk were to become increasingly peripheral to the lives of the folk.'[12] This chapter examines how far it is possible to sustain the dichotomies which inform this model of change, and then considers the consequences of the further commercialisation of the imagination in the context of the final drive to mass literacy.

Transition

The novelist, playwright and radical politician Thomas Holcroft began his working life helping his mother and father peddle small wares from door to door in the Berkshire villages of the 1750s. He became familiar with the interiors of every sort of poor man's house, and never forgot the wealth of imaginative literature which looked down upon him: 'Even the walls of cottages and little alehouses would do something; for many of them had old English ballads, such as Death and the Lady, and Margaret's Ghost, with lamentable tragedies, or King Charles's golden rules, occasionally pasted on them.'[13] From the very beginning of the period, printed verses and tales were as common a possession as the pots and trinkets Holcroft and his family were trying to sell. They were merely one item amongst the stock of basic needs and minor luxuries which the least prosperous of households sought to obtain as time and circumstances permitted. Just as a purchased item of clothing would extend rather than displace an existing wardrobe, so a ballad or a chapbook would feed into rather than expel the established repertoire of songs and verses. The labouring poor could not afford the luxury of counterposing the oral and the written in the way of subsequent folklorists. If we are to understand the complex and evolving balance between the performed and the made, between the produced and the reproduced, we must begin by recognising that for those with little money and less education, the only division that really mattered was between having something and having nothing at all.

Whilst orally transmitted songs and stories were far more hard-wearing and widely available than almost any other possession, there were always limits to their scope and durability. The opportunity to extend the stock of material held in the memories of older members of the family and community was always welcome, particularly if the young lacked the patience to wait until parents or neighbours could find the time to give voice to their mental archives. A turning point in the growth of Holcroft's imagination was the gift of two battered chapbooks, *Parismus and Parismenes* and *The Seven Champions of Christendom*, which were to him 'an inestimable treasure'.[14] He pored over these ancient stories, which had been in circulation since at least the late sixteenth century and had another hundred years of life in them, until they were lodged as firmly in his memory as 'my catechism, or the daily prayers I repeated kneeling before my father'.[15] Print was still too rare a commodity to be consumed and discarded in one sitting. The precious, dog-eared pages were read and reread, borrowed and reborrowed until imperceptibly they merged back into the communal oral tradition whence most had originally come. Conversely those who became specialist performers, or who moved beyond reinterpreting traditional material to creating songs and stories of their own, would not hesitate to use more formal means of preserving both their sources and their innovations. Manuscript song books, collections of ballads, broadsides and newspaper cuttings reinforced the memory of one generation and provided a secure bequest for the next.[16]

John Harland's account of the work of the Wilsons, an early-nineteenth-century dynasty of Lancashire dialect composers, captures something of the problems of preservation, which were becoming more acute as communities began to expand and break up. The father, Michael Wilson, was known to have made up numerous songs 'relating to local events, scenes and manners', but since he was 'content to sing them in social life', no record was made, and fifty years later they were beyond recall. His most prolific son, Thomas, took the precaution of writing down his *oeuvre*, but then he lent his notes to one Thomas Brotherton, who managed to mislay them, and Harland was reduced to offering a £2 reward for their return.[17]

The constant movement backward and forward between the oral and the printed greatly complicated the work of the folklorists, though few realised just how impure most of their material was. Recent research suggests that as much as four-fifths of the folk-songs gathered in the major early-twentieth-century surveys ultimately derived from published broadsides.[18] Only the handful of uneducated collectors whose contact with the written word had made them realise the wealth of the spoken were properly aware of the tangled roots of their heritage. Here, for instance, Clare describes how he came to record an item: 'I met with a poetical Story tother day "The Foundlings Lamentation" told by a neighbour some of the things struck me so much as to copy them she tracd its origin to a "penny book" from which she had gotten it by heart years afore.'[19] What had been printed, possibly from an oral source, then remembered and repeated and written down once more, became part of the reserves upon which Clare drew as he made the transition from composing verses in his head to becoming a published poet. At least one of his pieces eventually found its way into the catalogues of the broadside entrepreneur Catnach,[20] and set in the context of the essential heterogeneity of the popular imagination, the rough and ready approach of those who opened up the mass market in cheap literature becomes easier to recognise. Catnach was said to have held court in the back room of his premises, a pot of ale and a pipe to hand,

> receiving ballad-writers and singers, and judging of the merits of any production which was brought to him by having it sung then and there to some popular air played by his fiddler. His broad-sheets contain all sorts of songs and ballads, for he had a most catholic taste, and introduced the custom of taking from any writer living or dead whatever he fancied, and printing it side by side with the productions of his own clients.[21]

Working in this fashion, Catnach was not so much disrupting as dramatically compressing the time-honoured procession of material from one form to another.

In the most successful enterprises of the period, the inequalities of reward available to those engaged in the expansion of popular literature were as extreme as any to be found in capitalist manufacture. Catnach, who, according to his biographer, 'had a tenacious love for money',[22] began life as a printer's apprentice and retired at forty-six with more than £10,000,[23] and the dominant figure of the next generation, Edward Lloyd, who introduced the penny dreadful and then the mass circulation Sunday newspaper, started with nothing and left half a million.[24] By contrast, those who were employed to create and distribute their products were for the most part remunerated at a level well below that of the average factory worker. It was a trade founded on pennies. The ballads and broadsides, and then the eight-page stories, the songbooks and the Sunday newspapers were bought for coppers and their vendors were paid in the same currency.[25] A common thread of poverty ran through Mayhew's elaborate classification of the retailers of imaginative literature.[26] The running, lurking and standing patterers, the chaunters and ballad singers, the long song and wall song sellers and the death hunters might all enjoy bouts of good fortune when a new item suddenly caught the public fancy, but then the market or the weather would turn against them and their prosperity would evaporate. The street sellers of newspapers, who were the later-nineteenth-century successors of Mayhew's men, enjoyed a more regular income, but one which placed them near the bottom of the manual occupations.[27]

Bringing print to the people was at once a last refuge for the respectable and a first opening for the destitute. Trade depressions would increase the volume of music and verse in the streets. Edwin Waugh drew attention to one of the side-effects of the Cotton Famine in Manchester: 'Swarms of strange, shy, sad-looking singers and instrumental performers, in the work-worn clothing of factory operatives, went about the busy city, pleading for help in touching wails of simple song – like so many wild birds driven by hard weather to the haunts of men.'[28] Those who supplied new material for the publishers fared little better. At the bottom end of the market, there was no cash transaction at all: 'If one of the patterers writes a Ballad on a taking subject, he hastens at once to Seven Dials, where, if accepted, his reward is "a glass of rum, a slice of cake, and five dozen copies," – which, if the accident or murder be a very awful one, are struck off for him while he waits.'[29] The recognised professional writers of broadsides, most of whom belonged to the same stratum of society as their readers, could expect no more than a shilling for a successful piece, over which they then lost all copyright.[30] As the size of the products increased, so did the pay, but a five-thousand-word penny dreadful would earn for its author no more than the weekly wage of an unskilled labourer.[31] It required immense prolixity to attain a substantial income. Of all those engaged in the mass production of imaginative literature below the level of the major publishers, only the time-served, unionised printers enjoyed anything like a secure standard of living.

There were, however, two important factors which obstructed the emergence of a full capitalist mode of production in this sector of the economy. The first was that the key technological innovation at the beginning of the nineteenth century, the invention of the Stanhope iron frame press, extended rather than inhibited the possibilities of small-scale, decentralised manufacture. Elsewhere new machinery destroyed the artisan workshop; here it opened the field to anyone who could find as little as £30 to purchase a press and hire a small room in which to instal it.[32] The consequence was the proliferation of printing establishments in the early decades of the century until every town in the country possessed the means of reproducing its own literature at a rate of at least 200 sheets an hour.[33] Subsequent developments served only to emphasise the hybrid nature of the industry. Those possessing capital and enterprise were able to consolidate their position in national or regional markets by exploiting further breakthroughs, ranging from the installation of steam power by *The Times* in 1814 to the purchase in 1856 of the first rotary press in Britain for printing *Lloyd's Weekly News*,[34] whilst at the same time the iron frame press remained the workhorse of jobbing printers until well into this century. There was thus a line of continuity between the earliest of the Blackburn weaver poets Joseph Hodgson, one of the dying race of self-sufficient ballad singers, who 'published almost everything he wrote as soon as it was written, depositing the whole edition in the crown of his hat, and hawked them wherever he went', and James Duxbury, one of his successors in the last quarter of the century, who bought a press out of his savings whilst working at a mill, and set himself up in business as the producer of his own and other writers' works when laid off during the strike of 1878.[35]

The second impediment was the intervention of the performer. The most striking characteristic of the first phase of the expansion of imaginative literature was the sheer volume of noise which accompanied it. As in the elementary schools, where silence did not descend upon the classroom until final decades of the nineteenth century,[36] so with the encounter with print by the newly literate. At every level, the sound of the human voice was magnified rather than quelled by the mass production and distribution of prose and verse. The simple relationship between the faceless publisher and the soundless reader was disrupted by men and women reciting, singing, shouting, chanting, declaiming and narrating. The predominance of the public and vocal over the private and withdrawn was

a consequence of the tactics and the limited opportunities of the producers, and the tastes and the restricted means of the consumers. The early
entrepreneurs faced immense difficulties in establishing adequate lines of
supply and distribution. The best way of overcoming a shortage of new
material was to tap both the established oral tradition and the songs
performed in parallel forms of popular entertainment, the multiplying
musical theatres, and free and easies.[37] And the most efficient means of
coping with the absence of both a network of shops to sell their wares and
a structure of cheap newspapers in which to advertise them was to
intensify rather than displace time-honoured means of reaching the
public. Thus the street book sellers cried out their wares to passers-by,[38]
and the broadside sellers and ballad singers attracted a crowd on street
corners by performing songs and narratives which may have found only a
temporary resting place in a printed form. Those who stopped to listen
were long accustomed to exercising their imagination in public. They
found it natural to respond to an unfamiliar song or story in the company
of others, and the casual group gave them the opportunity of saving their
pennies if the item did not appeal. Where a purchase was made and taken
to the home or workplace, the shortage of reading material and the
uneven distribution of literacy meant that sooner or later it was likely to
be read aloud once more.

At the very least the reliance on the human voice forced an awareness of
the revolution in popular literature on every inhabitant of the growing
towns. The eventual displacement of the broadside sellers by the newspaper boys did nothing to reduce the volume of sound. Charles Knight
described the consequence of the growth in mass communication:

> The penny newspapers, '*Daily Telegraph*', '*Daily News*', '*Globe*,
> sir?', *Standard*, sir?' assail our ears at every hour in all our leading
> thoroughfares; and after mid-day little boys in the Strand, in
> Holborn, in Tottenham Court Road, and along the chief omni-
> bus routes, bawl '*Echo, Echo*', '*Special Echo*', till long after
> sundown. Nor are these cries confined to the great Metropolis;
> every country town shares in them, thanks to the wide-spread
> ramifications of our railway system.[39]

However, where the noise represented performance rather than merely
advertisement, it was evidence of the participation by both distributors
and consumers in the creative process. Every broadside and ballad
publisher knew that his material had yet to take its final form when it left
his presses. The success or failure of an item was in the last resort
determined by how well it could be sung or recited, and how successfully
the singers and narrators rose to the challenge. The music of a ballad was
rarely printed, and although the sheet sometimes suggested an appropriate

tune, selection was frequently at the discretion of the singers, who took their responsibility very seriously. 'I was told, on all hands', wrote Mayhew, 'that it was not the words that ever "made a ballad, but the subject; and, more than the subject,– the chorus; and, far more than either,– *the tune!*" Indeed, many of the street-singers of ballads on a subject have as supreme a contempt for words as can be felt by any modern composer.'[40] Where the seller had only prose upon which to work, much still depended on his capacity to adopt a fitting and moving tone for its recitation, and his ability to embroider the text with suitable exclamations and elaborations.

The continuing role of performance, both before and after the point of sale, enhanced the spoken word at the expense of the printed in two senses. It preserved, at least partially, the communal act of interpretation which is associated with transmission in the oral tradition, and at the same time it exercised a powerful influence over the form and content of what was being written. Mayhew was emphatic about what he termed 'the *necessity* which controls street authorship': 'It must be borne in mind that the street author is closely restricted in the quality of his effusion. It must be such as the patterers approve, as the chaunters can chaunt, the ballad-singers sing, and – above all – such as street-buyers will buy.'[41] The central characteristic of the market to which the authors and publishers had to conform was its sense of transition. Those whom the patterers and singers sought to detain were on the move in several senses. Not only were they hurrying about their business or strolling between occupations, but they were also undergoing an evolution from an oral-cum-written to a written-cum-oral means of exercising their imagination,[42] as at the same time they were in passage between a rural existence conditioned by intermittent contact with the towns to an urban way of life which retained strong links with the countryside.

The influence of the still incomplete engagement with literacy amongst those who stopped to buy the wares of the street sellers can be seen most clearly in the construction of the broadsides. It is instructive to compare an item such as Catnach's *Account of a Dreadful and Horrible Murder Committed by Mary Bell Upon the Body of Her Mother*[43] with the primers children were then encountering in the Church schools. Where, for instance *The Child's First Book and Sunday School Primer*[44] encouraged the progress of the pupil towards full literacy by presenting first the alphabet and disconnected syllables, and then isolated words graded by length rather than sense, with a handful of prayers and Biblical extracts as the ultimate destination, the broadside achieved the same end by presenting on a single page the one dramatic story in three different dimensions. The fluent reader could enjoy a compact and plainly written 250-word account of the crime (in which the mother's gruel was poisoned with arsenic after she had disapproved of her daughter's lover), those less certain of their abilities could commit to memory or have recited to them five four-line verses on the subject, and the wholly illiterate could still gain some impression of the story from the crude woodcut which adorned the page. The stories were circumstantial and self-sufficient; the fact that Mary Bell had yet to be tried was no obstacle to the attribution of motive and guilt. The verses had a simple metre and frequently commenced, as in this case, with a formulaic, if carelessly set down, invocation:

> You pretty maids where'er You be,
> Draw near & Listen unto me,
> Whilst I to You a tale unfold,
> Will make Your heart's blood to run.

The pictures matched their subject matter in their eye-catching simplicity, although as it took longer to make a woodcut than compose a text, publishers frequently sacrificed accuracy to speed. Catnach, for instance, selected from his shelves the same block to illustrate the *Dreadful Account of a most Barbarous, and Shocking Murder Committed by William Burt Upon the Body of his Infant Child,* and *the cruel manner in which he wounded his Wife, at Brighton and The Dreadful Murder Committed by Nicholas Steinburg, in the Body of his Wife and four children.*[45] Innovation in the design of typeface in the first two decades of the nineteenth century[46] led to the adoption of a far wider range of size and design of headings and sub-heads, making the entire document as vigorous in appearance as in content. The transition from an image to a print culture which had been in motion since the Reformation[47] was left deliberately incomplete by these publishers. The chapbooks had always possessed some visual indication of the story, and as their blocks finally wore out,[48] the penny dreadfuls began to appear, each one of which, Lloyd insisted, had to carry an illustration, however crudely executed.[49] Only the blind and the stone deaf can have failed to derive some pleasure from the outpouring of cheap literature. The material was ideally suited to those who emerged from their education with the slightest grasp of the tools of reading and writing, providing an immediate opportunity to practise their uncertain skills, and every incentive to develop them into fluent literacy.[50]

Where the school primers until late in the century patrolled a narrow courtyard paved with morally uplifting fables and religious texts, the material on sale to the newly educated constituted a fairground of noise and colour. The immense variety of subjects and genres crammed into the catalogues of the larger publishers or scattered through the random collections of casual readers had in common only the vigour of their treatment. There was no market for plain tales of plain people; 'such topics as they love to hear', observed the *Quarterly Review*, are 'of men and women great in goodness or in vice, of life and death in their widest sense, of crime and disaster, of human sorrows and joys whether in Chick Lane or Windsor Castle'.[51] The seemingly insatiable appetite for sensation which so dismayed the promoters of mass education had its origins far back in the history of popular taste. The chapbooks had relied for their appeal on dense accounts of extraordinary deeds and heroes. Packed into their five to seven thousand words was enough spectacle to sustain over a long period imaginations which could not expect a regular diet of fresh stories. For instance, the first sentence of *The Pleasant and Delightful History of Jack and the Giants* indicates the riches in store: 'King Arthur's only son desired his father to furnish him with a certain sum of money, that he might go and seek his fortune in the principality of Wales, where a very beautiful lady lived, whom he heard was possessed with seven evil spirits.'[52] Some of the hostility to the broadsides and penny dreadfuls was merely a consequence of publishers making visible what previously had been hidden in the oral tradition. According to Francis Grose, 'ghosts, fairies and witches, with bloody murders, committed by tinkers, formed a principal part of rural conversations, in all large assemblies, and particularly those in Christmas holydays'.[53] The delight in the bizarre and the violent long predated mass literacy;[54] the achievement of the new era was the infusion of the fabulous with a particular sense of everyday reality.

Although earlier imaginative forms had often featured common people with recognisable motives and aspirations, none were grounded in the familiar in the way in which was now demanded by the expanding readership.[55] Observers looking down on the phenomenon were inclined to explain it in terms of the material deprivation suffered by those who could only afford penny publications; in the view of *Blackwood's Magazine*, 'People working face to face with the primitive powers – people in whose understanding poverty does not mean a smaller house or fewer servants, or a difficulty about one's butcher bill, but means real hunger, cold, and nakedness, are not people to be amused by abstractions.'[56] However patronising, there was some substance in this explanation, yet the labourers who had bought the wares of the seventeenth- and eighteenth-century chapmen had been no more insulated from the harsh realities of existence. The dimensions of the new aesthetic were determined less by the absolute level of hardship and more by the character of the expanding centres of population, where the bulk of the literature was produced and sold. Popular taste was conditioned by the twin forces of confidence and crisis. There was a sense of pride, of collective self-assertion amongst the urban dwellers, and at the same time a deep uncertainty about the relevance and resilience of the inherited value structures. What was required was a form of expression which would reflect their own lives in their own circumstances, yet provide a dramatic working out of the moral dilemmas with which they were constantly faced. It was not enough to describe. As social relations came under increasing pressure, intractable problems had to be simplified and displaced to a realm in which there was always a resolution.[57]

The heightened sense of drama which pervaded the penny fiction, the speed with which new material was written, produced and presented, seemed appropriate to the accelerated existence of the towns. The bustle of the streets was conveyed by both the substance and the texture of the writing. 'The main reliance of the publishers now', observed Ludlow and Jones, 'is on unnatural and violent incidents thickly crowded, and developed by dialogue that runs on with a rattle like the stick of a London boy drawn along a row of area-railings.'[58] At the heart of the material was the conviction that the commonplace was suffused with the tragic, and that extremes of emotion and fortune were best conveyed through the detail of daily life. Thus every effort was made to locate the characters and events in concrete settings by means of what a leading exponent, J. M. Rymer, described as 'a recollection of *little facts*'.[59] At times the identity of person and place was conveyed with a precision which would have delighted the Post Office: here for instance we are introduced to the fateful heroine of the *The last Farewel to the World, and Confession, of John Hogan*:

> Ann Hunt, a blooming country girl,
> In Mary-le-bone lived a servant,
> Near Portland-Place in Charlotte-street,
> At No. 4, subservient.[60]

Time was less often given as completely, the hour of the day having greater import than the month, and the month than the year, which reflected the depth of focus of those for whom they were written. Other 'little facts' – occupation, dress, diet, domestic arrangements – were sketched in as the occasion demanded. In exchange for a penny the barely educated expected to meet themselves in their own world.

The range of themes treated in the publications was as diverse as the experience of the readers. At their most quotidian, the ballads and broadsides celebrated or bewailed the intensity of their pleasures and tribulations. The sense of identification with the scenes and events was frequently enhanced by the use of dialect. Here, a London street seller is portrayed with exuberant delight:

> I Deals in Costermongery,
> And in my calling makes some noise,
> And to them wot is hungry,
> I sarves out 'taters and sawoys,

> Some may sport a boney poney,
> Or lean knacker for a job,
> But I've a randy, dandy, tear up, flare up,
> Moke that cost eleven bob,
> Stow your gab and guffery,
> To every fakement I am fly,
> I am regular – AX MY EYE![61]

In the North, dialect representations of the sufferings and resilience of the growing urban population were already reaching a wide market.[62] The immensely popular 'Jone o' Grinfilt' series, which began with an account of a weaver travelling to Oldham to enlist in the Napoleonic Wars as a last defence against starvation, was soon circulating indiscriminately through printed, manuscript and oral forms.[63] Its appeal lay in the combination of recognisable poverty and compensating humour as the eponymous hero struggled to survive his endless misfortunes. In the early post-war *Jone O' Grinfilt Junior*, 'taken down from singing' by John Harland, husband and wife can no longer pay their debts:

> Neaw, owd Bill o' Dan's sent bailies one day,
> Fur t'shop scoar aw'd ow'd him, 'ot aw' couldn't pay;
> But he just to lat, fur owd Bill o' Bent,
> Had sent tit un' cart, un' ta'en goods fur rent;
> They laft nowt bur a stoo' 'ot 're seeots fur two;
> Un' on it keawrt Marget an' me.[64]

The dialect constituted a mode of expression capable of asserting both the continuity of the expanding communities and their viability in the face of hardship and upheaval.

The pleasure taken by those immersed in domestic hardship in the yet more extreme troubles of others was at once surprising and perfectly comprehensible. There was nothing new about it. For John Clare it was an indication of a saving humanity in a population which often appeared indifferent to finer feelings and higher art: 'it is a paradox yearly witnessed of the apparent apathy & unconsern with which they witness the tragedy of death displaying faces as seemingly happy as on an holiday excursion yet these very people will stand around an old ballad singer & with all the romantic enthusiasm of pity shed tears over the doggerel tales of imaginary distress'.[65] As the pressures on the home became more acute, the treatment of the problems became more dramatic. Sensational though it was, much of the natural or man-made disasters of the broadsides was reducible to the working-class family, whose members fell into bad company, committed acts of violence on each other, or suffered accident, ill-health or ruin. Domestic morality was reinforced either by an appeal to the natural feelings of parent, child or spouse, or by an exposure of the consequences of neglecting the responsibilities each bore the other. Catnach's *Dreadful Life, and Confession of a Boy Aged Twelve Years, Who was Condemned to Die at the last Old Bailey Sessions*[66] managed to combine both. The 'New Copy of Verses' commenced with a ritual invocation to maternal sympathies:

> Give ear ye tender mothers dear,
> And when this tale you read,
> Of a little boy of twelve years old,
> 'Twill make your heart to bleed

whilst the accompanying prose description of the seamy events proclaimed the moral which was to be drawn from them: 'With horror we attempt to relate the progress of evil, generally prevailing among children, through the corrupt example of wicked parents.' The subsequent development of the penny fiction of the 1840s enabled the domestic situations to be explored in more detail without in any way compromising the simple morality which they represented.[67] However acute the pressures bearing down on the heroes and heroines, the choices they faced were never complicated, their outcome never ambiguous.

To many alarmed commentators, the growth of the reading public during the first half of the century was characterised by the million-selling execution broadsides[68] and the subsequent and apparently inexhaustible catalogue of murder and seduction in the penny fiction. However, those who so eagerly bought the latest drama did not necessarily confine their reading to this category, and the impact of technical and commercial innovation was not limited to the sensational. At this early stage the barriers between popular and classical literature were less visible than they were later to become. Catnach, like Cluer and Dicey before him, himself was not above raiding the established canon of great authors,[69] and many of those engaged in translating oral forms into print also drew upon more literary sources of inspiration. Joseph Hodgson, for instance, the voluminous Bradford broadside publisher and writer, was also known in his community for the possession of a 'wonderfully extensive library for a person of his humble station, the apartments on the ground floor being literally wainscotted with books'.[70] If few working men's cottages were as well endowed, serious self-taught readers were capable of gaining access to a surprisingly wide body of literature. In his recent survey of artisan poets of the period, Brian Maidment draws attention to the 'profound knowledge of British poetry' which they displayed in their writings.[71] With the price of new polite literature still running at a guinea and a half for a three-decker novel,[72] men like Hodgson had to rely on the development of two established modes of disseminating print.

Firstly, where the performer and his audience stood between the writers and consumers of ballads and broadsides, so a network of collective enterprises bridged the gap between the publishers and readers of major works of literature. Through informal contact between individuals known in the neighbourhood as 'readers', who would pool their random collections of battered volumes, to the growth of more structured self-improvement societies, ways were found of at least reducing the problem of the cost of full-length books.[73] Those who wished to read sooner or later found themselves in conversation with those who had already done so. Secondly, a handful of publishers began to combine opportunities for cheap printing with what initially were traditional forms of distribution to open up a new market. In 1836, an Owenite named William Milner set himself up as a general printer in the Swine Market in Halifax, and the following year began a business of republishing prose and fiction in sixpenny or shilling volumes, loading editions of Pope, Defoe and Bunyan into a horse-drawn van and touring the villages and country fairs in the district.[74] His Cottage Library was soon imitated, particularly by John Dicks' English Library of Standard Works,[75] and by mid-century, most of the standard repertoire up to and including the Romantics was available in shilling editions.

Those who had discovered the pleasure of the literary imagination could now range freely. Thomas Okey, for instance, acquired the 'reading habit' through encountering as a schoolchild ' "Penny Bloods" and other Weeklies issued in penny sheets, such as *Sweeney Todd the Barber*'.[76] Soon he was finding it difficult to combine his developing taste for literature and his increasing duties in the workplace. 'To read in secret I encamped to the washhouse and I well remember during early apprenticeship days at Spitalfield my grandfather, catching sight of me reading there a copy of Dicks' shilling edition of Shakespeare – the whole a marvellous feat of cheap publishing – sternly reproachful, exclaimed: "Ah Tom, *that*'ll never bring you bread and cheese." '[77] His grandfather was of course right, but for those for whom reading was progressing from a pastime to a passion, Shakespeare was as familiar a figure as the Demon Barber of Fleet Street.

The dramatic expansion in the production and consumption of imaginative literature in the first half of the nineteenth century conformed to no simple pattern of development. It was a revolution without discontinuity, innovation shot through with tradition which generated fantasy suffused with a new sense of realism. The introduction of new techniques of production paved the way both for major capitalists and a multitude of small enterprises; it at once challenged the oral tradition and gave fresh voice to the singers of songs and the tellers of tales. Semi-literate and non-literate bought prose and verse which celebrated the burgeoning urban communities by dwelling extensively on their evils. In place of the polarities of speech and print, folk and business, producer and consumer, high and low art, we are faced with a culture of transition, in which the physical journeys between country and town had their counterpart in the constant movement between the categories. If it is too much to regard commercialisation as the begetter of a brief 'golden age of traditional popular culture', as Peter Burke has argued,[78] the diverse and multiplying imaginative forms possessed a protean quality which became increasingly difficult to sustain as the period wore on.

Commercialisation

Observers at mid-century were frequently uncertain how to respond to the developments in the market for cheap fiction.[79] The forces for progress and regression were not only evenly balanced but often interchangeable. On which side, for instance, were they to place a man like John Dicks, who in addition to his pioneering cheap reprints of the classics was making a small fortune out of Reynolds' *Mysteries of London*, the offspring of Eugene Sue's sensational *Mysteries of Paris* and parent in turn to a host of deplorable English imitations?[80] The problem of evaluation was compounded by the instability of the structure of production and consumption. Mayhew's elaborate delineation of the street singers and patterers was in part an obituary for a world which was disappearing as he discovered it. The agencies which had produced the complex body of written and spoken forms were still in motion. Cash transactions were becoming ever more central to the use of the imagination,[81] and the proportion of the population able to make some use of the printed word was becoming ever larger. In the event, the pattern of change was to be determined by two questions: firstly, whether the material resources of potential readers and writers of imaginative literature could keep pace with the possibilities for commercial expansion; secondly, whether their mental resources, in particular their command over the tools of literacy gained in the classroom, could match the opportunities which lay ahead.

In terms of volume and price, the trade in imaginative literature during the second half of the nineteenth century represented a copybook example of the progress of the capitalist economy. Increasing demand stimulated competition which in turn extended the market. The cottage industries of Seven Dials were challenged by older established firms prepared to lower their sights to increase their profits, and by new enterprises capable of exploiting modern techniques of mass advertising and selling.[82] The pioneering efforts of Milner and Dicks in the field of cheap reprints had attracted as many as ninety imitations by the 1890s. Only the guinea-and-a-half three-decker, cushioned by the circulating libraries, held out, but eventually its price too was forced down to 6s. There were two general consequences. Firstly, with every year that passed, more could be bought for less. A penny would buy a 250-word broadside in the 1840s, a fifty-page songbook or a 7,000-word serial by the 1860s, a 20,000-word novelette by the 1880s, and from 1896, with the appearance of Newnes' Penny Library of Famous Books, unabridged versions of classic texts.[83]

Secondly, the relationship between the producer and consumer gradually became more formal.[84] Those who had mediated the shift from the spoken to the printed word lost their place to the more specialised singers and reciters, or to more impersonal modes of distribution. The engine of change, as *The National Review* recognised, was purely commercial:

> The decay of the street ballad-singer, which is a fact beyond question, and which we attribute more to the establishment of such places of amusement as Canterbury Hall and the Oxford, and the sale of penny songbooks, than to the advance of education or the interference of the police, will probably be followed by the disappearance of the broad-sheet, and may silence the class of authors who wrote the street ballads.[85]

Performance survived, but it was taken off the streets and increasingly confined to reproduction rather than re-creation. Although the early music halls absorbed much of the broadside tradition and maintained a close rapport with their audiences, their material was translated back into print in penny songsters which were sold in shops and read in the home.[86] A contemporary innovation, the penny readings, encouraged a new generation of working men and women to listen to, and, in spite of the development of a circuit of professionals, often to sing or recite an immense range of classic and contemporary material, but in a manner which enhanced rather than undermined the status of the fixed text.[87] The leading proponent of the movement explained that the success of the enterprise depended on the 'habit of careful study on the parts of the readers, and a desire, on their part, to make their elocution as perfect as possible'.[88] In their attitude to received English they were an adult version of the literacy lessons in the inspected schools, which in time were equipped with literary anthologies of similar scope and substance.[89]

The increasing reliance upon print to stimulate the imagination was a reflection of the improvement in the standard of living of the majority of the labouring population during the second half of the nineteenth century. The growth of new forms of organised and private consumption of prose and verse were a consequence of the availability of more money and more time in which to spend it. Initially the labouring poor were excluded from some of the more dramatic innovations of the new era. They could no more purchase the shilling or two-shilling 'yellow-back' railway fiction of the 1850s than they could afford to use the stations on which they were sold.[90] But gradually cash wages rose to meet the falling cost of all forms of mass communication, and by the last decade of the century, transports of delight appeared accessible to all, regardless of class or gender. Agnes Repplier observed the new travelling public: 'The clerks and artisans, shopgirls, dressmakers, and milliners, who pour into London every morning by the early trains, have, each and every one, a choice specimen of penny fiction with which to beguile the short journey, and perhaps the few spare minutes of a busy day.'[91] Such a balance of work and pleasure, need and satisfaction was, however, difficult to sustain. There were persisting tensions between opportunity and fulfilment which became more marked if readers moved from light to serious fiction, and frequently unmanageable if they attempted a transition from consumers to producers of the written word.

To begin with, there remained at the end of the period sections of the population too poor to afford general access to books or newspapers, cheap though they had now become. In Rowntree's careful classification of income and expenditure in York in 1899, it was not until he reached Class 'D', skilled labourers and their families, that he found widespread use of the skills taught in the schools. Even here, the horizons were limited: 'for the most part, the reading of Class 'D' is confined to the evening papers, to more or less sentimental or sensational novels, or to the endless periodicals made up of short stories, scrappy paragraphic comments upon men and events, columns of jokes and riddles, and similar items of merely trivial character'.[92] The struggle for existence for Classes A to C, which comprised nearly half the working class in York, was still so desperate as to preclude regular expenditure on such luxuries. Should any pence become available, the first priority would be newspapers, particularly the sporting press.[93] The now well-established public libraries, which might have met the needs of this sector of society, remained a hostile environment to those who lacked confidence in their appearance and manner. As Lady Bell observed: 'A woman who lives in a distant part of the town, whose outer garment may be a ragged shawl, fastened with a pin, may not like going up an imposing flight of stairs, getting a ticket, giving a name, looking through a catalogue, having the book entered etc; whereas many of these, if the book were put into their hands, would read it.'[94]

The durability of print, and sheer scale of the industry by the last quarter of the century, with the sale, for instance, of sensational serial fiction calculated at two million copies a week in the late eighties,[95] meant that even the most destitute might sooner or later come across a fragment of prose to take their minds off their troubles. The central problem was one of control. The very poor could not ensure a constant supply of the cheapest material, and the marginally more prosperous experienced severe restrictions on their patterns of reading, particularly if their initial contact kindled serious intellectual ambitions. Sections of the market remained the preserve of the middle class despite the fall in prices. The purchase of new full-length fiction was a luxury denied to the bulk of the population, even after the guinea-and-a-half three-deckers had finally been overthrown. The most prosperous artisan was reduced to joining the queue at the library, or, as was most often the case, resorting to reprints, which became cheaper as the material was more distant from the present.

Once literature had been acquired, the obstacles to sustained reading were acute, notwithstanding the improvement in conditions since the first half of the century. If the home was less frequently also the place of labour,[96] it continued to be too crowded to afford the privacy in which to concentrate upon a book.[97] Despite a marginal increase in average house size, it was still next to impossible to withdraw from the noise and bustle of the family. As George Humphery recognised, 'very few can afford a separate room for study, which has to be conducted in surroundings not at all conducive to clear and constructive thought'.[98] The young miner Thomas Burt, whose taste for literature had been fired by youthful encounters with sensational fiction, found that the study of the volumes of Pope and Milton which he subsequently acquired was far from easy in his crowded home:

> One great drawback which I keenly felt was the want of seclusion. There was, of course, no study or library into which I could retire. The cottage in which we lived, though it compared not unfavourably with other colliery houses of the period . . . contained but one room – a fairly large one, which served for kitchen, bedroom, washhouse, sitting-room and all other household purposes.[99]

It was quieter in the evenings, but if the quality of candles had improved, and gas lighting was beginning to appear in better artisan housing,[100] reading after dark remained for the most part a threat to eyesight and pocket alike. If the male members of the household worked a shorter week and enjoyed more clearly defined free time, it was as it always had been difficult to stay awake in front of a long book after many hours of physical toil.[101] 'To be wearied at the day's end', commented a piece on 'The Reading Public', 'and read nothing that demands more concentrated attention than an illustrated magazine, is only human nature.'[102] The womenfolk, whose labours never finished, found it yet more difficult to set aside 'definite intervals of leisure', as Lady Bell observed, 'and not so many of them care to read'.[103] The constant pressure on the newly literate was towards the light and the fragmentary – 'Simply "snippets" and penny novels', wrote J. H. Haslam, '– always "snippets" and penny novels. These invariably go well among a class that reads by fits and starts.'[104]

By means of hunting through second-hand bookstalls, joining libraries and pooling resources with the occasional neighbour or workmate with similar intellectual tastes, the determined and not yet destitute reader could put together some sort of programme of study, albeit at the cost of forgone mealtimes, foreshortened sleep, and forsworn luxuries of every kind.[105] It was when he, or much less often she, thought to turn a passion for fiction or poetry into a source of income rather than expenditure that difficulties began to become insurmountable barriers. In common with other industries of mass communication in the nineteenth century, the profession of letters expanded far more rapidly than most forms of manufacture and commerce. The most recent survey has calculated that the population of full-time writers grew about fifteen-fold during this period.[106] As publishers started to move into the popular market in the middle decades of the century and the street authors went into a corresponding decline, new opportunities for making a living out of the increasing demand for imaginative literature appeared to open up.[107] There was, as we have seen, little sense of intellectual property amongst those who wrote instant verses of paragraphs for the broadside entrepreneurs. All future rights were ceded for the equivalent of about three pints of beer, and the material would in turn face widespread piracy if it was successful. The subsequent formalisation of relations between audience, writers and publishers, accompanied by an extension and tightening up of copyright,[108] suggested that manual workers who had discovered a literary talent might consider an alternative and more prosperous means of supporting their families. In practice, such expectations were rarely fulfilled.

Whereas for most modern writers the first step towards getting into print is often the most difficult, for the ill-educated, inexperienced working-class writers of the mid nineteenth century, this was much the easiest stage in the journey. The loss of access caused by the decline of street literature was more than compensated for by the rise of the provincial press, which constituted at once a nursery and a shop window for new literary talent. The confines of their columns matched the limited time and energy of their contributors. They had just enough space to publish the short poems which tired working men could manage to set down at the end of a working day. Such was the eagerness for self-expression that an aspiring writer might have to endure numerous rejections,[109] but once he had caught the editor's attention, he was instantly translated into a published if as yet unpaid writer. Thus, for instance, the mill-worker William Billington, who had made the acquaintance of Chaucer, Spenser, Shakespeare, Milton, Dryden, Pope, Scott and the Romantics in his early youth and dreamed of joining their ranks, started on his way when his work appeared in the 'Poet's Corner' of the *Blackburn Standard* in 1850.[110] His slowly increasing local reputation and the gradually mounting pile of press cuttings heightened his ambition, but at this point, market forces intervened. A largely middle-class reading public which would buy the productions of local labourers when they were merely a diversion in a sixpenny newspaper were not prepared to spend money on a full-length volume in sufficient quantity to attract a commercial publisher. As was to happen time and again in this period, Billington found that further progress was dependent on the intervention of a patron, which simultaneously deprived him of both the status and artistic independence of a professional writer.[111]

The local gentry or, increasingly, the urban middle class, who took up a poor but promising versifier, exacted a price. Unlike their eighteenth-century predecessors, they were cautious about attempting to remodel the surroundings of a new discovery, whom they now wished to see as a representative figure of the newly literate working class, but felt no compunction about reshaping their writings.[112] Whether the writer possessed major talent, like John Clare, who suffered endless difficulties with interference in his vocabulary and rhyme schemes from those who helped him into print,[113] or was a more modest figure like the woolcomber John Nicholson, whose first sponsor, J. G. Horsfall Esq., took it upon himself to suggest suitable topics and supervise the correction of 'many orthographical errors, arising from the author's imperfect education',[114] he was threatened by a loss of control over his creative activity in return for seeing his work between hard covers. Constantly reminded of his dependency on those who assisted him, the struggling poet found it impossible to develop a clear sense of either his own identity or that of his audience. Even when his book was published, it would not yield sufficient financial return to emancipate the author from either his employment or his patron, and he was left with a future precariously balanced between the uncertainties of the labour market and the whims of prosperous literati who had scant sympathy for any signs of social or ideological deviancy on the part of their humble muses. The reed-maker John Critchley Prince enjoyed a brief moment of fame and prosperity when his *Hours with the Muses*, published under the patronage of the future MP for York, was well received, but thereafter led a life of increasing material difficulty, blaming his patrons for failing to find him a suitable alternative to manual labour, whilst his biographer shared 'the opinion entertained by many of poet's friends, that he trusted too implicitly to the success of his works for that independence which he should, rather, have sought as the reward of thrift and industry'.[115] Such friends were alienated not only by his drinking but also by his willingness to write poetry for money rather than at the behest of his muse and his patrons. 'You cannot believe how tired I am of writing poetry', wrote Prince towards the end of his life, 'except for occasional solace and from my own impulses. I have leaned on a reed, and it has pierced me instead of sustaining me.'[116]

The expanding body of full-time novelists during the second half of the century remained very largely a middle-class preserve.[117] Writers from working-class backgrounds lacked the resources to begin composing full-length fiction and the outlets in which to publish it. The few who managed to contribute to serial fiction were rarely able to make a living out of it. Just as newly literate readers could not afford copyright books, so those amongst them who became authors could not afford to retain copyright in what they wrote. The conflict between the aspirations kindled by the increasing possession of literacy and the obstacles created by the diminishing opportunities for publication became ever more acute. In an article on 'The Difficulties of Appearing in Print' in 1850, the self-taught poet and handloom weaver Charles Fleming drew attention to a situation which was to become worse as the century wore on:

> The diffusion of knowledge through out our country, and the correct principles that have been introduced into the method of teaching the arts and speaking and reading in the very remotest nooks of our land, have in many instances, given birth to the desire of appearing in print ... Yet what of all this, when he is told by a bustling man of the world behind a counter, that his work, if published, would only facilitate the process of trunk making, or make good enough envelopes for rolls of tobacco? ... The desire of appearing in print is replete with difficulties to the candid and ardent mind. Repulsed on all hands, and sometimes treated as a dreaming enthusiast, he has often to explain the stanzas of a poem to a careless patron, or, it may be, show the sections of an essay to the gratification of idle curiosity, with the view of honeying down a name to a subscription list.[118]

Beyond the special case of dialect literature, to which I shall return, the bulk of imaginative activity was carried on independently of the literary market place.[119] The failure of men like Billington and Nicholson to break into the ranks of full-time authors did not destroy their passion for versifying. If the increasing access to provincial newspapers held out a misleading vision of escape from manual labour, the incentive it gave to composition was genuine. In the northern industrial centres in particular, there grew up a noisy throng of self-educated writers who met sometimes formally, more often in public houses, and poured out extempore verses, satires and epitaphs on each other, on their neighbours and on local dignitaries of varying repute.[120] Their excessive consumption of alcohol, which dismayed their patrons and has exercised the sympathy of more recent observers, may have been a consequence of frustrated hopes and irreconcilable tensions, but it was also a product of their continuing participation in their own culture. Those who bought them drinks in return for verses were engaging in the only absolutely reliable, even-handed transaction that was available. And at least in the short term, there was no necessary antithesis between alcohol and the imagination. As Nicholson's biographer was forced to admit, 'when under the influence of intoxicating liquor, he seldom misbehaved in any other manner than raving in poetry'.[121]

The difficulties experienced by readers and would-be authors in establishing adequate command over access to an increasingly commercialised system of producing imaginative material were only part of the explanation of the quality of the literature which found its way into shops, newsagents and station book-stalls. In an open market place, with prices falling and the disposable income of the bulk of the population rising, it was reasonable to ask questions of the discrimination of the reading public. Many observers were inclined to lay the blame for shortcomings in the fiction offered for sale at the feet of consumers rather than, or as well as, producers. According to John Parker in a prize essay in 1853, '*The Mysteries of London*, and *The Mysteries of the Court of London*, both penny weekly publications from the pen and press of G. W. M. Reynolds, are extensively circulated and sold to young men and young women of imperfect moral education.'[122] Whether or not contemporary serials were 'in harmony with the worst instincts of our own nature', as Parker claimed, he had a point in drawing attention to the audience for whom Reynolds was writing, and in particular to the training it had received in the classroom. Just as the exercise of the imagination was ever more dependent on reading rather than listening, so the task of equipping the population with the tools of literacy was, as we have seen, increasingly the responsibility of the inspected schools. In the past, ways of gaining access to stories and verse had been learned by the child as it began to talk and to listen to the speech of others. But as the role of performance declined, professional teachers sought to establish a monopoly of transmitting the new skills of communication. An ever larger proportion of the public for whom Reynolds and his successors were labouring, from which Nicholson and his fellow bards were drawn, had been taught how to read and what to read, how to write and in what context, by means of the systems of instruction whose content and application were traced in chapter 3.

The children who emerged from the schools before and after the Revised Code had to overcome three handicaps. Firstly, they had little sense of how to employ the skills with which they had been equipped to extend the body of tales, ballads and rhymes which they had already absorbed in the home and which they would continue to pick up, albeit in a less pervasive form, from those with whom they lived and played. So far from their receiving an imperfect moral education, as Parker claimed, it seemed all too often as if the sole application of their instruction was to a body of arid and intimidating behavioural values. Secondly, until the last quarter of the century they received little or no guidance on how to choose and derive benefit from the fiction and poetry which was thrust at them from an increasingly wide variety of shops and stalls outside the school gates. Even when the anthologies of approved literature began to make their appearance in the classroom, only a tiny proportion of children spent any time with them, and only a fraction of the available and affordable forms of contemporary literature was to be discovered within their pages. Finally, as we have seen, the pen was for copying the sentences of others, not inventing your own. Composition was eventually admitted to the official curriculum in 1871, but as a means of exploiting the Penny Post, not of imitating penny dreadfuls. In the face of the growing commercialisation of the imagination, the difficulty of bridging the gap between possessing and wielding the tools of literacy both paralleled and compounded the problem of reconciling the poverty of the readers and writers and the apparent wealth of opportunity which lay at their feet.

The interaction between the aptitude of the audience and the prose which was written for it can be glimpsed in the work of one of the most prolific mid-nineteenth-century serial authors, Thomas Prest, whose successes included the introduction of Sweeney Todd to popular melodrama.[123] A characteristic production was *Evelina, the Pauper's Child; or, Poverty, Crime, and Sorrow, A Romance of Deep Pathos*, published by Edward Lloyd in 1851. As its title indicated, the tale combined the classic ingredients of the gothic novel, with an innocent heroine enduring extremes of misfortune at the hands of heartless villains and sightless fate until, as the final page announced, 'Evelina, once the pauper child, became the Countess of Westbourne Sidley.'[124] In one sense its appeal was obvious enough. The novel was packed with dramatic incident, and until the narrative reached the sunny uplands of the landed gentry, was grounded in recognisable working-class life, including a harsh account of conditions in a workhouse, and much, albeit generalised and frequently misprinted, concern for the lot of the underprivileged: as one of the characters is made to remark, 'The world is bad enough, and there is but little sympathy in it with the suffering victims of poverty.'[125] What is of particular interest, however, is how Prest sought to meet half-way the semi-literate, half-educated state of his readership.

The text is pervaded by a sense of its own limitations. Time and again a crisis in the story overcomes the power of the pen. When, for instance, Evelina's father is (wrongfully) arrested for murdering the rapacious

Colonel Ormond, 'No words could do justice to the feelings of the wretched Mrs. Marsden and Evelina'; at the subsequent trial, 'Vainly would we seek to give even a faint idea of the anguish, the maddening anguish of mind and body that Mrs. Marsden and Evelina were suffering.'[126] In part this was merely a stock device of appealing over the footlights to the emotions of the audience, but it also represented a deliberate admission of the inadequacy of written language in the process of communication. The prose could aspire to do no more than supply the raw materials upon which the readership could go to work. The final climax is left typically unfinished: 'O, how vain would it be for us to attempt to portray the agony of Evelina and Mr. Langton when they received this intelligence; or to give anything like an adequate idea of the scene which followed when father and daughter met once more after the lapse of so many years within the gloomy walls of a dungeon. We must leave it to the imagination of the reader.'[127]

This withdrawal by the author was a response to both the continuing vitality of oral modes of entertainment and the prevailing weakness of the new tools of literacy. Songs and stories had gained their effect, as Prest sought to, by conveying the outline of an event or character, and expecting the listeners, who shared a frame of reference, to develop appropriate emotions and dialogues in their heads. Those who now bought the penny serials would not be at a loss when thrown back on their own powers of invention. At the same time, minimal demands were made of the skills of reading. Faced with a weekly deadline, and expected to produce if not value than at least bulk in return for money, Prest and his fellow authors supplied plenty of words, but made small use of them. The scene-setting was stereotyped, the speech highly stylised. Here, for instance, a moment of crisis is presented with a familiar blend of reticence and convention: 'Colonel Ormond had retreated nearer towards the door, and the rage that filled his bosom needs no description to bring it to the imagination. "And so, Richard Marsden", he said, gnashing his teeth and frowning frightfully.'[128] The inexperienced or inattentive reader missed little; the more fluent or careful one gained scant reward. Very rarely was an effect gained through the quality of the prose alone. It was writing by numbers for those for whom the printed word was still an artificial mode of communication.

On their own terms, the products of Prest and his contemporaries, especially the immensely popular G. W. M. Reynolds, could be effective. The balance between the inherent orality and the hesitant literacy of the readers was maintained by the vivid colour and relentless pace of the story. The conventions of melodrama were the only means of bridging the gap between the expectations and capabilities of those who bought the penny fiction.[129] When handled with energy and skill, the texts could integrate social comment with high adventure and provide the newly educated with a hugely entertaining return for the investment of limited skills and scarce pennies. Yet the device of appealing to real emotions through artificial language, of appropriating the strengths of the old forms of communication to compensate for the shortcomings of the new, was difficult to sustain. The complementary forces of the mechanisation of production and the systemisation of education gradually emptied the genre of the life it once contained. The writers employed to meet the escalating demand for new fiction found it all too easy to recycle plots and prose in increasingly sterile forms, while the audience trained more comprehensively yet no more deeply by the schools found it all too difficult to make more ambitious demands of the material they found on sale. As a result, the language and the situations became ever more predictable and ever less recognisable. Penny fiction came to display, in the words of one commentator,

> A gentle and unobtrusive dullness; a smooth fluency of style, suggestive of the author's having written several hundred of such stories before, and turning them out with no more intellectual effort than an organ-grinder uses in turning the crank of his organ; an air of absolute unreality about the characters, not so much from overdrawing as from their deadly sameness.[130]

'Love Leads to a Fortune', in the *Monthly Magazine of Fiction* of 1885, has exactly the same plot as Evelina, with a poor girl courted by a gentleman and discovering in the final chapter that because of a family feud and a forged will, she is heir in her own right to her fiancée's estates. However, the depiction of poverty, which gave some sense of scale and movement to Prest's equally contrived story, is vestigial to the point of non-existence, and rather than provoking the imagination, the prose forecloses the possibility of any mental activity outside the printed page. There were no longer any answers to be made to the appeals to the reader: 'It was lovely spring weather', the story concludes, 'when the bells of Pilsby church rang out for Sir Adrian Warburton and his bride. Health and youth and wealth were their portion, and what more has earth to give?'[131]

Taught as they were that literacy was a tool for promoting self-discipline, that the written word was a vehicle for absorbing disconnected facts rather than developing powers of free thought and fancy, the newly educated readers found it extremely difficult to bridge the gap between what the State forced them to learn and the market asked them to buy. The less parents participated in the transmission of the skills of communication to their children, and the less their children as they grew up were able to participate in the production and reproduction of their imaginative resources, the greater was the problem of retaining contact with more indigenous oral and literary forms of expression. As education became comprehensive and then compulsory, the circus of cheap fiction seemed ever more attractive over the walls of the school courtyard, the relation between the two ever more distant. Where the systematic curriculum offered one pretence of wholeness, the penny serial with its stereo-typed characters and happy endings[132] offered another. In neither case was it possible to establish a basis for reworking the experience of daily life.

At the same time, both in the classroom and on the bookstalls, the classics of fiction and poetry were becoming more available. However, instead of enriching the long-established diversity of popular culture, the increase in access was threatening to impoverish it by driving a wedge between the serious and the sensational. It was not that in the past, every English labourer possessed his own well-thumbed copy of Milton, or spent every evening reading Pope or Dryden. Of the Augustan texts, only *Robinson Crusoe, Moll Flanders* and *Gulliver's Travels* found their way into chapbook form.[133] Rather it was that the leading names in the literary heritage were no strangers to the half-educated and the self-educated, and they felt no embarrassment or undue deference if they encountered a fragment of a text on a bookstall or a scene from a play in the repertoire of travelling actors. 'The common people', wrote Clare in 1825, 'know ... the name of Shakespeare as a great play writer because they have often seen him nominated as such on the bills of strolling players that make shift with barns for theatres.'[134] Shakespeare was a familiar presence in the reading lists of autobiographies in the first half of the century,[135] and the less committed readers might come across his poetry in the eclectic outpouring of the 'Seven Dials publishers: 'On turning over a massive bundle', wrote C. M. Smith of such material, 'we find them to embrace lyrical selections from the works of Shakespeare, Herrick, Suckling, Rochester, Burns, Byron, Moore, Dibdin, Russell, Eliza Cook and a number of other names well known in literature.'[136]

Clare, however, was concerned that the 'common fames' of the bard and 'paltry balladmongers' had bred indifference to their relative merits, and looked forward to the development of a more informed literary judgment. Yet when in the last quarter of the century the schools began to teach 'literature' to children who could then afford to go out and buy unabridged editions, it seemed to some observers less a matter of deepening a long-held involvement and more one of rescuing a popular taste corrupted by the very success of the schools. Compared with Clare's time, 'Elementary education in its more merely mechanical sense', as Thomas Wright put it, had transformed the opportunities of the common people: 'An overwhelming and now constantly increasing majority of them can read; and, broadly speaking, it may be said that in the present day who can read may read, and have choice of reading.'[137] However, in the absence of proper guidance the freedom had become a licence, and the mass of new readers were by this time insulated from the material which in more relaxed if less literate decades they might have glimpsed sight of: 'the tremendous increase in the lower kinds of prose reading that recent times have witnessed, has, among its other evil effects, led to the neglect of the works of poets who could be understood of the people – works the perusal of which could certainly tend to elevate the taste of any whose previous reading had been in the poorer or lowest forms of serial publications'.[138] Only 'elderly readers among the working-classes'[139] could display an easy acquaintance with such literature.

This reduction of 'choice' to a stark contrast between the elevating and the corrupting was both misleading and perceptive. In one sense it was a gross over-simplification of the confusion which still reigned in the imaginative resources of the labouring poor. The sheer durability of print, together with the continuing inability of the most dedicated autodidact to control access to new copyright literature, constantly disordered the chronology of publishing in this period. By the second half of the nineteenth century, the literary world of the common reader represented a vast, cluttered, uncatalogued second-hand bookshop. Forms of fiction and verse long thought to be obsolete survived in forgotten corners to be rediscovered by fresh generations anxious to practise their recently acquired skills. As late as the 1890s there could be found outside the railway station in Nottingham a broadside seller whose stall contained a selection of Catnach's ballads.[140] Categories of books initially produced for the wealthiest end of the market were in time begged, borrowed or resold into the hands of far less prosperous consumers. At the end of the century, John Eldred, a stonemason's son growing up in a London tenement devoid of any literature save a Sunday paper, found his mental universe suddenly transformed through the purchase by his enterprising mother of the small library of emigrating neighbours:

> I open each of the newly-purchased volumes with a thrill, handle it gently and reverently. I remember all the titles – a mixed assortment: *Pilgrim's Progress*; *Don Quixote*; Defoe's *Journal of the Plague Year*; Darwin's *Voyage of the Beagle*; Hakluyt's *Voyages*; Cook's *Voyages*; J. H. Speck's *Discovery of the Sources of the Nile*; Hugh Miller's *Old Red Sandstone*; Herbert Spencer's *First Principles*; a volume of Emerson's *Essays*; *The Old Curiosity Shop*; Reade's *It's Never Too Late to Mend*; *The Vicar of Wakefield*; George Eliot's *Mill on the Floss*; Harrison Ainsworth's *Old St. Paul's*; Bulwer Lytton's *Last Days of Pompeii*; *Treasure Island*; *Masterman Ready*; *Children of the New Forest*; *Gulliver's*

Travels; Carlyle's *Sartor Resartus* – and a bound volume of *Ally Sloper's Half-Holiday*.[141]

Three centuries of books stood side by side and amidst them, the oral tradition still survived, at once extending and collapsing the imaginative perspective of the growing child. Thomas Jackson, a compositor born in 1879, derived his early entertainment from a collection of literature he found at the bottom of a cupboard, and from listening to his father's singing: 'Some of his songs were ballads I have since seen in "broad-sheets", some were ballads I have not met in print – such as the seaman's song (probably derived from the brother of my grand-father's grandfather who was supposed to have fought both at St. Vincent and the Nile).'[142]

The variety was inescapable, particularly in the first few years after leaving school, but at the same time the opportunities for discrimination were growing. As Wright indicated, by the last quarter of the century, an experienced reader could choose between a penny serial and a reprinted classic or an improving monthly, and perhaps of equal importance, could form an opinion of those who displayed a different taste. Those facing this dilemma were doubly disqualified by their education from effectively resolving it. In the first instance, the encounter with serious literature, even for the small minority who lasted through to the sixth and later seventh grades, was too slight and ended too soon to equip them with the means of charting a successful course across the sea of literature they might encounter beyond the classroom. The complaints which echo through the accounts of early-nineteenth-century readers who had received little or no formal schooling[143] are still present in the autobiographies of those born late enough to enjoy the full fruits of compulsory education. Jack Lawson, a miner's son born in 1881, attended day schools until he was twelve, when he left to go down the pit. Despite the rigours of his work, he was able to practise his literacy on adventure stories which led to more substantial material, including Dickens, Scott, Eliot, and the Brontës: 'Then came Shakespeare; the Bible; Milton and the lives of the poets generally. I was hardly sixteen when I picked up James Thomson's *Seasons*, in Stead's "Penny Poets" '.[144] The variety and novelty of the literature was at once exciting and bewildering. It suddenly appeared possible to ready everything and understand nothing. The problem was, as he later wrote, 'there were no persons to act as guides to men who desired to study'.[145] Intermittent encounters with similarly committed but inexperienced readers might help, as might the occasional mutual improvement society, but neither could bridge the gap between the limited and mechanical skills with which the child was equipped at school and the boundless and subtle demands of the now widely available cheap reprints.

Secondly, the attempts which began in the aftermath of Forster's Education Act to broaden the range of literature encountered in the classroom and to encourage children to write themselves tended to force alternative forms of imaginative expression still further apart.[146] In one sense the innovation represented a major advance on the curriculum prior to and immediately following the Revised Code. Pupils who were given, for instance, Stevens and Hole's *The Grade Lesson Books in Six Standards Especially adapted to meet the Requirements of the New Code*, 1871, would, unlike any of their predecessors, find themselves reading Chaucer, Spenser, Shakespeare, Milton, Pope, Cervantes, Goldsmith, Gilbert White and Dickens if they survived the course. Yet the approach to this material, and to the new art of composition, remained essentially oppositional. The texts were intended to promote the 'mental culture of youth', as Stevens and Hole explained: 'By introducing those who may use their book to an acquaintance with some of the best English classics they seek to contribute to the formation in them of a pure literary taste.'[147] This purity of taste bore no relation to the aesthetics of either the oral tradition or street literature. The engagement with great writers was expected to elevate the pupil above the stories and songs learned in the home, and to give protection against the 'veritable mountian of pernicious trash'[148] on sale outside the classroom. 'If we wish, therefore, to get rid of the worse and weaker forms of penny fiction', wrote the *Quarterly Review* in 1890, 'we must begin in the school-room – not necessarily by yielding to the popular cry for technical education for boys and cookery classes for girls at public expense – but by encouraging the growth of something resembling culture.'[149]

'Culture' was designed to achieve by a more secular and less arid means the long-held ambition of reconstructing the judgment of working-class children through the promotion of new modes of communication. In the 1890s, the reading of good poetry was still encouraged as a means of instilling 'an increased desire to eradicate habits of pronunciation'.[150] Composition was also seen as a form of expression alien to the child's background. The early reports on the introduction of the subject were pessimistic; the Rev. C. F. Johnstone sought to explain the failures of pupils in his area:

> They cannot write English because they do not understand English. They have had no homes, perhaps, in which they could associate with educated persons, and no familiarity with educated speech, and the want has never been made good by any training in their schools which could give them the understanding of their language and a facility in the use of it.[151]

The expansion of the curriculum was making the rising generation more rather than less uncertain of its capacity to create new material, and more rather than less deferential to the great authors of the past.

Within the schools the consequence was to heighten the difficulty of moving between the categories of expression. Johnstone found, for instance, that those who tried composition were unable to find their own voice: 'In the places where it is attempted it is marred by the ambition of fine writing, and becomes intolerable from its affectation and bad taste.'[152] In the world beyond the classroom the increasing efforts to instil a better literary taste in the new readers compounded the long-established problem of reconciling literary forms which transcended class, region and time with the demands and capacities of newly educated local audiences. The first generation of industrial muses had been forced into the confining arms of middle-class patrons and the restricting columns of provincial newspapers by their failure to establish a market amongst the barely literate for verses which aspired to the high seriousness and refined language of the classics.[153] By the final decades of the century compulsory schooling and commercial enterprise had significantly increased access to authors who had so excited the early autodidacts, but in such a way as to reduce rather than increase their familiarity. Mass publishing had driven the facile penny productions further away from the more demanding literature, and mass education had immured the prestigious authors in a pantheon which too few of its pupils were equipped or willing to visit. The farm labourer Fred Kitchen enjoyed reading *Police News* and *Ally Sloper* with his workmates, but could go no further: 'So we got sensation, entertainment, and jollification; but never a line of good reading, for which I longed. I was too timid to bring my school prizes out for the other lads to jeer at ... So I shut myself out of the world of books and hunted rats.'[154] Others ploughed on regardless. At the end of the century, one of the more enthusiastic products of the new curriculum, the compositor Thomas Jackson, found that a sustained course of serious reading was divorcing him from the commonplace setting of his father's ballads which he had once so much enjoyed:

> Insensibly, pre-occupation with these 'classics' treated as a single category – the Best – caused a student to slip into regarding Culture as a fixed Mind-world in which one either ascended with the geniuses to supreme heights or sank with the dullards and the dunces to the uncultured slime. Insensibly, in this way, one acquired a complete detachment from – if not a downright contempt for – the uncultured vulgarity and sordidness of everyday life and actuality.[155]

In the employment of his imagination, all that he had in common with the consumers of cheap serials was his inability to use his literacy to engage with rather than turn away from the world in which he lived.

Conclusion

In the middle of the eighteenth century, the publisher William Dicey was in the habit of attaching the following note to his broadsides:

> the use of these Old Songs is very great, in respect that many Children never would have learn'd to Read, had they not took a delight in poring over Jane Shore, or Robin Hood &c. which has insensibly stole into them a Curiosity and Desire of Reading other the like Stories, till they have improv'd themselves more in a short time than perhaps they would have done in some Years at School.[156]

Despite the dramatic expansion in both the scale of the industry and the size of the reading public in the intervening period, this claim remained as true in 1914 as it had been in 1750. The exercise of the imagination was the greatest and most persistent incentive for gaining a command of the tools of literacy, and their first and most satisfying application. Without the chapbooks and broadsides, and later the penny dreadfuls and the cheap reprints, rather more than 5 per cent of the population would still have been illiterate by the time compulsory education was finally imposed; without the buoyant and later rapidly increasing number of signatures in the marriage registers, Dicey and his successors would not have made their fortunes. Beneath this seemingly fruitful partnership of commercial endeavour and consumer satisfaction, however, lay a complex process of change whose outcome was determined by the evolving relationship between the organisation of production and the skills and practices of the newly created readers and writers.

The imagination, as with other forms of cultural activity, is a way of managing experience. Through the use of oral or written language, events and emotions are given shape and value, and alternative visions of hope or despair are called into being.[157] The gradual extension of the realm of print at the expense of speech or song offered a more diverse and profound means of interpreting and reworking daily life, but its potential was dependent on how far those who wished to employ the new mode of communication could exercise control over it. There had always been some division of labour in the oral tradition, which was neither as anonymous nor as collective as folklorists liked to believe,[158] and commercially published ballads and stories had long commingled with those transmitted by word of mouth. The difficulties of participating fully and effectively in imaginative expression were not unprecedented, but as the process became more dependent on formal cash transactions and formal language training, they became more acute. Initially the incomplete state of both the commercialisation of manufacture and the training of the audience prolonged the role of performance in the structure of production and reproduction and generated material which had a genuine if crude relevance to the circumstances of the readers. Subsequently, as the industry became more intensively capitalised and the market more intensively educated, it grew increasingly difficult to prevent fissures opening up within the body of literary genres, and between them and the life which the mass of the population lived outside the printed page.

In many ways the success of the dialect movement from the mid-century onwards provided a negative illustration of the forces which were at work elsewhere. Older oral forms were combined with a growing confidence in the use of literacy to produce a diverse and vibrant category of material which consolidated the identity of the industrial communities, celebrating their values and achievements, and deploying myths about their past to condemn sufferings in their present.[159] This was made possible by the continuing existence of small-scale production, the revived vitality of performance in contexts more appropriate to the growing prosperity and leisure time of the workforce and their families, and by the resistance of the readership to attempts by the schools to standardise their employment of written language. At the height of the movement, William Billington, the millworker whose transition we have traced from a young enthusiast for the classics to a patronised poet of high feeling to an unpublishable versifier in public houses, found himself in print once more. After a lapse of twenty-two years he produced *Lancashire Songs, Poems and Sketches*, a collection of dialect verses, satire, squibs and humour which needed no middle-class intervention to help it sell. His abandonment of 'the deep questioning, the glowing imagery, the reverential spirit, the yearning for a glimpse of the unseen'[160] was a form of defeat for both Billington and his community, but as his biographer was now forced to accept, his new volume spoke to its audience: 'Its contents were, doubtless, more to the popular taste than the solemnly sonorous verse of Billington's first book; and, whilst his claim to be a true poet must rest chiefly upon the latter, the dialect rhymes of the second volume are likely to secure many more readers and admirers.'[161]

7

POLITICS

The Life and Opinions of Thomas Preston, Patriot and Shoemaker;
containing much that is useful, more that is true, and A great deal more,
(perhaps), than is EXPECTED! provides a succinct account of the
awakening of its author's political consciousness in the 1790s. Preston was
set on the road which was to take him through Spencean radicalism to a
trial for High Treason following the 1816 Spa Fields riots by the
destruction of his belief in the necessity of the established order:

> The increase of reading had dissipated the delusion, and people
> now knew the meaning of words, whether spoken in the Senate,
> wrote in a lawyer's bill of costs, or printed on an impress warrant.
> The charm of *Ignorance* which had so long lulled my mind into a
> *comparative* indifference at the people's wrongs, was now begin-
> ning to disappear.[1]

He was able to use the skills picked up during a 'contracted' education
to engage in an ultimately far-reaching critique of the language which
clothed and protected the distribution of power.[2] The impact of the new
forms of communication on old forms of authority has been widely
observed. 'Democracy as we know it', write Goody and Watt, 'is from the
beginning associated with widespread literacy.'[3] Reading and writing
promote political participation. Those who have been to school or who
have educated themselves are able to demystify authoritarian regimes and
gain access to the information upon which the effective exercise of their
newly won rights depends.[4]

However, if we look no further than the radical patriot and shoemaker,
it is evident that the application of the tools of literacy to politics was
fraught with difficulty. His new-found ability to discover the meaning of
words led not to liberty but to the foot of the gallows, from which he was
only rescued by the stubborn integrity of a London jury. The 'armour of
coercion', as Gramsci put it,[5] could be an effective response to unarmed
assaults on the hegemony of the State. At the same time Preston was not
making his voyage of intellectual discovery alone. Between the insubordi-
nate artisan on the one side, and the frightened and vengeful Government

on the other, lay a growing body of unenfranchised readers and sometimes writers whose debates, letters, pamphlets and occasional books gave a context for the use of his literacy; whose emerging corporate identity gave a shape to the demands he formulated; and whose organised strength, reinforced by key legal safeguards, provided such defence as was available against physical counter-attack. The passage from oral to literate modes of communication relied on and in turn demanded new ways of relating individual and collective forms of identity and behaviour. In 1913, R. A. Scott-James conducted a pessimistic review of the key agent in the development of the mass electorate, the newspaper press, 'the means by which Governments and other powers within a State acquired the information, the knowledge of facts and events, on which they acted'.[6] 'The only real democracy', he wrote in conclusion, 'is an actively conscious and self-expressive community.'[7] The actual or potential voter depended on the skills of reading and possibly writing to establish an effective relationship with entities larger than the family or immediate neighbourhood. What was at issue was the dimension, the coherence and the substance of the new, conscious community. Throughout the period those striving for reform and those seeking to contain it were engaged in a debate about the ways in which the newly literate could constitute and give effect to a common political culture.

The manner in which the tools of reading and writing created the 'informed, participant citizen' thus resolves itself into three related issues. Firstly it is necessary to examine how the State attempted to reconstitute the political nation through the promotion and control of mass literacy. Then there is the question of how the new skills were put into practice, particularly in respect of the most widely and consistently employed form of political communication in the period, the newspaper press. Finally there remain the successors of Thomas Preston, the minority of serious readers, those whom Gramsci hoped would become 'the whalebone in the corset'[8] of the working-class movement as it attempted to redefine the political in the interests of the labouring poor.

The State

The policy of the State towards the political implications of the growth of a reading and writing public underwent a series of transitions over the period. Between the first appearance of an autonomous radical movement in the 1790s, at a time when two in five men and three in five women were still illiterate, and the establishment of the Labour Party in 1906 on the eve of the virtual disappearance of marks from the marriage registers, the range of expectations and fears associated with the application of literacy altered very greatly. We can perhaps best establish the conjunction of ambition and apprehension which in varying proportions characterised official behaviour by glancing at a revealing crisis which blew up almost exactly half way through the period.

The introduction of the Penny Post in 1840 was, as we have seen, designed to transform the relationship between the individual and the nation.[9] The mass of the population were to be encouraged to acquire and above all to use the skills of literacy to establish regular and effective contact with each other regardless of distance. The constellations of private neighbourhoods, bounded by their dependence on the spoken word, were to be translated into an integrated society of freely communicating citizens. For the first time Britain would exist as a single entity, the elaborate and ever more extensive bureaucracy of the Post Office ensuring that every last village and hamlet would be brought into the stream of national life at a cost the poorest man or woman could afford. The campaign for reform took place against a background of deepening economic depression and rising working-class unrest. Its proponents argued that by exposing to rational intercourse the delusions which flourished unchecked in orally bounded communities, and by strengthening the ties of the basic authority structure of the family, the innovation would do much to avert the danger of violence and revolution in a way which would avoid overt and provocative physical repression. Yet the political risks were almost as great as the financial. Whether or not literate men would now use the post for pleasure, they had long employed it to foment unrest. At the moment when Rowland Hill succeeded in democratising correspondence, those advocating greater democracy by means of correspondence were still on the wrong side of the law. Sending threatening letters, a capital offence until 1823, was now punishable by transportation for life,[10] and under the Seditious Meetings Act of 1817, it remained illegal for political societies, their members or officers, to write to each other.[11]

The question of whether this extension of the use of literacy would strengthen or undermine the security of the State was brought out into the open four years later in the form of a major public controversy over the secrecy of the post. Since at least the middle of the seventeenth century, governments had been interfering with the mail to gain information on criminal or seditious activity.[12] The turmoil of the Revolutionary wars and their aftermath had caused an extension of the practice, with warrants being issued by the Home Secretary either for opening the correspondence of named individuals, such as Horne Tooke, Despard, Thistlewood, Watson and Orator Hunt, or for detaining any suspicious correspondence passing through particular post offices.[13] There was another flurry of warrants during the Reform Bill crisis, and again in 1838 and 1839 as Chartism grew in strength.[14] By this time, all leading working-class politicians assumed as a matter of course that any letter sent by post was liable to be read by or on behalf of the Home Office.[15] As the authorities chose individuals with the widest range of contacts in the movement, letters to or from a very large number of Chartists were at risk.[16] The sense of mistrust was intensified by the long-standing fear of police spies, and by the fact that usually the only sign that a letter had been opened was an unexplained delay in transit, which given the inefficiency of the unreformed Post Office was a common occurrence at the best of times.

The early months of the Penny Post coincided with a resurgence of Chartism, and the Home Office was quick to exploit the opportunities presented by a possible increase of correspondence amongst its enemies. In the first three complete years of the system a record number of warrants were issued.[17] Eventually the Italian republican Joseph Mazzini, then staying in London, was caught in the net.[18] Suspecting he was the victim of espionage, he encouraged William Lovett and Henry Hetherington, themselves the subjects of earlier warrants, to write him a specimen letter,[19] and when it was delivered with a tampered seal, took the evidence to the MP Thomas Duncombe, who presented a petition on his behalf to the House of Commons. The Home Secretary, Sir James Graham, at first refused on the grounds of national security to discuss the matter at all, and when he was eventually forced by mounting public clamour to appoint a Select Committee, insisted that its proceedings be held in private. Its report sought to defend official policy by appealing partly to precedent[20] and partly to the ease with which disaffected elements could now communicate in private with each other. The reduction in the cost of postage, together with the spread of literacy, demanded more rather than less State surveillance. If the powers of the Home Office were removed,

> every criminal and conspirator against the public peace would be publicly assured that he should enjoy secure possession of the easiest, cheapest and most unobserved channel of communication, and that the Secretary of State could not under any circumstances interfere with his correspondence.[21]

In opposition, Duncombe's campaign initially aroused great indignation in the national press, whose shock at the exposure of a practice so familiar to its victims was itself revealing. 'It is clear', wrote *The Times*, 'that however uninterrupted and undisputed this tradition may be in the Home Office, its discovery is a surprise to the nation.'[22] The protest took the form of an appeal not to an abstract notion of human rights, but to a national tradition of liberty. 'It was disgraceful to a free country', thundered Duncombe, 'that such a system should be tolerated – it might do in Russia, ay, or even in France, or it might do in the Austrian dominions, it might do in Sardinia; but it did not suit the free air of a free country.'[23] While Graham sought to defend civilisation from the dangers of privacy, his critics placed the sanctity of private expression at the centre of a civilised state.[24] The essence of the conflict was whether an individual extended or qualified his realm of privacy by engaging in written communication. In the Commons, Macaulay was in no doubt about the matter:

> I cannot conceive how we can make out that there ought to be any difference in principle in the way in which we should treat a letter in transit, and a letter after it has been delivered . . . they are both alike my property; and the exposure of my secrets is the same and attended with the same consequences, whether from the reading of a letter which is yet to be delivered, or from the reading of a letter which has been delivered.[25]

It was a principle which overrode any short-term considerations of national defence: 'So I say in the case before us, the experience of many years shows us that the benefits arising from the strict observation of the security of private life, without the exercise of arbitrary power, much more than counterbalances all the advantages to be derived from a contrary system.'[26]

In the event, the Government weathered the storm. *The Times* accepted the Select Committee's arguments that the powers were only exercised in a national emergency, and that by implication their use would now be confined to threats from below.[27] The only administrative reform was that the Home Office prudently ceased to keep a record of the warrants that were issued. Nothing was settled, least of all the tensions which had been exposed in the equation between the expansion of communication and the growth of political liberty. The attempt to replace the pattern of enclosed communities with a network of communicating citizens threatened on the one side the security of the State and on the other the security of the individual. But whereas the unresolved issues could be re-interred under a cloak of precedent and official secrecy in a way which is not unfamiliar in our own times, elsewhere they remained matters of continual debate and compromise. Since 1792, when Pitt's Government found itself simultaneously banning the distribution of radical literature and sponsoring, through the Reeves' Associations, the dissemination of political tracts, the State had been faced with the problem of reconciling demands to both expand and restrict the use of literacy.[28] The Whig theory of liberty, although seriously at variance with the practice of successive Whig and Tory governments, could not countenance permanent comprehensive censorship; at the same time no responsible ministry could permit the undisciplined employment of the tools of reading and writing.

The prosecution of the war against Napoleon postponed further consideration of the problem, but in the aftermath of Waterloo it returned to confront the Liverpool Administration. At the end of the decade, as the post-war radical movement reached its height, the Government was presented with the first serious legislative proposal to create a national system of elementary education, just after it had rushed through the Publications Act,[29] which further tightened restrictions on the radical press. In the event, Brougham's attempt to set up a network of parish-based schooling foundered on religious controversy, and the imposition of security bonds on printers, together with an extension of the scope of the stamp duty, represented the high-water mark in the history of attacks on opposition newspapers which went back to the reign of Queen Anne. Yet the terms of the debate looked forwards rather than backwards. The inquiries into the state of elementary education which preceded Brougham's Parochial Schools Bill placed the matter firmly in the public domain and gave implicit official recognition to the work of the National and British School Societies, and the arguments upon which the Stamp Duties Bill was based had much in common with the reasoning which led to the dismantling of all repressive legislation on news during the subsequent three and a half decades.

The question, stated Ellenborough in the Lords, was whether it was right to 'deprive the lowest classes of society of all political information?'[30] The short answer was yes: 'he saw no possible good to be derived to the country from having statesmen at the loom and politicians at the spinning jenny'.[31] However, the long-term prospect was characterised by three assumptions which would later be taken over by liberal reformers. Firstly it was recognised that by one means or another the common people had already gained sufficient command of the tools of reading and writing to engage in widespread political discourse. If Eldon's claim that 'there was now scarcely a village in the kingdom that had not its little shop in which nothing was sold but blasphemy and sedition'[32] bordered on the hysteri-cal, we now know from the analysis in chapter 4 that amongst the artisans who comprised the bulk of organised radicalism there was and had been for generations high levels of adult male literacy,[33] and beyond their ranks there was more than a sufficient distribution of reading skills to constitute a conduit for the writings of Paine and Cobbett. Lowe's oft misquoted injunction in 1867 to 'prevail on our future masters to learn their letters'[34] was half a century late, particularly in respect of the section of the labouring population enfranchised by the Second Reform Bill. From the 1790s onward, the greater problem was the possession rather than the absence of literacy.

Secondly, whereas the newspaper stamp originally had been imposed to quell criticism from within the ruling class, the concern was now exclusi-vely with the threat from below. 'It was not against the respectable press that this bill was directed', explained Ellenborough, 'but against a pauper press.'[35] Just as the educationists were attempting to devise a system of schooling adapted exclusively to the assumed needs of the lower orders, so the freedom to use the skills of literacy was conditional on class status.[36]

Finally, as much as the key question in educational reform became not whether teaching should take place but how and by whom it was supplied, so the basic issue in the development of political communication was the character of those who controlled it. The point of imposing a bond, explained Castlereagh, was that 'The times . . . in which we lived, seemed to him to require, that persons exercising the power of the press should be men of some respectability and property.'[37] If in the end it was impossible to prevent the lower orders, given their propensity to club together in the face of financial hardship, from reading newspapers, it did appear feasible to determine who wrote and published them.

Between the Reform Bill crisis and the mid 1850s, the financial relationship between the State and the use of literacy was transformed. Ensuring the responsible employment of reading and writing ceased to be a reliable source of revenue and became a mounting form of expenditure. The stamp duty, together with taxes on paper and advertisements, which in all had yielded a net income of a million pounds a year, was repealed,[38] and instead successive governments became committed to an annual subsidy of elementary education which was rising at an alarming rate.[39] Although the rhetoric of free speech was now much more to the fore, the major change was not in principle but in tactics. The argument with earlier repressive measures was over means rather than ends. The outpouring of unstamped papers in the early 1830s,[40] and the persistent difficulty of enforcing the reduced stamp after 1836, indicated that the devices adopted by Pitt and his successors were counter-productive. So far from guaranteeing the respectability of publishers, printers and editors, the restrictions were ensuring that those who communicated with the politically literate had in common only their poverty and their disrespect for the law, and so far from dispersing the enclosed working-class communities and binding their members to a new national polity, the shared experience of repression and high costs was uniting as never before the mass reading public in opposition to the State.

The solution was to abandon the use of corporate authority, and rely instead on a combination of private enterprise and private families. In the debate surrounding the reduction of the stamp in 1836, and its abolition in 1855 following a Select Committee four years earlier, it was pointed out that market forces would be far more effective than the law in driving the pauper press out of existence.[41] Whereas the illegal papers could be kept going by highly motivated volunteers, and small-scale legal ventures required cheap machinery and could obtain paper on credit, a mass circulation penny paper would need extensive capital reserves to acquire premises, buy presses and raw materials, hire staff, set up a distribution network and meet the costs of promoting the new product.[42] Not only would this ensure that only the right sort of person was attracted to the business, but once he had invested his money, he would not put it at risk by falling foul of the law. As the Select Committee pointed out, 'capitalists will not embark on an illegal proceeding'.[43] What inevitably would be a smaller number of papers would in turn be able to pay good rates to their writers, and contribute to the necessary professionalisation of journalism. And whilst the entrepreneurial resources of the unstamped publishers were underestimated,[44] Edward Lloyd's payment immediately following the abolition of the penny stamp of £10,000 for the country's first rotary press to print the largest circulation paper of the second half of the century appeared to validate the argument.

Once it had been established, the penny press, like the Penny Post, would strengthen the ties of domestic life, which would in turn ensure a more rational and disciplined employment of the tools of literacy. Reducing the cost of newspapers would remove the need for working men to club together to acquire political information. 'For his part', explained the Chancellor of the Exchequer in 1836, 'he would rather that the poor man should have the newspaper in his cottage than that he should be sent to a public house to read it.'[45] The problem was not so much the consumption of alcohol, although one witness to the 1851 Committee claimed to know personally 'the cases of men who never would have been drunkards but for going to the public houses to read the newspaper',[46] but rather that in such surroundings the news was not only read, but listened to and talked about in the company of those who were neither respectable nor sober. The ambition now was to place as much distance as possible between the oral and the literate, and between one politically conscious working man and another. The long-established tradition, prevalent in polite society as well as amongst the lower orders,[47] of multiple readers of single copies, was to be replaced by one individual, or at least one family, per paper.

Ensuring that the poor man in his cottage made the right choice and the correct use of a newspaper then became the responsibility of the school-master. Cheap newspapers, like cheap correspondence, would increase the demand for schooling, and when the children were inside the classroom, the teachers could commence the task, which was examined in chapter 3, of rebuilding the working-class family as the basic unit of moral order in society. It was the responsibility of the inspected curriculum not to inculcate the children in specific political truths, but rather to equip them with the cognitive skills which would enable them to understand, clearly but uncritically, the material placed before them in later life by the market economy. Neither could achieve the stable progressive society alone. Whilst it was evident by the time of the establishment of the Penny Post that religion could not supply an all-embracing, self-sufficient training in the schools, it was not clear whether it was possible or desirable to substitute an equally fixed and comprehensive secular programme of facts and values. There was too much hostility to the principle of the State defining and imposing a set of political truths, and too much uncertainty about the capacity of the barely literate, frequently absent children to grasp them. The Revised Code struck a new balance by retreating from the transmission of religious or secular bodies of knowledge, and placing the emphasis on the skills of reading and writing, which were to be directed specifically to the task of coping with the new press. The rubric of Standard VI, which was the summit of achievement in the early years of the Code, required that pupils display the ability to read 'a short ordinary paragraph in a newspaper or other modern narrative'.[48]

The construction of the partnership between the schoolmasters and the capitalist proprietors and editors, bound together by mass literacy, made possible a striking absence of direct political censorship, despite the possibilities of espionage by the Home Office, and of direct political indoctrination, despite some attempt to teach civic duties as the Revised Code was modified and extended in the last quarter of the century. Whilst those who campaigned against the residual penny stamp were justified in their complaints of a restriction on the freedom of the press, the extent of Government intervention was mild by comparison with many other European countries. After 1855, with the exception of the employment of the blasphemy laws against the secularists,[49] it was the bankruptcy rather than the criminal courts which threatened the existence of radical journalists and their editors. Equally, whilst those children who encountered the proliferating history textbooks received unambiguous instruction in the achievements of imperial Britain,[50] these fell far short of the kind of detailed 'lessons in the government and constitution under which we live'[51] that the more advanced reformers were demanding. In this way neither the acquisition nor the application of reading and writing could have overt political implications. By emptying the field of confrontation, successive governments sought to maximise the potential of mass literacy for creating a new sense of nationhood, whilst minimising the danger of equipping their enemies with yet more powerful weapons of subversion.

The hopes of success for such a strategy were not always shared by the agencies which were given the central role in its implementation. Teachers and school inspectors were in practice often less sanguine than politicians about the impact of schooling on the working-class family, and in the debate over the creation of a cheap press, it was *The Times*, fearful of competition from below, which was most in favour of the continuation of taxation, and the leading newspaper distributor W. H. Smith who was least optimistic about the good necessarily driving out the bad in a free market. The principal grounds for hope were derived, paradoxically, from the long history of the public engagement with literacy by the lower orders. The political function of reading and writing had never been confined to the corresponding societies, infidel tracts and unstamped press, vigorous and alarming though they had been. Since at least the 1760s, constitutional electoral politics had involved the production and dissemination of an increasing volume of literature whose form and content were designed for an audience far larger than the elite of enfranchised voters. The key innovator was John Wilkes, whose series of confrontations with the administrations of George III were conducted through the medium of pamphlets, newspapers, handbills and ballads deliberately aimed at the humble as well as the middling sort of people.[52] Both his propaganda techniques and the arguments he raised pointed towards the emergence of the artisan radical movement of the 1790s, yet it remains the case that Wilkes was for the most part engaged in what he claimed was the legal Parliamentary process, and his legacy was at least as influential in conventional constituency activity during the succeeding century.

An indication of the scope and function of the written word in the operation of the unreformed system may be gleaned from the extensive collection of material which has survived for the seat of Newcastle under Lyme.[53] A contested borough election was as much a bonanza for the local printers as it was for the publicans and innkeepers. It is difficult to be certain whether 'the consumption of literature by the unenfranchised matched their intake of alcohol, but there is no doubt that they constituted part of the audience for the barrage of material produced by the competing interests. For the writers of the addresses, satires, broadsheets and songs, the campaign was a long one, beginning with the jockeying for position between potential candidates before the election began and continuing beyond the poll as the successful party publicly thanked its supporters, and the defeated attempted to have the new MPs unseated for electoral malpractice. They were an integral element in the combination of drawing-room conspiracy and street theatre which characterised electoral politics until the professionalisation of the parties later in the nineteenth century, accompanied by the Ballot Act of 1872 and, more importantly, by the Corrupt Practices Act of 1883. Until then the non-electors were mobilised to dramatise the scale of support for candidates at the hustings, to intimidate, verbally or physically, opponents and their canvassers, and more generally to supply by means of ritual a sense of participation in the political process otherwise denied by the restricted franchise.

The broadsheets, vigorous in both appearance and language, were used to announce meetings, rally the faint-hearted, celebrate victorious skirmishes and condemn the character and behaviour of the opposition camp. The efficiency of the printers and distributors was such that an attack on a candidate published in the morning would find a response circulating through the streets later in the same day. Oral and written modes of campaigning reinforced each other at various levels. Some broadsheets were issued to counter alleged slanders, others to replenish the stocks of verbal abuse. The rowdy drama of the hustings was heightened by the regular display of the state of the poll during the two-week election. And the spirits of the crowd were sustained by the composition of political songs identical in style and format to the penny ballads with which the semi-literate were so familiar. Some of these were generalised versions of the rhetoric of the more formal broadsheets. In 1792, for instance, the opponents of the Stafford camp were supplied with the eight verse 'Fletcher & Liberty. Tune of, *Gee ho Dobbin*':

> He's generous, he's open, and free from all guile,
> And imperious upstarts he'll ever revile.
> He's the friend of the poor and belov'd by mankind,
> And true to our Interests we'll always him find.
> CHORUS. For he's honourable and worthy he's chosen to be,
> The guard of our Rights and of our liberty.[54]

Others were rhyming versions of the elaborately coded squibs and satires which were devised as parodies of open letters, race bills, recipes, lost and found notices, or, as in this example, public announcements:

> Worthy of Admiration, And appeared last Night. A wonderful Tom Cat with a Blue Tail, this Animal is of rare production from Lang-tang-rang, a newly discovered Island in China near Potters Land. He will be shown gratis tomorrow on his way to the Town Hall, and exhibits a beautiful spotted hump on his back. He will be attended by the Grand Master of the Coal Mart and his Suit, famed for their agility and sleight of hand in the Coal Trade, he has likewise in his keeping a fascinating curiosity from the Land of Ape's Dale, and never exhibited here before. A grand procession will attend this company on the way to the place of exhibition, where Radicals and Reformers will be admitted gratis.[55]

The impenetrable local references enhanced the sense of common membership of a local political community in which the divisions between the voters and the non-voters and between the competing factions were mediated by a shared partly literate, partly oral discourse.

In Newcastle, as elsewhere, tensions between conflicting class interests were proving increasingly difficult to contain by the 1830s, and the area was to be the scene of serious violence in 1842.[56] Yet in spite of the polarisation achieved by the First Reform Act and subsequently embodied in Chartism, the established modes of using formal communication to extend the political nation beyond the boundary of the franchise were still maintained, albeit in an increasingly modified form. This was partly because in its central tactics Chartism represented not the beginning of a new mode of political action but the culmination of the old. The constitutional device of collecting signatures to exert pressure on Parliament was carried to its logical conclusion, and the licensed disorder of the General Elections was formalised by the promotion of 'hustings candidates' who conducted a parallel mock contest, complete with published addresses and songs.[57] And it was partly because the enlarged and more consistently defined electorate created by the Reform Act complicated rather than transformed the existing practice of constituency politics. The outpouring of literature continued as before, plastering the walls and encouraging the newly educated to practise their skills. However, a combination of a doubling of the number of eligible voters and the development of new forms of mass communication, particularly the related ventures of the railways and the Penny Post, gradually led to the adoption of more centralised and bureaucratic means of employing the printed word.

As much as it was middle-class businessmen and holiday-makers, rather than manual workers and their families, who made the first and most extensive use of the Penny Post, so it was the contemporary political movements which reaped the most immediate and substantial benefit. The League's reserves and expertise enabled it to pioneer the large-scale use of the mail to educate the electorate and influence the conduct of actual or potential MPs.[58] In 1844 it sent over 300,000 letters together with over two million 'stamped and other publications'.[59] The League had assisted Rowland Hill in his campaign, and in the aftermath of the reform Richard Cobden was able to write to him acknowledging the value of a 'terrible engine for upsetting monopoly and corruption: witness our League operations, the *spawn of your penny postage*'.[60]

Such efforts required a systematic attempt to distinguish between voters, who could now be reached inside their homes, and non-voters, upon whom the League wished to avoid unnecessary expenditure. In this sense it represented a more divisive use of formal communication than the older forms of constituency politics. Yet the drive to compile and exploit a comprehensive and reliable register of electors which underpinned the League's campaign and became the basic task of the growing party organisations[61] necessarily affected a larger proportion of the population than was envisaged by those who redefined the franchise at the successive

Reform Acts. Whilst the Act of 1832 standardised the property qualification in the boroughs, its application proved less than straightforward.[62]
Potential voters were frequently apathetic or uncertain about their rights,
and the eligibility of those who made the effort to be registered, or had it
made for them, varied from year to year as their housing conditions
changed. The introduction to the boroughs in 1867 of the simple concept
of the householder, and its extension to the counties in 1884, merely
compounded the difficulties. The family circumstances of an electorate
which now reached well into the working class were yet more variable, the
problems of establishing and updating an accurate register yet more acute.
The consequence was that those who wished to communicate with the
electorate through some form of street literature, or, on the infrequent
occasions when the funds were available, through the post, were forced to
address a wider public than was strictly necessary, which in turn hastened
the transition, which was well under way by the 1850s, towards the more
generalised medium of the newspapers as a means of cutting down on
election expenses.[63]

It also meant an extension of the traditional practice of engaging the
indigent and ill educated to assist in the political process at elections. To
the continuing work of distributing or pasting up printed material was
added the remunerative if temporary task of assisting the party registration agent. The occupation attracted the growing army of politically
conscious labouring men unable to find permanent employment in trade
unions or other working-class bodies who enjoyed both the involvement
in the constituency organisation and the temporary respite to their
financial problems. One such was the energetic George Meek, whose wide
reading in his youth had prepared him for little more than a string of
casual jobs in and around his native Eastbourne. In the election of 1886 he
was able to earn 'an occasional shilling distributing circulars and so on',[64]
and then was given part-time work on the register. The election of 1890
brought renewed employment:

> In July and August I assisted the Liberal agent, as usual, with the
> registration work, looking up occupiers who had moved, getting
> 'old lodgers' to renew their claims to the vote and 'new lodgers' to
> fill in and sign claims. This work generally lasted four weeks and
> three days, and as I was paid five shillings a day it was very
> welcome, as it enabled me to get badly needed boots and
> clothing – to say nothing of regular meals.[65]

Meek was the product of what was by now a national system of
elementary education, where the State, as elsewhere, had eventually
succeeded in extending its presence without provoking unmanageable
dissent. When finally it had intervened to make schooling compulsory in

1880, following a decade in which school boards were allowed discretion in the imposition of bye-laws, the experience had demonstrated both a sophisticated ability of parents to manipulate the regulations and a surprising willingness by the authorities to respond to the problems families were experiencing in adjusting their child-rearing strategies to the new system. Head teachers and attendance officers used newspaper advertisements, public notices and frequent correspondence, as well as personal interviews, to communicate with parents who themselves appear to have been neither intimidated nor unduly confused by their encounters with the new bureaucracy.[66] Friction was still widespread, but it was never sufficient to amount to a generalised rejection of the enforced involvement of the State in the transmission of basic skills of communication.

Given the absence of direct taxation at this level of society, and with the Poor Law demanding elaborate paperwork for its internal administration but not for its dealings with applicants, the provision of literacy involved the most complex relations with central and local government bureaucracy that the working class, particularly the poorer sections, who experienced the greatest difficulties with attendance, were likely to encounter. The strategy of undermining the unofficial, collective forms of provision without embarking on a full-scale confrontation with alternative education, of abrogating the absolute rights of parents in the interest of reinforcing the working-class family, was consistent with the policy which had evolved towards the use of literacy during the century. Just as the vote was now being conceded to the head of the household, so his authority would be strengthened by and would in turn police the employment of written communication. Through a combination of controlled expenditure and selective discipline, backed up by market forces, successive governments sought to establish the State as a neutral entity, connected to the individual citizen and his wife and children through the institutions and practices of rational discourse.[67]

The press

The strategy for containing the use of literacy in which the State intervened only to compel the children of its citizens to undergo a comparatively brief period of education lacking in systematic indoctrination remained full of risk. If it avoided the danger inherent in overt repression of associating any employment of reading and writing with radical protest, the dependency on the schoolmaster to train and the commercial publisher to control the audience for political communication offered no absolute guarantee of success. That dedicated canvasser for the Eastbourne Liberals, George Meek, whose cast of mind belied his name, had for years been an avid reader of *Reynolds' News*, the most left-wing mass circulation Sunday paper. When he then encountered the *Clarion, Justice* and the *Workman's Times*, he was converted to socialism and began to hold meetings in the town advocating membership of the newly formed Independent Labour Party, which resulted, not surprisingly, in his expulsion from the local Liberal Association.[68] Henceforth his newspaper reading, particularly of the *Clarion*, and his organisational activity reinforced each other throughout the founding years of the Labour Party. The fortunes of the political application of the written word by the newly educated are most visible in the history of the press. Whereas it proved impossible to set up a permanent political bureaucracy until the ILP in 1893, and the exploitation of the post, for legal and practical reasons, was slow by comparison with rival middle-class movements, there was a diverse and continuing tradition of newspapers claiming to speak for or to working-class radicals which stretched from the appearance of Cobbett's *Twopenny Trash* in 1816 through to the launching of the *Daily Herald* in 1912.

In the creation of a separate working-class public, formal communication had a dual application. Firstly, it had to promote a sense of collective identity which extended beyond the limits of the orally bounded community but resisted incorporation into a concept of nationhood articulated by an increasingly ambitious middle class. Secondly, it had to assist in developing a sense of the political that retained a fertile relationship with other forms of cultural expression which were themselves making increasing use of the written word. Newspapers lay at the heart of both processes. Their function in connecting those still separated by diverse economic experience and by the continuing difficulty and expense of physical movement was apparent from the moment when Cobbett succeeded in establishing a rudimentary national distribution system for his *Pamphlet*,[69] whilst their potential for subverting the established order rested in large part on their identity as a literary form. The persistent problems encountered by the Home Office up to the final abolition of the stamp in enforcing a legally watertight definition of a newspaper were a product not only of deliberate manipulation of the regulations by ingenious radical journalists, but also of a critical uncertainty about the appropriate scope and language of a genre which was at once a cut-price alternative to the journals of educated society and a formalised version of oral modes of transmitting and debating information prevalent amongst the uneducated.

From the outset, the most striking aspect of the radical press was the confidence of its address to its readership. 'Friends and Fellow Countrymen', began the epochal first edition of *Cobbett's Political Register*. 'Friends, Brethren and Fellow-Countrymen', commenced each of the leaders of the *Poor Man's Guardian*, the most successful of the unstamped papers of the Reform period. And in the early years of the *Northern Star*, O'Connor directed his weekly epistles to 'My Beloved Friends'. In many ways the friendship which was claimed between the journalists and their readers encapsulated the strengths and the difficulties of the radical press between 1816 and the related demise of Chartism and the *Northern Star*. It indicated the remarkable ease with which the writers were able to establish a community of interests with ill-equipped and inexperienced readers, but at the same time it reflected the ambiguity of the relationship between the papers, most of which were privately owned, and the organised presence of the working class which in the end had to constitute something more than a group of well-disposed individuals.

The self-consciously personal tone of so much of the radical journalism served three broad functions. Most obviously it was a means of facilitating the transition from oral to literate modes of forming political opinion. Cobbett, like his successors, was intensely aware that for reasons of cost, custom and the uneven distribution of literacy, his writings were likely to be more often read aloud than silently,[70] and deliberately adopted a style which reflected the pace and rhythms of everyday speech.[71] It was not just that the arguments would translate easily from the printed word to the spoken voice, but that those whose principal communication skill had always been oral would feel no loss of confidence in their reasoning powers when they encountered what became the first mass circulation newspaper. His hard-won vernacular prose, which received a full practical and theoretical exposition in his best-selling *Grammar* two years later,[72] reflected a respect for his audience in many ways more profound than his indignant and compassionate defence of their interests in the articles themselves. Subsequent journalists endowed with less talent and smaller egos than Cobbett were nonetheless willing to operate within a smiliar structure. At a time when the levels of nominal literacy were at best static,[73] the radical press could only prosper by encouraging the labouring poor to make greater use of dormant skills. As the campaign for electoral reform gained momentum, the rhetorical style of the newspapers derived strength from and reinforced the public meetings through which the bulk of the political process was conducted. When the Six Acts closed the loophole which Cobbett had exploited to publish the *Pamphlet* legally and cheaply, he was able to transfer his energies to the outdoor gathering without checking his stride. By the same measure, the papers which defied the regulations as the Reform movement reached its climax had no difficulty integrating addresses to the readership through their leader columns and verbatim reports of speeches which constituted the bulk of their news reporting. *The Poor Man's Guardian* was at once the *Hansard* of the National Union of the Working Classes as it met each week at the Rotunda and an arresting source of information and ideology which could inform subsequent conversation and debate. In O'Connor Chartism had a leader and the *Northern Star* a proprietor who made every effort to minimise the distance between the spoken and the printed word. Thomas Frost's summary of his journalism applied equally to his platform technique: 'His style was vigorous, but coarse, being well sprinkled with expletives, often set forth in capitals, and spiced for the taste of the "fustian jackets" of the Midlands and the North.'[74]

The second function of the personal voice which echoed through the radical press was the provision of a source of authority which was at once convincing and easily recognisable. Those attempting to politicise the labouring poor in this period faced the dual problem of the weakness of collective means of asserting doctrine and the vulnerability of all forms of organisation to prosecution for secret activity. Where the machine-breakers and arsonists sought to inflate their strength and protect their identity by adopting the device of the anonymous threatening letter,[75] those committed to constitutional means of protest had everything to gain from making individual names as public and as resonant as possible. The dramatisation of the personality through print at once enhanced the impact of the message and diminished the capacity of the Government to stigmatise its transmission as seditious conspiracy. If, as was the case with the *Poor Man's Guardian*, a paper was more directly associated with a structured, if geographically limited, organisation, it was possible to supplant the editorial 'we' for the proprietorial 'I', but the tone of face-to-face address remained, as did the reluctance to withhold the names of contributors: 'these are times when all good men should be known to each other'.[76] The *Northern Star*, as concerned as its predecessors to resist charges of secrecy and also infiltration by secret agents, found it more difficult to reconcile the democratic with the charismatic, and settled for a combination of an unsigned leader and a highly idiosyncratic letter from O'Connor.

Finally, the elaboration of the authorial persona heightened the accessibility of the realm of the political. It was easier to grasp the meaning and the relevance of abstract rights when they were embodied in the larger-than-life figure of Cobbett. His use of his own experiences and thoughts as a practising farmer as a point of reference for every attack on Old Corruption rendered his demands for reform immediately comprehensible to those with no training in intellectual inquiry. The carefully cultivated style of argument by seemingly random association of observations about the weather, the beauties of nature, his health, his family, the state of the crops, his tastes in food and drink, leavened with jokes, reports of chance encounters with strangers met on the road or in the market, snippets of news garnered from gossip or newspapers replicated the forms of conversation which took place in the pubs or in breaks during the working day.

At the same time his ventures into other fields of writing, including history, farming, gardening, emigration and child-rearing treatises, grammars and dictionaries encouraged the more literate and mentally ambitious not to compartmentalise their approach to formal knowledge. Although Cobbett lacked the close involvement with chapbook and broadside literature displayed by contemporaries such as Spence and Hone, he shared their essentially catholic approach to the transmission of political material. There were no necessary boundaries to the form or the substance of the assertion of the rights of the dispossessed.

The immediate post-war period was marked not only by Cobbett's unprecedented achievements in the field of journalism, but in a resurgence of all forms of popular printed commentary on the state of the nation and its institutions. In some respects the drama of the war of the unstamped has distracted attention from the full range of writing and publishing which was taking place. It was as commonplace to hear the iniquities of the Government as the crimes of a condemned prisoner sung on street corners. Instantly manufactured, speedily forgotten verses were as much a part of radical politics as they were of the Parliamentary elections we have already examined, and in the case of a handful of boroughs with a wide franchise, such as Westminster, the two categories merged into one. Entrepreneurs like Catnach moved with ease between the eloquence of Sir Francis Burdett and the confessions of the latest murderer.[77] The printers and their distributors were an integral part of the commercial exploitation of every level of political activity. When the young John Buckley was taken to his first open-air political gathering in the 1820s, he found the fringe of the meeting 'occupied with conjurors, political ballad-singers and players, and gingerbread stalls'.[78]

The ballads were less discriminating than the newspapers in both their use of language and their exploitation of the market, but all forms were brought together in 1820, when George IV unwisely attempted to divorce his wife on the grounds of adultery. Cobbett, who had been forced by the Six Acts to suspend his twopenny *Pamphlet*, threw himself into the fray, turning himself into Queen Caroline's personal legal advisor and his *Register* into her exclusive mouthpiece. As the divorce had to receive Parliamentary consent, he had no difficulty in yoking the cause of the wronged woman to his long-standing preoccupation with Old Corruption in all its aspects. For their part the ballad-mongers were able to combine as never before moral outrage with sexual titillation, obsequious support of royalty with irreverent satire of the monarch, and sweeping demands for reform with loyal support for the constitution. As ever, Catnach was able to make money with a succession of items including *The Rose of Albion*:

> Be hush'd ev'ry rumour which malice invented
> Her fair spotless fame still triumphantly shines
> The fair *Rose* of *Albion* its sweets yet untainted,
> Still blooms in our much-loved Queen Caroline.[79]

The intersection of political journalism and commercial sensationalism was paralleled by the convergence of the middle- and working-class reform movements which had been forced apart by the war with revolutionary France. Both survived the death of the much-exploited Queen in 1821, but were exposed to new strains as the campaigns for Parliamentary and press reform reached their climax in the following decade.

At the outset the *Poor Man's Guardian*, the most widely read unstamped paper of the Reform Bill crisis, whose sales of up to 15,000 copies a week were exceeded only by Cobbett's *Register* and the *Northern Star* amongst radical journals in the first half of the century,[80] marked a refinement in the conception of political communication. It retained the style of personal address of its notable predecessor, without requiring its succession of editors and regular contributors to dwell at length on their own personalities. During the first two years of its existence, as the reform of Parliament was debated and decided, the paper consisted of three main elements, an unsigned leader, correspondence in the form of political statements from individuals and communications from secretaries of other organisations, and lengthy reports of the weekly meetings of the National Union of the Working Classes. The 'news' items were largely confined to the guerilla warfare over the paper's own existence. It kept apart from the less reputable forms of street literature, and viewed with mounting mistrust the middle-class reform movement. However, by 1833, the battle to extend the franchise to the labouring poor had been lost, and the future of the papers which had supported it looked increasingly uncertain. The *Guardian* maintained its format as sales fell, but its proprietor and publisher, Hetherington, was forced to change his approach in another of his ventures, the *Destructive*, which in June 1834 announced that it would

> henceforward be a repository of all the gems and treasures, and fun and frolic and 'news and occurrences' of the week. It shall abound in Police Intelligence, in Murders, Rapes, Suicides, Burnings, Maimings, Theatricals, Races, Pugilism, and all manner of moving 'accidents by flood and field'. In short it will be stuffed with every sort of devilment that will make it sell.[81]

This was in fact a fair summary of the contemporary character of the unstamped press as a whole. In Wiener's definitive finding list, no more than half the titles could loosely be called political, and many of these employed satire, literary and dramatic criticism, or theological debate to attack the status quo.[82] Another three in ten were miscellanies of literature and useful and entertaining knowledge, and the remainder included periodical versions of the ballads and sensational accounts of real or imaginary crimes and disasters which, as we have seen, were the staple fare of the street-sellers. What Hetherington, and even more successfully John Cleave in his *Weekly Police Gazette*, now did was to amalgamate the forms into publications which were recognisable forerunners of the mass circulation papers which developed in the second half of the century and are with us today. In doing so they sacrificed the consistently direct address to the readership, and the sharp edge of their radicalism. In return they mounted the first serious challenge to both the street literature and the papers catering for the growing middle-class reading public.

In this context, the *Northern Star* was both a progression and a throwback. It rapidly achieved a more secure national presence than its unstamped predecessors, and, especially in the first year of its existence, made a serious attempt to attain the width of coverage of a full-scale newspaper. O'Connor employed talented journalists and encouraged the inclusion of news about every sort of radical debate and activity from every part of the country. Contributors were now paid for material which extended beyond the immediate concerns of Chartism.[83] There were paragraphs of domestic and foreign news, some of it, such as an account of a suicide in a workhouse, or the repression of liberal protest in Spain, having political implications, but much else included merely for human interest, or, at worst, just to fill a space. As Chartism gained momentum in the autumn of 1838, the paper's readership may have wished to relax with a report of a 'Dreadful Crash Accident – The Passengers Thrown into the Sea' or a list of the runners and odds at York races, or even, for a few months, with a weddings column, but it is difficult to imagine their pleasure in discovering 'Lord Marlborough appointed to Captaincy of Deal Castle', or their need to read a dense half page of 'Market News'.[84]

However, by the time of the Second Petition, the balance had shifted back to an earlier model of radical journalism. The bulk of the news was confined to Chartist meetings and other activities, and the readers were now expected to derive such further information or entertainment as they required from other printed or oral forms. Only the advertisements for proprietary medicines, the source of much-needed income, flourished as before.[85] Less attempt was now made to attract the attention of those not already wholly committed to the cause. Instead the paper relied for the breadth of its appeal on the established technique of emphasising the sense of personal address in the columns of print. O'Connor's strident voice echoed through the pages, both in his signed contributions and the detailed reports of his speeches and other doings during the preceding week, and although the paper was legally stamped and not subject to direct persecution, the constant references to its own role in the movement and to its struggles to maintain sales made it a leading member in its own right of the *dramatis personae* of Chartism. In turn the dignity of every individual member of its audience, even if their grasp of literacy was so poor that they could only listen to a reading of the paper, was enhanced by the dire', unpatronising tone of the prose, and the encouragement which was giv..n to participate in the process of communication by contributing to the vigorous correspondence section.

The change in format accompanied a fall in sales. From a peak of around 50,000 in the heady days of 1838, the circulation dropped to 12,500 a week in 1842 and 6,000 by 1846. Even in the dramatic year of 1848, the average sale was no more than 12,000, and the paper finally went out of existence in 1852.[86] Throughout the first half of the century, the radical press was at once dependent on and a substitute for the strength of the organisations whose cause they championed. The complexity of the relationship was evident from the beginning.[87] As the *Political Register* suddenly acquired a national, lower-class readership, so the Hampden Clubs ceased to be a forum for middle-class debate and expanded rapidly across the country and down the social scale. Yet Cobbett, who was doing so much to politicise and integrate the post-war discontent, was profoundly unenthusiastic about the appearance of the first nationwide radical movement, patchy and uncoordinated as it was, and refused to associate himself with it:

> since the question of *reform* has been so much agitated, I have taken particular pains to endeavour to discourage all sorts of *combinations, associations, affiliations,* and *correspondencies* of *societies* having that object in view; and I have said, upon these occasions, that if the object were not to be obtained by the general, free, unpacked, unbiased, impression and expression of the public mind it never could be, and never ought to be obtained at all.[88]

In his view all forms of organisation would either lead to violence, or would attract the violent attention of the law. Ironically, it was Cobbett and the other unstamped editors of the period who had the greatest trouble with the courts, and from the suspension of Habeas Corpus in 1817 to the Six Acts of 1819, the Government did more to unite political communication and organisation than either the journalists or the club secretaries could have achieved themselves.

By contrast, the relation between the unstamped press and the radical movements of the Reform Bill crisis had a substance which was not solely the product of continuing repression, important though that was. There was a genuine reciprocity of function, which added greatly to the impact of each. The fledgling newspapers, permanently threatened by prosecution, bankruptcy or both, needed the new organisations and their members to provide free copy, volunteer vendors, sales outlets, contributions to the Victims Fund and articulation of the campaign against the Stamp Act. For their part, the rapidly growing political movements relied on the journals to display announcements and advertisements, to develop and integrate political consciousness, to co-ordinate their separate branches and to extend their influence beyond their geographical base. The only sense in which the National Union of the Working Classes lived up to its grandiloquent title was through the circulation of its principal mouthpiece, the *Poor Man's Guardian*, over a half of whose sales were in the provinces.[89] Within London, the Union's structure of over eighty classes was too complex to be held together by informal contact, but too basic to generate an efficient bureaucracy. The privately owned papers could exercise this responsibility without raising further problems of administration and expenditure. Their staff took upon themselves the risks of prosecution, leaving the societies they supported free to reap the benefit of their dramatisation of the repressive character of the pre- and post-Reform administrations. It was a sophisticated solution to the still primitive state of both organisation and communication. Literacy was employed to bridge the gap between local grievance and national agitation, and in turn the atmosphere of crisis offered the most compelling incentive to integrate the possession and the use of the skills of reading and writing.[90]

The compromise between autonomous newspaper and official spokesman was replicated in a more dramatic but in the end less satisfactory form in the *Northern Star*. The complex and still confused story of its foundation is indicative of its subsequent history. The paper was the joint initiative of O'Connor, increasingly frustrated at the inadequate coverage of his radical touring, and a group of Yorkshire radicals, anxious to extend the width and range of the campaign against the New Poor Law, and to protect it from misrepresentation by the middle-class press. They resorted to an established democratic device of issuing shares to raise money, but O'Connor feared that the £690 which was eventually collected would be insufficient to guarantee the financial stability of a national weekly[91] and that, in the words of the most detailed first-hand account, persuaded his collaborators that 'the mixed authority of a committee would hamper the editor and render the paper inefficient'.[92] Instead he borrowed the capital for a private enterprise, in return for a promise of interest and a subvention from his own funds.[93] The consequence was a newspaper which at once counterbalanced and reflected the weakness of Chartism as an organisation. Its rapid success in attaining a circulation in excess of 50,000 copies paved the way for the emergence of the first movement to overcome, if only temporarily, the deep regional and occupational divisions within the labouring population.[94] Although the railway network was now being constructed, and the postage system about to be reformed, the former was both expensive and incomplete, and use of the latter rendered federated bodies subject to prosecution and private individuals open to surveillance.[95] Thus, as with earlier, less ambitious societies, the National Charter Association relied heavily on the radical press for the bulk of its internal communication, and the *Northern Star* played a key role in building up the organisation, publicising and reporting its meetings and activities, broadening and strengthening the ideological consensus, and sustaining the enthusiasm of its growing number of supporters.[96] Selling the paper was less of an adventure than in the days of the unstamped, but more often a source of income, encouraging the growth of a cadre of semi-professional local leaders, who supported their work as secretaries and speakers with their income as newsagents.[97] Reading it every week in the workplace, public house or meeting of the local association was the most regular and effective means of renewing commitment to the cause, the paper acting as a great flywheel to the movement as it endured extreme vicissitudes of fortune after the failure of the first petition.

No major working-class movement has ever owed as much to a single newspaper as Chartism did to the *Northern Star*. Yet this most political use of literacy rested on a series of compromises which were endemic to the radical press of the first half of the century, and seriously weakened its legacy to the second half. In common with most of its predecessors, O'Connor's journal was partly a political pamphlet and partly a full-scale newspaper, partly a personal venture and partly the servant of an organisation. Just as Chartism was much the most ambitious movement, so its principal publication displayed most clearly the ambiguities of this form of communication in the first phase of working-class protest. Its financial arrangements, for instance, which were and have remained the cause of considerable controversy, were merely a more acute form of a long-standing dilemma. From the *Twopenny Trash* onwards, those radical journalists who suddenly broke into the mass market were faced with conflicting commercial and political pressures. There were big profits in prospect as circulations grew far faster than costs, but at the same time the proprietors were committed to causes greater than their own incomes. The consequence was that Cobbett, Hetherington and O'Connor all at some point found themselves in charge of a large flow of cash,[98] but Cobbett was bankrupt by 1820, Hetherington died so poor that his estate could barely meet the debts charged to it, and in the long run there was a substantial redistribution of money from O'Connor to the *Northern Star* and from the paper to both the pockets of those engaged in its production and sale, and the coffers of the movement in the various phases of its existence. The financial problems reflected deeper tensions within Chartism, and it may be argued that the failure of the paper successfully to resolve its contradictions stemmed ultimately from the movement itself.

The uneven development of Chartism, with so much emphasis placed on its newspaper at the expense of its bureaucracy, was a direct result of the compromise which the State had by this stage reached in its treatment of the right to protest. Having tightened the laws on seditious libel and retained a penny stamp, it was prepared to countenance a radical press, but it refused to abandon its reserve powers of postal espionage or to legalise any form of organisation outside the particular case of the friendly societies. Thus the terms on which the Chartist journalists set about defining and promoting an alternative sense of a public sphere were already circumscribed. Their newspaper had to be both privately owned and urgently committed to the movement which so desperately needed it. It was too bound up in the day-to-day struggles of the organisation to sustain its development as a full-scale newspaper, and too dependent on the position of its proprietor to escape the negative aspects of the personalisation of address which had been so characteristic of the working-class political papers. O'Connor's 'My Dear Friends' of his open letters in the first period of Chartism had become 'My Dear Children' by the time of the Third Petition in 1848. As the bureaucracy and the paper had failed to sustain an equal relationship, so the paper and its readership had lost their equality of respect. In the end the appeal of the paper was too narrow, its dependency on one voice too great, to survive the demise of the movement it had done so much to sustain. A working-class political reading public had been created, but had been unable to develop a tradition of journalism which could incorporate the wider areas of popular culture which could now make use of the printed word.

It was in these circumstances that the commercial forces upon which governments had pinned their hopes since their change in policy after the Reform Bill now began to come to the fore. While the *Northern Star* was still struggling to keep Chartism going, the Sunday papers had started their rise to dominance in the market, a position which they were not to lose until after the Second World War.[99] *Lloyd's Illustrated London Newspaper* (1842), the *News of the World* (1843), the *Weekly Times* (1847), and *Reynolds' Weekly Newspaper* (1850) were from the outset cheaper than the national dailies or political weeklies, and with the exception, to its cost, of the *News of the World*, were quick to take advantage of the abolition of the stamp in 1855 and reduce their price to a penny. Privately owned, staffed by professional journalists, making full use of developments in transport and marketing techniques, the papers not only achieved, but more importar.. sustained circulations well in excess of Cobbett or O'Connor's ventures at the height of their political careers. As the State sacrificed its tax revenues and poured money into elementary education, so their sales and their profits rose. Private enterprise reaped the benefit of public expenditure, and in return the threat of revolution receded over the horizon.

The papers, particularly *Lloyd's* and *Reynolds'*, had their roots deep in the world of sensational fiction, and their success in translating the dissemination of news into a completely new category of popular leisure coincided with the virtual disappearance of independent working-class politics. Yet it remains the case that none of these highly capitalised ventures was a wholehearted supporter of the status quo, and one of them, *Reynolds' Newspaper*, was as consistent an advocate of the interests of the working man as any of its more idealistic predecessors, and a fiercer, not to say more abusive, critic of the working man's enemies than any of the radical journals founded during the early years of socialism and the Labour Party. Reynolds himself had been an active Chartist as well as a best-selling novelist, and long after he had relinquished control of the paper it constituted, in the words an early historian of the press, 'a formidable spokesman for the most irreconcilable portions of the community'.[100]

The explanation of this apparent paradox lies in three crucial elements of continuity between the old radical weeklies and the new Sunday press. Firstly, the working man with a passing interest in the world and an adequate command of literacy had long been accustomed to moving from politics as reasoned arguments to politics as entertainment to entertainment alongside politics. After the Napoleonic Wars this meant buying broadsides as well as the *Twopenny Trash*; during the 1830s it meant choosing between a range of unstamped and other penny publications which eventually were combined in *Cleave's Weekly Police Gazette*. Although the *Northern Star*'s attempt to provide a similar range of material eventually fell away, literate Chartists still had at their disposal an immense variety of political ballads and broadsides,[101] as well as the purely sensational penny literature. What was new about the Sunday papers was not their ambition but their success, built upon skilled journalism and the exploitation of a rapid expansion of the reading public and a parallel growth in its disposable income and leisure time. They consolidated the mixture of political comment, fiction, reports of crime and other human tragedy, literary news and theatre reviews, and extended it into new areas such as sport and gardening.[102] The real break with the past came with the demise of the street-sellers whose stock-in-trade of executions, crimes and disasters could not compete with the newspapers which now carried in a more authoritative though equally salacious form the contents of fifty broadsides for the same price.

Secondly *Reynolds' Newspaper* in particular retained something of the tone of personal address upon which its predecessors had based their success. Although there were fewer meetings to report, the journalism preserved the direct, vigorous, demotic style of the open-air speech. The paper deliberately avoided the cadences of the establishment press, whilst at the same time losing no opportunity of criticising the class bias of its rivals. Even more so than the unstamped, it was explicitly an anti-newspaper newspaper, called into being by the shortcomings of the existing coverage of working-class affairs, and refusing to replicate the polite discourse of its corrupt opponents. Here, for instance, a signed leader by Reynolds comes to the defence of the newly formed but beleaguered Amalgamated Society of Engineers:

> In conclusion, let me congratulate the workmen in the dispute for the calm, dignified and even noble demeanour which they have hitherto maintained. Despite the *Times* – despite the banded organs of the press against them – despite the unscrupulous recourse which has been had to misrepresentation the most flagrant and scurrility the most vile – they have obtained the respect and the good wishes of all liberal-minded and conscientious persons.[103]

Elsewhere in the paper it encouraged active communication with its readership by running a substantial correspondence column.

Finally, the commercial element of the new press was largely an extension of earlier practices rather than a decisive break. Most of the important radical papers had been privately owned, had established national distribution networks by offering regular discounts to wholesalers, and particularly in the case of the *Northern Star* had looked for and carried extensive advertising of no relevance to the political struggle. Whilst the proportion of advertisements now increased, their source was too varied, and their contribution to the papers' solvency too small for outside businesses to exercise a direct influence over editorial content.[104] Not until the Harmsworth revolution did the news become simply a means of keeping the advertisements apart. What mattered was the volume of sales, which made the major contribution to income and determined the attraction of the paper to those prepared to buy space for their goods or services. This did encourage the biggest of the Sundays, *Lloyd's*, to appeal to a lower-middle-class readership with greater purchasing power, but although *Reynolds'* was forced to accept material from dubious sources, it did prove possible to stay afloat on the basis of sales to the literate labouring poor.

The key change was not the introduction of market forces, which proprietors from Cobbett onwards had wrestled with throughout their careers in journalism, but rather a transformation in the relationship between the papers as commercial ventures and the organised presence of the working class. *Reynolds' Newspaper* was from the outset an active supporter of the trade union movement in particular, carrying detailed accounts of disputes, and in the case of some of the more important strikes of the period, organising appeals for funds. Yet however sympathetic its attitude, and however useful its dissemination of information, which included from 1853 a regular 'Labour and Wages' column, it was a voice outside the various forms of class struggle. This was partly because the paper, like its rivals, was increasingly produced by writers whose identity was confined to their membership of the emerging profession of journalism.[105] Although Reynolds himself had some Chartist credentials, his staff and his successors as editor confined their activities to the paper itself. It was no more necessary to be a trade unionist to report the conduct of a strike than it was to be a criminal to relay the details of a robbery. Partly also it was because in the aftermath of the failure of Chartism, collective forms of working-class activity were too segmented, and the political movements too weak, to generate a closer partnership between those who created news of resistence and aggression, and those who disseminated it to a national audience.

The consequence of this detachment of practice from communication was most apparent in the growing tension between the support the paper gave to the more advanced forms of class protest, and the theory of society which informed its reporting. Whilst the substance of the news often involved crucial developments in industrial and later political conflict, the conceptual framework of the accounts and the language in which they were conveyed remained locked in a theatrical analysis of Old Corruption with which Cobbett would have been perfectly at home.[106] An indication of the resulting incoherence can be gained from this spirited defence of the unions at the time of the Sheffield Outrages:

> Indeed it would not be difficult to show that neither the principle nor the system of working-class trades' unionism is in the slightest degree responsible for those deplorable outrages. On the other hand, it is quite easy to show that the royalist and aristocratic systems, whose organs attempt to implicate the whole of the working classes in the Broadhead crimes, are directly and immediately responsible for the Sheffield atrocities. The fact is, that Broadhead has been only a faithful copyist of the hereditary rulers of the English people. To protect their trade interests,

royalty and aristocracy never scrupled to perpetuate any amount of murders, or any quantity of crime.[107]

Rather than the reporting of class conflict informing the other categories of news and entertainment in the paper, the style and preoccupations of popular melodrama inherited from street literature invaded the presentation of organised struggle. The separate sections were held together only at the level of rhetoric. The account of the latest strike was connected to the report of a murder or review of a play by little more than an appeal to the reader's pleasure in the sensational, and to his confidence in the moral worth of himself and his class as a whole.

The fragmentation of the labour movement was replicated in a dispersal of the means of conveying information. In an era of rising literacy rates and falling newspaper prices, it was no longer possible to complain of a conspiracy of silence, but the increasing body of print constituted a disjointed picture of the world of the newly educated. Readers with a strong predilection for the sensational would buy the aggressively written and marketed *Lloyd's* and disregard its pallid Liberal politics, those with a more developed class consciousness and more fastidious literary taste would purchase the *Bee-Hive*, in spite of its restricted appeal. The latter's awkward subtitle, 'A Weekly Newspaper of General Intelligence, And Trades', Friendly Society and Co-operative Journal', betrayed its difficulty. In an effort to respond to the full range of the working man's interests it eschewed the ghetto of the proliferating trade union journals[108] by being privately owned and professionally edited, but in order to overcome its lack of capital and avoid the trivialising style of *Reynolds'*, it set out to be the responsible and wordy spokesman for a range of working-class organisations.[109] The consequence was that its 'General Intelligence', despite the obligatory crime reporting, lacked sufficient scope and interest to attract the uncommitted, whilst its relations with organised labour were often uneasy and finally, when its founder Potter fell out with the Junta, broke down altogether. The internal communications of the individual unions were now too sophisticated, but their sense of collective endeavour still too primitive to demand the success of a hybrid enterprise such as the *Bee-Hive* which at its peak was selling 8,000 copies a week when *Reynolds'* and *Lloyd's* had passed 300,000.

In those sections of the press untrammelled by obligations to organised labour or traditional popular culture, attempts were made to superimpose an invented community on the newly literate. The provincial newspapers, also the product of the reforms of the 1850s and parallel advances in the technology of communication, particularly the telegraph-based news agencies, projected a vision of regional society in which industrial and political conflict was localised and contained within boundaries set by an increasingly confident middle class.[110] The Liberal national dailies occasionally gave valued support to particular working-class campaigns which could be resolved without major redistributions of power,[111] but for the most part preferred to restrict their coverage to what Thomas Wright called 'an all-inclusive generalisation, which takes in and uses the working classes without distinctly specifying them'.[112] The grievances of the lower orders were called into being to validate the attitudes of their superiors:

> Some opinion or feeling that may really be general among the upper or middle classes, or that, on the other hand, may merely be invented to suit the passing and special purpose of the minister, or party or interest whose organ asserts their existence, but which, in any case, is in opposition to the views entertained by the working classes – some opinion or feeling of this kind is by a deft use of expressions of universality made to appear universal.[113]

The *Poor Man's Guardian* had famously carried to the right of its masthead a miniature printing press framed by the slogan 'Knowledge is Power', with 'Liberty of the Press' inscribed on its platen. By the final quarter of the century such optimism was at once obsolete and still relevant. Caught between the weakness of collective forms of resistance and the strength of commercial forms of exploitation, the free press had been unable to constitute a sense of the political which was both integrated with other forms of popular culture and consistently independent of the world view of middle-class papers. At the same time it is too much to argue that the newsprint which the products of the elementary schools were now consuming constituted 'the effective means of social control which the establishment had always hoped the popular press might be'.[114] This was partly because *Reynolds' Newspaper* at least had managed to keep alive the spirit of aggressive insubordination which had characterised radical journalism since the time of Cobbett. In spite of its outmoded social theory and trivialising literary style, it refused to become an acolyte of Gladstonian Liberalism, and instead supported the reappearance of autonomous radical politics, welcoming in turn the SDF, the ILP and the LRC, although in the spring of 1900 it was mainly preoccupied with a vigorous campaign against the Boer War.[115] It was partly also because it remained possible for penurious and unqualified writers to begin to communicate with the increasing number of working-class readers. Between 1890 and 1910 the multiplying labour organisations generated and were sustained by as many as eight hundred papers, half of them explicitly socialist.[116]

The experience of these final two decades constituted less a reversal of earlier defeats than a re-encounter in a more acute form with the problems with which the unstamped and Chartist journalists had wrestled. At one level the most important paper of the period, Blatchford's *Clarion*, founded in 1891, marked a closer achievement of the synthesis between the popular and the political which had been the objective of radical journalists for most of the century. It was written in lively and direct prose which never lost sight of either the gravity of its cause or the recreational needs of its readership. A genuine attempt was made to connect the news and the features to the preoccupations of the comment columns. Blatchford himself, a successful graduate of the school of 'New Journalism', was capable of being serious without being solemn, personal without being patronising. In the words of one reader, 'His articles in the *Clarion* were so simple and lucid that even a half-timer in a cotton factory, who was eager to understand something of the world in which he lived, could understand them.'[117] Unlike the Sunday papers of the third quarter of the century it was as visually attractive as the old broadsides, and with 'Our Woman's Column' and 'Our Children's Column' it made at least a token effort to appeal beyond the head of the working-class household.

Yet in spite of its success the paper was still hamstrung by the familiar difficulties of uncertain relations with political organisation and inadequate safeguards against commercial pressure. In its early years, when, together with Joseph Burgess's *Workman's Times* it played a key role in launching the ILP,[118] it seemed to have established a fruitful, reciprocal partnership with the most important radical movement of the day. In the event, however, the dependency of the ILP on the *Clarion* and other journals for a public voice concealed its weakness as a national movement,[119] and in turn the reliance of the paper on a network of politically committed agents disguised its shortcomings as a business venture. At a time when the launch costs of a daily paper were well into six figures, Blatchford began his enterprise with £350 raised by mortgaging the insurance policies of himself and his partner A. M. Thompson, plus a loan of £50.[120] The enormous impact of *Merrie England*, which sold 750,000 copies within a year of publication in 1893, boosted both the ILP and the paper, but the book's emphasis on propaganda rather than organisation and its antipathy towards all forms of industrial progress indicated tensions between the journalist who had trained in Fleet Street and the Party which had emerged from the class struggle in the textile factories.

The *Clarion*, the *Workman's Times* and the *Labour Leader*, which although more often seen as a spokesman for the ILP was in fact the property of Keir Hardie until 1904 and deeply influenced by his personality,[121] were privately owned yet dedicated to the spread of democratic politics.[122] Blatchford saw political organisation as no more than an extension of the newspaper's educative function. It was there to make socialists rather than constitute a bureaucratised alternative to the existing parties. Like Cobbett before him, Blatchford instinctively distrusted structure and discipline. Almost from the outset he was at odds with the growing centralisation of the ILP and its increasing tendency to subordinate cultural activities to the political struggle.[123] His difficulties culminated in the defection of the *Clarion* over the Boer War and finally in its involvement in a breakaway from the Labour Party in 1911. The more puritanical Hardie, forced in the end to choose between the commercialism of 'new journalism' and the rigours of the political struggle, settled for the latter, and his paper suffered accordingly.[124] The ILP which at its peak had no more than 35,000 members, was not large enough to guarantee the solvency of either the privately owned *Clarion* or the host of journals launched by its branches,[125] and Blatchford's enterprise, for all the quality of the journalism, was too undercapitalised to mount a serious challenge to the hold of the purely commercial papers which were in a much better position to exploit the expanding market and consequent increase in the availability of advertising revenue. When the working class finally gained its own daily in 1912, in the form of the *Daily Herald*, this deliberately kept itself independent of any one organisation in a still weak and segmented labour movement. As a consequence it raised only £300 launch capital and faced competition a year later from an official Labour paper, the *Daily Citizen*.[126] In 1914, with universal nominal male literacy at last achieved, and universal manhood suffrage within sight, both were on the verge of bankruptcy.

The earnest worker

As he walked round Ancoats in 1906 trying to discover the readership of the press amongst the working-class population, J. H. Haslam received a mixed response. There was an established market for labour periodicals and other self-improvement material, but it did not extend far into the slum districts. 'Eh mester', replied one newsagent in surprise, 'they dunnat want anythin' as'll do 'em good here! . . . What they want here is love an' romance.'[127] In the year that the Labour Party was founded, its leading supporter amongst the political weekly papers circulated to no more than one in a hundred voters. Whilst total illiteracy was now mostly confined to the old and the very young, there was, as there always had been, a marked variation in the employment the newly educated were able and willing to make of their skills. Only a minority of manual workers could find the mental and material resources to engage in the pursuit of book knowledge. From the first cohort of radicals who used Paine as a guiding light through to the later generations whose encounters with Ruskin, Morris and Marx destroyed their deference to the tenets and institutions of Liberalism, the history of working-class politics is strewn with men and occasionally women studying late into the night and going back to the fields or the workbench the next morning with their heads full of theory and analysis. These were the 'organic intellectuals' whom Gramsci hoped would educate the organisations they helped to found and run.[128] Their capacity to do so depended on the ways in which they were able to extend their use of literacy, and in particular on their relations with those who remained more inclined to confine their attention to light fiction. It was at this level of personal endeavour that the parameters of the emerging working-class political culture, and the fissures within it, finally became apparent.

The sustained reading of substantial political argument, and even more so, the occasional attempts to add to the body of radical literature, were by their nature private activities. They demanded at least a temporary abstraction from the communal noise of the family or the public house, and their successful completion generated inescapable tensions with those less committed to such pursuits. Yet throughout the period there were a number of powerful forces counteracting the tendencies towards with-drawal and isolation. In the first instance, the persistent inadequacy of formal elementary education, even after the introduction of compulsion and successive modifications to the teaching of literacy, meant that every working man's child set upon becoming a serious student would be forced to rely on the resources of the community to acquire the necessary command of the tools of reading and writing. Thomas Burt's résumé of his schooling said as much as any curriculum vitae of the time could have done: 'When deductions are made for interruptions by strikes, sickness, and other unavoidable causes, I could not have been altogether more than a year and a half or two years at school. Something, however – indeed, much – had been accomplished. I had very imperfectly no doubt, learned to read, write, and do easy sums in arithmetic. The key of knowledge had thus been put into my hands, and the use I was to make of it depended largely upon myself.'[129] The element of self-sufficiency, however, was confined to the sphere of motivation. Once his education ended at about the age of nine, there was no external authority to force him to continue reading. He was free to let his newly acquired tools rust away. But once he decided to sharpen them further, he was immediately thrust into formal and informal contact with other like-minded individuals. His journey to full literacy involved a Primitive Methodist Sunday school where he took further classes, his father, who lent him books, fellow colliers with whom he discussed literature in breaks in work underground, and one friend in particular with whom he formed a close, mutually supportive intellectual friendship.

The self-educated reader was as much a myth as the self-made million-aire. If it was true that no working man could depend on his schooling to equip him with the necessary level of competence, it was equally true that he could not depend on his own unaided efforts to make good the deficiency. Thus Walter Hudson, one of the first generation of Labour MPs, summarised his intellectual training: 'Richmond National Schools gave me my elementary education, but I started work at the age of nine, and, to all intents and purposes, I have educated myself, grabbing the learning I could at Sunday schools, evening classes, and debating societies.'[130] Mutual assistance was the only practicable response to the cost of books and to the problem of knowing what to read, how to read, and what to make of the literature that had been read.[131] In between the classes and the conversations would be bouts of private study, but the need for help, advice and encouragement always remained. The structure of support varied in its formality, and, as was argued above, nothing was a substitute for a coherent programme of full-time secondary or University education.[132] Yet as with the humble task of deciphering an unexpected letter, so with the ambitious attempt to understand political economy or natural selection, the poor pooled their efforts to reduce their shortcomings.

The second factor broadening the impact of private study was the necessary interaction between literary and non-literary forms of learning. No working-class politician seeking to account for the development of his consciousness ever supposed that the process was confined to the acquisition and use of literacy. 'I had a little education at a national school', explained the engineer and Labour MP George Barnes, 'but on the whole I have had to educate myself, and my most valuable lessons have been learned in the great free school of hard work.'[133] 'My best book', wrote Arthur Henderson, 'has been my close contact with, and deep interest in the spiritual, moral, social and industrial affairs of life.'[134] Behind the cliché was a reality at once common to but always different in the lives of every labour leader. At the outset, as was argued in chapter 3, the initial impact of the written word in the classroom had to be set in the context of the complex and profound teaching the child was receiving in his home and neighbourhood.[135] Like Thomas Burt, Frank Hodges grew up in a mining community in the throes of bitter class conflict: 'The first chapter in my life, my school life, was closed in an atmosphere of industrial war. I had tasted poverty to the very dregs. I became a potential rebel.'[136] Whether the instruction came directly from a father or mother, or more diffusely from the parents' struggle to maintain their household, the child already knew a great deal more than the schoolmaster could ever teach him, and equally had a sense of the possible application of the skills transmitted in the classroom which bore little relation to the intentions of those who supplied his education.

As the child grew into a man, the 'school of adversity and hard work', as another MP, W. C. Steadman put it,[137] continued its lessons as the young worker discovered his place in the economy and picked up his work training by a variety of means, few of which were based on the printed word. Yet however necessary and inescapable the direct experience of the relations of production, it was never sufficient to turn the dissatisfied worker into the committed activist. 'All the time I was an apprentice', continued Steadman, 'I attended night-schools, and did everything I could to improve my general knowledge.'[138] Barnes also took care to supplement his free school of hard work with evening classes, and became one of the many literate labourers of his generation whose outlook was transformed by Henry George's *Progress and Poverty*: 'This famous work made a great impression upon me, and attracted me into the general movement for social reform.'[139] There was no set pattern in the conjunction of literature and work. Timing depended on the accident of stumbling across a book or a newspaper, or on the eruption of a more general economic or political crisis. The weight given to the alternative forms of instruction was conditioned by the inclination of the individual concerned. Some read to make sense of action, like the future TUC leader Walter Citrine, who was thrown into industrial conflict as soon as he started work, and then 'set about learning as much as I could about the theory and practice of trade unionism';[140] others, like John Wilson, studied first and acted later: 'So I put myself through a systematic course of grammar, history, logic, and political economy, John Stuart Mill and Henry George being perhaps the writers who most influenced me, and in 1869 I began my public career by helping to found the Miners' Association.'[141]

All that connected the accounts of emerging commitment to causes beyond the immediate needs of the workplace or the family was the essential presence of both poverty and print. On the one side was material deprivation, which curtailed or in some cases abolished altogether the chances of formal education, on the other a range of formative texts, most notably the works of Carlyle, Ruskin, J. S. Mill and Henry George.[142] Will Thorne, who, as we have seen, led his first strike before he could read,[143] summarised his development when asked by an engineer in his gas works where he had acquired the 'foolish rubbish' of his socialism: 'I told him that I had learnt it from books and pamphlets that I had bought with the few shillings I had to spare; that I had learnt it in the works in which I had been employed; that I had learnt it from bitter experience.'[144] Deprivation gave relevance to the reading, and the literature gave meaning to the conflict. Jack Lawson, like Hodges, had begun his political education during his schooldays, which coincided with a three-month miners' strike: 'Grim, desperate, savage, the men and women had fought for months. All unconscious of it, I had even as a boy of eleven become class conscious.'[145] However, it was not until he was a young man that an encounter with the journalism generated by the revival of socialism performed the vital task of giving form and dimension to his work experience: 'The *Labour Leader* had linked me to the great industrial world, and it and the *Clarion* had shown me that I had long been a socialist without knowing it.'[146]

The third breach of the insularity of the working-class intellectual was the constant presence of the human voice in his pursuit and application of political knowledge. All the forms of collective instruction referred to above, ranging from the casual conversation with a fellow enthusiast to lectures in an evening class or debates in a mutual improvement society, involved talking and listening. It was not merely a matter of the committed reader recharging his batteries or sharpening his ideas; often the crucial first encounter with a writer or a body of ideas took place well away from the printed page. Vere Garratt, for instance, owed his introduction to socialism to discussions with a fellow operative in the gas meter factory in which he was employed: 'I occupied the footstool for many a pleasant hour and heard the gospel according to Morris, Keir Hardie, and Robert Blatchford.'[147] Only then did he extend his reading beyond his existing preoccupation with poetry and drama. A similar effect could be achieved in a more impersonal setting. Joseph Stamper first discovered radical politics when he came across a man standing on a chair in the street haranguing passers-by.[148] More formally, the turning point for the future Labour MP Charles Duncan came when he attended a public meeting: 'I was only twenty-two when I was converted to Socialism by Mr. Tom Mann and Mr. Jack Williams, the well-known leaders of the unemployed. They came to Newcastle to lecture on social and labour problems; I heard them, and was greatly impressed.'[149] The impact of such events was not confined to the abstract quality of the arguments. Great oratory was capable of moving the most sober and rational of men. The critical moment in Henry Snell's intellectual development occurred when he joined the crowd being addressed by Charles Bradlaugh in the market place at Nottingham in 1881: 'His energy on the platform was cyclonic, and his power to sway the emotions of a great audience had to be witnessed to be understood.'[150] It was not until after such events that men like Duncan and Snell began to read their way into causes to which they were now committed.

If the spoken word could lead to the written word, then the reverse was equally true. Those who had studied all the books, pamphlets and newspapers they could lay their hands on would sooner or later find themselves discussing their findings with fellow readers, conversing on doorsteps or in pubs with hesitant neighbours or workmates, and finally venturing out themselves to take their place on a chair in the street or a platform in a hall.[151] Frank Hodges' account of his life in the ILP would have been recognised by any participants in the labour movement in the preceding century:

The local branches of the Independent Labour Party were always centres of education and culture, none more so perhaps than any other local organisations. The men gathered together week by week and discussed the political items of the day, probed deeply into social and industrial problems, read propaganda literature and took part in debates, and later went forth into the highways, byways and street corners to preach the gospel of Socialism.[152]

The dramatic advances in all forms of mass communication since the 1790s had intensified the level of activity, but done little to change its basic outline. However pejorative the term might appear when employed by middle-class critics, working-class politicians were and always had been agitators, as reliant on the power of their lungs as the strength of their reasoning to achieve their objectives.[153] Their principal source of printed propaganda, the radical press, was, as we have seen, dependent for its content and style on reports of the speeches and meetings which comprised the bulk of the political discourse. But whilst the sophisticated use of literacy would point the reader towards a platform, it did not necessarily equip him with the skills he would need in front of an audience, which was one of the major reasons why lay preachers were so frequently found in the ranks of labour leaders. 'A Wesleyan by persuasion', recalled Arthur Henderson, 'I became a lay preacher, and my work as such undoubtedly had a great influence on my career, not only as a factor in the strengthening and development of my moral character, but in fitting me for the public life I was destined to lead.'[154] The Methodist churches provided the only formal training for making the necessary transition from communing with books to communicating with people.[155]

The reciprocal relationships between individual and collective inquiry, between books and deprivation, and between literary and oral communication ensured that the working-class intellectual was unable to abstract himself completely from the lives of those with whom he lived and worked. However unlimited his mental horizon may have become, there was little prospect of using his reading to escape the confinements of his background. Although the establishment of the Labour Party and the growth of a cadre of professional trade union leaders were creating the possibility of using a sophisticated grasp of communication to exchange a workbench for a desk, the opportunities were small and the material rewards negligible. As we saw in chapter 4, the generation which grew to maturity in the final decades of our period witnessed only marginal improvements in upward mobility through study. In the words of Robert Roberts,

> Such people in a more equitable system would, of course, have found a place far more fitted to their abilities: but only a very few,

aided by luck and determination, succeeded in breaking through their environment. The vast majority, half conscious often of talents wasted, felt a frustration they could hardly have explained ... They talked more, read more and possessed a much larger vocabulary than their neighbours in general.[156]

As they attempted to squeeze a few spare pence out of their hard-pressed family economies to spend on newspapers or cheap books, as they struggled to find the time and energy to read what they had bought in the midst of the physical demands of their homes and their work, and as they risked dismissal and blacklisting for attempting to apply the conclusions of their reading, such men had every incentive to take an active part in campaigns against inequalities of power and privilege.

For their part, those who through circumstance of inclination were less confident in their command of the tools of reading and writing had good cause to look to the more literate for assistance and leadership. As Thomas Burt observed, 'In the sphere of social organisation and education advancement there was ample room for earnest workers.'[157] The attraction of the 'earnest worker' was two-fold. Firstly he was an individual whose engagement with literature had both developed and displayed a moral seriousness, a responsible concern for matters beyond the day-to-day demands of work and leisure. This might be expressed in terms of a religious commitment, but not necessarily to a particular sect, and indeed could with equal force apply to a confessed secularist. Secondly he was a working man who through quality of personality and, very frequently, the good fortune of a stable occupational and home life, had acquired the capacity to work long hours in front of a book or with pen in hand without the expectation of financial reward. His function was exercised at both a general and a practical level. The bulk of the discourse of every working-class community was still oral, and the influence of the serious reader was felt first through conversation. 'The top-class natural leaders of the workers', noted Roberts, ' – the good, intelligent talkers – acted above else as assessors, arbiters and makers of the common conscience ... The pressure of their beliefs, prejudices and errors seeped slowly through the social layers of working-class life and conditioned the minds of all.'[158] At the same time there were a range of necessary tasks which the literate could perform in the neighbourhood at large and in the context of particular structures. We have seen at various points in this study how the tools of literacy were borrowed when the need arose, and this dependency on the skills of specific individuals was more acute when collective action was in prospect. Well accustomed to formal or informal association in his pursuit of books, the practised reader possessed both the instinct and the talent for organisation.[159] Thomas Wright charted the progress from the unofficial workplace leader to the specialised officer in a larger bureaucracy:

> A working man who is moderately well read, who is capable of expressing himself in proper and appropriate language, of writing a well-phrased letter, of drawing up an address or the heading of a subscription list in suitable terms, is a rarity in a workshop, and is regarded and honoured as such by his fellow-workmen, who speak for him as a great 'scholard', refer to him to decide disputes for them, or tell them how to write their most particular letters, put their grievances into addresses or petitions, act as secretary to their meetings and associations, and be their spokesman when occasion shall require.[160]

In this sense the union officials whose duties were examined in chapter 4 were well prepared for the world of constitutions, minutes, correspondence and addresses they discovered as the permanent political organisations were established in the closing years of the century.

Yet if the 'serious-minded people'[161] were never a race apart, major obstacles remained to their integration with the less studious. The political culture which sponsored the ILP and the Labour Party was confined and divided by the uses of literacy which it inherited. At the outset, there were the limitations imposed by the educational system through which an increasing proportion of enfranchised and unenfranchised alike had passed. The leading characteristic of those who had struggled through to Standard III or IV was not that they had been taught to believe in a middle-class God or a middle-class state, but rather that they were for the most part incapable of using their mental training to develop beliefs in anything else. Such control as the inspected, compulsory curriculum exercised over the political consciousness of the lower orders was achieved less through indoctrination than through restriction of intellectual inquiry. The teachers gained their most profound effect through their failure rather than their success. And whilst schooling was for its duration a levelling process, once it was over, an increasing gap opened up between the minority who were able to build upon their meagre foundation of skills and the majority whose grasp of the tools of literacy was still superficial and mechanical.

At the very least, it might be argued that compulsory education had successfully exposed the rising generations to the influence of market forces. R. A. Scott-James concluded in 1913 that 'It is not too much to say that capital controls the doling out of knowledge to the masses almost as completely as the Roman Church controlled it seven hundred years ago.'[162] In an important sense, however, this was a gross over-statement. Commercial journalism had yet to achieve any sort of monopoly in the dissemination of political information. Access to printing presses had not been completely denied to extra-Parliamentary radicals; there was still a pauper press. Working-class readers could buy a multitude of small periodicals advocating local or sectional causes, plus successful national weeklies like the *Clarion*, plus, by the time Scott-James was writing, the *Daily Herald* and the *Daily Citizen*, which in spite of their problems had circulations in excess of a million just before the war. In addition, sections of the press run unashamedly for profit, particularly *Reynolds' News*, continued to perform a valuable service. Beyond the printed word, moreover, there remained the still powerful lines of oral communication within neighbourhoods and between the informed and the less informed. The real impact of commercial exploitation was more indirect, though no less significant. Developments in the second half of the century began to consolidate a division between the serious and the trivial, the improving and the entertaining. It was not so much that capitalism controlled the flow of information, but rather that it deeply influenced its definition and status. Just as the growth in penny fiction had widened the gap between the 'classics' and the 'popular', so the multiplication of penny newspapers had made it increasingly difficult to assimilate the instructive with the sensational. Blatchford made a brave effort with his newspaper and the clubs which it spawned, but he failed to appeal much beyond the ranks of the committed activists. For *Clarion* readers, leisure was an extension of politics; for purchasers of *Reynolds'* and even more so the now million-selling *Lloyd's*, politics was a disposable supplement of recreation. Whilst the 'earnest workers' could still keep in touch with their communities, the continuing distinction between the 'serious minded' and the remainder of a now almost universally literate working-class population had a disabling effect on the prospects of mobilising its full strength against the liberal State.[163]

For its part, the State also gained its most profound influence in an oblique fashion. If commercial forces had yet to achieve the scale of hegemony exercised by medieval Catholicism, neither had the governments which had given the capitalists their opening. The tactical withdrawal from direct censorship which was completed in the 1850s, together with the caution with which compulsory education was introduced and implemented, ensured that except in limited instances, the acquisition and use of literacy were not in themselves intrinsically political acts. The situation contrasted sharply with contemporary Germany, where pervasive state intervention compounded the effects of poor housing and limited commercialised recreation and led to the creation of a nation-wide network of socialist cultural organisations.[164] The *Clarion* Fellowship and its related ventures could scarcely compete with the mass membership of the SPD's gymnastic, choral, church, rambling and educational clubs.

English recreational associations which to a greater or lesser extent employed the skills of reading and writing neither relied on nor necessarily led to socialist organisation. The tools of communication put into the hands of working-class children in the schools and sharpened through subsequent mutual instruction could be put to subversive ends, but equally they could be employed to extend the realm of the constitutional electoral process. Of equal importance, the related concessions of the franchise and freedom of speech to the propertied undermined the possibility of forging a permanent alliance between disaffected middle-class intellectuals and discontented working-class readers. The forces which came together in the campaign against 'Taxes on Knowledge' were dispersed following its success.[165] Only in the last quarter of the century was it possible for young labourers struggling to gain a wider perspective on their economic experience to receive theoretical and practical guidance from educated socialists. 'What helped me more than the books even', recalled Will Thorne, 'was the personal contact I had with great thinkers and working class leaders', who in his case included Liebknecht, Bebel, Singer, Adler, Engels, Aveling, Eleanor Marx, Morris and Hyndman.[166] Even then it remained difficult to insist that all those engaged in free inquiry through the medium of the printed word had a common and necessary enemy in the capitalist state.

In terms of overt repression, the most potent Government action was against freedom of organisation rather than freedom of expression. This caused undue emphasis to be placed on the achievement and employment of a notionally free press, and a persistent difficulty in establishing a successful relationship between bureaucracy and journalism. When, for reasons which extend beyond the confines of this study, Chartism was not replaced by a body of equivalent scope and independence, the increasing numbers of working men now able to both read and contribute to radical literature lacked a practical, disciplined context in which to test out their conclusions and connect them with the outlook of the less literate. It was almost inevitable that when the Independent Labour Party finally did emerge, its most effective national presence should be in the form of a privately run newspaper rather than a comprehensive organisation. The host of smaller journals attached to local bodies did as much to sectionalise as to integrate the Party. To recall Gramsci's homely metaphor, for much of this period the problem was not that the corset of the working-class movement had no bones, but rather the reverse. Despite the existence in 1914 of both the Labour Party and two labour daily papers, one of them official, the achievement of a conjunction between mass literacy and mass action remained unfulfilled.

Conclusion

The organisation of this book into discrete chapters on family, education, work, the natural world, imagination and politics reflects divisions which belonged to the mental universe of the literate rather than the pre-literate. It was precisely the inability of the oral tradition to distinguish between these categories which rendered its supersession necessary. None were more anxious than the self-educated artisans that fact and fancy, history and folklore, science and magic be divorced. Any challenge to inherited structures of power required the overthrow of orally transmitted patterns of belief. Yet once the political had been abstracted from the superstitious, the problem remained of re-establishing the relationship between the realms of the public and the private. By the beginning of the twentieth century, an increasing number of literate working men were able to describe themselves as 'politicians' in the way that previously had not been possible. The men who wrote the addresses and took the minutes of the succession of organisations from the London Corresponding Society to Chartism could find at best only temporary employment as full-time agitators before the necessity of keeping their families forced them back to the workbench.[167] It was not until the related growth of first the permanent trade union bureaucracies and then the Labour Party that those who had established an effective control over the tools of reading and writing could hope to devote all their time to defining and asserting the Parliamentary rights of their class. But as their subsequent autobiographies made clear, the task of translating the new sense of the political into a comprehensive reworking of the role of the State remained radically incomplete.

Ben Turner was a handloom weaver's son who began his working career as a mill-hand and ended it as a junior member of the 1929–31 Government, having served variously as a journalist, trade union official, founder member of the ILP and long-time member of the National Executive of the Labour Party. At one level his *About Myself, 1863–1930* demonstrated the breadth and the vitality of the culture from which the first cohort of Labour MPs was drawn. His 'untutored, unlettered father'[168] introduced him to radical politics by encouraging him to read *Reynolds' Newspaper* aloud to his family and neighbours, and at the same time immersed him in the dialect songs and stories which were frequently sung and recited in the home and in the pubs and clubs of his native Holmfirth.[169] Although he entered the mill as a half-timer at the age of ten, he was able to extend the education he had received at dame and national schools through attendance at a secular Sunday school, evening classes and debating societies. He became a voracious reader, and gradually learned how to express himself with a pen, encouraged in the mid 1880s by the possibility of contributing 'Labour notes for a radical newspaper run by a working printer'.[170] As reader, writer, singer and orator he moved easily between dialect and standard English, and between recreation and agitation. In his dual capacity as a journalist on the *Workman's Times* and a member of Leeds Trades Council he was at the centre of the formation of the ILP and thereafter was able to maintain his wife and five daughters through his skill as a communicator and organiser.

At the same time his account is pervaded by a sense of limitation. Despite his achievements at self-education, he recognised that he was not 'as sound a reader as I should have been',[171] lacking as he did the training and opportunity to give focus and system to his study. Although as a politician he never lost his links with organised labour or his pleasure in literature of every sort, his career in the Labour Party was devoid of the sense of all-embracing change which had characterised his first encounters with the written word. His personal success, and that of the movement to which he devoted his skills, was characterised in terms of the adaptation rather than the transformation of the political order. As the 1929 Government took office, he took pride in the fact that

> All the Party talk about Nationalisation of Women, Atheists, Infidels, etc., is now worn out for the Labour Party has amongst its leaders, more local preachers, more teetotallers than any other party can number, and whilst there will be a mental scallywag or two in our midst, the Movement compares favourably in honour and honesty with any other of the old parties of the State.[172]

The political game was still played by the rules of the 'old parties of the State', and the minority of working men who now joined in still found it difficult to see the remainder of their community as more than occasional spectators. It is appropriate that Turner's memoir should end with a discussion of the prospects of the *Daily Herald*, of which he had become a director. Whilst the paper was surviving in the face of intense competition from the commercial press and their 'immoral insurance schemes'[173] and was playing a key role in the continuing growth of the Labour Party, it was still under-capitalised and under-read, hampered by the Party's failure to break out of its minority position in spite of the universal franchise, and by its own failure to appeal to more than a million working-class readers, despite universal literacy.

8

LITERACY AND ITS USES

The future of this study is the past which provides the point of departure for Hoggart's classic account, *The Uses of Literacy*.[1] The generation which went to school in the decades before the First World War grew up to form the culture whose subsequent erosion by mass communication Hoggart sought to analyse. Approached through the perspective of the eighteenth and nineteenth centuries, *The Uses of Literacy*, which is now over thirty years old, has an air of great familiarity. This is partly because its preoccupation with the exploitation of inexperienced readers by unprincipled capitalists had been current in one form or another since at least the appearance of Matthew Arnold's *Culture and Anarchy* in 1868. At the very end of the period covered by this book, R. A. Scott-James delivered the following verdict on the consequences of the final drive to mass literacy: 'a careful observer of the workings of the Education Act [of 1870], basing his judgment upon the circulation of literature, might come to the general conclusion that it was contributing to the intellectual debauchery of the working classes, and that its influence was more subtly deleterious than that of the public house'.[2]

Yet this section of the population, so close to the moral abyss on the eve of the First World War, reappears in the 1930s as the upholders of 'a decent, local, personal, and communal way of life'[3] which is to be threatened by forms of journalism and fiction only in their infancy before 1914. Perhaps the first importance of *The Uses of Literacy* is the sense of proportion it forces upon the hopes and fears which were articulated with increasing stridency as the marks in the marriage registers fell towards 1 per cent. Whilst Hoggart might have been more aware of the difficulties which were apparent long before the time of his childhood, his repeated emphasis on the resilience of older cultural forms and of the oral tradition in which they were embodied is one of the abiding strengths of his account. Neither those who rejoiced in the virtual attainment of universal nominal literacy in the Registrar General's reports nor those who proclaimed the imminent disintegration of working-class culture were justified in supposing that the Edwardian period represented some sort of terminus in the history of mass literacy. As we saw in chapter 2, the most obvious factor prolonging the period of transition was the persisting generational variation in the command of literacy. Around one in ten were still unable to write at all, and behind them were the middle-aged and the old, particularly if they came from the ranks of the unskilled, or from the countryside, or were women, whose grasp of the tools of reading and writing could be extremely limited and would remain so for the rest of their lives. In the Hunslet of Hoggart's youth, and in towns and villages across England, children grew up in the company of grandparents and elderly neighbours whose mental resources were still largely dependent on the spoken word.

The consequences of this stratification by age and background were compounded by the sheer variety of the application by the common people of the basic skills taught in the elementary schools. Central to Hoggart's book, as to any adequate account of the subject, is the plurality of the functions of literacy. Despite the increasing body of pedagogic theory and cultural analysis, reading and writing remained simple tools which in the hands of those with the most limited training and experience were put to the most diverse range of tasks. This study has pursued its quarry from valentines to blacklists, from magical spells to political pamphlets, from dialect poetry to arbitration awards, and has been prevented by space or evidence from following it down many more lanes and alleyways. As a category of cultural practice, literacy permitted a breadth of engagement which could never be matched by the subsequent revolutions in mass communication of the cinema, radio and television. Although the tendency to divide production from consumption in the field of the printed word was well advanced by 1914, it was still far from complete, and in some areas, such as the postal system, active employment of writing was dramatically increasing just before the war. In the cinema, by contrast, which was becoming established as a rival form of entertainment, there was little to do except buy a ticket and sit in the dark to consume a product frequently manufactured in another continent. Only in the early years, when the short-sighted and the illiterate took children with them to read the captions, was there scope for serious audience participation. 'When the picture gave place to print on the screen', recalled Robert Roberts, 'a muddled Greek chorus of children's voices rose from the benches, piping above the piano music. To hear them crash in unison on a polysyllable became for literate adults an entertainment in itself.'[4]

The existence of so many categories of activity, each with its own trajectory over time, argues strongly against too schematic a model of change. Notwithstanding the attempts by generations of inspected teachers to regiment the mental processes of their pupils, and the increasing tendency of publishers and newspaper proprietors to standardise the reading matter available outside the classroom, the culture of the newly literate remained a sprawling, multi-layered entity. Even where clear developments had taken place, their conclusion and implications often remained extremely uncertain. This was partly because those institutions which appeared to have the greatest opportunity to shape the outcome, such as the State or private enterprise capitalism, were not always acting in consort, were frequently unsure of their strengths and tactics, and at all times faced resistance and appropriation; the rise of gambling as a direct consequence of the attempt to promote through the use of literacy a more rational response to the uncertainties of life was a case in point. It was partly also because by their nature no final form could be given to the diverse ways reading and writing could be employed to generate systems of meaning in the rapidly changing industrial society, or in turn to the range of meanings which could be attached to literacy itself.

What we can do, however, is establish the dimensions of the changes which had taken place by 1914, and identify those possibilities which were still open, and those which had been closed down. Here the strengths and weaknesses of *The Uses of Literacy* are most apparent. On the one hand its combination of a sympathetic response to the intricacies of social behaviour and a fierce critique of the impact on them of capital-intensive modes of literary production led to the foundation of a new school of cultural studies. On the other, as some of Hoggart's successors have pointed out, his analysis was restricted by its preoccupation with leisure and related forms of consumption.[5] In this study, the examination of the growing uses of literacy since the mid eighteenth century has revealed both the breadth and the interdependence of the categories of practice which were involved. It has become evident that an understanding of the function of reading and writing over time requires that equal attention be paid to education, the State, private enterprise capitalism, and the structures of working-class activity in both the home and the workplace. If we take, for instance, the issue of acquiring the skills of literacy, it may be argued that in spite of Gardner's recent work,[6] the historiography of education is still too confined to the official institutions of teaching, and in spite of Sutherland's pioneering research,[7] still too concerned with organisation and funding rather than the processes of cognitive training which went on during the lessons. The significance of the growth of a 'schooled society' rests in part on the complex relationship between the classroom and the economy and curriculum of the working-class home, and in part on the connection between the ways in which literacy was taught and the ways in which it might be employed in later years. Just as the implications of the aridity of official pedagogy only became evident as pupils sought to apply their skills to areas such as the multi-coloured world of sensational fiction, so the consequences of the growing centralisation of the production of cheap literature which were traced in chapter 6 took on their particular form only in conjunction with the training the readership had received. 'Commercialisation', which features so largely in accounts of publishing and journalism in the period, had no autonomous power of its own, but was particularly dependent on the role of the State both in its intervention in education and its tactical withdrawal from the control and supply of reading matter. For their part, the capacity of the newly literate to overcome the shortcomings of their training and to resist the twin forces of capital and the State was deeply influenced by the ways in which they could use their skills in various modes of collective action.

The precise nature of the interaction between the categories in the century and a half under review becomes clearer if we return to the related issues of coherence, community and power which were raised at the end of the first chapter. At one level, as has been suggested, a sense of discipline and order in the culture of the newly literate is neither to be expected nor desired. Reading and writing did not drive out the spoken word but rather set up increasingly complex relations between the modes of communication, in the same way that in this century the radio and then television have co-existed with print, altering but not necessarily abolishing its functions.[8] The absence of a neat pattern of change reflected the widespread ability of the labouring poor to find their own uses for this relatively simple technology, and, as for instance in the case of labour relations, to make sophisticated shifts between written and oral forms in order to advance or defend their interests. However, it is possible to draw a distinction between heterogeneity and incoherence, and to argue that the period as a whole witnessed a decisive transition from the former to the latter.

The initial difficulty was that the Churches and then the State eventually succeeded in reducing the variety of ways in which reading and writing might be acquired, but failed to find a means of teaching the skill which would equip the pupils to meet the growing diversity of challenges they would meet in life after school. As the applications of literacy grew, the consequences of the inability of the newly educated to make effective connections between bodies of knowledge became more serious. Their grasp of the tools of written communication was so mechanical that only the very gifted or those who could establish an organised context within which to sharpen and apply their reading and writing skills stood any chance of resisting the fissiparous pressures of middle-class professionals, politicians, employers and entrepreneurs. It was not that they were wholly excluded from any area of cultural practice. Readers were found for every form of prose, fiction and poetry, and attempts were made at creative writing in virtually every genre. Participation in bureaucratised trade union and political activity gradually became more widespread, the pauper press still showed signs of life, and in the fields of medicine, religion and history there were working men and sometimes women manipulating the printed word. What was missing was a broadly disseminated ability to employ the tool of reading, and much more so, writing, to move with ease and purpose between the categories. Despite belated attempts to reduce the distance between them, home and school, school and work remained widely separated forms of learning and activity, and over time it became more rather than less difficult to integrate practical and abstract work knowledge, sensational and 'classic' literature, oral and written history, botanic and 'scientific' medicine, formal and informal labour relations, recreation and politics. Too often multiplication of function meant fragmentation rather than enrichment. The cultural forms sustained by the use of literacy were increasingly divorced from each other, and from the structures of material inequality within which the readers and writers lived and worked.

Much of the evidence for this study is derived from sources which naturally emphasise the tendency of literacy to erode traditional forms of community. The quantitive data – the marriage registers and the postal returns – can be broken down to individual units or grouped at will into regional or national figures. The most fertile category of qualitative material, the autobiographies, were written in private and focused on the developing persona of the author. Over the period as a whole, and in particular from the second quarter of the nineteenth century onwards, the increase in the possession and use of literacy eroded differentials between sectors in the labouring population. Whereas the marriage registers of the 1830s and 1840s reflected the sharp variations in literacy by occupation, gender and residence which had been features of societies throughout early modern Europe, within little more than two generations, labourers and skilled artisans, husbands and wives, country and town dwellers, had become virtually indistinguishable. Children were exposed to a State-supervised education system, and their parents to nationally circulating newspapers and mass-produced fiction.

Yet if the registers and the memoirs and the other sources are examined carefully, it is possible to detect strong currents running against the expected reduction of orally defined communities to aggregates of private individuals and their families in the context of an enhanced sense of nationhood. The claims for the isolating effects of literacy to be found in so many studies of the subject are a function partly of an over-estimation of the gulf between print and speech, and partly of an under-estimation of the effects of poverty on the recently trained readers and writers. It may be that where, as is the case with most modern researchers, the individual has full command of the tools of literacy and unrestricted access to reading matter, where he or she has undergone fifteen to twenty years' full-time education culminating at a university far from the family home, the encounter with the written word takes the form of endless hours of private study and an accelerating withdrawal from the relatives and neighbours of childhood. But where, as was the case for at least the first century covered by this study, parents either taught their children or organised or bought a temporary, interrupted sequence of formal schooling, where, in spite of the rising levels of literacy and falling costs of literature, the skills and the artefacts on which to practise them remained in short supply, the acquisition and application of reading and writing naturally lent themselves to joint endeavour. With literacy, as with any other material or cultural good, deprivation meant mutual dependence.

At the casual level of writing or reading the occasional letter, working through a chapbook, broadside or newspaper, compiling or paying a bill of goods or services, the tools of literacy were borrowed within the home, neighbourhood or workplace. Those whose ambitions for more substantial intellectual inquiry had been kindled by native wit or by unusually supportive parents or teachers might require more privacy, but self-improvement had to involve informal or structured assistance. And whatever the task, reading and writing almost always led to and followed from the spoken word, whether in the form of children repeating their lessons in the classroom, literates spelling out texts to illiterates, neighbours telling over stories once read and now remembered, broadside-sellers shouting their wares, autodidacts sharing their discoveries, trade unionists reading minutes of the last meeting to a meeting which would generate more, or politicans reading speeches in newspapers then making their own to waiting reporters. As the number of total illiterates fell and the range of penny publications grew, it became easier to regard literacy as a private and silent possession, but the shift was marginal. No community at the end of the period was without a small minority who had missed schooling altogether, and a much larger number whose education had endowed them with slight skills and little confidence in using them, and no reader with any serious desire for literature could afford to purchase all that he or she wanted. For most individuals for most of the period, reading and writing fostered personal contact, and magnified, rather than stilled, the sound of the human voice.

The extent to which the literate could combine a continuing connection with the local and the oral with a fuller involvement with the world beyond depended on the efficacy of the tools at their disposal. A major reason for the disinclination of the educated to allow their time in the classroom to disrupt inherited ways of communicating and associating was the generally correct perception that many of the claims made for abstract learning were either false or inapplicable. Although the opportunities for upward social mobility were slowly increasing during the second two thirds of the nineteenth century, the chances of a working man's child using his education to move out of his class remained slim. The Education Act of 1902 created the prospect of some form of secondary education, but the era of the 'scholarship boy', which gave birth to Richard Hoggart, did not commence until after the First World War. Not only was the realm of higher education and the middle class largely out of sight, but it was still difficult, for reasons which were examined in chapter 4, to use schooling to overcome the substantial barriers which existed within the working class. In other, equally important areas, there was a yawning gap between promise and delivery. The doctors poured scorn on folk remedies but then could not prevent a child dying of consumption or whooping cough. The fully educated teachers and clergy preached thrift at the newly educated labourers but did not explain how they could afford the regular contributions to a friendly society. Small wonder that the schoolmaster and the minister saw their former pupils turning back to local wise women, publicans, book-keepers and the informal support networks of family and neighbours to cope with their troubles. By contrast, when rising prosperity, cheaper transport and improved facilities for acquiring and using literacy all came together, then the consequence, in the form of the halfpenny postcard, was a sudden and massive extension of the boundaries of the family and the community.

The only effective way in which the newly educated could hope to make a serious impact on the constricting bonds of hardship and inequality was through some form of collective action. Without literacy, there could be little organisation; without organisation, little effect could be given to literacy. The most successful example of the application of reading and writing to break down the isolation of the working-class community throughout the period was the growth of the trade union movement from primitive town-based democracies to elaborate national, and in some cases international, organisations by the early twentieth century. Here correspondence, rule books, ledgers, membership cards, blacklists, circulars and newspapers were used to overcome the deference, ignorance and immobility of the orally defined locality. Through the structures which they made possible, reading and writing transformed the perspective of at least a section of the workforce. Yet the use of literacy could not of itself create organisations where legal or other physical and ideological obstacles rendered them impossible, neither could it compensate fully for weaknesses in those which were formed. Despite their increasingly professional bureaucracies and their intricate manipulation of formal and informal rules, the unions were unable to establish a stable relationship between centralised discipline and localised autonomy; nor were they able to break out of a largely defensive industrial strategy. In the political arena, the employment of the written word in the form of the radical press disguised and was in turn undermined by the persistent difficulty of developing effective national movements. For most of the period, much of the labouring population found that the problems of bridging the gap between the individual possession and the collective use of literacy rendered them relatively more isolated in a society in which so much could now be gained by those who could exploit the new forms of communication.

This was particularly true of the brides, whose literacy levels at last caught up with the grooms. During the second half of the period their rate of increase often outstripped their marriage partners, and for several decades they actually managed to attain higher scores than their new husbands in wide areas of the country. Yet the exclusion of women from most forms of working-class organisation during the nineteenth century made it extremely difficult for them to employ their new skills to compensate for the loss of status and authority caused by the erosion of oral means of storing, transmitting and endorsing information. Caught between the increasingly rigid official regulations in areas such as education and medicine, and the increasingly elaborate rule books of trade unions and other self-help bodies, they had much less chance of making the transition from nominal to functional literacy, and a much smaller prospect of mounting an effective counter-attack against the pressures of the State and the market. Their loss was not absolute. In spite of the competition of mass-produced fiction and non-fiction, mothers still told stories to their children and passed on substantial bodies of domestic knowledge; notwithstanding compulsory school attendance and medical registration, unofficial teaching and health care did not disappear altogether. And there were those whose determination and ability enabled them to write poetry and autobiography.[9] But taken as a whole, the realities of power and opportunity in the use of literacy mocked the display of growing equality in the tables of the Registrar General.

What was left to both men and women was the freedom enjoyed by all those who survived the lessons in one-, two- and three-syllable words to travel outside the walls of their homes and beyond the streets of their neighbourhoods through the agency of the fiction and non-fiction which became increasingly available. There is no doubt that this capacity to journey in the mind was a powerful incentive to gain a working command of literacy, and that with the passage of time the destinations which might be reached became ever more numerous and distant. As the quantity of fantasy which could be bought for a penny grew, as the variety of cheap periodicals widened and the national and foreign coverage of the Sunday newspapers became more extensive, the labourer sitting before the fire after work and even his wife snatching a few minutes from the endless domestic routine could transport themselves with greater facility than once they had possessed. The problem was one of finding a consistent focus for their mental perspective, and of readjusting their sights when faced once more with the material realities of their daily lives.

At this point, the issues of coherence, community and power begin to merge. Because the readers experienced such trouble controlling the world before their eyes, the exploration of distant landscapes tended to lose its sense of scale and meaning. This was true not only of 'escapist' fiction, but of supposedly factual matters such as news of scientific discoveries or political crises abroad where the items were difficult to connect to each other or to any categories of undertaking open to the newly literate. The central problem was the true nature of the apparent profusion of uses associated with the printed word. In the relations of authority within which universal literacy was achieved, the diversity became a disorder, and, most critically, the plurality became a hierarchy. Some men could do more things with the tools of reading and writing than most others, and most men could do more than most women. Equally the status attached to some literate actions, and by extension to those who performed them, was set above that of actions undertaken by or associated with the remainder of the population.

The strategy of those who promoted mass literacy and the institutions in which it was to be gained was based on the hope that the formal channels of communication would be a means of bypassing the irreducible material inequalities of the industrialising society and the tensions which they engendered. Those charged with defending the liberal State and the market economy would gain access to the communities of the labouring poor with which they seemed to be in danger of losing all contact, and the disaffected elements would through the acquisition and practice of their new skills absorb values and discover diversions which would reconcile them to the new order. In an important sense this ambition failed. It was partly that the tradition of using literacy which the uneducated inherited gave them more confidence in their capacity to find their own applications than those who taught them ever expected. It was partly that the State and the economy were slow in developing, and neither the politicians nor the employers had sufficient confidence in their own strength or in the power of the schoolmaster. And it was partly that in virtually every area the use of literacy could not be insulated from the pressures of physical deprivation. Thus despite the huge increase of public involvement in the provision of education and of private exploitation in the market for reading matter, it is difficult to detect a successful imposition of a middle-class world view through the creation and manipulation of a literate labouring population.

Instead the achievement of those who exercised such power in the schools and in the production and employment of literature was of a more negative order. There was always a danger that through their increasing expertise in what was after all a common language, and through their growing access to what could be seen as a common literary heritage, the newly literate would subvert the distinctions upon which the divide between polite and popular culture was based. What prevented this happening was firstly the exposure of the working man's child to an educational system which rendered the tools of literacy both strange to handle and difficult to employ for any but the most mundane tasks, and then the confinement of the literate adult to a limited field of practices and a subordinate system of meanings. In a particular sense literacy could not have a single use. As the disparity between middle-class and working-class signatures in the marriage registers dwindled into insignificance, so the gap between the efficacy and status of the literacy of separate sections of the population widened. The children who spent more and more of their lives in school were denied the opportunity of connecting their basic training to higher forms of learning or to most of the problems they would face beyond the classroom. Their parents, who had glimpsed the prospect of extending through intellectual inquiry their control of their environ- ment, were excluded by the growth of the professions from access to advanced bodies of 'scientific' knowledge, and from the power, prestige and income which accompanied their application. The artisans who made ever more intricate use of the written word in their conduct of labour relations found themselves subordinated to a new breed of paper-qualified engineers, architects, surveyors and accountants and increasingly stigma- tised as manual rather than mental labourers. Those who sought to exercise their imaginations after work discovered that Shakespeare and Milton were becoming more accessible but less familiar as the 'classics' were divorced from mass-produced literature and from oral and literary categories of creativity practised by the mass of the population.

Over the period the tools of literacy were not so much appropriated as blunted. It was a process of disablement rather than theft. A mode of communication which could have provided the basis for a single, egalitar- ian culture instead became the means of reinforcing the distinction between those who worked with their 'brains' and those who worked with their 'hands'. The subsequent expansion of opportunities for a handful of gifted children to change sides merely consolidated the divide. The danger that the newly literate would employ their accomplishments to re- articulate the structures of economic and political authority was seen off, but at a cost to the long-term development of both industry and the state. The post-war inheritance was of a workforce which was educated but increasingly ill trained, of a population which was enfranchised but devoid of a clear sense of citizenship, and of generations of schooled children still struggling to bridge the gap between the possession and use of skills ever more relevant to the task of making sense of their world and giving voice to their conclusions.

A notable character in John Sykes' *Slawit in the 'Sixties* was a billposter who

> could neither read or write, neither did he give a straw for those who could. At one place he had posted a bill the wrong way up, and when a bystander asked him how the folks were to read the bill, he walked away swearing that they could do as they liked, 'they could stand on their heads if they wanted to'.[10]

It is difficult not to sympathise with this illiterate and irascible Yorkshireman. There was no reason why lack of education should prevent him making a living out of the increasing demand for reading matter, neither was there good cause to feel unduly deferential towards those who could now make out their letters. Yet the bystander also had a point. Too often in the history of the coming of mass literacy the newly educated were left facing unnecessary obstacles, few of which could be resolved by the simple expedient of standing on their heads.

APPENDIX A

MARRIAGE REGISTER SAMPLE

Through the work of R. S. Schofield up to 1840 and of the Registrar General from 1839 onwards, the general pattern of literacy in the period covered by this study has already been established. The purpose of this sample was to exploit the more detailed system of recording marriages established in 1837 in order to make a closer examination of the more important determinants of literacy during the final transition to a nominally literate society.

The major obstacle to the analysis of marriage registers after 1837 is the continuing unavailability of the records of all non-Anglican ceremonies. Although it is possible to purchase a copy of any specified marriage in the period, the Registrar General forbids access to complete registers held in his possession, which prevents any form of sampling across the entire population of marriage partners. In the early years of the new system, only a small proportion of brides and grooms chose to marry outside the parish church, but gradually the practice became more widespread, until by 1914, 17.6 per cent of marriages in England and Wales were conducted in Catholic, Nonconformist, Quaker or Jewish places of worship, and 24.1 per cent in the local registrar's office.

However, throughout the period, the incidence of non-Anglican marriages varied extensively across the country, and it was thought that it might be possible to counteract the dangers of drawing an increasingly unrepresentative sample by concentrating on Registration Districts with particularly high levels of ceremonies in the Established Church. Using Registration Districts rather than individual parishes as the basic unit of analysis generated a number of advantages.

Firstly, the Registrar General's practice of publishing aggregate returns of the form of marriage and the proportions of marks and signatures for each Registration District up to 1884 made it possible to identify the areas in which the custom of marrying outside the parish church remained very low. The factors determining the choice of venue for a wedding in this period are still not properly understood, but Olive Anderson's work on civil marriages suggests that whilst in the early years of the system the practice was confined to the very poor, thereafter a variety of local conditions and traditions influenced the decision.[1] A further inspection of the returns indicated that the Anglican/non-Anglican division did not correspond to any simple urban/rural, industrial/non-industrial or high/low literacy levels. The situation was further complicated by the fact that some Nonconformist sects continued to use the local parish church for weddings long after it was necessary to do so. Thus, for instance, a Methodist stronghold like Stoke-on-Trent had 82 per cent church marriages in 1874, whereas Rochdale, equally industrialised, had only 44 per cent. Macclesfield, in the same year, had 13 per cent illiteracy and 88 per cent Anglican marriages, whereas Bury (Lancashire) had 17 per cent illiteracy and only 58 per cent marrying in the Church of England.

Secondly, by working at the level of Districts (which were usually co-extensive with the Poor Law Unions), rather than individual parishes, it was possible to use the Registrar General's returns to check the accuracy of the sample up to 1884. As levels of literacy are strongly associated with social status, it was thought likely that if the literacy sample was accurate, the occupation sample would also be reliable. No check was available for the remaining three decades, except the very rough indicator of whether the sample returns continued to represent the same proportion of the County returns which were still published.

Thirdly it was hoped that by selecting Districts with contrasting social and economic characteristics it would be possible to illuminate the significant features of the move from 34 per cent male and 50 per cent female illiteracy to levels of 0.7 and 1.1 per cent in 1914.

Ten Registration Districts were selected: the industrial centres of Dudley, Macclesfield, Sheffield and Stoke-on-Trent, the more traditional urban communities of Bethnal Green and Lichfield, the mixed urban and rural areas of Nuneaton and Wokingham, and the rural areas of Cleobury Mortimer in Shropshire and Samford in Suffolk. For the non-industrialising communities it was relatively easy to identify the parishes which comprised the new Registration Districts, but considerable difficulty was encountered in the rapidly growing towns, where the map of parishes was redrawn several times during the sample period.

A sample of at least 1,000 marriages was taken for each District, based on every fifth year from 1839 to 1914. As the data were, for this purpose, already recorded randomly, it was sufficient to undertake a systematic sample designed to yield an average of 62.5 marriages for each of the sixteen years. In the larger Districts it was necessary to err on the side of caution, and the final total of marriages was 10,835. Details of the age of marriage partners, marital status, and literacy of bride, groom and both witnesses were coded for computing as they were recorded, and occupations of the groom, groom's father and bride's father were transcribed and coded later on the basis of a slightly modified version of the four-digit system devised for the 1951 census.[2] It had been hoped to make use of the residential evidence, but categorisation required such detailed local knowledge as to render the exercise impracticable. The data sheets, compiled from the registers of a total of 174 parishes, were transferred to punched cards at the University of Keele Computer Centre, and analysed through the SPSS programme.

In 1884, the level of Anglican marriages in the ten selected Districts stood at 90.4 per cent as against an average for England and Wales of 70.7 per cent. If the subsequent decline in the national level was mirrored in the sample, we would expect to find an Anglican rate of around 75 per cent in 1914. Up to 1884, the sample closely followed the aggregate returns for each District, the male illiteracy level being just 0.13 per cent above the average for the ten Districts, the female 0.7 per cent.

APPENDIX B

LITERACY NETWORKS

Literacy networks at weddings

Groom	Bride	First witness	Second witness	All period Number	%	1839–1854 Number	%	1859–1874 Number	%	1879–1894 Number	%	1899–1914 Number	%
L	L	L	L	5,852	55.5	815	28.8	1,021	39.9	1,620	64.6	2,396	90.7
L	L	L	X	408	3.9	113	4.0	138	5.4	127	5.1	30	1.1
L	L	X	L	395	3.7	62	2.2	108	4.2	133	5.3	92	3.5
L	L	X	X	117	1.1	36	1.3	44	1.7	29	1.2	8	0.3
X	X	X	X	698	6.6	432	15.2	211	8.2	50	2.0	5	0.2
X	X	X	L	209	2.0	126	4.4	61	2.4	22	0.9	0	0
X	X	L	X	385	3.7	233	8.2	116	4.5	32	1.3	4	0.2
X	X	L	L	301	2.9	126	4.4	105	4.1	62	2.5	8	0.3
L	X	L	L	542	5.1	213	7.5	154	6.0	133	5.3	42	1.6
L	X	L	X	408	3.9	191	6.7	150	5.9	58	2.3	9	0.3
L	X	X	L	155	1.5	63	2.2	69	2.7	20	0.8	3	0.1
L	X	X	X	243	2.3	138	4.9	73	2.9	31	1.2	1	0
X	L	L	L	413	3.9	123	4.3	137	5.4	121	4.8	32	1.2
X	L	L	X	139	1.3	47	1.7	68	2.7	19	0.8	5	0.2
X	L	X	L	154	1.5	51	1.8	61	2.4	36	1.4	6	0.2
X	L	X	X	123	1.2	64	2.3	44	1.7	14	0.6	1	0
				10,542	100.1	2,833	99.9	2,560	100.1	2,507	100.1	2,642	99.9

Missing observations 293
L – signature; X – mark

Literacy networks – unskilled labourers

Groom	Bride	First witness	Second witness	All period Number	All period %	1839–1854 Number	1839–1854 %	1859–1874 Number	1859–1874 %	1879–1894 Number	1879–1894 %	1899–1914 Number	1899–1914 %
L	L	L	L	856	34.0	61	7.5	131	19.8	267	47.3	397	83.8
L	L	L	X	98	3.9	21	2.6	32	4.8	34	6.0	11	2.3
L	L	X	L	119	4.7	21	2.6	37	5.6	41	7.3	20	4.2
L	L	X	X	35	1.4	8	1.0	13	2.0	9	1.6	5	1.1
X	X	X	X	299	11.9	204	25.0	74	11.2	20	3.5	1	0.2
X	X	L	X	107	4.2	70	8.6	29	4.4	8	1.4	0	0
X	X	X	L	150	6.0	95	11.6	42	6.3	11	2.0	2	0.4
X	X	L	L	115	4.6	47	5.8	41	6.2	25	4.4	2	0.4
X	X	L	L	110	4.4	44	5.4	34	5.1	20	3.5	12	2.5
X	X	L	X	79	3.1	35	4.3	29	4.4	10	1.8	5	1.1
X	X	X	L	57	2.3	25	3.1	23	3.5	8	1.4	1	0.2
X	X	X	X	72	2.9	40	4.9	22	3.3	10	1.8	0	0
X	L	L	L	193	7.7	51	6.2	68	10.3	60	10.6	14	3.0
X	L	L	X	68	2.7	25	3.1	30	4.5	11	2.0	2	0.4
X	L	X	L	100	4.0	36	4.4	39	5.9	23	4.1	2	0.4
X	L	X	X	60	2.4	34	4.2	19	2.9	7	1.2	0	0
				2,518	100.2	817	100.3	663	100.2	564	99.9	474	100

Literacy networks – skilled labourers

Groom	Bride	First witness	Second witness	All period		1839–1854		1859–1874		1879–1894		1899–1914	
				Number	%	Number	%	Number	%	Number	%	Number	%
L	L	L	L	2,644	54.8	358	27.7	449	37.8	734	65.1	1,103	90.6
L	L	L	X	213	4.4	65	5.0	85	7.1	50	4.4	13	1.1
L	L	X	L	171	3.5	29	2.2	45	3.8	52	4.6	45	3.7
L	L	X	X	61	1.3	19	1.5	25	2.1	16	1.4	1	0.1
X	X	X	X	314	6.5	179	13.8	109	9.2	22	2.0	4	0.3
X	X	X	L	78	1.6	40	3.1	26	2.2	12	1.1	0	0
X	X	L	X	173	3.6	98	7.6	55	4.6	18	1.6	2	0.2
X	X	L	L	131	2.7	60	4.6	49	4.1	18	1.6	4	0.3
L	X	L	L	328	6.8	131	10.1	93	7.8	83	7.4	21	1.7
L	X	L	X	228	4.7	114	8.8	79	6.6	31	2.8	4	0.3
L	X	X	L	70	1.5	27	2.1	32	2.7	10	0.9	1	0.1
L	X	X	X	138	2.9	80	6.2	39	3.3	18	1.6	1	0.1
X	L	L	L	138	2.9	40	3.1	40	3.4	45	4.0	13	1.1
X	L	L	X	55	1.1	19	1.5	29	2.4	5	0.4	2	0.2
X	L	X	L	36	0.7	10	0.8	16	1.3	7	0.6	3	0.2
X	L	X	X	49	1.0	25	1.9	18	1.5	6	0.5	0	0
				4,827	100.0	1,294	100.0	1,189	99.9	1,127	100.0	1,217	100.0

NOTES

1 INTRODUCTION

1 J. Mayett, Autobiography, unpublished MS, Buckinghamshire Record Office, n.d., 1–3, 49–50.
2 R. S. Schofield, 'Dimensions of Illiteracy in England 1750–1850', in H. J. Graff (ed.), *Literacy and Social Development in the West* (Cambridge, 1981), p. 207; L. Stone, 'Literacy and Education in England 1640–1900', *Past and Present*, 42 (1969), 105.
3 *Seventy-seventh Annual Report of the Registrar General*, PP 1916, V, table 10.
4 F. Furet and J. Ozouf, *Reading and Writing: Literacy in France from Calvin to Jules Ferry* (Cambridge, 1982), p. 15.
5 W. J. Ong, *Orality and Literacy* (London, 1982), p. 78. For a concise summary of his view, see W. J. Ong, 'Writing is a Technology that Restructures Thought', in G. Baumann (ed.), *The Written Word* (Oxford, 1986), pp. 23–50.
6 J. Goody, *The Domestication of the Savage Mind* (Cambridge, 1977), pp. 2–16, 148–60; J. Goody and I. Watt, 'The Consequences of Literacy', in J. Goody (ed.), *Literacy in Traditional Societies* (Cambridge, 1968), pp. 28–67.
7 E. L. Eisenstein, *The Printing Press as an Agent of Change* (Cambridge, 1980), p. 688 and *passim*.
8 First explored on a large scale in M. McLuhan, *The Gutenberg Galaxy* (London, 1962).
9 J. Oxenham, *Literacy: Writing, Reading and Social Organisation* (London, 1980), p. 14; Unesco, *Literacy 1965–1967* (Paris, 1968), p. 11; Unesco, *Literacy 1972–1976* (Paris, 1980), p. 14. Despite these achievements, the levels in 1980 of the forty-four countries with 'very high infant mortality' stood at 42 per cent for men, and 19 per cent for women: Unicef, *The State of the World's Children 1984* (Oxford, 1984), p. 120.
10 Unesco, *The Experimental World Literacy Programme, a Critical Assessment* (Paris, 1976), p. 115.
11 Unesco, *Experimental Programme*, pp. 19–20. The relevance of literacy campaigns to revolutionary struggle is examined in P. Friere, *Cultural Action for Freedom* (Harmondsworth, 1972), pp. 19–47. Also *The Pedagogy of the Oppressed* (Harmondsworth, 1972).
12 The emergence of the notion of 'functional literacy' is discussed in D. P. Resnick and L. B. Resnick, 'The Nature of Literacy: An Historical Exploration', *Harvard Educational Review*, 47, no. 3 (August 1977), 383.
13 H. J. Graff, *The Literacy Myth* (London, 1979).
14 E. Johansson, 'The History of Literacy in Sweden, in comparison with some other countries', *Educational Reports, Umea*, 12 (1977), pp. 2–42.
15 Schofield, 'Dimensions'.
16 Amongst the numerous local studies see W. P. Baker, 'Parish Registers and Literacy in East Yorkshire', *East Yorks Local History Society* (1961); V. A. Hartley, 'Literacy at Northampton 1761–1900', *Northamptonshire Past and Present*, 4 (1966), 379–81; J. S. Hurt, *Bringing Literacy to Rural England: The Hertfordshire Case* (Chichester, 1972); R. Smith, 'Education, Society, and Literacy: Nottinghamshire in the Mid-Nineteenth Century', *University of Birmingham Historical Journal*, 12 (1969), 42–56; W. B. Stephens, 'Illiteracy and Schooling in the Principal Towns, 1640–1870: A Comparative

Approach', in D. A. Reeder (ed.), *Urban Education in the Nineteenth Century* (1977), pp. 27–48.

17 See appendix A.

18 *Seventy-seventh Annual Report of the Registrar General*, PP 1916, V, table 10.

19 A. Bullock, *A Language for Life* (London, 1975), pp. 14–15.

20 However, a number of official bodies concerned with education and literacy treated England and Wales as one unit, and it has not always been possible to separate the data on the two countries.

21 On Scotland, see R. A. Houston, *Scottish Literacy and the Scottish Identity* (Cambridge, 1985).

22 C. Geertz, 'Thick Description: Toward an Interpretative Theory of Culture', in C. Geertz (ed.), *The Interpretation of Cultures* (London, 1975), p. 17; B. Martin, *A Sociology of Contemporary Cultural Change* (Oxford, 1981), pp. 30–6; R. Chartier, 'Culture as Appropriation: Popular Cultural Uses in Early Modern France', in S. L. Kaplan (ed.), *Understanding Popular Culture* (Berlin, 1984), pp. 233–5.

23 R. Pattison, *On Literacy* (Oxford, 1982), pp. 20–1.

24 P. Burke, *Popular Culture in Early Modern Europe* (London, 1978).

25 J. Hall, *The Olde Religion* (London, 1628), p. 167.

26 J. Brand, *Observations on Popular Antiquities* (Newcastle upon Tyne, 1777), p. iv. See also R. M. Dorson, *The British Folklorists* (London, 1968), pp. 10–34.

27 Brand, *Observations*, p. iv (Brand's italics).

28 S. Trimmer, *The Oeconomy of Charity* (London, 1801), I, p. 10.

29 L. Soltow and E. Stevens, *The Rise of Literacy and the Common School in the United States* (Chicago, 1981), p. 49.

30 J. Kay-Shuttleworth, 'An Explanation of the Intentions of her Majesty's Government entitled Recent Measures for the Promotion of Education in England', in *Four Periods of Public Education* (London, 1862), p. 229.

31 B. Brierley, *Home Memories and Recollections of a Life* (Manchester, 1886), p. 44; R. Story, *The Poetical Works of Robert Story* (London, 1857), p. vi; Henry Price, 'Diary' (MS 1904), 30. See also John Younger, *Autobiography of John Younger, Shoemaker. St. Boswells* (Kelso, 1881), p. 121; William Lovett, *Life and Struggles of William Lovett* (London, 1876), p. 35; L. James, *Print and the People 1819–1851* (London, 1976), pp. 20–1; D. Riesman, 'The Oral and Written Traditions', in E. Carpenter and M. McLuhan (eds.), *Explorations in Communication* (London, 1970), p. 113.

32 B. Mandeville, *The Fable of the Bees*, ed. F. B. Kaye (Oxford, 1966 edn), p. 268.

33 *Ibid.*, p. 270.

34 *Ibid.*, p. 270.

35 *Ibid.*, p. 308.

36 W. B. Hodgson, 'Exaggerated Estimates of Reading and Writing', *Transactions of the National Association for the Promotion of Social Science* (1867), 399. The paper was published as a separate pamphlet in 1868. Hodgson was a former headmaster and Assistant Commissioner to the Newcastle Commission, and was later to become Professor of Commercial and Mercantile Law at Edinburgh.

37 *Ibid.*, 397.

38 *Ibid.*, 397, 398.

39 M. Stubbs, *Language and Literacy. The Sociolinguistics of Reading and Writing* (London, 1980), p. 160.

40 A. R. Luria, *Cognitive Development. Its Cultural and Social Foundations* (Cambridge, Mass., 1976), p. 55 and *passim*. Luria is not always clear whether the effect is a consequence of literacy or of the whole process of collectivisation. For the Soviet drive against illiteracy, see R. Pethybridge, *The Social Prelude to Stalinism* (London, 1974), pp. 132–95.

41 A. Inkeles and D. H. Smith, *Becoming Modern* (London, 1974), pp. 15–35, 152, 315.

42 D. Lerner, *The Passing of Traditional Society* (Glencoe, 1958), p. 64.

43 E. Todd, *The Causes of Progress* (Oxford, 1987), p. 131.

44 M. J. Bowman and C. A. Anderson, 'Concerning the Role of Education in Development', in C. Geertz, *Old Societies and New States* (New York, 1963), p. 252.

45 S. Scribner and M. Cole, *The Psychology of Literacy* (Cambridge, Mass., 1981), p. 7. Harvey Graff makes much the same observation: Graff, *Literacy Myth*, p. 304. See also Bowman and Anderson's comments on the shortage of case studies in the study of literacy and economic growth: 'Concerning the Role of Education', p. 250.

46 C. Critcher, 'Sociology, Cultural Studies and the Post-War Working Class', in J. Clarke, C. Critcher and R. Johnson (eds.), *Working Class Culture* (London, 1979), p. 19.

47 M. Spufford, 'First Steps in Literacy: the Reading and Writing Experiences of the Humblest Seventeenth-century Spiritual Autobiographers', *Social History*, 4, no. 3 (October, 1979), 412.

48 J. Lancaster, *Improvements in Education as it Respects the Industrious Classes of the Community* (London, 1803), p. 58.

49 R. K. Webb, 'Working Class Readers in Early Victorian England', *English Historical Review*, 65 (1950), 350. His findings are confirmed by M. J. Campbell in his unpublished D.Phil. thesis, 'The Development of Literacy in Bristol and Gloucestershire 1755–1870', Bath University, 1980, 14, 209–15.

50 See below, chapter 3, p. 90.

51 Furet and Ozouf, *Reading and Writing*, p. 112. This separation was also a feature of Russian elementary education: J. Brooks, *When Russia Learned to Read* (Princeton, 1985), p. 47.

52 A valuable start has now been made by Keith Thomas in his 'Numeracy in Early Modern England', *Transactions of the Royal Historical Society*, 5th series, 37 (1987), 103–32.

53 M. Twyman, *Printing 1770–1970* (London, 1970), pp. 5–59; S. H. Steinberg, ·*Five Hundred Years of Printing* (3rd edn, Harmondsworth, 1974), pp. 277–91.

54 C. Knight, *The Old Printer and the Modern Press* (London, 1854), pp. 238, 260–1, 263.

55 D. Cressy, *Literacy and the Social Order* (Cambridge, 1980), p. 146.

56 R. A. Houston, 'The Development of Literacy: Northern England, 1640–1750', *Economic History Review*, 35, no. 2, 206.

57 Schofield, 'Dimensions', p. 211; Stone, 'Literacy and Education', pp. 110–11.

58 In the Early Modern period, reading was taught prior to and apart from writing. For this reason Thomas regards Cressy's literacy figures as a 'spectacular underestimate' of the numbers who had a basic reading ability. K. Thomas, 'The Meaning of Literacy in Early Modern England', in G. Baumann (ed.), *The Written Word* (Oxford, 1986), p. 103.

59 T. Laqueur, 'The Cultural Origins of Popular Literacy in England, 1500–1800', *Oxford Review of Education*, 11, 3 (1976), 255. Houston, *Scottish Literacy*, p. 195.

60 Cressy, *Literacy*, pp. 76–7.

61 M. Spufford, *Small Books and Pleasant Histories* (London, 1981), pp. 111–28.

62 Spufford, 'First Steps', p. 247.

63 C. J. Sharp, *English Folk Song, Some Conclusions* (4th edn, Wakefield, 1965), p. 4.

64 D. F. McKenzie, 'The Sociology of a Text: Oral Culture, Literacy and Print in Early New Zealand', in P. Burke and R. Porter (eds.), *The Social History of Language* (Cambridge, 1987), pp. 161–79.

65 For a broader discussion of the dangers of polarising 'oral' and 'literate' cultures, see R. Finnegan, *The Oral Tradition* (Cambridge, 1977), p. 24; B. V. Street, *Literacy in Theory and Practice* (Cambridge, 1984), pp. 20–4. 45–9, 97–9, 110–20. For the complex interconnections between literate and illiterate as early as the twelfth century, see B. Stock, *The Implications of Literacy* (Princeton, 1983), p. 522; M. T. Clanchy, *From Memory to Written Record* (London, 1979), pp. 175–201.

66 D. Vincent, 'The Decline of the Oral Tradition in Popular Culture', in R. D. Storch (ed.), *Popular Culture and Custom in Nineteenth Century England* (London, 1982), pp. 20–47; Burke, *Popular Culture*, p. 245.

67 First published *c.* 1538. See the facsimile reprint ed. R. S. Shuckburgh (London, 1889).

68 G. Wells, *Language Development in the Pre-school Years* (Cambridge, 1985), pp. 395–6; Bullock, *Language for Life*, pp. 10–11.

69 Evidence of Jonathan Taylor, in *Report from the Committee on . . . the Apprentice Laws of the Kingdom* (1813), PP 1812–13, IV, pp. 16–17.

70 C. More, *Skill and the English Working Class, 1870–1914* (London, 1980).
71 W. S. Gray, *The Teaching of Reading and Writing* (Paris and London, 1956), p. 24. See also Bullock, *Language for Life*, p. 9.
72 Unesco, *Literacy 1972–1976* (Paris, 1980), p. 12; Resnick and Resnick, 'The Nature of Literacy', p. 383; K. Levine, *The Social Context of Literacy* (London, 1986), pp. 25–35; Stubbs, *Language and Literacy*, p. 97.
73 Thomas, 'Meaning of Literacy', p. 97; Pattison, *On Literacy*, p. viii.
74 H. A. Jones and A. H. Charnley, *Adult Literacy* (London, 1980), p. 3.
75 C. St. J. Hunter and D. Hunter, *Adult Illiteracy in the United States* (New York, 1979), pp. 26–30.
76 Bullock, *Language for Life*, pp. 6, 16, 24. The report advocated the creation of an entirely new system of measurement which would at least permit the monitoring of progress in the future. The content and limitations of the post-war literacy surveys are examined in K. B. Start and B. K. Wells, *The Trend of Reading Standards* (Windsor, 1972).
77 The findings of these surveys are summarised in D. Vincent, 'Reading in the Working Class Home', in J. K. Walton and J. Walvin (eds.), *Leisure in Britain 1780–1939* (London 1983), pp. 209–14.
78 The data are examined in R. Rawson, 'An Enquiry into the Condition of Criminal Offenders in England and Wales, with respect to Education', *Journal of the Statistical Society of London*, III (1840), 331–52.
79 R. S. Schofield, 'The Measurement of Literacy in Pre-Industrial England', in J. Goody (ed.), *Literacy in Traditional Societies* (Cambridge, 1968).
80 See below, chapter 2, pp. 46–8.
81 The limitations of the data in the US census are discussed in Soltow and Stevens, *Rise of Literacy*, p. 3.
82 In particular Flora Thompson, in *Lark Rise to Candleford* (Harmondsworth, 1982), p. 80. Also, J. E. Vaux, *Church Folklore* (London, 1894), p. 103.
83 *Third Annual Report of the Registrar General*, PP 1841, VI, p. 9; *Thirty-second Annual Report of the Registrar General*, PP 1871, XV, p. xiii.
84 Furet and Ozouf reach a similar conclusion about the validity of marriage signatures in France: *Reading and Writing*, pp. 10–18.
85 The 180 signatures represented just under 30 per cent of marriage partners.
86 See below, chapter 3.
87 A point strongly argued in Levine, *Social Context of Literacy*, p. 85.
88 Cf. the model of literacy set out by Brian Street in *Literacy in Theory and Practice*, p. 8. Also Scribner and Cole, *Psychology of Literacy*, pp. 236, 258; H. Graff, *Legacies of Literacy* (Bloomington, 1987), p. 4.
89 Discussed in D. Vincent, *Bread, Knowledge and Freedom* (London, 1981), pp. 14–38.
90 For the necessary association of writing with power, see Pattison, *On Literacy*, pp. 61ff.; Graff, *Legacies of Literacy*, pp. 11–12.

2 FAMILY

1 *Second Annual Report of the Registrar General*, PP 1840, XVII. The report covered the year ending 30 June 1839. The first annual report made no reference to this subject.
2 See appendix B.
3 For the periodisation of the sample, see appendix A.
4 For the final period of Schofield's sample (1815–44), the literacy of 'labourers and servants' was 34 per cent; for the first period of my sample (1839–54), the literacy of unskilled labourers was 32 per cent: Schofield, 'Dimensions', p. 211.
5 W. B. Stephens, *Education, Literacy and Society, 1830–1870* (Manchester, 1987), pp. 13–14.
6 Cressy, *Literacy*, p. 145. Also G. Parker, 'An Educational Revolution? The Growth of Literacy and Schooling in Early Modern Europe', *Tijdschrift voor Geschiedenis*, XCIII (1980), 212; R. A. Houston, 'Literacy and Society in the West 1500–1850', *Social History*, 8, no. 3 (1983), 271.

7 In France, although women had made rapid advances, they still lagged a few points behind their spouses. Furet and Oxouf, *Reading and Writing*, pp. 23–44.

8 The variations between the genders are also discussed in Stephens *Education*, pp. 16–17. On the more general tendency for differentials to be maintained as literacy levels rise, see Graff, *Legacies of Literacy*, p. 286. In the modern world, apart from South Africa and Botswana, women are behind men in every country except those with literacy levels in the upper nineties. Unesco, *World's Children*, p. 120.

9 There is some suggestion that prior to 1750, there may have been a positive correlation between age and literacy, perhaps explained by the incidence of post-school self-teaching of literacy. D. W. Galenson, 'Literacy and Age in Pre-industrial England: Quantitative Evidence and Implications', *Economic Development and Cultural Change*, 29, no. 4 (July 1981), 13–29.

10 *Twenty-seventh Annual Report of the Registrar General*, PP 1866, XIX, pp. 2–5; *Forty-seventh Annual Report of the Registrar General*, PP 1886, XVII, pp. 2–5; *Seventy-seventh Annual Report of the Registrar General*, PP 1916, V, table 12.

11 D. Levine, 'Education and Family Life in Early Industrial England', *Journal of Family History*, 4, no. 4 (Winter 1979), 373–9.

12 Literacy levels represent the mean of the rates of brides and grooms. The returns for the first period of the sample, 1839–54, were made unreliable by the widespread practice, especially amongst those marrying for the second time, of entering 'Of full age' rather than the actual age. For inter-generational differences elsewhere in Europe, see C. Cipolla, *Literacy and Development in the West* (Harmondsworth, 1969), pp. 92–4.

13 The lower literacy of young marriage partners may be a result of their lower than average social class. Only 0.3 per cent of teenage grooms were from social class 1, as aginst 1.33 per cent for the whole sample, and only 0.9 per cent of teenage brides as against 1.6 per cent.

14 Lady F. Bell, 'What People Read', *Independent Review*, 7, pt 27 (1905) 435.

15 Cf. Furet and Ozouf, *Reading and Writing*, p. 47, on slightly higher rates of residual illiteracy in early-twentieth-century France.

16 Roberts, *The Classic Slum*, p. 177.

17 D. Vincent, 'Love and Death and the Nineteenth Century Working Class', *Social History*, 5, no. 2 (May 1980), 223–47.

18 Cramer's V for the association between the literacy of grooms and networks of literacy at weddings was .70717, whereas the value for the association between networks at weddings and social mobility at weddings was .09377.

19 This may have been a consequence of a purely random choice of witnesses, which would have pulled in men and women from higher and thus more literate sectors of the population. However, it seems more probable that marriage partners would have chosen witnesses from amongst their close family or immediate neighbours, who are likely to have been of similar social status.

20 Oxenham, *Literacy*, p. 6.

21 [M. D. Hill] 'The Post Office', *Fraser's Magazine*, LXVI (1862), 330–1; *Twenty-seventh Annual Report of the Postmaster General* (1881), p. 11; *Thirty-seventh Report* (1891), p. 17; *Forty-seventh Report* (1901), p. 25; H. Robinson, *Britain's Post Office* (Oxford, 1953), p. 221. The figures relate to letters only, and do not include postcards, of which over 926 million were carried in 1913.

22 [J. W. Croker] 'Post Office Reform', *Quarterly Review*, LXIV (1839), 558; B. R. Mitchell and P. Deane, *Abstract of British Historical Statistics* (Cambridge, 1971), pp. 393, 396.

23 [M. D. Hill] 'Post-Office Reform', *Edinburgh Review*, LXXX (1840), 554. On the campaign for the Penny Post, see M. Daunton, *Royal Mail* (London, 1985), pp. 8–11.

24 *Second Report from the Select Committee on Postage*, PP 1837–8, XX, pt II, p. 303.

25 A. Wynter, *Peeps into the Human Hive* (London, 1874), II, p. 10.

26 J. H. Heaton, 'Postal and Telegraphic Progress under Queen Victoria', *The Fortnightly Review*, CCCLXXVI (June 1897), 839–49.

27 *S.C. on Postage*, p. 215.

28 Robinson, *Britain's Post Office*, p. 100. By the mid 1830s, however, 356 Post Towns were providing a penny post within their delivery area.

29 D. Jerrold, 'The Postman', in *Heads of the People* (London, 1878 edn), I, p. 254. Also J. Routledge, *Chapters in the History of Popular Progress* (London, 1876), p. 583.

30 *S.C. on Postage*, p. 215.

31 *Postal History*, 202 (November–December 1977), 10–11.

32 Daunton, *Royal Mail*, p. 6.

33 *S.C. on Postage*, p. 199.

34 *Ibid.*, p. 49.

35 For an example of the fulfilment of this expectation, see the account given by the young Edward Harvey of his uncles William and John coming to his house to have letters written for them in the late 1850s. E. Harvey, *A Postman's Round 1858–61*; selected and introduced by Tony Mason (Coventry, 1982), pp. 7, 9.

36 Croker, 'Post Office Reform', p. 532.

37 *S.C. on Postage*, p. 134.

38 *Ibid.*, p. 41.

39 R. Hill, *Post Office Reform, its Importance and Practicability* (London, 1837), p. 67.

40 *S.C. on Postage*, p. 105. See also J. Arch, *Joseph Arch, The Story of His Life, told by Himself* (London, 1898), p. 9.

41 For a more extended discussion of the relationship between literacy and the family in the political crisis of the late 1830s, see Vincent, 'Reading', pp. 207–26.

42 R. Hill, *Post Office Reform*, p. 93.

43 *S.C. on Postage*, p. 200. The political implications of the introduction of the Penny Post are examined at greater length in D. Vincent, 'Communication, Community and the State', in C. Emsley and J. Walvin (eds.), *Artisans, Peasants and Proletarians, 1790–1860* (London, 1985).

44 R. and G. B. Hill, *The Life of Sir Rowland Hill and the History of the Penny Postage* (London, 1880), 1, p. 395.

45 R. Hill, 'Results of the New Postage Arrangements', *Quarterly Journal of the Statistical Society of London* (July 1841), 85; Robinson, *Britain's Post Office*, p. 155; A. Clinton, *Post Office Workers* (London, 1984), p. 29.

46 *Report from the Select Committee on Postage*, PP 1843, VIII, p. 15.

47 *1843 S.C. on Postage*, p. 13.

48 H. Ashworth, *Recollections of Richard Cobden, M.P. and the Anti-Corn Law League* (2nd edn, London, 1878), p. 185. In one election in London alone, 40,000 tracts were posted to electors. *The Administration of The Post Office from the Introduction of Mr. Rowland Hill's Plan of Penny Postage up to the Present Time* (London, 1844), pp. 59–60.

49 R. and G. B. Hill, *Life of Rowland Hill*, p. 478.

50 *Administration of the Post Office*, p. 196.

51 *Twenty-seventh Annual Report of PMG*, appendix A; *Forty-seventh Annual Report* (London, 1901), appendix A.

52 If all the items sent by mail are included, however, Britain was overtaken by the USA in the 1890s: Union Postale Universelle, *Statistique générale du Service Postal, Année 1890* (Berne, 1892), p. 2; UPU, *Année 1900* (Berne, 1902), p. 2.

53 *Tenth Annual Report of the Postmaster General on the Post Office* (London, 1864), p. 27.

54 See below, chapter 7.

55 M. D. Hill, 'The Post Office', p. 332.

56 Robinson, *Britain's Post Office*, pp. 153, 167–9.

57 *Tenth Report of PMG*, p. 15.

58 For similar ambitions in the United States see the discussion of the growth of its postal service in Soltow and Stevens, *Rise of Literacy*, p. 75.

59 Soltow and Stevens, *Rise of Literacy*, pp. 34–8.

60 'Return of the total number of letters posted at the Head Post Offices in England and Wales during the week beginning 3 May, 1891', Post Office Archives (hereafter POA), Post 19/127.

61 A marked seasonal increase in correspondence has been evident in spa towns such as Tunbridge Wells from as early as the mid eighteenth century: B. Austen, *English Provincial Posts 1633–1840* (London, 1978), pp. 88–90.

62 W. Southgate, *That's the Way it Was* (London, 1982), p. 19.

63 The proportion of 'Letters posted in the District for Delivery in the District in the Year 1863' were 5 per cent in Oldham, 7 per cent in Ashton and Dudley, 25 per cent in Manchester and 28 per cent in Birmingham.

64 *Eleventh Annual Report of the Postmaster General on the Post Office* (London, 1865), p. 8.

65 *Seventeenth Annual Report of the Postmaster General on the Post Office* (London, 1871), table XI.

66 *Tenth Report of PMG*, p. 35.

67 'Estimated Total Number of Letters posted at every Post Office in the United Kingdom founded upon an account taken for the week commencing the 15th January, 1838', POA, Post 19/36; 'Returns of the Number of Letters, Book Packets and Free Newspapers, delivered from the Head Post Offices in England and Wales during the week commencing the 15th and ending the 21st January, 1861', POA, Post 19/81.

68 'Total Number of Letters posted at every Post Office in England and Wales for the week ended 23 Jan, 1842', POA, Post 19/40; 'Number of Letters ... delivered from Head Post Offices during one Week in the Year ended 31st March, 1901', POA, Post 19/127.

69 *1838 S.C. on Postage*, p. 209. Scribner and Cole found that letter writing amongst the Vai in Liberia was similarly confined to practical family matters: *Psychology of Literacy*, pp. 71, 73.

70 Furet and Ozouf, *Reading and Writing*, p. 77.

71 J. Sykes, *Slawit in the 'Sixties* (Huddersfield, 1926), p. 86.

72 Robinson, *Britain's Post Office*, pp. 198, 204.

73 *1843 S.C. on Postage*, p. 282.

74 *Seventh Annual Report of the Postmaster General on the Post Office* (London, 1862).

75 *Thirty-fourth Annual Report of the Postmaster General on the Post Office* (London, 1888), pp. 4–5.

76 W. H. Cremer, *St. Valentine's Day and Valentines* (London, 1971), pp. 10–13; F. Staff, *The Valentine and its Origins* (London, 1969), pp. 25–38.

77 Letter from Sir Frederick Freeling to the Postmaster General, quoted in Staff, *The Valentine*, p. 49. William Hone claimed that by 1838 the figure was already as high as two hundred thousand: W. Hone, *The Every-Day Book* (London, 1838), 1, p. 215.

78 Hill, 'Results', p. 89.

79 'The Post Office', *Fraser's Magazine*, XLI (February 1850), 227.

80 *Ninth Annual Report of the Postmaster General on the Post Office* (London, 1863), p. 11; *Seventeenth Report of the Postmaster General on the Post Office* (London, 1871), p. 20. It might be noted that the numbers posted from London to the country were consistently twice those coming in.

81 For a cross-section of this material, see the twenty-box set in the John Johnson Collection, Bodleian Library.

82 On the poor quality of much of the material see C. M. Smith, 'The Press of the Seven Dials', in *The Little World of London* (London, 1857), p. 262.

83 S. Bamford, *Early Days* (London, 1893 edn), pp. 149–59.

84 *Twelfth Annual Report of the Postmaster General on the Post Office* (London, 1866), p. 15.

85 Thompson, *Lark Rise*, p. 486.

86 *Twenty-fourth Annual Report of the Postmaster General on the Post Office* (London, 1878), p. 10.

87 *Twenty-sixth Annual Report of the Postmaster General on the Post Office* (London, 1880), pp. 9–10.

88 G. Buday, *The History of the Christmas Card* (London, 1964), pp. 72–137.

89 N. Alliston, 'Pictorial Post Cards', *Chambers Journal* (October 1899), 745–8.

90 *Forty-seventh Annual Report of the Postmaster General on the Post Office* (London, 1901), p. 26.

91 F. Staff, *The Picture Postcard and its Origins* (London, 1966), pp. 7–91. For an account of the living to be made selling the early postcards see T. Kenney, *Westering. An Autobiography* (London, 1939), p. 92.

92 Heaton, 'Postal Progress', p. 839. See also A. Wynter, *Our Social Bees* (London, 1861), p. 4; C. Redding, *Yesterday and Today* (London, 1863), III, p. 187.

93 *Fourth Annual Report of the Postmaster General on the Post Office* (London, 1858), p. 17. He was referring to a return for 1855.

94 Cipolla, *Literacy*, pp. 14, 128.

95 For literacy in Sweden, see E. Johansson, 'The History of Literacy in Sweden', in Graff, *Literacy*, p. 180.

96 Hill, 'Results', pp. 87, 99. By 1841 the Birmingham and Grand Junction Railway alone was earning £32,000 a year from its postal business, which was almost a third of the entire cost of postal transport before the Penny Post. The mutually beneficial but often fraught relationship between the Post Office and the railway companies in the nineteenth century is traced in Daunton, *Royal Mail*, pp. 122–33.

97 R. and G. B. Hill, *Life of Rowland Hill*, pp. 16, 22.

98 P. O'Brien, 'Transport and Economic Development in Europe, 1789–1914', in P. O'Brien (ed.), *Railways and the Economic Development of Western Europe, 1830–1914* (London, 1983), pp. 2–6.

99 M. Horler, *The Early Recollections of Moses Horler* (Radstock, 1900), p. 8.

100 Levine, *Social Context of Literacy*, p. 45; Thomas, 'Meaning of Literacy', pp. 106–7.

101 Thompson, *Lark Rise*, pp. 58, 258, 471. Also W. Tinsley, *Random Recollections of an Old Publisher* (London, 1900), I, p. 8; G. Haw, *From Workhouse to Westminster – The Life Story of Will Crooks, M.P.* (London, 1911), p. 18.

102 K. Dayus, *Her People* (London, 1982), p. 167.

103 *Ibid.*, p. 31.

104 Heaton, 'Postal Progress', p. 839.

105 E. Hall, *Canary Girls and Stockpots* (Luton, 1975), p. 5.

106 *Ibid.*, p. 5. See Roberts, *Classic Slum*, pp. 168–9 for the penetration by the picture postcard of the least literate section of the community.

3 EDUCATION

1 *Second Annual Report of the Registrar General*, PP 1840, XVII, p. 4.

2 Schofield, 'Dimensions', pp. 206–8.

3 Mitchell and Deane, *Abstract of British Historical Statistics*, pp. 396–8.

4 *Forty-seventh Annual Report of the Registrar General*, PP 1881, XXVII, p. xi.

5 *Seventy-seventh Annual Report of the Registrar General*, PP 1916, V, table 10.

6 Cf. the similar sequence in France, where 'the great educational laws of the 1880s were enacted at a time when the cause of universal literacy was, if not entirely so, at least pretty well won, as can be seen from the figures': Furet and Ozouf, *Reading and Writing*, p. 45.

7 For the importance of demand in the growth of elementary schooling in France see Furet and Ozouf, *Reading and Writing*, p. 66.

8 A more detailed exposition of this point is made in T. Laqueur, 'Working Class Demand and the Growth of English Elementary Education 1750–1850', in L. Stone (ed.), *Schooling and Society* (Baltimore, 1976), p. 192.

9 See Vincent, *Bread, Knowledge and Freedom*, chs. 4 and 5.

10 In *Father and Son* he describes his experience in early infancy as a mute witness to the theft by the family dog of a leg of mutton (London, 1907 edn). pp. 18–19.

11 H. Bee, *The Developing Child* (3rd edn, New York, 1981), pp. 170–220.

12 A. Ireson, 'Reminiscences', in J. Burnett (ed.), *Destiny Obscure* (London, 1982), p. 84.

13 Ireson, 'Reminiscences', pp. 86–7.

14 *Ibid.*, p. 87.

15 T. Cooper, *The Life of Thomas Cooper* (London, 1872), p. 5.

16 More, *Skill*, esp. pp. 181–94.

17 W. Cobbett, *A Spelling Book with Appropriate Lessons in Reading and with A Stepping-Stone to English Grammar* (London, 1831), p. 103.

18 A. Bell, *Extract from a Sermon on the Education of the Poor* (2nd edn, London, 1807), p. 10.

19 A. Errington, MS Autobiography, 1. For a more general discussion of the working-class knowledge of their family's past see D. Vincent, ' "to inform my famely and the world": Autobiography and Ancestry in the Nineteenth Century', in *English Genealogical Congress, Selected Papers Given at the Congresses of 1978 and 1984* (London, 1986), pp. 95–108.

20 J. Gutteridge, *Lights and Shadows in the Life of an Artisan* (London, 1969 edn), p. 90.

21 E. G. Robinson, 'I Remember', MS, 5. Also, T. Burt, *Thomas Burt, MP., D.C.L., Pitman and Privy Councillor. An Autobiography* (London, 1924), p. 26; F. Kitchen, *Brother to the Ox* (Horsham, 1940), pp. 3–4.

22 The title of chapter 3 of *When I Was a Child* (London, 1903).

23 P. Inman, *No Going Back. An Autobiography* (London, 1952), p. 14. Also Haw, *Workhouse to Westminster*, p. 4.

24 F. Place, *The Autobiography of Francis Place*, ed. Mary Thale (Cambridge, 1972), p. 61.

25 J. J. Bezer, 'The Autobiography of One of the Chartist Rebels of 1848', in D. Vincent (ed.), *Testaments of Radicalism* (London, 1977), p. 157.

26 'William Bowyer' [William Bowyer Honey], *Brought Out in Evidence: An Autobiographical Summing-Up* (London, 1941), pp. 63–4. See also H. Snell, *Men, Movements and Myself* (London, 1936), p. 6; J. Saunders, *The Reflections and Rhymes of an Old Miller* (London, 1938), p. 86. Notwithstanding the most recent survey of the teaching of literacy: 'Parents with very little or no educational background ... would be unable to use the spoken word as a means of precise communication, or as a vehicle for interesting conversation': A. Ellis, *Educating our Masters* (Aldershot, 1985), p. 170.

27 J. Clare, 'Autobiographical Fragments', in E. Robinson (ed.), *John Clare's Autobiographical Writings* (Oxford, 1983), p. 33.

28 M. K. Ashby, *Joseph Ashby of Tysoe 1859–1919* (London, 1974 edn), p. 15.

29 R. Blatchford, *My Eighty Years* (London, 1931), p. 13.

30 W. Lovett, *Life and Struggles of William Lovett* (London, 1967 edn), p. 7.

31 G. Marsh, 'A Sketch of the Life of George Marsh, Yorkshire Collier. 1834–1921', TS, 7.

32 A. Foley, *A Bolton Childhood* (Manchester, 1973), pp. 17–18. Also W. E. Adams, *Memoirs of a Social Atom* (London, 1903), I, p. 67; Robinson, 'I Remember', p. 3.

33 J. Harris, *My Autobiography* (London, 1882), p. 9.

34 Cited in F. J. Harvey Darton, *Children's Books in England* (3rd edn, Cambridge, 1982), p. 233.

35 Blatchford, *My Eighty Years*, p. 4.

36 Foley, *Bolton Childhood*, p. 11.

37 J. Lawson, *A Man's Life* (London 1932), p. 11.

38 Lovett, *Life and Struggles*, p. 3.

39 A. Ellis, *A History of Children's Reading and Literature* (Oxford, 1968), pp. 35, 77; J. R. Townsend, *Written for Children* (Harmondsworth, 1967), p. 36; Harvey Darton, *Children's Books*, pp. 127–213.

40 Ellis, *Children's Reading*, p. 62.

41 Bamford, *Early Days*, p. 87.

42 *Ibid.*, p. 87. See also J. Bowd, 'The Life of a Farm Worker', *The Countryman*, 51, pt 2 (1955), 293–4; J. Myles (ed.), *Chapters in the Life of a Dundee Factory Boy. An Autobiography* (Dundee, 1850), p. 31.

43 Spufford, *Small Books*, pp. 219–57.

44 Clare, 'Autobiographical Fragments', p. 56. Bamford was born in 1788, Clare in 1793.

45 Clare, 'Autobiographical Fragments', p. 2. On 'Mother Bunch', see below, chapter 5, p. 176.

46 J. A. Leatherland, *Essays and Poems with a brief Autobiographical Memoir* (London, 1862), p. 5. Leatherland had also read many chapbooks, of which he was 'passionately fond'.

47 Bamford, *Early Days*, p. 90. Also Kitchen, *Brother to the Ox*, p. 11.

48 M. Grossek, *First Movements* (London, 1937), p. 44. Grossek was born in 1888.

49 Inman, *No Going Back*, p. 13.

50 Saunders, *Reflections and Rhymes*, pp. 12–13. Also Haw, *Workhouse to Westminster*, pp. 6, 18.

51 D. Barr, *Climbing the Ladder: the Struggles and Successes of a Village Lad* (London, 1910), p. 16. Also Adams, *Social Atom*, I, p. 35; J. Sexton, *Sir James Sexton, Agitator* (London, 1936), p. 229; W. Citrine, *Men and Work* (London, 1964), pp. 12–13; G. N. Barnes, *From Workshop to War Cabinet* (London, 1923), p. 2. On the more general influence of women as moral educators, see Lawson, *A Man's Life*, p. 59.

52 G. Edwards, *From Crow-Scaring to Westminster. An Autobiography* (London,1922), p. 21.

53 H. Snell, *Men, Movements and Myself* (London, 1936), p. 5. See also Foley, *Bolton Childhood*, p. 8; T. Okey, *A Basketful of Memories. An Autobiographical Sketch* (London, 1930), pp. 15–16; T. Tremewan, *Cornish Youth. Memories of a Perran Boy (1895–1910)* (Truro, 1968), p. 14; T. W. Wallis, *Autobiography of Thomas Wilkinson Wallis* (London, 1899), p. 10.

54 Errington, MS Autobiography, 4.

55 These are examined in more detail in Vincent, 'Reading', pp. 210–11.

56 Bowd, 'Life', p. 4.

57 Shaw, *When I Was a Child*, p. 139. Also A. Rushton, *My Life as a Farmer's Boy, Factory Lad, Teacher and Preacher* (Manchester, 1909), p. 32; F. Hodges, *My Adventures as a Labour Leader* (London, 1925), pp. 5–6; Bowyer, *Brought Out*, p. 82.

58 Snell, *Men, Movements*, p. 20.

59 P. McCann (ed.) *Popular Education and Socialisation in the Nineteenth Century* (London, 1977), pp. x-xi.

60 W. Heaton, *The Old Soldier; The Wandering Lover; and other poems; together with A Sketch of the Author's Life* (London, 1857), p. xvi; E. Green, MS Autobiography, *c.* 1880, 5.

61 M. Collier, *Poems on Several Occasions ... with some remarks on her life* (Winchester, 1762), p. vii.

62 N. Dale, *The Eventful Life of Nathaniel Dale* (Kimbolton, *c.* 1871), p. 6. Also B. Taylor, *About Myself* (London, 1930), p. 23; Heaton, *The Old Soldier*, p. xvi.

63 J. Nicholson, *Poems by John Nicholson, The Airedale Poet with a Sketch of his Life and Writings by John James FSA* (Bingley 1878), p. 4.

64 Darton and Harvey, *Books for Youth* (London, 1805).

65 M. L. Pearl, *William Cobbett, A Bibliographical Account of his Life and Times* (Oxford, 1953), p. 68; G. Spater, *William Cobbett, The Poor Man's Friend* (Cambridge, 1982), II, p. 372.

66 As an example of the long-term impact of Cobbett's work, his *Grammar* was cited by the leading member of the early Labour Party, Jimmy Clynes, as one of the formative influences on his career. W. T. Stead, 'The Labour Party and the Books that helped to make it', *Review of Reviews*, XXXIII (1906), 572.

67 For the wide availability of Mavor and other cheap primers on bookstalls at mid-century, see Smith, 'The Press of the Seven Dials', p. 261.

68 J. Wood, *Autobiography of John Wood, an old and well known Bradfordian, Written in the 75th Year of his Age* (Bradford, 1877), p. 5.

69 Mayett, MS Autobiography, 1. See also above, chapter 1, p. 1.

70 Mayett, MS Autobiography, 2.

71 Laqueur, 'Working-Class Demand', p. 192.

72 F. Smith, *A History of English Elementary Education 1760–1902* (London, 1931), pp. 220–2. Gardner's careful reworking of the official statistics casts doubt on the validity of any precise figures. His general conclusion is that private working-class schools declined more gradually than outside observers claimed and expected. P. Gardner, *The Lost Elementary Schools of Victorian England* (London, 1985), ch. 2.

73 *Report of the Commissioners Appointed to Inquire into The State of Popular Education in England*, PP 1861, XXI, pt III, p. 29.

74 Gardner, *Lost Schools*, p. 194.

75 T. W. Laqueur, *Religion and Respectability. Sunday Schools and Working Class Culture* (New Haven, 1976), p. 49.

76 E. G. Davis, *Some Passages from My Life* (Birmingham, 1898), p. xxx.

77 J. P. Edwards, *A Few Footprints* (2nd edn, London, 1906), p. 5. See also J. Harris, *My*

Autobiography (London, 1882), p. 25; W. Farish, *The Autobiography of William Farish* (1889), p. 10; R. Hampton, *Foolish Dick: An Autobiography of Richard Hampton, the Cornish Pilgrim Preacher*, ed. S. W. Christophers (London, 1873), p. 16.

78 J. Lancaster, *Improvements in Education as it Respects the Industrious Classes of the Community* (London, 1803), p. 12.

79 For an account of educational change caused by parental debt, see J. Basset, *The Life of a Vagrant* (London [1850]), p. 2.

80 Gardner, *Lost Schools*, p. 117.

81 I. Anderson, *The Life History of Isaac Anderson. A Member of the Peculiar People* (n.d.), pp. 5–6.

82 B. Madoc-Jones, 'Patterns of Attendance and their Social Significance', in P. McCann (ed.), *Popular Education and Socialisation in the Nineteenth Century* (London, 1977), p. 47.

83 H. Burstow, *Reminiscences of Horsham, being Recollections of Henry Burstow, the celebrated Bellringer and Songsinger* (Horsham, 1911), p. 5; J. Child, 'The Autobiography of a Dedicated Gardener', TS, 1; H. Herbert, *Autobiography of Henry Herbert, a Gloucestershire Shoemaker, and Native of Fairford* (Gloucester, 1866), pp. 6–7; J. H. Powell, *Life Incidents and Poetic Pictures* (London, 1865), p. 5; Saunders, *Reflections*, p. 25.

84 Lancaster, *Improvements in Education*, p. 16.

85 J. Kay-Shuttleworth, *Four Periods of Public Education* (London, 1862), p. 177.

86 *Report of the Committee of Council on Education 1872–3* (London, 1873), p. 98.

87 J. Blacket, *Specimens of the Poetry of Joseph Blacket, with an account of his life* (London, 1809), p. 15.

88 *Minutes of the Committee of Council on Education 1851–52*, vol. II (London, 1852), p. 384. The only adequate account of parental attitudes to education in this period is to be found in Gardner, *Lost Schools*, pp. 91–100. Cf. Jeffrey Brooks' account of the nature of parental demand in contemporary Russia. Brooks, *When Russia Learned to Read*, p. 43.

89 Thompson, *Lark Rise*, p. 44.

90 Trimmer, *Oeconomy of Charity*, I, p. 10.

91 *Ibid.*, I, p. 12.

92 S. Wilderspin, *A System for the Education of the Young* (London, 1840), p. 16.

93 *Ibid.*, p. 16.

94 *Minutes of the Committee of Council* (1847), p. 239, cited in A. Digby and P. Searby, *Children, School and Society in Nineteenth-Century England* (London, 1981), p. 120. Also R. Colls, ' "Oh Happy English Children!": Coal, Class and Education in the North-East', *Past and Present*, 73 (1976), 86–91, 96.

95 J. Talbot, *The Christian School-Master* (new edn, London, 1811), pp. 133–4.

96 *Second Report from the Select Committee on the Education of the Lower Orders*, PP 1818, IV, p. 14. Evidence of Rev. T. T. Walmsley.

97 J. Fletcher, *Minutes of the Committee of Council* (1846), p. 287, cited in Digby and Searby, *Children, School and Society*, pp. 77–8.

98 Talbot, *Christian School-Master*, p. 99.

99 *Ibid.*, p. 18.

100 M. G. Jones, *The Charity School Movement* (Cambridge, 1938), pp. 74–80.

101 Especially Hannah More's much-quoted statement, 'I allow of no writing for the poor.'

102 Trimmer, *Oeconomy of Charity*, I, p. 99.

103 *Manual of the System of Primary Instruction Pursued in the Model Schools of the British and Foreign Schools Society* (London, 1831), p. 8.

104 *Report from the Select Committee on the State of Education*, PP 1834, IX, p. 706. Cf. a similar set of priorities in contemporary French elementary schools: R. D. Anderson, *Education in France 1848–1870* (Oxford, 1975), p. 32.

105 Cited by James Kay-Shuttleworth, in *Recent Measures for the Promotion of Education in England* (1839), republished in *Four Periods*, p. 239.

106 (London, 1816), p. vii.

107 J. Kay-Shuttleworth, *Second Report on the Schools for the Training of Parochial School-Masters at Battersea* (London, 1843), republished in *Four Periods*, p. 411.
108 See Graff, *Legacies of Literacy*, p. 72, on medieval teaching techniques, which were much the same as those used up to the nineteenth century.
109 E. M. Field, *The Child and his Book* (2nd edn, London, 1892), pp. 113–225; M. F. Thwaite, *From Primer to Pleasure in Reading* (2nd edn, London, 1972), pp. 4–7. The most recent survey of methods of teaching reading and writing in this period is in A. Ellis, *Educating Our Masters* (Altershot 1985), pp. 87–102.
110 T. Dyche, *A Guide to the English Tongue* (2nd edn, London, 1710).
111 W. Markham, *An Introduction to Spelling and Reading English* (5th edn, London, 1738).
112 H. Innes, *The British Child's Spelling Book* (London, 1835).
113 C. W. Johnson, *The English Rural Spelling-Book* (London, 1846). Also, G. Vasey, *The Excelsior Reading Made Easy, or Child's First Book* (London, 1855).
114 For the early history of teaching literacy, see M. M. Matthews, *Teaching to Read, Historically Considered* (Chicago, 1966), pp. 19–74.
115 *Manual of B.F.S.S.*, p. 15.
116 *Minutes of the Committee of Council on Education 1840–41* (London, 1841), pp. 18–22; H. Dunn, *Popular Education; or The Normal School Manual* (London, 1837), pp. 69–71.
117 For a particularly clear account of writing as a set of purely physical skills see the curriculum outlined in W. Lovett and J. Collins, *Chartism. A New Organisation of the People* (London, 1840), pp. 97–100.
118 *1840–41 Minutes*, p. 22; J. H. Cowham, *Cowham's Mulhauser Manual of Writing* (London, 1888).
119 *1840–41 Minutes*, p. 22.
120 Gardner, *Lost Schools*, pp. 107–8.
121 Kay-Shuttleworth, *Four Periods*, p. 104.
122 S. Trimmer, *The Charity School Spelling Book* (9th edn, London, 1805), p. 73.
123 *Manual of the System of Primary Instruction Pursued in the Model Schools of the British and Foreign Schools Society* (London, 1831), p. 21; Dunn, *Popular Education*, p. 69.
124 Innes, *Spelling Book*, pp. 35, 81. Properly handled, the Bible could also serve as a basis for lessons in arithmetic. Thus: 'Of Jacob's four wives, Leah had six sons, Rachel had two, Bilhah had two, and Zilpah had also two; how many sons had Jacob?' Cited in 'Church and State Education', *The Edinburgh Review*, XCII (1850), 126.
125 Hodgson, 'Exaggerated Estimates', p. 400.
126 *1834 Select Committee on Education*, p. 25. Evidence of Henry Dunn.
127 Ellis, *Children's Reading*, pp. 39–40.
128 F. H. Spencer, *An Inspector's Testament* (London, 1938), p. 51.
129 Talbot, *Christian School-Master*, p. 91.
130 D. Leith, *A Social History of English* (London, 1983), pp. 33–57; O. Smith, *The Politics of Language* (Oxford, 1984), pp. 1–34; M. Cohen, *Sensible Words. Linguistic Practice in England 1640–1785* (Baltimore, 1977), pp. 88–95.
131 On the way in which the classes were becoming 'more elaborately distinguished' by their pronunciation, see K. C. Phillips, *Language and Class in Victorian England* (Oxford, 1984), p. 84. Also, P. J. Waller, 'Democracy and Dialect, Speech and Class', in P. J. Waller (ed.), *Politics and Social Change in Modern Britain* (Brighton, 1987), pp. 1–14.
132 H. Innes, *The Rhetorical Class Book, or the Principles and Practice of Elocution* (London, 1834), p. 12.
133 J. Gill, *Introductory Text-Book to School Management* (2nd edn, London, 1857), p. 56. Also, J. A. St John, *The Education of the People* (London, 1858), p. 224.
134 The scale of the change in communication skills embodied in the move from the home to the classroom is discussed in J. Cook-Gumpertz and J. J. Cook-Gumpertz, 'From Oral to Written Culture; The Transition to Literacy', in M. F. Whiteman (ed.), *Writing* (New Jersey, 1981), I, p. 98.
135 W. Cobbett, *A Grammar of the English Language in a Series of Letters Intended for the use of Schools and of Young Persons in General; but more especially for the use of Soldiers, Sailors, Apprentices and Plough-Boys* (London, 1835), Letter I.
136 Cobbett, *Grammar*, Letter III.

137 *Minutes of the Committee of Council on Education, 1851–52* (London, 1852), II, pp. 388–9. Table of subjects studies at 40 selected schools in the North Midlands.

138 Cobbett, *Grammar*, Letter II.

139 *Ibid.*, Letter XXII.

140 See, for instance, A. Allen and J. Cornwell, *A New English Grammar, with very copious exercises and a systematic view of the formation and derivation of words* (London, 1841), p. viii. Cornwell was a tutor at the BFSS Normal School. The book had reached its twenty-third edition by 1855.

141 *1851–2 Minutes*, II, p. 30. Report on Melksham National Girls' School, Wiltshire.

142 *Report of the Commissioners Appointed to Inquire into the State of Popular Education in England*, PP 1861, XXI, pt III, p. 148. For an unsuccessful proposal by a school inspector in 1890 to include the Lancashire dialect in the curriculum, see B. Hollingworth (ed.), *Songs of the People* (Manchester, 1977), pp. 1–2.

143 *Report on Popular Education*, pt I, p. 28.

144 *1840–1 Minutes*, p. 22.

145 Kay-Shuttleworth, *Four Periods*, pp. 43–4. On the attempt to reinforce the hierarchical society by teaching the working class to know its place, see B. Simon, 'Systemisation and Segmentation in Education: The Case of England', in D. F. Muller, F. Ringer and B. Simon, *The Rise of the Modern Educational System* (Cambridge, 1987), p. 92.

146 For the relationship between education, intelligence and communication skills in nineteenth-century American education, see C. Calhoun, *The Intelligence of a People* (Princeton, 1973), chs 1 and 2.

147 *1851–2 Minutes*, II, p. 48. See also C. W. Connon, *A First Spelling-Book* (1851), p. 4.

148 W. F. Richards, *Manual of Method for the Use of Teachers in Elementary Schools* (London, 1854), p. 66. For the parallel development of this theory in the United States, see Matthews, *Teaching to Read*, pp. 75–101; and in Russia, Brooks, *When Russia Learned to Read*, p. 50.

149 J. Gill, *Introductory Text-Book to School Management* (2nd edn, London, 1857).

150 J. S. Laurie, *First Steps to Reading* (London, 1862).

151 See above, ch. 1, p. 7.

152 Dunn, *Popular Education*, p. 116.

153 *Ibid.*, p. 14 (italics in original).

154 The events of 31 May 1838 caused a greater loss of life than the Peterloo Massacre. Their significance is discussed in Vincent, 'Reading', pp. 207–26. See also P. G. Rogers, *Battle in Bossenden Wood* (London, 1961).

155 F. Liardet, 'State of the Peasantry in the County of Kent', in Central Society of Education, *Third Publication* (London, 1839), p. 128.

156 J. M. Goldstrom, *The Social Content of Education, 1808–1870* (Shannon, 1972), pp. 94–151.

157 St John, *Education of the People*, pp. 50, 93–107; 'Church and State Education', p. 127.

158 For the growing crisis, see M. Sturt, *The Education of the People* (London, 1967), pp. 238–58; A. J. Marcham, 'The Revised Code of Education 1862: Reinterpretations and Misinterpretations', *History of Education*, 10, no. 2 (1981), 87–90; Ellis, *Educating our Masters*, p. 93.

159 *Report on Popular Education*, pt 1, p. 34.

160 *Ibid.*, pt 1, p. 35.

161 Kay-Shuttleworth, *Four Periods*, p. 590. For a similar attack see M. Arnold, *The Twice Revised Code* (London, 1862).

162 J. S. Hurt, *Elementary Schooling and the Working Classes 1860–1918* (London, 1979), pp. 30–4.

163 *Final Report of the Commissioners Appointed to Inquire into the Elementary Education Acts, England and Wales*, PP 1888, XXV, p. 135.

164 *First Report of the Commissioners Appointed to Inquire into the Elementary Education Acts, England and Wales*, PP 1886, XXIX, p. 129.

165 For a survey of the expansion in this literature, see A. Ellis, *Books in Victorian Elementary Schools* (London, 1971), pp. 21–32.

166 J. S. Laurie, *Laurie's Graduated Series of Reading Lesson Books* (London, 1866), bk 2, p. 54.

167 See also E. T. Stevens and Rev. C. Hole, *The Grade Lesson Books in Six Standards* (London, 1871).

168 Thompson, *Lark Rise*, p. 180.

169 Textbooks had been available since the early 1840s. See, for instance, J. Cornwell, *The Young Composer; or, Progressive Exercises in English Composition* (London, 1844).

170 *Report of the Committee of Council on Education 1872–3* (London, 1873), pp. 6–10; *Report of the Committee of Council on Education, 1882–3* (London, 1883), pp. 200–2. Figures are for the years ending August 31 1872 and 1882, for England and Wales.

171 The first period covers the sample years 1859, 1864, 1869 and 1874 and corresponds to the schooling received up to c. 1860; the second covers the sample years 1879, 1884, 1889 and 1894 corresponding to the school period up to c. 1880.

172 *Report of the Committee of Council on Education 1882–3* (London, 1884), pp. 200–2.

173 *Report of the Committee of Council on Education 1883–4* (London, 1884), pp. 205, 214–15.

174 'Penny Fiction', *The Quarterly Review*, 171 (1890), 150.

175 *Report of the Committee of Council on Education 1880–1* (London, 1881), p. 339.

176 *Ibid.*, p. 339.

177 Report of P. le Page Renouf, Inspector for Middlesex, in *1872–3 Report on Education*, pp. 121–2.

178 Hurt, *Elementary Schooling*, p. 180.

179 G. Collar and C. W. Crook, *School Management and Methods of Instruction* (London, 1900), p. 1.

180 *Ibid.*, p. 1. See also Digby and Searby, *Children, School and Society*, pp. 90–1.

181 Collar and Crook, *School Management*, pp. 3–4.

182 *Ibid.*, pp. 100–1.

183 A point strongly argued in a contemporary manual, J. Gunn, *Class Teaching and Management* (London, 1895), pp. 12–13.

184 Thompson, *Lark Rise*, p. 182. For a more general discussion of the alienation of children from elementary schools at the end of the nineteenth century, see S. Humphries, *Hooligans or Rebels?* (Oxford, 1981), pp. 34–61.

4 WORK

1 D. Hudson, *Munby, Man of Two Worlds* (London, 1972), p. 40.

2 R. Rawson, 'An Enquiry into the Condition of Criminal Offenders in England and Wales, with respect to Education', *Journal of the Statistical Society of London*, IV (1841), 351.

3 Schofield, 'Dimensions', pp. 212–13; Sanderson, 'Social Change', pp. 131–54; Sanderson, 'Literacy and Social Mobility', 82–9; Stephens, 'Illiteracy', pp. 3–4, 6, 58.

4 Graff, *Literacy Myth*, esp. pp. 195–233.

5 See below, appendix A, p. 282.

6 The composition and characteristics of this group are discussed in more detail below, pp. 127–32.

7 Cf. the similar finding of Stephens' survey of local case studies: Stephens, *Education*, p. 29.

8 The age-specific nature of this evidence is examined in ch. 3, p. 26.

9 Cf. Sewell's comparative study of occupational literacy from marriage registers in Marseilles. Between 1821–2 and 1869, the rates for 'Business and Professional' moved from 100 to 98, 'Sales and Clerical' from 97 to 100, 'Small Business' from 96 to 99, 'Artisan' from 65 to 90 and 'Unskilled' from 27 to 69. W. H. Sewell, *Structure and Mobility* (Cambridge, 1985), p. 254.

10 Conversely, it may be argued that these groups were most disadvantaged by the earlier absence of adequate education provision. Campbell, 'Development of Literacy', pp. 153, 192–9.

11 T. Laqueur, 'The Cultural Origins of Popular Literacy in England, 1500–1800', *Oxford*

Review of Education, 11, no. 3 (1974), 96–107; E. G. West, 'Literacy and the Industrial Revolution', *Economic History Review*, 2nd series, XXXI (1978), 371.

12 The vicars of the parish of St Peter's Stoke, which covered virtually the whole of the subsequent Registration District, kept up the practice until the early 1830s. In Prestbury, which included the whole of Macclesfield until new urban parishes began to be created in the 1830s, occupations were not recorded in the 1750s, but were continually thereafter.

13 The returns for Stoke and Macclesfield are from the parishes of St Peters Stoke and Prestbury until 1834, and for the Registration Districts thereafter. The absence of occupational data from St Peter's in the early 1830s rendered the samples of miners and labourers too small for analysis. The returns for Dudley are for the parish of Dudley until 1834, the Registration District from 1839.

14 J. Grayson, 'Literacy, Schooling and Industrialisation: Worcestershire, 1760–1850', in Stephens, *Studies in the History of Literacy*, pp. 54–67, esp. table 5.1.

15 M. W. Greenslade and D. G. Stuart, *A History of Staffordshire* (2nd edn, Chichester, 1984), pp. 88–9; R. Haggar, 'Pottery', in M. W. Greenslade and J. G. Jenkins (eds.), *A History of the County of Stafford* (Oxford, 1967), II, pp. 12–27.

16 Greenslade and Jenkins, *History of Stafford*, II, pp. 239–41.

17 S. Davies, *A History of Macclesfield* (1961), p. 45.

18 Sanderson, 'Literacy and Social Mobility'. See also the tables on pp. 82 and 83.

19 S. A. Harrop, 'Literacy and Educational Attitudes as Factors in the Industrialisation of North-East Cheshire, 1760–1830', in Stephens, *Studies in the History of Literacy*, pp. 37–53.

20 A. Redford, *Labour Migration in England 1800–1850* (3rd edn, Manchester, 1976), pp. 40–1; M. Anderson, *Family Structure in Nineteenth Century Lancashire* (Cambridge, 1971), pp. 38–40.

21 This may be equally true of rural areas. M. J. Campbell has found that in the districts outside Bristol, 'substantial differences of levels of literacy in geographically adjacent parishes may be explained in terms of the occupational distribution of the sample'. Campbell, 'Development of Literacy', p. 133. On the central importance of the occupational make-up of communities as a factor determining variations in literacy rates for the 1830–70 period, see Stephens, *Education, Literacy and Society*, p. 28 and *passim*.

22 Stephens, *Education, Literacy and Society*, pp. 10–11.

23 See appendix A for the characteristics of the Registration Districts in the sample.

24 Classes 1 and 2 grouped together. 'Literate' trades included in handicraft (H). Textile workers, potters, metal workers, miners incorporated into a single 'industrial' group (Ind). 'All' is literacy of complete sample, including illegible, missing and uncoded occupations.

25 In the 1864 returns the ratios were Samford, 65 (literate grooms): 83 (literate brides); Bury St Edmunds, 68:32; Ipswich, 56:44; Mildenhall, 52:48. *Twenty-seventh Annual Report of the Registrar General*, p. 13.

26 Lichfield 74:73; Tamworth, 77:81. *Twenty-seventh Annual Report of the Registrar General*, p. 17.

27 Stephens, *Education, Literacy and Society*, pp. 21, 79–80, 191–2, 247–50, 265.

28 The theory of the bureaucratisation of the labour process is surveyed in C. Littler, *The Development of the Labour Process in Capitalist Societies* (London, 1982), pp. 36–44.

29 W. Cooper, *Crown Glass Cutter and Glaziers Manual* (Edinburgh and London, 1835), p. v.

30 *The Taylor's Complete Guide ... The Whole Concerted and Devised By a Society of Adepts in the Profession* (London 1796), pp. 82–3, 130.

31 Jones, *Charity School Movement*, pp. 88–95.

32 *Report of the Committee of Council on Education* (1852), p. 16.

33 J. Devlin, *The Guide to Trade. The Shoemaker*, part 1 (London, 1839), p. 18.

34 *Report from the Committee on ... the Apprentice Laws of the Kingdom*, PP 1812–13, IV, p. 25.

35 F. Bower, *Rolling Stonemason. An Autobiography* (London, 1936), p. 43.

36 I. Prothero, *Artisans and Politics in Early Nineteenth-Century London* (London, 1981), pp. 25, 55; J. Rule, 'The Property of Skill in the Period of Manufacture', in Joyce, *Historical Meanings of Work*, p. 11.

37 J. A. St John, *The Education of the People* (London, 1858), p. 283.

38 R. Samuel, 'The Workshop of the World: Steam Power and Hand Technology in Mid-Victorian Britain', *History Workshop*, 3 (1977), 13.

39 R. Lloyd, *Lloyd's Treatise on Hats* (2nd edn, London, 1819), p. 22. Also Cooper, *Crown Glass Cutter*, p. vi.

40 M. Cook, *A Sure Guide Against Waste in Dress; or The Woollen Draper's, Man's Mercer's and Tailor's Assistant, Adapted also to the Use of Gentlemen, Tradesmen and Farmers shewing The Exact Quantity of Cloth, &c. necessary to make any Garment from a Child to a full sized Man* (London, 1787), pp. iii–iv.

41 G. Dodd, *The Textile Manufactures of Great Britain* (London, 1844), pp. 7–8.

42 J. Devlin, *The Guide to Trade. The Shoemaker*, pt 2 (London, 1841), p. 7.

43 T. Carter, *The Guide to Trade. The Plumber, Painter and Glazier* (London, 1838), p. 30.

44 T. Tredgold, *Elementary Principles of Carpentry* (London, 1820), p. vii. Amongst the works he claimed to supersede was P. Nicholson, *The Carpenter's New Guide: Being a Complete Book of Lines for Carpenting and Joinery* (3rd edn, London, 1801).

45 Devlin, *Guide to Trade*, pt 1, p. 8. Devlin's book was part of a series launched by Charles Knight in an attempt to invade the apprenticeship market. See also R. Whittock, *The Complete Book of Trades* (London, 1837). The genre is discussed in N. Cross, *The Common Writer. Life in Nineteenth-Century Grub Street* (Cambridge, 1985), p. 151.

46 See for instance W. Pain, *The Practical House Carpenter; or, Youth's Instructor* (London, 1794), which contained twenty-two pages of prices of various building processes.

47 M. Bowley, *The British Building Industry* (Cambridge, 1966), pp. 335–9; R. Postgate, *The Builders' History* (London, 1923), p. 9.

48 *The Builder's and Contractor's Price-Book* (London, 1856). See also the long-running series of Lockwood & Co.'s *Builder's and Contractor's Price-Books*. Later in the century, as the firms grew still larger, guides were published specifically for the use of builder's clerks. See T. Bales, *The Builder's Clerk. A Guide to the Management of a Builder's Business* (London, 1877).

49 See below, pp. 145–52.

50 J. Weale, *Catalogue of Books on Architecture and Engineering, Civil, Mechanical, Military, and Naval, New and Old* (London, 1854).

51 Vincent, *Bread, Knowledge and Freedom*, pp. 136–9, 141–9, 155–65; J. F. C. Harrison, *Learning and Living* (London, 1961), pp. 62–5; E. Royle, 'Mechanics' Institutes and the Working Classes, 1840–1860', *The Historical Journal* (1971), 305–21.

52 W. Pain, *The Builder's Companion and Workman's General Assistant* (London, 1758); W. Pain, *The Practical Builder* (London, 1774); W. Pain, *The Carpenter's and Joiner's Repository* (London, 1778). For a robust defence of the combined Architect and Handicraftsman, see R. Neve, *The City and County Purchaser, and Builder's Dictionary* (2nd edn, London, 1726), pp. iv–vi.

53 H. Perkin, *The Origins of Modern English Society 1780–1880* (London, 1969), p. 225.

54 Cf. R. Armstrong, *The Modern Practice of Boiler Engineering* (London, 1856), on the practice of boiler-making, also written by a qualified civil engineer. For similar attacks on non-experimental methods of practice, see G. R. Burnell, *Rudimentary Treatise on Limes, Cements* (London, 1850), pp. iii, v; E. Dobson, *A Rudimentary Treatise on Masonry and Stonecutting* (London, 1849), pp. 2–3.

55 C. Tomlinson, *Cyclopaedia of the Useful Arts* (London, 1854), I, p. vii.

56 T. Carter, *The Guide to Trade. The Printer* (London, 1838), p. 71.

57 Cf. the discussion of the 'mechanical arts' practised by contemporary French workers in W. H. Sewell, *Work and Revolution in France* (Cambridge, 1980), pp. 21–5.

58 C. Hutton, *A Treatise on Mensuration, both in theory and practice* (Newcastle upon Tyne, 1770; 4th edn, London, 1812). The practical section covered the calculations used by land surveyors, bricklayers, masons, carpenters and joiners, slaters and tilers, plasterers, printers, glaziers, pavers, plumbers and forestry workers.

59 G. Sturt, *The Wheelwright's Shop* (Cambridge, 1963), p. 19. A felloe was the rim of a wheel.
60 Sturt, *Wheelwright's Shop*, pp. 73–4.
61 For a pessimistic view of Britain's prospects in the field of research in the aftermath of the Exhibition, see J. Hole, *An Essay on the History and Management of Literary, Scientific, & Mechanics' Institutions* (London, 1853), p. 111. Also 'Emigration and Industrial Training', *Edinburgh Review*, XCII (1850), 499–500.
62 *Schools Inquiry Commission. Report Relative to Technical Education*, PP 1867, XXVI, p. 263. Also S. Cotgrove, *Technical Education and Social Change* (London, 1958), p. 19.
63 *Schools Inquiry Commission*, pp. 6–7. Ironically, in France those urging further effort were hampered by manufacturers content to imitate the apparently successful 'English' system of learning on the job. Anderson, *Education in France*, p. 203.
64 Although there was now a small but growing genre of 'do-it-yourself' manuals. See for instance S. T. Aveling's *Carpentry and Joinery. A Useful Guide for the Many* (London, 1871).
65 P. W. Musgrave, 'The Definition of Technical Education: 1860–1910', *The Vocational Aspect*, 34 (1964), 105–11.
66 *Second Report of the Royal Commissioners on Technical Instruction*, PP 1884, XXXI, p. 60.
67 The problems posed by the sheer variety of labour processes are discussed in Booth's chapter on 'Characteristics and Training of London Labour': C. Booth, *Life and Labour of the People in London*, 2nd series, vol. 5 (London, 1905), pp. 120–35.
68 *Report from the Select Committee on Scientific Instruction*, PP 1867–8, XV, p. 237. For a fuller discussion of this approach, see Cotgrove, *Technical Education*, pp. 34–6.
69 *Copies of Answers from Chambers of Commerce to Queries of the Vice-President of the Council as to Technical Education*, PP 1867–8, LIV, p. 38.
70 *S.C. on Scientific Instruction*, p. 87.
71 *Ibid.*, p. 305.
72 *Ibid.*, p. iii. For the problems of educating foremen, see P. W. Musgrave, *Technical Change, the Labour Force and Education* (Oxford, 1967), pp. 27, 38.
73 *Second Report of the Royal Commissioners on Technical Instruction*, PP 1884, XXIX, p. 83. For a more general discussion of the impact of the division of labour on employers' attitudes to work training, see S. and B. Webb, *Industrial Democracy* (London, 1902), p. 476.
74 *R.C. on Technical Instruction, Second Report*, p. 442.
75 An apprentice school was started at Salford Iron Works in 1873. M. J. Cruikshank, 'From Mechanics' Institution to Technical School 1850–92', in D. S. L. Cardwell (ed.), *Artisan to Graduate* (Manchester, 1974), p. 146.
76 *S.C. on Scientific Instruction*, p. 234. Mundella had organised a survey of 'large numbers of the people employed in various trades in our locality, based on a standard form'. Male literacy in Nottingham at this time stood at 83 per cent, three points above the national average. *Thirty-second Annual Report of the Registrar General*, PP 1871, XV, p. 19.
77 *S.C. on Scientific Instruction*, p. 239.
78 Musgrave, *Technical Change*, pp. 92–3; Cotgrove, *Technical Education*, p. 33.
79 The survey was carried out by J. Fitch, a Senior Schools Inspector. *R.C. on Technical Education*, XXIX, p. 411. In 1887, figures given in the House of Lords revealed that below Standard VI, 20,000 elementary schools gave English, 12,000 geography, 375 history and 43 elementary science. Musgrave, *Technical Change*, p. 93.
80 P. Magnus, *Educational Aims and Efforts 1880–1910* (London, 1910), p. 152.
81 *Ibid.*, p. 158.
82 This was much more effective than the Technical Instruction Act of 1889, which had permitted County and Borough Councils to levy a penny rate for technical and manual instruction; few did so. G. W. Roderick and M. D. Stephens (eds.), *Scientific and Technical Education in Nineteenth Century England* (Newton Abbot, 1972), pp. 12, 113.
83 Musgrave, *Technical Change*, p. 89; P. L. Robertson, 'Technical Education in the British

Shipbuilding and Marine Engineering Industries 1863–1914', *Economic History Review*, 2nd series, XVII (1974), 228.

84 M. Sanderson, *Educational Opportunity and Social Change in England* (London, 1987), p. 25.
85 N. B. Dearle, *Industrial Training* (London, 1914), p. 341.
86 K. McClelland, 'Time to Work, Time to Live: Some Aspects of Work and the Reformation of Class in Britain, 1850–1880', in Joyce, *Historical Meanings* of Work, p. 192.
87 More, *Skill*, p. 64.
88 In his careful study of shipbuilding, Robertson concludes that up to 1914, the levels of productivity at the yards were outstripping those of German and American competitors. The real problems began after the war. Robertson, 'Technical Education', pp. 234–5.
89 *R.C. on Technical Education*, XXIX, p. 506.
90 *Ibid.*, p. 236.
91 G. N. Barnes, 'Pushed into Fame', *Pearson's Weekly* (8 March 1906), 633, provides an account of this hybrid form of occupational learning. Also Tremewan, *Cornish Youth*, pp. 81–2. Apprentices were frequently expected to work from 6 a.m. to 5 p.m. before going to the classes. Robertson, 'Technical Education', p. 228.
92 K. Marx, *Capital* (Everyman edn, London, 1933), pp. 451–2.
93 Cf. H. Braverman, *Labor and Monopoly Capital* (New York, 1974), pp. 444–5; 'The worker can regain mastery over collective and socialised production only by assuming the scientific, design and operational prerogatives of modern engineering; short of this, there is no mastery over the labour process.'
94 For the widening gap between 'mental' and 'manual' labour in engineering and shipbuilding, embodied in the rise of the professional engineer and naval architect, see McClelland, 'Time to Work', p. 191.
95 Discussed in P. Dodd, 'Englishness and the National Culture', in R. Colls and P. Dodd (eds.), *Englishness. Politics and Culture 1880–1920* (London, 1986), pp. 8–9.
96 Dearle, *Industrial Training*, p. 338.
97 *S.C. on Scientific Instruction*, pp. 293–4.
98 *Ibid.*, p. 292.
99 *Ibid.*, p. 234.
100 On the role of parents in recruitment to the Preston textile factories, see Anderson, *Family Structure*, p. 122. Also R. Price, *Labour in British Society* (London, 1986), p. 72.
101 Price, *Labour*, pp. 81–2.
102 McClelland, 'Time to Work', p. 183; S. Pollard, 'Factory Discipline in the Industrial Revolution', *Economic History Review*, 16 (1963), esp. 254–8; N. McKendrick, 'Josiah Wedgwood and Factory Discipline', *Historical Journal*, IV, no. 1 (1961).
103 Daunton, *Royal Mail*, p. 193; Robinson, *Britain's Post Office*, p. 223.
104 *Report upon the Post Office* (1854), p. 10. Postmasters were also to satisfy themselves as to the 'character' of applicants.
105 *First Annual Report of the Postmaster General on the Post Office* (1855), pp. 29–30. Also Daunton, *Royal Mail*, pp. 238–46. Before taking the exam, candidates had to receive a 'nomination', and the role of patronage was not eliminated from the rural districts until 1892.
106 They had to make a daily record of their activities.
107 C. Steedman, *Policing the Victorian Community* (London, 1984), p. 103.
108 G. Howell, 'Trade Unions, Apprentices, and Technical Education', *The Contemporary Review*, XXX (June–November 1877), 852.
109 Dearle, *Industrial Training*, pp. 193, 258. Also, Booth, *Life and Labour*, 2nd series, vol. 5, p. 290. In 1911, R. A. Bray proposed an elaborate scheme of 'Juvenile Labour Exchanges', whose work would be based on a form filled up by the school showing the child's 'position in the school, and any particular ability he may have displayed'. R. A. Bray, *Boy Labour and Apprenticeship* (London, 1911), pp. 224–5.
110 F. McKenna, *The Railway Workers 1840–1970* (London, 1980), p. 50; K. Hudson, *Working to Rule* (Bath, 1970), pp. 60–1.

111 Barr, *Climbing the Ladder*, p. 7. He had attended a village school for five years. Later he left the railway, and eventually became an estate agent.

112 Levine, *Social Context of Literacy*, p. 149.

113 *Eleventh and Final Report of the Royal Commissioners Appointed to Inquire into the Organisation and Rules of Trades Unions and other Associations*, PP 1868–9, XXXI, appendix, p. 252. See also the procedures for the Carpenters (p. 224) and Compositors (p. 239). The masons had pre-printed 'initiation forms': OSM, *Fortnightly Returns*, 11–25 June 1857.

114 The paper ran a series of twenty-three biographies of union officials at fortnightly intervals between 8 March 1873 and 17 January 1874.

115 Cited in Webbs, *Industrial Democracy*, pp. 196–9. The first union to introduce competitive examinations were the cotton-weavers in 1861.

116 Prior to the Labour Exchanges, the halfpenny evening papers such as the London *Echo* began to provide a job-finding service through their situations vacant columns, but the bulk of the positions were in the retail or servant sectors.

117 Prothero, *Artisans and Politics*, p. 30.

118 H. Broadhurst, *Henry Broadhurst, M.P., the Story of His Life from a Stonemason's Bench to the Treasury Bench. Told by Himself* (London, 1901), p. 21. Also Bower, *Rolling Stonemason*, p. 44; T. Wright, *Habits and Customs of the Working Classes* (London, 1867), p. 50; E. J. Hobsbawm, 'The Tramping Artisan', in *Labouring Men* (London, 1968). For the use of 'certificates' at the beginning of the century, see an account of the woolcombers' tramping system in *The Book of Trades* (London, 1804), I, pp. 6–7.

119 W. Kiddier, *The Old Trade Unions from Unprinted Records of the Brushmakers* (London, 1930), p. 143. The brushmakers also published 'The Tramping Route'. This gave the list of towns to be visited, the number of miles the man had to walk, and the exact money due at each stage (p. 13).

120 *Report of the Select Committee on Artizans and Machinery*, PP 1824 V, p. 98. Evidence of John Lang.

121 Pattison, *On Literacy*, p. 174.

122 Graff, *Literacy and Social Development*, p. 234.

123 See above, table 4.4.

124 R. Rawson, 'Enquiry into Criminal Offenders', p. 333. In 1837, 1838 and 1839 54.2 per cent of prisoners could 'read and write imperfectly', 10.0 per cent could 'read and write well', and 0.4 per cent 'had acquired a superior degree of instruction'. Also, W. B. Neale, *Juvenile Delinquency in Manchester* (Manchester, 1840), p. 26; P. Priestley, *Victorian Prison Lives* (London, 1985), pp. 107–8; Campbell, 'Development of Literacy', pp. 41–5, 165–7.

125 On the endemic insecurity of artisans in even the most advanced trades, see McClelland, 'Time to Work', p. 185.

126 'Characteristics and Peculiarities of Trades. The Tailor and Shoemaker', *The London Saturday Journal* (April 1839), 270–1. See also Devlin, *The Guide to Trade. The Shoemaker, part 2*, p. 156.

127 Daunton, *Royal Mail*, p. 259; Robinson, *Britain's Post Office*, p. 231.

128 McKenna, *Railway Workers*, pp. 135, 156.

129 *Ibid.*, p. 232.

130 A. Williams, *Life in a Railway Factory* (London, 1915), p. 282. Also p. 289.

131 J. Melling, ' "Non-Commissioned Officers": British Employers and their Supervisory Workers, 1880–1920', *Social History*, 5, no. 2 (May 1980), 189–91.

132 *S.C. on Scientific Instruction*, p. 233.

133 *Ibid.*, p. 292.

134 T. Wright, 'Working Class Education and mis-Education', in *Our New Masters* (London, 1873), p. 117.

135 W. A. Abram, 'Social Conditions and Political Prospects of the Lancashire Workman', *Fortnightly Review* (1868), 432. A smiliar practice was followed by French manufacturers. Anderson, *Education in France*, p. 203.

136 *R.C. on Technical Instruction*, XXIX, p. 217.

137 D. Dunkerley, *The Foreman* (London, 1975), pp. 142, 152–3.
138 Webbs, *Industrial Democracy*, p. 493.
139 More, *Skill*, p. 216.
140 See the forthcoming Ph.D. thesis of Andrew Miles, under the aegis of the Keele Life Histories Centre. For a preliminary attempt to examine the process as revealed in the occupations of fathers and sons in the Census, see B. Preston, *Occupations of Father and Son in Mid-Victorian England* (Reading, 1977).
141 Cf. Sewell, *Structure and Mobility*, p. 247 on Marseilles, where in the absence of large numbers of industrial and agricultural workers, the increase of movement into the middle class was more rapid, the rates rising from 8 per cent in 1821–2 to 12 per cent in 1846–51 to 19 per cent in 1869.
142 Cf. the similar findings in D. Mitch, 'The Spread of Literacy in Nineteenth-Century England', Ph.D. thesis, University of Chicago (1982), 63.
143 In Marseilles, Sewell found that the rate of mobility for literate sons began to rise at the same time as in this sample, although more sharply. As his study proceeds no further than 1869, no comparison is possible with the later fluctuations found here. Sewell, *Structure and Mobility*, pp. 255–7.
144 G. Crossick, 'The Emergence of the Lower Middle Class in Britain: A Discussion', in G. Crossick (ed.), *The Lower Middle Class in Britain*, (London, 1977), p. 19. Also Mitch, 'Spread of Literacy', p. 123, table 27.
145 J. Keating, *My Struggle for Life* (London, 1916), esp. pp. 117–66.
146 For accounts of working as a paper boy, see Kenney, *Westering*, pp. 17–19; S. Shaw, *Guttersnipe* (London, 1946), pp. 26, 28; Citrine, *Men and Work*, p. 26. Also J. H. Haslam, *The Press and the People* (Manchester, 1906), p. 19.
147 The comparatively small number of teachers in the table is partly a consequence of the absence from the calculations of women. The numbers of female teachers increased much faster than the occupied population, but male teachers only kept pace with it.
148 Bowyer, *Brought Out in Evidence*, p. 95. By the end of the period, banks, insurance companies and central and local government were using exams to recruit clerks. Bray, *Boy Labour*, p. 141. On the limited opportunities see also the findings of R. D. Anderson's careful study of education and social mobility in nineteenth-century Scotland, where he finds only a tiny proportion of the urban working class reached university and the professions beyond it. R. D. Anderson, *Education and Opportunity in Victorian Scotland* (Oxford, 1983), pp. 117–61.
149 Learner, *Passing of Traditional Society*, p. 48; Inkeles and Smith, *Becoming Modern*, p. 23.
150 Clerks under 30 totalled 85.7 per cent, as against 58.1 per cent of farmers, 60 per cent of innkeepers and hotel managers, and 61.3 per cent of industrial managers. Cf. Sewell, *Structure and Mobility*, p. 236: in Marseilles in 1851, the mean age of business and professional grooms was 43.1, and for those in sales and clerical occupations, 37.8.
151 Wright, 'Working Class Education', p. 116.
152 J. Zeitlin, 'From Labour History to the History of Industrial Relations', *Economic History Review*, 2nd series, XL, 2 (1987), 177–8.
153 A. Flanders, *Industrial Relations* (London, 1965), pp. 10 and 7–33 *passim*.
154 *Mechanics' Magazine*, 20 December 1823, 270–2. Cited in Prothero, *Artisans and Politics*, p. 34. Also, Rule, 'The Property of Skill', p. 100.
155 Wright, *Habits and Customs*, p. 84.
156 *S.C. on Artizans and Machinery*, p. 139.
157 Lloyd, *Hats*.
158 *Ibid.*, p. xxx.
159 National Association for the Promotion of Social Science, *Trades' Societies and Strikes* (London, 1860), p. 116.
160 For a detailed account of the maintenance of customs by the coopers, see B. Gilding, *The Journeyman Coopers of East London* (Oxford, 1971), pp. 49–53.
161 *R.C. on Organisation of Trade Unions*, p. 53.
162 On the relationship between modes of communication and the attempts to maintain control in the workplace, see C. Behagg, 'Secrecy, Ritual and Folk Violence: The

Opacity of the Workplace in the First Half of the Nineteenth Century', in R. E. Storch (ed.), *Popular Culture and Custom in Nineteenth Century England* (London, 1982), pp. 154–79.

163 See the account of the hatter John Lang of the interception of letters to his society's 'town-house' and the subsequent court case. *S.C. Artizans and Machinery*, p. 92.

164 Not until the Friendly Societies Act of 1846 could any national working-class organisation gain immunity from prosecution. E. Yeo, 'Some Practices and Problems of Chartist Democracy', in J. Epstein and D. Thompson (eds.), *The Chartist Experience* (London, 1982), pp. 360–2. See also Vincent, 'Communication, Community and the State', pp. 166–86.

165 Postgate, *Builders' History*, p. 21.

166 Kiddier, *Old Trade Unions*, p. 20. For the development of box clubs, see C. R. Dobson, *Masters and Journeymen* (London, 1980), pp. 38–45; Webbs, *Industrial Democracy*, pp. 3–8.

167 *S.C. on Artizans and Machinery*, p. 574. See also M. Plant, *The English Book Trade* (2nd edn, London, 1965), p. 386 for the printers making loans to other unions, and Webbs, *Industrial Democracy*, pp. 90–1 for the breadth of the practice of cash transfers in the late eighteenth and early nineteenth centuries.

168 Bower, *Rolling Stonemason*, p. 46. Also Wright, *Habits and Customs*, pp. 100–2.

169 *S.C. on Artizans and Machinery*, p. 135.

170 See above, pp. 42–3.

171 *S.C. on Artizans and Machinery*, p. 135.

172 *S.C. on Postage*, p. 209.

173 *Ibid.*, p. 221.

174 *R.C. on the Organisation of Trade Unions*, p. 52.

175 OSM, *Fortnightly Returns*, 26 May–9 June 1836, p. 81. For the Brushmakers' equivalent *Circular*, see Kiddier, *Old Trade Unions*, pp. 54–65.

176 Twenty-three union newspapers appeared in the 1830s, and a further thirty-two in the 1840s. The masons waited until 1911 before starting the short-lived *Journal of the Operative Stonemason's Society*. R. Harrison, G. B. Woolven and R. Duncan, *The Warwick Guide to British Labour Periodicals* (Hassocks, 1977).

177 OSM, *Fortnightly Returns*, 9 June–23 June 1839, p. 81.

178 J. Buckley, *A Village Politician: The Life Story of John Buckley* (London, 1897), p. 84; W. Farish, *The Autobiography of William Farish. The Struggles of a Hand Loom Weaver. With Some of His Writings* (1889), p. 299; Herbert, *Autobiography of Henry Herbert*, pp. 21, 52; J. Hopkinson, *Victorian Cabinet Maker. The Memoirs of James Hopkinson 1819–1894*, ed. J. B. Goodman (London, 1968), pp. 21–2, 32, 57–8; Lovett, *Life and Struggles*, p. 31; R. Lowery, *Robert Lowery, Radical and Chartist*, ed. B. Harrison and P. Hollis (London, 1979), pp. 82–3; H. E. Price, 'Diary', MS (1904), 65; C. Thomson, *The Autobiography of an Artisan* (London, 1847), pp. 72–3.

179 C. M. Smith, *The Working Man's Way in the World* (London, 1857), p. 188.

180 OSM, *Revised Black List from September, 1834, to April, 1853* (1853). Some of the names were incomplete, others gave an alias or nickname. Full details of the offence and fine were printed. Fourteen men were charged with indecency in different places, each being fined 5s. By 1868 the rules had been amended to permit defaulting names to be erased after twelve years.

181 *R.C. on the Organisation of Trade Unions*, p. 104. A new union was formed in 1848.

182 *Schools Inquiry Commission. Report Relative to Technical Education*, PP 1867, XXVI, p. 28.

183 *Ibid.*, p. 30. In the same way the masons extended their rule book to the substantive issue of 'chasing' in 1865, but deleted it three years later. R. Price, *Masters, Unions and Men* (Cambridge, 1980), p. 62.

184 *R.C. on the Organisation of Trade Unions*, p. 111.

185 *Ibid.*, p. 53.

186 *Ibid.*, p. 53. See also Price, *Masters, Unions and Men*, pp. 59–61; K. Burgess, *The Origins of British Industrial Relations* (London, 1975), p. 115.

187 Zeitlin, 'Labour History', p. 172.

188 Webbs, *Industrial Democracy*, p. 58.
189 *R.C. on the Organisation of Trade Unions*, appendix 227. See also Rule 10 of the National Union of Agricultural Workers, cited in full in Arch, *Joseph Arch*, pp. 115–16.
190 NAPSS, *Trades' Societies*, p. 117. The only conditions were that the majority of the lodge members supported the strike, and that an attempt at a negotiated settlement should be made first.
191 R. Kettle, *Strikes and Arbitration* (London, 1866), pp. 14–15.
192 OSM, *Fortnightly Returns*, 11 June–25 June 1857.
193 W. Thorne, *My Life's Battles* (London, 1925), p. 43.
194 *Ibid.*, p. 70. On Thorne's work for the Gasworkers' Union see G. and L. Radice, *Will Thorne. Constructive Militant* (London, 1974), pp. 28–43.
195 Thorne, *Life's Battles*, pp. 98–9. See also the experiences of the Weavers' leader, Ben Turner: *About Myself* (London, 1930), pp. 99–102.
196 Thorne, *Life's Battles*, pp. 78–9.
197 For an account of Mundella's pioneering work in Nottingham, see W. H. G. Armytage, *A. J. Mundella 1825–1897* (London, 1951), pp. 319–20. For Kettle's objectives, see *Strikes and Arbitration*.
198 V. L. Allen, 'The Origins of Industrial Conciliation and Arbitration', *International Review of Social History*, IX, pt 2 (1964), 240; Plant, *Book Trade*, p. 392; J. R. Hicks, 'The Early History of Industrial Conciliation in England', *Economica*, X (1930), 27–32; J. H. Porter, 'Wage Bargaining under Conciliation Agreements, 1860–1914', *Economic History Review* 2nd series, XXIII (1970), 461–2; V. Gore, 'Rank-and-File Dissent', in Wrigley, *British Industrial Relations*, p. 51.
199 Webbs, *Industrial Democracy*, p. 224; Zeitlin, 'Labour History', p. 171.
200 *Potteries Examiner*, 9 August 1879.
201 E. J. Hobsbawm, 'Custom, Wages and Work-Load', in *Labouring Men* (London, 1968), pp. 344–50; P. Joyce, 'Introduction', in Joyce, *Historical Meanings of Work*, pp. 10–11.
202 Kettle, *Strikes and Arbitration*, p. 9.
203 Webbs, *Industrial Democracy*, p. 229.
204 Staffordshire Potteries Board of Arbitration, *Minutes of Evidence Taken and Award of Arbitration Held at the Queen's Hotel, Hanley. 9th and 10th January, 1877, before J. E. Davis Esq. (Umpire), On Notice Given by Employers of a Ten Per Cent Reduction in Workmen's Prices* (1877), p. 36.
205 *Potteries Examiner*, 22 November 1879, 8, 15.
206 *Ibid.*, 58.
207 Staffordshire Potteries Board of Arbitration, *Award of Thomas Brassey, M.P.* (1880), pp. 2–4; F. Burchill and R. Ross, *A History of the Potters' Union* (Hanley, 1977), pp. 126–32; Hicks, 'History of Industrial Conciliation', p. 35.
208 Staffordshire Potteries Board of Arbitration, *Appeal of Workmen for an increase of Ten per cent and Appeal of Manufacturers for a reduction of Ten per cent in wages. Evidence and Award. Umpire, H. T. Hinckes, Esq., M.P.* (1891).
209 I. G. Sharp, *Industrial Conciliation and Arbitration in Great Britain* (London, 1950), pp. 11–20; Burgess, *British Industrial Relations*, pp. 173–213; Porter, 'Wage Bargaining', pp. 464–72. Also W. R. Garside and H. F. Gospel, 'Employers and Managers: Their Organisational Structure and Changing Industrial Strategies', in Wrigley, *Industrial Relations*, p. 105. On the difficulty experienced in the iron trades see J. H. Porter, 'The Iron Trade', in Wrigley, *Industrial Relations*, pp. 253–64.
210 *First Report of the Royal Commission on Labour*, PP 1892, XXXIV, p. 103.
211 Broadhurst, *Henry Broadhurst*, p. 43; Price, *Masters, Unions and Men*, p. 208. On the general decline of the rotation of union seats of government, see Webbs, *Industrial Democracy*, pp. 17–18.
212 Webbs, *Industrial Democracy*, pp. 189–90.
213 *Second Report of the Royal Commission on Labour*, PP 1892, XXXV, pp. 321–2.
214 Of eighty-one Labour or Lib-Lab MPs between 1874 and 1910, sixty had identifiable trade union links. Of these a third had been General Secretaries, or the equivalent, of their unions.
215 Staffordshire Potteries Board of Arbitration, *Brassey Award*, p. 4.

216 See for instance the miner Thomas Burt, who had to take a drop in pay when he left the coal face to become Secretary and Agent. Burt, *Thomas Burt*, p. 166.

217 Edwards, *Crow-Scaring*, pp. 39ff.

218 *Pace* the argument of Price, *Masters, Unions and Men*, esp. pp. 198–228.

219 The 1896 Conciliation (Trade Disputes) Act empowered the Board of Trade to select an arbitrator only if both parties requested its assistance. The most notable revelation of the Government's weakness was its failure to persuade the quarry owner Lord Penrhyn to accept arbitration in a series of disputes between 1896 and 1903. C. Wrigley, 'The Government and Industrial Relations', in Wrigley, *Industrial Relations*. Also E. H. Hunt, *British Labour History 1815–1914* (London, 1981), p. 325, who concludes that 'the absence of any means of enforcement was still the outstanding characteristic of official industrial relations policy when the pre-war strikes began'.

220 Porter, 'Wage Bargaining', p. 474; Gore, 'Rank-and-file Dissent', p. 66.

221 Children's Employment Commission, *Appendix to First Report*, PP 1842, XVI, p. 71. Delay had been at work since he was seven, but he had attended a Sunday school.

222 Roberts, *The Classic Slum*, p. 167.

223 Hudson, *Working to Rule*, pp. 59–61. For a similar attempt to regulate the use of the lavatory by the engineers Thorneycrofts see Price, *Labour in British Society*, pp. 100–1. Alfred Williams argued that recruitment practices at Swindon railway works were actually becoming less formal at this time. Williams, *Railway Factory*, pp. 215–17.

224 Littler, *Labour Process*, pp. 64–78.

225 J. R. Gillis, *Youth in History* (New York, 1974), p. 121.

226 Melling, ' "Non-Commissioned Officers" ', 194.

5 THE NATURAL WORLD

1 J. Lawson, *Letters to the Young on Progress in Pudsey during the Last Sixty Years* (Stanningley, 1887), p. 47. Also, Dayus, *Her People*, p. 1.

2 Unesco, *Literacy 1972–1976*, p. 25. Also Oxenham, *Literacy*, p. 45; Inkeles and Smith, *Becoming Modern*, p. 23.

3 W. Henderson, *Notes on the Folk Lore of the Northern Counties of England and the Border* (London, 1866), p. xvii.

4 *Ibid.*, p. xx.

5 J. Barker, *The History and Confessions of a Man* (London, 1846), I, p. 85.

6 R. A. Scott-James, *The Influence of the Press* (London, 1913), p. 133.

7 W. H. Mallock, *Studies of Contemporary Superstition* (London, 1895).

8 W. C. Hazlitt, *Faiths and Folklore* (London, 1905), p. ix.

9 Burne, *Shropshire Folk-Lore*, I, p. xi.

10 On 'Superstition' as beliefs unsanctified by those in official authority, see Larner, *Witchcraft and Religion*, p. 142.

11 Barker, *History and Confessions*, I, p. 50. Also Snell, *Men, Movements*, p. 4.

12 J. Brand, *Observations on Popular Antiquities* (Newcastle upon Tyne, 1777), p. xvii. Also, J. Aspin, *A Picture of the Manners, Customs, Sports and Pastimes of the Inhabitants of England* (London, 1825), pp. 12–13.

13 W. Hone, *The Table Book* (London, 1838), p. 421.

14 T. Oliver, *Autobiography of a Cornish Miner* (Camborne, 1914), p. 85. On Cornish ghosts see also Lowery, *Robert Lowery*, p. 130; Lovett, *Life and Struggles*, pp. 11, 13.

15 W. Thoms, 'Folk-Lore', *The Athenaeum*, 982 (22 August 1846), 863.

16 'The Autobiography of a Suffolk Farm Labourer', *Suffolk Times and Mercury* (1894–5), pt II, ch. 3.

17 Sykes, *Slawit in the 'Sixties*, p. 10.

18 E. E. Evans-Pritchard, 'The Morphology and Function of Magic', in J. Middleton (ed.), *Magic, Witchcraft and Curing* (New York, 1967), p. 3.

19 Snell, *Men, Movements*, p. 4. Also J. Saunders, *The Reflections and Rhymes of an Old Miller* (London, 1938), p. 32; Turner, *About Myself*, p. 42. Cf. W. Howitt, *The Rural Life of England* (London, 1838), I, p. 189.

20 Snell, *Men, Movements*, p. 4.
21 See above, ch. 3, p. 57.
22 Gutteridge, *Lights and Shadows*, p. 87.
23 *Ibid.*, p. 116. The book was William Withering, *A Botanical Arrangement of all the vegetables naturally growing in Great Britain . . . With an easy introduction to the study of botany*. It was first published in 1776; revised editions regularly appeared until 1852.
24 For a full account of the pleasures of the collective study of nature by self-educated artisans, see Heaton, *The Old Soldier*, pp. xviii–xix.
25 Gutteridge, *Lights and Shadows*, p. 139. Cf. the pleasure obtained by the Cornish miner Thomas Oliver from a microscope he saved up to buy. Oliver, *Autobiography*, pp. 60–1.
26 Gutteridge, *Lights and Shadows*, p. 131. See also the account given by Henry Snell of collecting herbs for sale as medicine: *Men, Movements*, p. 11.
27 R. Gamble, *Chelsea Childhood* (London, 1979), p. 94.
28 M. C. Balfour, *Examples of Printed Folk-Lore Concerning Northumberland* (London, 1904), p. 49; J. Burn, *The Autobiography of a Beggar Boy*, ed. D. Vincent (London, 1978), p. 67; C. S. Burne, *Shropshire Folk-Lore* (London, 1883), I, pp. 189–206; Henderson, *Folk Lore of the Northern Counties*, p. 264; W. Hone, *The Year Book* (London, 1839), p. 253; T. T. Wilkinson, 'On the Popular Customs and Superstitions of Lancashire', *Trans. Hist. Soc., Lancs. and Ches.*, XI (1858–9), p. 161. Also F. B. Smith, *The People's Health* (London, 1979), pp. 109–11; R. M. Dorson, *The British Folklorists* (London, 1968), pp. 93–4; S. X. Radbill, 'Whooping Cough in Fact and Fancy', *Bulletin of the History of Medicine*, XIII (1943), 39–52; J. Camp, *Magic, Myth and Medicine* (London, 1973), pp. 121–2.
29 'Popular Superstitions', *Working Man's Friend*, VI (1851), 176.
30 Hole, *Mechanics' Institutions*, p. 47. Also St John, *Education of the People*, p. 294.
31 L. Barrow, *Independent Spirits* (London, 1986), pp. 161–83; J. V. Pickstone, 'Medical Botany. (Self-Help Medicine in Victorian England)', *Memoirs of the Manchester Literary and Philosophical Society*, 119 (1976–7), 83–95.
32 W. Fox, *The Working Man's Model Family Botanic Guide* (10th edn, Sheffield, 1884), preface.
33 A. I. Coffin, *A Botanic Guide to Health* (Leeds, 1845), pp. xiii, ii.
34 D. E. Allen, *The Naturalist in Britain* (London, 1976), pp. 164–7.
35 Gutteridge, *Lights and Shadows*, p. 145.
36 N. Parry and J. Parry, *The Rise of the Medical Profession* (London, 1976); P. Vaughan, *Doctors' Commons* (London, 1959).
37 J. Lane, 'The Provincial Practitioner and his Services to the Poor, 1750–1800', *The Society for the Social History of Medicine Bulletin*, 28 (June 1981), 13.
38 M. W. Flinn, 'Medical Services under the New Poor Law', in D. Fraser (ed.), *The New Poor Law in the Nineteenth Century* (London, 1976), pp. 45–58; F. B. Smith, *The People's Health* (London, 1979), pp. 346–62; F. F. Cartwright, *A Social History of Medicine* (London, 1977), pp. 158–9; R. G. Hodgkinson, *The Origins of the National Health Service* (London, 1967), pp. 680–94.
39 The fullest account of the shortcomings of the reform is to be found in I. Loudon, *Medical Care and the General Practitioner, 1750–1850* (Oxford, 1986), pp. 228–48.
40 For an account of the impact of a Poor Law doctor on his community see D. Vincent, *Victorian Eccleshall* (Keele, 1982), pp. 94–5.
41 P. H. J. H. Gosden, *Self Help* (London, 1973), pp. 112–14; P. Johnson, *Saving and Spending* (Oxford, 1985), pp. 48–74.
42 Loudon, *Medical Care*, p. 255.
43 Snell, *Men, Movements*, p. 18. Also Okey, *A Basketful of Memories*, p. 16.
44 Johnson, *Saving and Spending*, p. 71.
45 J. Bowd, 'The Life of a Farm Worker', *The Countryman*, 51, pt 2 (1955), 293–4. The book was a chapbook version of *Bluebeard*. This took place in 1830 when Bowd was seven years old. In the same year the Buckinghamshire labourer Joseph Mayett managed to see three doctors, one in Oxford, when he fell ill: Mayett, MS Autobiography, 103–6. For the similar use of a doctor by an equally poor East Anglian family

see E. Green, MS Autobiography, *c.* 1880, 88, 95–6, 101; by a poor Sussex family, G. Meek, *George Meek. Bath Chair-Man. By Himself* (London, 1910), p. 7.

46 For a general account of doctors working in Lancashire, see T. Whittaker, *Life's Battles in Temperance Armour* (London, 1884), p. 11; Sykes, *Slawit in the 'Sixties*, pp. 129–30. For the doctor as a familiar member of a late-nineteenth-century Cornish mining community, see Tremewan, *Cornish Youth*, pp. 107–8.

47 F. B. Smith, 'Health', in J. Benson (ed.), *The Working Class in England 1875–1914* (London, 1985), pp. 36–7; Vaughan, *Doctors' Commons*, pp. 202–3; A. J. Youngson, *The Scientific Revolution in Victorian Medicine* (London, 1979), pp. 9–41.

48 Cartwright, *Social History of Medicine*, p. 91.

49 Ellis, *Educating Our Masters*, p. 37.

50 Porter, 'Before the Fringe', pp. 23–6; Turner, *Advertising*, pp. 40–3; P. S. Brown, 'Medicines Advertised in Eighteenth Century Bath Newspapers', *Medical History*, 20 (1976), 159–60.

51 G. A. Cranfield, *The Development of the Provincial Newspaper 1700–1760* (Oxford, 1962), pp. 221–3; J. J. Looney, 'Advertising and Society in England 1720–1820; A Statistical Analysis of Yorkshire Newspaper Advertisements', Ph.D. thesis, Princeton University (1983), 78, 249.

52 Loudon, *Medical Care*, pp. 11–28; R. Porter, 'Laymen, Doctors and Medical Knowledge in the Eighteenth Century: The Evidence of the *Gentleman's Magazine*', in R. Porter (ed.), *Patients and Practitioners. Lay Perceptions of Medicine in Pre-Industrial Society* (Cambridge, 1986), pp. 313–14; R. Porter, 'Before the Fringe', in R. Cooter (ed.), *Alternative Essays in the Social History of Irregular Medicine* (London, 1987), pp. 6–18.

53 R. Porter, 'The Language of Quackery in England 1660–1800', in Burke and Porter, *Social History of Language*, pp. 74–94.

54 Parry and Parry, *Medical Profession*, pp. 124–6; Loudon, *Medical Care*, pp. 297–301; Waddington, *Medical Profession*, pp. 96–132.

55 The number of doctors, it should be noted, did not keep up with the growth in the population in the second half of the nineteenth century. There were 107 medical practitioners per 100,000 people in 1841, 76 in 1861 and 65 in 1911. Loudon, *Medical Care*, appendix vii; I. Waddington, *The Medical Profession in the Industrial Revolution* (Dublin, 1984), pp. 148–9.

56 A. J. Lee, *The Origins of the Popular Press in England 1855–1914* (London, 1976), p. 85; L. Brown, *Victorian News and Newspapers* (Oxford, 1985), pp. 15–24.

57 'Advertisements', *Quarterly Review*, XCVII (1855), 212; E. S. Turner, *The Shocking History of Advertising* (London, 1952), pp. 63–6; Smith, *People's Health*, p. 344.

58 *S.C. on Patent Medicines*, pp. x, 376.

59 *Reynolds' News*, 22 June 1873, 7.

60 *Report as to the Practice of Medicine and Surgery by Unqualified Persons in the United Kingdom*, PP 1910, XLIII, p. 4. The Report was based on over 1,600 replies by Medical Officers of Health.

61 'Unqualified Practice Through the Post', *British Medical Journal* (27 May 1911), 1281–4; *S.C. on Patent Medicines*, pp. xx, 311–12, 316, 333.

62 Smith, *People's Health*, p. 341.

63 The British Medical Association, *Secret Remedies* (London, 1909), p. vii.

64 *Report on Unqualified Persons*, p. 21; J. H. Taylor, 'The Practice of Medicine and Surgery by Unqualified Persons', *British Medical Journal* (27 May 1911), 1243–5.

65 A second volume followed in 1913.

66 *S.C. on Patent Medicines*, pp. 114, 674.

67 V. Berridge, 'Popular Sunday Papers and Mid-Victorian Society', in Boyce *et al.*, *Newspaper History*, p. 251; J. Curran, 'The Press as an Agency of Social Control: An Historical Perspective', in Boyce *et al.*, *Newspaper History*, p. 63.

68 Curran, 'The Press', p. 63. On the almanacs, see below, p. 192–3.

69 *Report from the Select Committee on Patent Medicines*, PP 1914, X: Q2618.

70 Although the 1910 inquiry still found 'domestic remedies' were being handed down through families in rural areas. *Report on Unqualified Persons*, p. 21.

71 C. E. S. Flemming, 'Quackery in Rural Districts', *British Medical Journal* (27 May 1911), 1246.

72 Respectively the Rev. Dr Read, LLD, of Banstead Downs, and Dr J. Colbourne, MD, of 60 Maddox Street, London. The Smoke Ball would 'positively cure' fifteen other complaints as well.

73 L. S. Haggard (ed.), *I Walked by Night, Being the Life and History of the King of the Norfolk Poachers. Written by Himself* (London, 1948), pp. 16–17. For a survey of the variety of folk medicine, see R. Porter, 'Medicine and the Decline of Magic', unpublished paper (1986), 7–14.

74 The potential value of this form of medicine for providing relief from anxiety and stress, which might in turn lead to physical benefits, is emphasised in J. Devlin, *The Superstitious Mind. French Peasants and the Supernatural in the Nineteenth Century* (New Haven, 1987), p. 63.

75 Haggard, *I Walked by Night*, p. 15. Also E. Trimmer, 'Medical Folklore and Quackery', *Folklore*, 76 (Autumn 1965), 161–75.

76 *Report on Unqualified Persons*, p. 22.

77 *Ibid.*, p. 6.

78 Smith, 'Health', pp. 38–50; Cartwright, *Social History of Medicine*, p. 96.

79 Whittaker, *Life's Battles*, p. 27. Cf. Joseph Stamper, son of a Lancashire iron-moulder, whose youth some fifty years later was stretched backwards by his mother who 'In her childhood had spent different periods with relatives of her parents in isolated parts of Wales. She had a great store of supernatural stories she had gathered there.' J. Stamper, *So Long Ago . . .* (London, 1960), p. 47.

80 On the quality of the personal detail embodied in such beliefs, see Atkinson, *Forty Years*, p. 81.

81 C. Hole, *Witchcraft in England* (London, 1945), p. 147.

82 F. Grose, *A Provincial Glossary with a Collection of Local Proverbs and Popular Superstitions* (London, 1787), p. 17.

83 G. Sanger, *Seventy Years a Showman* (London, 1938), pp. 138–9. Also, G. Mitchell, 'Autobiography and Reminiscences', in S. Price (ed.), *The Skeleton at the Plough* (London, 1874), p. 110; C. Redding, *Yesterday and Today*, I, p. 100; Sykes, *Slawit in the 'Sixties*, p. 12.

84 J. C. Atkinson, *Forty Years in a Moorland Parish* (London, 1891), pp. 74–102; Vaux, *Church Folklore*, p. 310; E. Porter, *Cambridgeshire Customs and Folklore* (London, 1969), pp. 147–82; R. Hunt, *Popular Romances of the West of England* (London, 1916), pp. 314–15; 'Popular Superstitions', *Working Man's Friend*, VI (1851), 176; Wilkinson, 'On the Popular Customs and Superstitions of Lancashire', 159; Hole, *Witchcraft*, pp. 148–57; J. Harland and T. T. Wilkinson, *Lancashire Folk-Lore* (London, 1882), p. 154; C. S. Burne, *Shropshire Folk-Lore* (London, 1883), I, pp. 145–71; W. Hone, *The Year Book* (London, 1839), pp. 421–5, 1276; Hone, *The Table Book* II, 942, 1045–8. For more general discussions of the persistence of witchcraft in the nineteenth century, see J. N. Demos, *Entertaining Satan* (Oxford, 1982), pp. 369–400; J. Obelkevich, *Religion and Rural Society: South Lindsey 1825–1875* (Oxford, 1976), p. 283; Devlin, *Superstitious Mind*, pp. 100–19.

85 The 1910 inquiry, which found wise women active though declining in rural areas, concluded that 'In the more outlying rural districts, belief in witchcraft is still held by a few people.' *Report on Unqualified Persons*, p. 22.

86 'Popular Superstitions', pp. 176–7; see Devlin, *Superstitious Mind*, p. 45, on contemporary French healers making a substantial living out of their neighbours.

87 Henderson, *Notes*, p. 141; Hunt, *Popular Romances*, p. 34; Burne, *Shropshire Folklore*, I, pp. 146, 169, 172, 181; Hone, *The Year Book*, p. 252; Howitt, *Rural Life*, II, p. 221; Atkinson, *Forty Years*, pp. 103–25; Liardet, 'State of the Peasantry', p. 137; Lawson, *Progress in Pudsey*, p. 48; Sykes, *Slawit in the 'Sixties*, p. 10; Obelkevich, *Religion and Rural Life*, pp. 287–91.

88 Harland and Wilkinson, *Lancashire Folk-Lore*, p. 121. Also, Wilkinson, 'Popular Customs', pp. 157–8; Sykes, *Slawit in 'Sixties*, p. 10; T. Preston, *The Life and Opinions of Thomas Preston* (London, 1817), p. 35.

89 A. Haig, *The Victorian Clergy* (London, 1984), p. 3.
90 Numbers of ministers from O. Chadwick, *The Victorian Church* (London, 1970), II, p. 244. Ratio calculated on the assumption of a mean household size of 4.75. It excludes monks and nuns, but includes paid local preachers. England and Wales here includes the Channel Islands and the Isle of Man.
91 S. G. Green, *The Story of the Religious Tract Society* (London, 1899), p. 2.
92 For a wider discussion of these surveys and their findings, see D. Vincent, 'Reading', pp. 210–11.
93 C. B. Fripp, 'report of an Inquiry into the Condition of the Working Classes of the City of Bristol', *Journal of the Statistical Society*, II (1839), 368–75; Manchester Statistical Society, 'Report on the State of Education among the Working Classes in the Parish of West Bromwich', *Journal of the Statistical Society*, II (1839), 371; Manchester Statistical Society, 'Report on the Condition of the Working Class in the Town of Kingston-upon-Hull', *Journal of the Statistical Society*, V (1842), 212–21; C. R. Weld, 'On the Condition of the Working Classes in the Inner Ward of St. George's Parish, Hanover Square', *Journal of the Statistical Society*, VI (1843), 20; J. E. Martin, 'Statistics of an Agricultural Parish in Bedfordshire', *Journal of the Statistical Society*, VI, (1843), 255–6. The domination by the Bible of the serious literature of the poor at this time is discussed in L. James, *Print and the People 1819–1851* (Harmondsworth, 1978), p. 29.
94 See above, ch. 3, p. 85.
95 Liardet, 'State of the Peasantry', p. 124.
96 *Ibid.*, pp. 133, 137.
97 W. K. Lowther Clark, *A History of the S.P.C.K.* (London, 1959), pp. 172–86.
98 See below, ch. 6, pp. 199–200.
99 Green, *Religious Tract Society*, p. 8.
100 W. Jones, *The Jubilee Memorial of the Religious Tract Society* (London, 1850), pp. 246–7; W. O. B. Allen and E. McClure, *Two Hundred Years: The History of the Society for Promoting Christian Knowledge, 1698–1898* (London, 1898), p. 98; Ludlow and Jones, *Progress of the Working Class*, p. 184.
101 J. Parker, 'On the Literature of the Working Classes', in Viscount Ingestre (ed.), *Meliora, or Better Things to Come* (London, 1853), p. 183. The quote is from Proverbs I.20.
102 'Popular Superstitions', p. 177.
103 Burne, *Shropshire Folklore*, I, p. 146. The letter was duly written and sent. Oakengates and Wellington are part of the modern town of Telford.
104 Devlin, *Superstitious Mind*, pp. 93–5, 165–81.
105 *Napoleon's Book of Fate* (London and Otley, William Walker, n.d.) claimed that the text was a translation of a 500-year-old German book found in 'Bunoparte's Cabinet of Curiosities at Leipsic, during the confusion which reigned there after the defeat of the French army'.
106 *Napoleon Bonaparte's Book of Fate* (Glasgow, n.d.), 24. The letter was to be folded nine times, worn next to the heart until bed-time, then placed under the head in a left-hand glove, and the ensuing dream would indicate the future of the relationship. For other contemporary 'penny dreamers' see *The Dreamer's Oracle* (1850); *The Dreamer's True Friend* (1874), *The Golden Dreamer* (1840); and *The Universal Dreamer* (1850). On their circulation see Harland and Wilkinson, *Lancashire Folk-Lore*, p. 121; Lawson, *Progress in Pudsey*, p. 52.
107 *Mother Bunch's Golden Fortune-Teller* (Newcastle upon Tyne, n.d.), p. 7.
108 Obelkevich, *Religion and Rural Society*, pp. 259–312; K. Thomas, *Religion and the Decline of Magic* (Harmondsworth, 1973), p. 798; Vaux, *Church Folklore*, esp. pp. 293–311; Lawson, *Progress in Pudsey*, pp. 48–9.
109 Grose, *Provincial Glossary*, p. 52; G. Deacon, *John Clare and the Folk Tradition*, (London, 1983), p. 283; Vaux, *Church Folklore*, pp. 297–303; A. Smith, *The Established Church and Popular Religion 1750–1850* (London, 1981), pp. 19–21.
110 In Catholic France there was a greater emphasis on the relics of saints and other artefacts, but a similar sense of religion as an instrumental force which could be employed to resolve secular problems. Devlin, *Superstitious Mind*, pp. 1–42.

111 Hone, *The Every-Day Book*, 2, p. 181.
112 Vaux, *Church Folklore*, p. 298; Henderson, *Folk Lore of the Northern Counties*, p. 198; Wilkinson, 'Popular Customs of Lancashire', p. 158; Harland and Wilkinson, *Lancashire Folk-Lore*, p. 102; Hone, *The Year Book*, pp. 254–5; Burne, *Shropshire Folk-Lore*, I, pp. 173–4.
113 Burne, *Shropshire Folk-Lore*, I, p. 172.
114 Edwards, *From Crow-Scaring to Westminster*, p. 52. Also A. Rushton, *My Life as a Farmer's Boy*, pp. 49–50; Barker, *History and Confessions*, I, pp. 109–10; T. Cooper, *The Life of Thomas Cooper* (London, 1872), p. 71; C. Thomson, *The Autobiography of an Artisan* (London 1874), pp. 65–6; Hodges, *My Adventures as a Labour Leader*, p. 63.
115 S. Budd, *Varieties of Unbelief* (London, 1977), pp. 13–14; V. E. Neuburg, *The Reading of the Victorian Freethinkers* (London, 1973).
116 Snell, *Men, Movements*, p. 32.
117 H. Mayhew, *London Labour and the London Poor* (London, 1861), p. 259.
118 Cited in J. P. Harrison, 'Cheap Literature – Past and Present', *Companion to the British Almanack* (1873), p. 65.
119 Jones, *Religious Tract Society*, pp. 246–7. Also C. J. Hoare, 'The Penny Press', *The Englishman's Magazine*, N.S., V (December 1850), 721.
120 'Clericus Londinensis', 'The Public Press', *The Churchman's Monthly Penny Magazine*, I (1846), 58.
121 Allen and McClure, *Two Hundred Years*, p. 198.
122 E. G. Salmon, 'What the Working Classes Read', *Nineteenth Century*, XX (1886), 115.
123 W. C. E. Newbolt, *Apostles of the Lord* (London, 1901), p. 50.
124 The ways in which the aridity and perceived irrelevance of the school curriculum was exacerbating the problems of the clergy is examined in A. D. Taylor, 'Hodge and his Parson', *Nineteenth Century*, XXXI (1892), 359.
125 Berridge, 'Popular Sunday Papers', p. 252. For an account of the range of inquiries made to the *Family Paper* from a wide cross-section of the community, see T. Frost, *Forty Years' Recollections, Literary and Political* (London, 1880), pp. 233–4, 328–30.
126 On the similar erosion of the position of elderly people and women as repositories of knowledge in France, see Devlin, *Superstitious Mind*, p. 89.
127 Demos, *Entertaining Satan*, p. 395. Martine Segalen also examines how fear of women declined as their authority in the labour process was diminished. M. Segalen. *Love and Power in the Peasant Family* (London, 1983), p. 189.
128 H. McLeod, *Religion and the Working Class in Nineteenth-Century Britain* (London, 1984), p. 27; J. Rule, 'Methodism, Popular Beliefs and Village Culture in Cornwall', in R. D. Storch (ed.), *Popular Culture and Custom in Nineteenth-Century England* (London, 1982), p. 63.
129 D. Vincent, 'The Decline of the Oral Tradition in Popular Culture', in R. D. Storch (ed.), *Popular Culture and Custom in Nineteenth-Century England* (London, 1982), pp. 40–1.
130 J. Obelkevich, 'Proverbs and Social History', in Burke and Porter, *Social History of Language*, pp. 45–64.
131 Ong, *Orality and Literacy*, p. 97. Also, Burke, *Popular Culture*, p. 179; W. Muir, *Living with Ballads* (London, 1965), p. 48; D. Buchan, *The Ballad and the Folk* (London, 1972), p. 229.
132 The best surveys of the transformation in public attitudes to time in this period are to be found in D. S. Landes, *Revolution in Time* (Cambridge Mass., 1983), pp. 227–30, 285; Thompson, 'Time, Work-Discipline', 56–97.
133 The fullest account of Clare's work as a collector is to be found in Deacon, *John Clare*.
134 J. Clare, *The Shepherd's Calendar*, ed. E. Robinson and G. Summerfield (Oxford, 1973), p. 92.
135 Robinson, *Britain's Post Office*, pp. 102–17; Landes, *Revolution in Time*, p. 227.
136 McKenna, *Railway Workers*, pp. 243–51; Landes, *Revolution in Time*, p. 285.

137 *Fourth Report of the Postmaster General on the Post Office* (1858), p. 35. However, until 1872 County Post Offices could, 'for certain purposes', observe local time.

138 The first clause of this Act specified that 'Whenever any expression of time occurs in any Acts of Parliament, deed or other legal instrument, the time referred to shall, unless it be otherwise specifically stated, be held in the case of Great Britain, to be Greenwich Mean Time.'

139 See above, p. 39.

140 W. E. Adams, *Memoirs of a Social Atom* (London, 1903), I, p. 71. Also St John, *Education of the People*, p. 122; Jackson, *Solo Trumpet*, p. 40. This was a fear which went all the way back to Plato. See Pattison, *On Literacy*, p. 39.

141 Clare, *Shepherd's Calendar*, p. 3.

142 J. Clare, 'Essay on Popularity', in J. W. and A. Tibble (eds.), *The Prose of John Clare* (London, 1951), p. 208.

143 Scribner and Cole, *Psychology of Literacy*, p. 138: Oxenham, *Literacy*, pp. 46–8; Ong, *Reading and Writing*, pp. 57–68; Stubbs, *Language and Literacy*, p. 101.

144 Cooper, *Life*, p. 57. Although the outcome of his ambition was a breakdown, he persisted. In 1843, for instance, to raise funds to pay debts incurred in political activity, he mounted a production of *Hamlet*, 'as I knew the whole play by heart' (p. 228).

145 Clare, *Shepherd's Calendar*, p. 67.

146 *Ibid.*, p. 69.

147 *Ibid.*, p. 126.

148 Hone, *Every-Day Book*, vol. 1, 6 January. This sense was present amongst the earliest collectors. Grose in 1787 lamented that the practices he was describing were 'sliding into oblivion'. Grose, *Provincial Glossary*, p. vi.

149 'Autobiography of a Suffolk Farm Labourer', pt II, ch. 11.

150 B. Bushaway, *By Rite. Custom, Ceremony and Community in England 1700–1880* (London, 1982), pp. 107–15; D. H. Morgan, 'The Place of Harvesters in Nineteenth-Century Village Life', in R. Samuel (ed.), *Village Life and Labour* (London, 1975), p. 44; Howitt, *Rural Life*, I, p. 206; Hone, *The Year Book*, pp. 1064–5, 1069–70; J. Buckley, *A Village Politician: The Life Story of John Buckley* (London, 1897), pp. 26–8.

151 See, for instance, the details of the first of the new-style festivals held in the Staffordshire village of Eccleshall. Vincent, *Victorian Eccleshall*, pp. 150–1.

152 Laqueur, *Religion and Respectability*, pp. 85–6, 171–2, 177–9, 235–6.

153 G. Parkinson, *True Stories of Durham Pit-Life* (London, 1912), pp. 66–7.

154 Charlotte Brontë provides a vivid description of a Whitsun Sunday school feast in the West Riding towards the end of the Napoleonic Wars in *Shirley* (London, 1893 edn), 1, pp. 330–49. On the day, a procession of Church of England scholars from three parishes collides with a joint Baptist, Independent and Wesleyan march. The latter break into a hymn, but are routed by the former, who strike up 'Rule, Britannia!'

155 On the growth of day excursions by train, see H. Perkin, *The Age of the Railway* (London, 1971), pp. 213–14.

156 L. Jermy, *The Memories of a Working Woman* (London, 1934), p. 8. Also, Snell, *Men, Movements*, pp. 16–17, 20; P. B. Cliff, *The Rise and Development of the Sunday School Movement in England 1780–1980* (Redhill, 1986), pp. 56, 92, 100; Turner, *About Myself*, p. 40.

157 Hone, *Table Book*, pp. 583, 1135–6, 1286.

158 Cited in Chancellor, *History for their Masters*, p. 10.

159 Sturt, *Education of the People*, p. 271.

160 Chancellor, *History for their Masters*, pp. 35–6, 61–2.

161 M. E. Sadler and J. W. Edwards, 'Public Elementary Education in England and Wales 1870–1895', in Education Department, *Special Reports on Educational Subjects 1896–7* (London, 1897), pp. 58–9. On the generally poor state of history teaching in elementary schools, see J. G. Fitch, *Lectures on Teaching* (Cambridge, 1881), pp. 370–1.

162 Charles Rollin's *The Ancient History of the Egyptians, Carthaginians, Assyrians, Babylonians, Medes and Persians, Macedonians and Grecians*, appeared in English in 1738 and was continuously in print for the next century, as was A. M. Ramsay's *The Travels of Cyrus* (1st English edn, 1727), which followed its hero through the ancient

world, introducing a wide range of classical history, mythology and theology. See Burn, *Beggar Boy*, p. 130; Barker, *History of a Man*, I, pp. 138–9; Cooper, *Life*, pp. 33, 62; Gutteridge, *Lights and Shadows*, p. 226; Parkinson, *True Stories*, p. 64; W. Fairbairn, *The Life of Sir William Fairbairn, Bart*. (London, 1877), p. 74; T. Carter, *Memoirs of a Working Man*, pp. 74–5; Lowery, *Robert Lowery*, p. 45; Jackson, *Solo Trumpet*, p. 15.

163 This problem is discussed at greater length in Vincent, *Bread, Knowledge and Freedom*, pp. 25–9.

164 Lowery, *Robert Lowery*, pp. 39, 213, 215.

165 C. H. McCarthy, *Chartist Recollections* (Bradford, 1883), p. 2. See also G. J. Holyoake, *Bygones Worth Remembering* (London, 1905), I, p. 84. Frost, *Forty Years*, p. 97. For references to autobiographies containing accounts of Chartism see J. Burnett, D. Vincent and D. Mayall, *The Autobiography of the Working Class, Vol. 1, 1790–1900* (Brighton, 1984), p. 401.

166 Lancaster, *Improvements in Education*, p. 59. His contemporary and rival Alexander Bell claimed that 'economy of time' was a principal virtue of his Madras system. Bell, *Sermon on Education*, p. 19.

167 For a more general discussion of the promotion of time-thrift by schools, see Calhoun, *Intelligence of a People*, pp. 58–9; Inkeles and Smith, *Becoming Modern*, pp. 136, 140; Thompson, 'Time, Work-Discipline', pp. 24–5.

168 On contemporary concern about this problem, see P. Bailey, *Leisure and Class in Victorian England* (London, 1978), pp. 65, 97, 174; R. D. Storch, 'The Problem of Working-Class Leisure. Some Roots of Middle-class Moral Reform in the Industrial North: 1825–50', in A. P. Donajgrodski (ed.), *Social Control in Nineteenth Century Britain* (London, 1977), pp. 144–7; Rule, 'Methodism', p. 49.

169 For the part played by education in the attack on Saint Monday, see D. A. Reid, 'The Decline of Saint Monday 1766–1876', *Past and Present*, 71 (1976), 14.

170 Hole, *Mechanics' Institutions*, p. 70.

171 *Minutes of the Committee of Council on Education 1840–41* (1841), p. 72.

172 The tension between public traditional pastimes and the domestic alternatives is examined by R. W. Malcolmson in *Popular Recreation in English Society 1700–1850* (Cambridge, 1973), p. 156.

173 See the account of Adam Rushton breaking the rules to read in the silk mill in which he worked in the late 1840s: Rushton, *My Life*, p. 35; and Vere Garratt at the very end of the period erecting a pile of boxes on his bench at a gas meter factory to hide his reading from the supervisor: V. W. Garratt, *A Man in the Street* (London, 1939), p. 97.

174 B. S. Rowntree (ed.), *Betting and Gambling* (London, 1905), p. 185.

175 J. H. Haslam, *The Press and the People* (Manchester, 1906), pp. 8–11; Stamper, *So Long Ago*, p. 171; Brown, *Victoran News*, p. 244; R. McKibbin, 'Working-Class Gambling in Britain 1880–1939', *Past and Present*, 82 (1979), 148; T. Mason, *Association Football and English Society 1863–1915* (Brighton, 1980), pp. 187–95.

176 Central Society of Education, *Third Publication* (London, 1839), p. 122.

177 See Vere Garratt's account of the difficulties he experienced as a self-improving son of a gambling father as both sought to use the public library in the evenings. Garratt, *Man in the Street*, p. 95.

178 L. James, *Fiction for the Working Man* (Harmondsworth, 1974), p. 40.

179 Roberts, *Classic Slum*, p. 165.

180 J. G. Leigh, 'What Do The Masses Read?', *Economic Review* (1904), 175. See also Lady F. Bell, 'What People Read', *Independent Review*, 7, pt 27 (1905), 428–9, 431; R. A. Scott James, *The Influence of the Press* (London, 1913), pp. 183–4.

181 C. Booth, *Life and Labour of the People in London*, 17 (London, 1902), p. 47.

182 See R. Whipp, ' "A time to every purpose": an essay on time and work', in Joyce, *Historical Meanings of Work*, pp. 210–22 for a valuable critique of the view that Western society has seen a single progress towards abstract clock-time.

183 Fewer than one in ten extant nineteenth-century working-class autobiographies were written by women. Burnett, Vincent and Mayall, *Autobiography of the Working Class*, p. xviii.

184 Bell, 'What People Read', p. 435.

185 C. Blagden, 'Thomas Carman and the Almanack Monopoly', *Studies in Bibliography*, XIV (1961), 21–39; B. Capp, *Astrology and the Popular Press. English Almanacks 1500–1800* (London, 1979), pp. 238–69; M. Harris, 'Astrology, Almanacks and Booksellers', *Publishing History*, VIII (1980), 92–100.
186 The almanac street-seller interviewed by Mayhew complained that the abolition of the stamp had unleashed so many free almanacs that his trade was ruined. Mayhew, *London Labour*, I, p. 293. On the use of the post, see A. Wynter, *Peeps into the Human Hive* (London, 1874), pp. 1, 41–2, and ch. 2 above, pp. 41–2.
187 *The British Almanack* (1838), p. 2.
188 *Ibid.*, p. 107.
189 A. Heywood, *Three Papers on English Printed Almanacks* (1904), III, pp. 14–16; James, *Print and the People*, pp. 53–4.
190 P. Joyce, *Society Signified. Popular Conceptions of the Social Order*, forthcoming.
191 Published in Leeds, price 6d. Other almanacs tried 'Jennywerry', 'Jenewery', 'Jenewarry'.
192 Published in Bradford, price 1d.
193 For the continuing popularity of *Moore* in early-twentieth-century Salford, see Roberts, *The Classic Slum*, p. 166.
194 Published in Halifax.
195 Published in Halifax. The December entry discussed the pleasures of Christmas.
196 Price One Penny. See also Mungo Shoddy, *Dewsbre Back at Mooin Olmenac An T'West-Riden Historical Calendar for T'Year 1868*. Batley. 1d.
197 Cited in Heywood, *Three Papers*, vol. III, p. 29.
198 And even vice versa. Robert Roberts claimed that the desire to read the sporting papers was a crucial incentive to literacy. Roberts, *The Classic Slum*, p. 164.
199 Booth, *Life and Labour*, 17 (London, 1902), pp. 57, 58; Leigh, 'What Do The Masses Read?', p. 171; Bell, 'What People Read', p. 429; B. S. Rowntree, *Poverty, A Study of Town Life* (London, 1903), pp. 143–4; McKibbin, 'Working-Class Gambling', pp. 147–77; G. Stedman Jones, *Languages of Class* (Cambridge, 1983), p. 203.
200 Haggard, *I Walked by Night*, p. 13.

6 IMAGINATION

1 Vincent, 'Love and Death', 226–32.
2 See, *inter alia*, Brierley, *Home Memories*, pp. 21, 31; Lowery, *Robert Lowery*, p. 56; J. Harris, *My Autobiography* (London, 1882), pp. 24, 48; Cooper, *Life*, p. 22.
3 Adams, *Memoirs*, I, p. 101.
4 Hopkinson, *Victorian Cabinet Maker*, p. 18; Snell, *Men, Movements*, p. 15.
5 W. M. Gattie, 'What English People Read', *Fortnightly Review*, 52 (1889), 320. Also J. Ackland, 'Elementary Education and the Decay of Literature', *The Nineteenth Century*, XXXV (1894), 423. On the persistently high proportion of fiction lent by public libraries, see T. Kelly, *A History of Public Libraries in Great Britain 1845–1965* (London, 1973), pp. 85–8, 192–5.
6 J. Ginswick (ed.), *Labour and the Poor in England and Wales 1849–51*, I (London, 1983), p. 62; 'The Poetry of Seven Dials', *Quarterly Review* (1867), 405.
7 Bell, 'What People Read', p. 434; A. Lang and 'X' A Working Man, 'The Reading Public', *Cornhill Magazine* (1901), 794.
8 See above, pp. 89, 94.
9 M. Spufford, *Small Books and Pleasant Histories* (London, 1981), pp. 92–8.
10 M. Pickering, *Village Song and Culture* (London, 1982), p. 166.
11 Buchan, *The Ballad and the Folk*, pp. 171, 89. Also, W. Muir, *Living with Ballads* (London, 1965), p. 259.
12 Buchan, *The Ballad and the Folk*, p. 270.
13 T. Holcroft, *Memoirs of the late Thomas Holcroft* (London, 1816), p. 135.
14 *Ibid.*, p. 3.
15 *Ibid.*, p. 13.

16 A. L. Lloyd, *Folk Song in England* (London, 1975), p. 20; R. S. Thomson, 'The Development of the Broadside Ballad Trade and its Influence upon the Transmission of English Folksongs', Ph.D. thesis, Cambridge University (1974), 215.
17 J. Harland (ed.), *The Songs of the Wilsons* (London, 1865), pp. 11, 27.
18 Thomson, 'Broadside Ballad Trade'. For a more general discussion of this point see R. Elbourne, *Music and Tradition in Early Industrial Lancashire 1780–1840* (Woodbridge, 1980), pp. 55–6; Spufford, *Small Books*, p. 9.
19 Cited in Deacon, *Clare and the Folk Tradition*, p. 24. See also the extensive discussion of the response to the oral tradition of the 'Ettrick Shepherd' James Hogg in D. Vincent, 'The Decline of the Oral Tradition in Popular Culture', in R. Storch (ed.), *Popular Culture and Custom in Nineteenth Century England* (London, 1982), pp. 20–4, 31–42.
20 'The Meeting', which Catnach published as 'Here we meet too soon to part'. Catnach set it to the music of a popular aria from Rossini's *Tancredi*. Deacon, *Clare and the Folk Tradition*, p. 64.
21 'Street Ballads', *The National Review*, XXVI (July 1861), 416; C. Hindley, *The Life and Times of James Catnach* (London, 1878), p. 383; G. A. Sala, *The Life and Adventures of George Augustus Sala, written by himself* (London, 1895), I, pp. 96–7. Catnach's rival John Pitts collected folk-songs and ballads from Irish immigrants of Seven Dials. L. Shepard, *The History of Street Literature* (London, 1973), p. 69.
22 Hindley, *Life of Catnach*, p. 65.
23 Mayhew, *London Labour*, I, p. 234.
24 W. Roberts, 'Lloyd's Penny Bloods', *Book-collectors' Quarterly*, XVIII (1935), 3.
25 V. E. Neuburg, *Popular Literature. A History and Guide* (London, 1977), p. 140.
26 Mayhew, *London Labour*, I, pp. 234–317.
27 A. J. Lee, *The Origins of the Popular Press in England 1855–1914* (London, 1976), p. 65. For 'out-of-works and down-and-outs' singing as a means of begging in the last decade of the century see Stamper, *So Long Ago*, p. 35.
28 E. Waugh, *Home-Life of the Lancashire Factory Folk During the Cotton Famine* (London, 1867), p. 197.
29 'Poetry of Seven Dials', p. 404.
30 *Ibid.*, pp. 398–9; Smith, 'The Press of the Seven Dials', p. 254; C. Hindley, *Curiosities of Street Literature* (London, 1871), p. ii; 'Street Ballads', p. 399; Mayhew, *London Labour*, I, p. 234; Cross, *The Common Writer*, p. 126; V. E. Neuburg, 'The Literature of the Streets', in H. J. Dyos and M. Wolff (eds.), *The Victorian City* (London, 1973), I, pp. 200–1.
31 T. Catling, *My Life's Pilgrimage* (London, 1911), p. 39; Roberts, 'Lloyd's Penny Bloods', p. 14. Cf. the similar plight of the American dime novel writers: M. Denning, *Dime Novels and Working-Class Culture in America* (London, 1987), p. 20.
32 James, *Print and the People*, p. 23; M. Twyman, *Printing 1770–1970* (London, 1970), pp. 5–6, 51–2; C. Clair, *A History of Printing in Britain* (London, 1965), p. 210; S. H. Steinberg, *Five Hundred Years of Printing* (3rd edn Harmondsworth, 1974), pp. 279–80.
33 Thomson, 'Broadside Ballad Trade', p. 39.
34 On Lloyd's operation, see Catling, *Life's Pilgrimage*, p. 52.
35 G. Hull, *The Poets and Poetry of Blackburn* (Blackburn, 1902), pp. 17–18, 347. See also the autobiography of the last of the old self-sufficient ballad singers, D. Love, *The Life and Adventures of David Love, Written by Himself* (3rd edn, Nottingham, 1823), and Bamford's account of the composition and distribution of the first Jone o' Grinfilt song (below, n. 58). For a more general discussion of poets controlling the whole process of production and the problems they faced, see B. E. Maidment, *The Poorhouse Fugitives* (Manchester, 1987), pp. 328–9.
36 See above, ch. 3, pp. 79–80.
37 On the wholesale appropriation by ballad-printers of songs made popular in the Manchester theatres, see J. Harland, 'Songs of the Working Classes', *Manchester Guardian*, 4 December 1839, 4.
38 For the necessary vigour and eloquence of the street book seller, see T. Wright, *The Great Unwashed* (London, 1868), p. 222.

39 Knight, *London*, I, p. 144. Also, Lee, *Popular Press*, p. 35.
40 Mayhew, *London Labour*, I, p. 297. Also Smith, 'The Press of the Seven Dials', p. 253; J. Harland and T. T. Wilkinson, 'An Essay on Ballads and Songs', *Trans. Hist. Soc. Lancs. and Ches.*, XI (N.S.), (1870), 116.
41 Mayhew, *London Labour*, I, p. 234.
42 P. Joyce, *Society Signified. Popular Conceptions of the Social Order* (forthcoming), p. 24.
43 London, n.d. St Bride Coll.
44 T. Hogg, *The Child's First Book and Sunday School Primer* (London, 1838). See also above, ch. 3, p. 76.
45 St Bride Coll. See also C. Hindley, *Curiosities of Street Literature* (London, 1871), p. ii and Smith, 'Press of the Seven Dials', p. 261 on the general quality of the illustrations.
46 J. Holloway and J. Black (eds.), *Later English Broadside Ballads* (London, 1975), I, p. 4; James, *Print and the People*, p. 25.
47 R. W. Scribner, *For the Sake of Simple Folk. Popular Propaganda for the German Reformation* (Cambridge, 1981), p. 229.
48 See J. Ashton, *Chapbooks of the Eighteenth Century* (London, 1882), p. vii, for a description of the increasing use by unscrupulous publishers of irrelevant pictures in place of damaged or worn blocks.
49 Roberts, 'Lloyd's Penny Bloods', 6; G. P. Haining, *The Penny Dreadful* (London, 1975), p. 15.
50 On the role of the broadside in particular in assisting the transition to functional literacy, see M. Vicinus, *The Industrial Muse* (London, 1974), p. 26.
51 'Poetry of Seven Dials', p. 406. Also C. Mackay, *Memoirs of Extraordinary Popular Delusions* (London, 1841), I, p. 221.
52 From an undated, probably eighteenth-century version, published in Nottingham, 'printed for the Running Stationers'. John Johnson Coll.
53 Grose, *Provincial Glossary*, p. vii.
54 As also in French peasant culture. Devlin. *The Superstitious Mind*, p. 78.
55 See also Jeffrey Brooks' discussion of similar quality Russian Instalment Novels in *When Russia Learned to Read*, p. 148.
56 'The Byways of Literature. Reading for the Million', *Blackwood's Magazine*, LXXXIV (1858), 205.
57 See also the very useful discussion of contemporary American dime novels in Denning, *Mechanic Accents*, pp. 65–84.
58 J. M. Ludlow and L. Jones, *The Progress of the Working Class 1832–1867* (London, 1867), p. 181.
59 Rymer, 'Popular Writing', p. 101.
60 Reprinted in Holloway and Black, *Later English Broadside Ballads*, 2, p. 155.
61 *Axe My Eye*, St Bride Coll.
62 For surveys of the growth of the dialect movement see Joyce, *Society Signified*; B. Hollingworth (ed.), *Songs of the People* (Manchester, 1977), pp. 1–4.
63 On the origins of the series see S. Bamford, *Walks in South Lancashire* (Blackley, 1844), pp. 169–71; J. Harland, *Ballads and Songs of Lancashire* (London, 1865), pp. 212–13; Elbourne, *Music and Tradition*, p. 79.
64 Harland, *Ballads and Songs*, pp. 224–5.
65 Cited in Deacon, *John Clare*, p. 43.
66 London, n.d. St Bride Coll.
67 Haining, *Penny Dreadful*, p. 14.
68 According to Mayhew, at least six 'executions' enjoyed seven-figure sales: those of Rush, the Mannings, Courvoisier, Good, Corder and Greenacre. Mayhew, *London Labour*, I, p. 308. Also Neuburg, 'Literature of the Streets', pp. 193–4, 198–9.
69 Smith, 'Press of Seven Dials', p. 253.
70 G. Hull, *The Poets and Poetry of Blackburn* (Blackburn, 1902), p. 17.
71 B. E. Maidment, *The Poorhouse Fugitives* (Manchester, 1987), p. 98.
72 R. English, 'The Price of the Novel, 1750–1894', The *Author*, V (1894), 94–9; M. Plant, *The English Book Trade* (2nd edn, London, 1965), pp. 414–18.

73 The ways in which readers sought to overcome the problem of cost are surveyed in Vincent, *Bread, Knowledge and Freedom*, pp. 113–28.

74 H. E. Wroot, 'A Pioneer in Cheap Literature. William Milner of Halifax', *The Bookman*, 66 (1897), 174.

75 On Dicks, see 'John Dicks', the *Bookseller* (3 March 1881), 231; Burt, *Thomas Burt*, pp. 143–4; Neuburg, *Popular Literature*, pp. 174–7.

76 Okey, *Basketful of Memories*, p. 20.

77 *Ibid.*, p. 18. For other self-educated readers taking pleasure in Shakespeare see Barker, *History and Confessions*, I, p. 149; Fairbairn, *Life*, p. 74; C. Thomson, *The Autobiography of an Artisan* (London, 1849), p. 67; Nicholson, *Poems by John Nicholson*, p. 4; See also James, *Print and the People*, p. 83.

78 Burke, *Popular Culture*, pp. 245–6.

79 C. J. Hoare, 'The Penny Press', the *Englishman's Magazine*, N.S., V (December 1850), 721–3; F. Mayne, 'The Literature of the Working Classes', the *Englishwoman's Magazine*, N.S., V (October 1850), 619–21; 'New and Cheap Forms of Popular Literature', *The Eclectic Review*, N.S., XVIII (July 1845), 75–6; Parker, 'On the Literature of the Working Classes', p. 186; J. W. Ross, 'The Influence of Cheap Literature', *London Journal*, I (1847), 115; J. M. Rymer, 'Popular Writing', the *Queens' Magazine* (June 1842), 101.

80 The first volume of Reynolds' *Mysteries* was published by George Vickers. Dicks took over this and other writings of Reynolds after Vickers' death in 1846. Neuburg, *Popular Literature*, pp. 157, 174–7; James, *Fiction for the Working Man*, pp. 164–9.

81 As was the case in other areas of popular culture. E. Yeo and S. Yeo (eds.), *Popular Culture and Class Conflict 1590–1914* (Brighton, 1981), p. 274.

82 On the development of new techniques of marketing, see Plant, *English Book Trade*, pp. 404–9, 429–44; Cross, *The Common Writer*, p. 5.

83 R. D. Altick, *The English Common Reader* (Chicago, 1957), pp. 294–317; 'Penny Fiction', the *Quarterly Review*, 171 (1890), 168.

84 For a general discussion of this point see Elbourne, *Music and Tradition*, p. 88.

85 'Street Ballads', the *National Review*, XXVI (July 1861), 416.

86 For early penny song-books derived from the music halls see *The Great Exhibition Songster* (London, n.d.), and *March's Music Hall Pocket Companion and Bouquet of Songs* (London, n.d.). John Johnson Coll. Also, J. S. Bratton, *Victorian Popular Ballads* (London, 1975), pp. 25–9; James, *Print and the People*, p. 40.

87 Ludlow and Jones, *Progress of the Working Class*, pp. 189–90; T. Wright, *Habits and Customs of the Working Classes* (London, 1867), pp. 168–83; Stamper, *So Long Ago*, pp. 153–4; H. E. Meller, *Leisure and the Changing City, 1870–1914* (London, 1976), pp. 134–8; Vincent, *Victorian Eccleshall*, pp. 151–2.

88 J. E. Carpenter, 'Origin and Progress of the "Penny Reading" Movement', in *Penny Readings in Prose and Verse* (London, 1865), I, p. 6.

89 See above, ch. 3, p. 89.

90 On the 'yellow-backs', see Altick, *English Common Reader*, pp. 299–300; Plant, *English Book Trade*, p. 415.

91 A. Repplier, 'English Railway Fiction', in *Points of View* (Boston, 1891), p. 209.

92 Rowntree, *Poverty*, p. 75.

93 See above, ch. 5, pp. 190–1, 194–5.

94 Bell, 'What People Read', p. 433.

95 'The Literature of the Streets', *Edinburgh Review*, CCCXXVII (January 1887), 43.

96 For the problems to would-be readers caused by the presence of handlooms in the home see the account given of Spitalfields domestic life to the *Report of the Select Committee on Public Libraries*, PP 1849, XI, p. 51.

97 Between 1801 and 1901 the proportion of persons to a house fell only slightly from 5.67 to 5.20. House size increased over this period, but in 1901, 8.2 per cent of the population still lived two or more to a room, with much higher densities in many towns. G. R. Porter, *The Progress of the Nation*, new edn, rev. F. W. Hirst (London, 1912), pp. 91–6. On the problem of overcrowding and reading, see James, *Fiction for the Working Man*, p. 44.

98 G. R. Humphery, 'The Reading of the Working Classes', the *Nineteenth Century*, XXXIII (1893), 700.

99 Burt, *Thomas Burt*, p. 122.

100 Gas lighting in working-class homes became more common after 1892, when the penny slot meter was introduced. Ellis, *Educating Our Masters*, p. 16.

101 Barr, *Climbing the Ladder*, p. 26; Lawson, *A Man's Life*, p. 79; Bailey, *Leisure and Class*, p. 12.

102 Lang and 'X', 'The Reading Public', p. 794. Also, 'Byways of Literature', 205.

103 Bell, 'What People Read', p. 434. See also above, ch. 5, pp. 191–2.

104 Haslam, *Press and the People*, p. 15.

105 For accounts of the practical sacrifices entailing in serious reading see: Green, MS Autobiography, 21; Barker, *History and Confessions*, I, p. 55; Fairbairn, *Life*, p. 74; Nicholson, *Poems*, p. 5; Garratt, *Man in the Street*, p. 96; Snell, *Men, Movements*, p. 45; Vincent, *Bread, Knowledge and Freedom*, pp. 120–5.

106 Cross, *The Common Writer*, pp. 2–3. For an earlier and more limited survey see R. D. Altick, 'The Sociology of Authorship', *Bulletin of the New York Public Library*, 66 (1962).

107 Frost, *Forty Years*, p. 317.

108 Until 1814 copyright was fourteen years plus another fourteen if the author was still alive. It then became a minimum of twenty-eight and a maximum of the author's life; in 1842 it became a minimum of forty-two years or the author's life plus seven years; in 1911 it became the author's life plus fifty years.

109 See, for instance, the experience of the Halifax weaver William Heaton, who sent 'upwards of thirty poems to different papers, and received nothing in return but abuse' before at last a piece was accepted by the *Leeds Intelligencer*. Heaton, *The Old Soldier*, pp. xxi–xxii.

110 W. A. Abram, *Blackburn Characters of a Past Generation* (Blackburn, 1894), pp. 223–4. He also published in the *Blackburn Times*. See also the account of the iron turner James Powell winning 'an ephemeral local celebrity' when his poetry is accepted by the 'principal Brighton papers'. J. H. Powell, *Life Incidents and Poetic Pictures* (London, 1865), p. 41.

111 His book, *Sheen and Shade: Lyrical Poems*, was dedicated to 'Thomas Clough Esq., ... By generous aid at length I have succeeded in collecting the scattered offspring of my vagrant muse.' W. Billington, *Sheen and Shade: Lyrical Poems* (Blackburn and London, 1861), dedication. See also the similar progress of John Critchley Prince as chronicled in R. A. D. Lithgow, *Life of John Critchley Prince* (Manchester, 1880), pp. 40–58.

112 For a fuller discussion of the role of middle-class patrons, see B. E. Maidment, 'Essayists and Artisans – The Making of Victorian Self-Taught Poets', *Literature and History*, IX (Spring 1983), 83–5; Maidment, *Poorhouse Fugitives*, pp. 325–8; Cross, *The Common Writer*, pp. 126–47; Vicinus, *Industrial Muse*, pp. 168–79; Vincent, *Bread, Knowledge and Freedom*, pp. 30–5.

113 J. Clare, *Selected Poems and Prose of John Clare*, ed. E. Robinson and G. Summerfield (London, 1967), pp. xx–xxi.

114 Nicholson, *Poems*, pp. 7–8.

115 Lithgow, *John Critchley Prince*, p. 203; Vicinus, *Industrial Muse*, pp. 171–2.

116 Lithgow, *John Critchley Prince*, pp. 194–5.

117 Cross, *The Common Writer*, p. 6.

118 *The Working Man's Friend and Family Instructor*, April 1850, reprinted in Maidment, *Poorhouse Fugitives*, pp. 332–3.

119 This point is argued at greater length in B. E. Maidment, 'Class and Cultural Production in the Industrial City', in A. J. Kidd and K. W. Roberts (eds.), *City, Class and Culture* (Manchester, 1985).

120 The most detailed evocation of this world is to be found in Hull, *Poets and Poetry*.

121 Nicholson, *Poems*, p. 107. See also Lithgow, *John Critchley Prince*, pp. 123–34.

122 Parker, 'Literature of the Working Classes', p. 186. Also Mayne, 'Literature of the Working Classes', p. 620; C. Redding, *Yesterday and Today* (London, 1863), III, p. 179.

123 On Prest, see Neuburg, *Popular Literature*, p. 172; Altick, *English Common Reader*, p. 290.
124 T. P. Prest, *Evelina, the Pauper's Child; or, Poverty, Crime, and Sorrow. A Romance of Deep Pathos* (London, 1851), p. 158.
125 *Ibid.*, p. 50.
126 *Ibid.*, pp. 14, 15.
127 *Ibid.*, p. 158.
128 *Ibid.*, p. 8.
129 James, *Print and the People*, pp. 83–6.
130 Repplier, 'English Railway Fiction', p. 221. Also Frost, *Forty Years*, p. 320. Cf. J. H. Haslam's survey of the penny fiction bought by the working class of Ancoats: 'there was not a single item in it akin to the real lives of those Ancoats inhabitants'. Haslam, *Press and the People*, p. 6.
131 The *Monthly Magazine of Fiction*, December 1885, p. 128.
132 The approach of the penny novelettes in the *Bow Bells* series can be judged from the headings of the last chapters of each story. Those of 1879 included 'Found – Sunshine At Last' (p. 15), 'Sunshine Through The Clouds' (p. 223), and 'Sunshine After Clouds' (p. 272).
133 P. Rogers, 'Classics and Chapbooks', in *Literature and Popular Culture in Eighteenth Century England* (Brighton, 1985), p. 163.
134 J. Clare, 'Essay on Popularity', p. 207.
135 Vincent, *Bread, Knowledge and Freedom*, pp. 192–3.
136 Smith, 'Press of the Seven Dials', p. 253.
137 T. Wright, 'On a Possible Popular Culture', *Contemporary Review*, 40 (1881), 26, 27.
138 *Ibid.*, 28.
139 *Ibid.*, 29.
140 P. J. Cropper, *The Nottinghamshire Printed Chap-Books* (Nottingham, 1892), p. 7.
141 J. Eldred, *I Love the Brooks* (London, 1955), p. 45. When he had money of his own, he extended this collection by purchases from the second-hand bookshops in the Charing Cross Road. See also Meek, *George Meek*, p. 254 on the enforced irregularity of serious reading.
142 Jackson, *Solo Trumpet*, p. 37. Also Turner, *About Myself*, pp. 29–32.
143 Vincent, *Bread, Knowledge and Freedom*, pp. 127–8.
144 Lawson, *A Man's Life*, p. 78. On the impact of Stead's 'Penny Poets', see also Stamper, *So Long Ago*, p. 162.
145 Lawson, *A Man's Life*, p. 79. Also Hodges, *My Adventurers as a Labour Leader*, p. 15; Burt, *Thomas Burt*, p. 191; G. N. Barnes, *From Workshop to War Cabinet* (London, 1923), p. 16; Turner, *About Myself*, p. 49.
146 On the widening of the curriculum, see Ellis, *Children's Reading*, pp. 91–2, and above, ch. 3, pp. 88–9.
147 Stevens and Hole, *Grade Lesson Books*, Sixth Standard, p. v.
148 'Literature of the Streets', p. 43.
149 'Penny Fiction', p. 170.
150 *Report of the Committee of Council on Education 1891–92* (1892), p. 338.
151 *Report of the Committee of Council on Education, 1872–3* (1873), pp. 92–3.
152 *Ibid.*, p. 93.
153 Vicinus, *Industrial Muse*, pp. 141–7.
154 Kitchen, *Brother to the Ox*, p. 73.
155 Jackson, *Solo Trumpet*, pp. 21–2. For a similar view of the incompatibility of 'a higher sensibility' and the 'hardships of the toil', see Williams, *Railway Factory*, p. 290.
156 Cited in Deacon, *John Clare*, pp. 32–3.
157 Martin, *Contemporary Cultural Change*, pp. 30–49; Bratton, *Victorian Popular Ballads*, p. 9.
158 Elbourne, *Music and Tradition*, p. 110.
159 Joyce, *Society Signified*, pp. 22–43; Maidment, *Poorhouse Fugitives*, pp. 355–9.
160 Abram, *Blackburn Characters*, p. 226.
161 *Ibid.*, p. 228.

7 POLITICS

1 T. Preston, *The Life and Opinions of Thomas Preston* (London, 1817), p. 13.
2 He became a follower of Thomas Spence, the proponent of land and language reform. On Spence's critique of language, see Smith, *Politics of Language*, pp. 100–7.
3 Goody and Watt, 'Consequences of Literacy', p. 55.
4 L. W. Pye (ed.), *Communications and Political Development* (Princeton, 1963), pp. 3–23.
5 A. Gramsci, *Selections from the Prison Notebooks of Antonio Gramsci*, ed. and trans. Q. Hoare and G. Nowell Smith (London, 1971), p. 263.
6 R. A. Scott-James, *The Influence of the Press* (London, 1913), p. 33.
7 *Ibid.*, p. 318.
8 Gramsci, *Prison Notebooks*, p. 340.
9 See above, ch. 2, p. 43. Also Vincent, 'Communication, Community and the State', pp. 168–70.
10 E. P. Thompson, 'The Crime of Anonymity', in D. Hay *et al.*, *Albion's Fatal Tree* (Harmondsworth, 1977), p. 283.
11 In this case the penalty was seven years' transportation. On the problems this caused to the National Charter Association, see E. Yeo, 'Some Practices and Problems of Chartist Democracy', in J. Epstein and D. Thompson (eds.), *The Chartist Experience* (London, 1982), pp. 352, 360–2, 364–5.
12 Robinson, *Britain's Post Office*, pp. 25, 47, 55, 91–2; Lewins, *Her Majesty's Mails*, p. 223.
13 *Report of the Select Committee on the Post Office*, PP 1844, XIV, p. 13.
14 *Ibid.*, p. 11.
15 See for instance the caution of Robert Lowery on sending letters between Chartists in the aftermath of the 1839 Convention. Lowery, *Robert Lowery*, p. 155. Also F. C. Mather, *Public Order in the Age of the Chartists* (London, 1959), p. 221.
16 As the 1844 Select Committee explained: 'the object in issuing [the warrants] has been in many cases, to ascertain the views, not of the party receiving but the party sending the letter'. *Select Committee on the Post Office*, p. 14.
17 *Ibid.*, p. 11.
18 His suspicions were aroused when he noticed that the original postmark had been over-printed with a later one in an attempt to conceal the delay in transit. J. Mazzini, *Life and Writings of Joseph Mazzini* (London, 1891), III, pp. 186–7.
19 Lovett, *Life and Struggles*, pp. 247–8.
20 See in particular the 100-page appendix to the Commons Select Committee in which the history of the practice was set out in detail.
21 *Select Committee on the Post Office*, p. 19.
22 *The Times*, 26 June 1844, 6.
23 *Hansard*, 3rd series, LXXV (1844), col. 899.
24 See in particular the attacks by the *Westminster Review* and by Denman, the Lord Chief Justice. 'Mazzini and the Ethics of Politicians', *Westminster Review*, LXXXII (September, 1844), 255–61; *Hansard*, 3rd series, LXXV (1844), cols. 980–1.
25 *Hansard*, 3rd series, LXVII (1844), col. 841.
26 *Ibid.*, cols. 842–3.
27 *The Times*, 4 August 1844, 4.
28 In May 1792 a Royal Proclamation against Seditious Writings was issued, aimed principally against Paine. In November, John Reeves, with much official encouragement, formed his Association for the Preservation of Liberty and Property against Republicans and Levellers, which, together with its provincial counterparts, published tracts in the vernacular designed to counter the influence of Paine. A. Goodwin, *The Friends of Liberty* (London, 1979), pp. 264–5.
29 *Hansard*, 3rd series, XLI (1820), col. 1589.
30 One of the 'Six Acts' of 1819. For details see W. H. Wickwar, *The Struggle for the Freedom of the Press* (London, 1927), pp. 138–40.
31 *Hansard*, 3rd series, XLI (1820), col. 1589.
32 *Ibid.*, col. 1589.

33 See above, ch. 4, p. 97.
34 Usually rendered as 'We must educate our masters.'
35 *Hansard*, 3rd series, XLI (1820), col. 1589.
36 P. Hollis, *The Pauper Press* (Oxford, 1970), pp. 27–9.
37 *Hansard*, 3rd series, XLI (1820), col. 1177.
38 J. Crawfurd, *Taxes on Knowledge* (London, 1836), pp. 49–50.
39 To the losses must be added the cost of the reform of the postal system (see above, ch. 2, p. 38), although the ever-hopeful Rowland Hill argued that like the Penny Post, abolishing the newspaper stamp would ultimately increase Government revenue. *Report from the Select Committee on Newspaper Stamps*, PP 1851 XVII, pp. 266–72.
40 On the impossibility of enforcing the legislation, see H. Brougham, 'Taxes on Knowledge', *Edinburgh Review*, LXII (October 1835), 130–1.
41 *Hansard*, 3rd series, XXXIV (1836), col. 627; *S.C. on Newspaper Stamps*, pp. 98, 115, 204.
42 Crawfurd, *Taxes on Knowledge*, p. 59; Hollis, *Pauper Press*, p. 38.
43 *S.C. on Newspaper Stamps*, p. 137.
44 J. Curran, 'The Press as an Agency of Social Control: an Historical Perspective', in Boyce *et al.*, *Newspaper History*, p. 63.
45 *Hansard*, 3rd series, XXXIV (1836), col. 625. For the close association between reading the unstamped press and public houses, strengthened by the establishment of unlicensed beer-houses after the Beer Act of 1830, see Hollis, *Pauper Press*, p. 38.
46 *S.C. on Newspaper Stamps*, p. 351.
47 I. Asquith, 'The Structure, Ownership and Control of the Press 1780–1855', in Boyce *et al.*, *Newspaper History*, pp. 100–1; L. Brown, *Victorian News and Newspapers* (Oxford, 1985), p. 27.
48 In 1871 this became Standard V. The specific reference to newspapers was dropped from the Code of 1875.
49 The blasphemy laws were used with increasing frequency after the prosecution of the editor, manager and printer of the *Freethinker* in 1882–3. Royle, *Radicals*, pp. 32–4, 271–83.
50 Chancellor, *History for their Masters, passim*, especially pp. 7–14.
51 Fitch, *Lectures on Teaching*, pp. 390–1.
52 J. Brewer, *Party Ideology and Popular Politics at the Accession of George III* (Cambridge, 1976), pp. 167–72; G. Rudé, *Wilkes and Liberty* (Oxford, 1962), pp. 181–4.
53 *Newcastle Elections 1790–1850.*
54 *Ibid.*, f. 41.
55 *Ibid.*, 110.
56 R. Fyson, 'The Crisis of 1842: Chartism, the Colliers' Strike and the Outbreak in the Potteries', in Epstein and Thompson, *Chartist Experience*, pp. 194–220.
57 D. A. Hamer, *The Politics of Electoral Pressure* (Hassocks, 1977), pp. 305–6.
58 N. McCord, *The Anti-Corn Law League 1838–1846* (London, 1958), pp. 163–87.
59 H. Ashworth, *Recollections of Richard Cobden, M.P. and the Anti-Corn Law League* (2nd edn, London, 1878), p. 185. In one election in London alone, 40,000 tracts were posted to electors. *Administration of the Post Office*, pp. 59–60.
60 Hill and Hill, *Life of Sir Rowland Hill*, p. 478.
61 H. J. Hanham, *Elections and Party Management* (London, 1959), p. 233.
62 Hamer, *Electoral Pressure*, pp. 11–23.
63 Brown, *Victorian News*, p. 70.
64 Meek, *George Meek*, pp. 113–14.
65 *Ibid.*, p. 155.
66 G. M. Belfiore, 'Family Strategies in Essex Textile Towns 1860–1895: The Challenge of Compulsory Elementary Schooling', D.Phil. thesis, Oxford University, 1987, 212–42, 331–73.
67 For a more general discussion of this point, see P. Corrigan and D. Sayer, *The Great Arch* (Oxford, 1985), pp. 114–65.
68 Meek, *George Meek*, pp. 169–70.
69 J. Sambrook, *William Cobbett* (London, 1973), p. 83; Wickwar, *Struggle*, pp. 52–5.

70 On coming together to read aloud the early radical press, see Farish, *Autobiography*, pp. 11, 12: J. Routledge, *Chapters in the History of Popular Progress* (London, 1876), pp. 512–13; Curran, 'Capitalism and Control', p. 204; Sambrook, *Cobbett*, p. 85. It was a practice which continued for much of the century. See Turner, *About Myself*, p. 27 on reading out *Reynolds' Newspaper* to the neighbours.

71 D. Green, *Great Cobbett. The Noblest Agitator* (Oxford, 1985), pp. 381, 447–50.

72 Smith, *Politics of Language*, pp. 202–47. Also above, ch. 3, p. 81.

73 Schofield, 'Dimensions', p. 207. For the levels of different sections of the working class see above, ch. 4, p. 97.

74 Frost, *Forty Years*, p. 181. Also, J. A. Epstein, 'Feargus O'Connor and the Northern Star', *International Review of Social History* (1976), 70, 84; D. Thompson, *The Chartists* (London, 1984), p. 52.

75 Thompson, 'Crime of Anonymity', p. 283; E. Hobsbawm and G. Rudé, *Captain Swing* (Harmondsworth, 1973), pp. 73, 88, 93, 94, 104, 111–16, 132, 166; Vincent, 'Communication, Community and the State', pp. 170–3.

76 *Poor Man's Guardian*, 12 May 1832, 391. Pseudonyms were permitted, but only if the editors were informed of the identity of the writer.

77 See for instance, Catnach's undated broadside, *Account of Sir Francis Burdett's Speech last Night In the House of Commons Respecting the late Westminster Election*. St Bride Coll.

78 Buckley, *Village Politician*, p. 53.

79 One of three songs on a broadside entitled *Caroline Queen of our Island*. St Bride Coll.

80 Hollis, *Pauper Press*, pp. 118–20.

81 *Destructive*, 7 June 1834. Cited in Hollis, *Pauper Press*, p. 122.

82 J. H. Wiener, *A Descriptive Finding List of Unstamped British Periodicals 1830–1836* (London, 1970). Given the propensity of the unstamped to exploit every form of contemporary journalism, it is difficult to place the material in precise categories, but 41 per cent of the periodicals may be said to have been predominantly political in their concerns, some of which were anti-reform, and a further 7 per cent were predominantly religious, usually with strong political implications.

83 Epstein, 'Feargus O'Connor', p. 83.

84 *Northern Star*, 13 October 1838.

85 See above, ch. 5, pp. 166–71.

86 Epstein, 'Feargus O'Connor', p. 11.

87 For an account of the scale of Cobbett's impact, see S. Bamford, *Passages in the Life of a Radical* (London, 1893), pp. 11–12.

88 *Weekly Political Register*, March 1817, reprinted in J. M. Cobbett and P. Cobbett, *Selections from Cobbett's Political Works* (London, 1835), V, p. 155. Also, Green, *Great Cobbett*, p. 386.

89 Hollis, *Pauper Press*, p. 120.

90 See Lovett's verdict on the seminal impact of the 'unstamped publications' on the whole field of cheap literature. Lovett, *Life and Struggles*, p. 51.

91 Lowery, *Robert Lowery*, p. 124; E. Glasgow, 'The Establishment of the *Northern Star* Newspaper', *History*, XXXIX (1954), 54–67; Epstein, 'Feargus O'Connor', pp. 55–60.

92 Lowery, *Robert Lowery*, p. 124. Also, following Lowery, Lovett, *Life and Struggles*, p. 173.

93 Lowery and Glasgow state that O'Connor reneged on his undertaking to invest his own money, but Epstein has more recently argued that he is likely to have given the paper substantial financial support.

94 Curran, 'Capitalism and Control', pp. 201–3.

95 The Corresponding Societies Act of 1799, reworked in the Seditious Meetings Act of 1817, made it illegal on pain of seven years' transportation for societies, their members or officers to correspond with each other. Newspapers, now stamped, were the most obvious means of maintaining legal communication. Yeo, 'Practices and Problems', pp. 360–2.

96 For an assessment of the contribution of the *Northern Star* to Chartism see Thompson, *The Chartists*, pp. 45–56.

97 A full account of acting as both agent for the *Northern Star* and secretary of the local Chartist association is given by T. Dunning, 'Reminiscences of Thomas Dunning', in D. Vincent (ed.), *Testaments of Radicalism* (London, 1977), pp. 135, 140–1. Dunning, once a shoemaker, remained a newsagent for the rest of his working life.

98 Hetherington's *London Despatch* was yielding profits of £1,000 a year in 1837, and in its best year of 1839, the *Northern Star* made £13,000. Curran, 'Capitalism and Control', p. 210.

99 The circulation of daily papers did not overtake the Sundays until 1947. Roberts, *Classic Slum*, p. 165.

100 H. R. Fox Bourne, *English Newspapers* (New York, 1966), p. 348.

101 On Chartist poetry see Y. V. Kovalev (ed.), *An Anthology of Chartist Literature* (Moscow, 1956); Vicinus, *Industrial Muse*, pp. 94–112; Maidment, *Poorhouse Fugitives*, pp. 23–94.

102 For the way in which the Sunday papers refined the concept of a newspaper, see R. Williams, 'The Press and Popular Culture: An Historical Perspective' in Boyce et al., *Newspaper History*, p. 48.

103 *Reynolds' Newspaper*, 25 January 1852.

104 Asquith, 'Structure, Ownership and Control', p. 10; Brown, *Victorian News*, p. 17.

105 Lee, *Origins of the Popular Press*, pp. 104–5.

106 The fullest account of the ideology of *Reynolds'* is to be found in V. S. Berridge, 'Popular Journalism and Working Class Attitudes 1854–1886: A Study of Reynolds' Newspaper, Lloyd's Weekly Newspaper and the Weekly Times', Ph.D. thesis, London University, 1976, 321–75.

107 *Reynolds' Newspaper*, 7 July 1867, 1.

108 Lee, *Structure and Ownership*, p. 123.

109 On the launching of the *Bee-Hive*, see S. Coltham, 'The Bee-Hive Newspaper: Its Origin and Early Struggles', in A. Briggs and J. Saville (eds.), *Essays in Labour History* (London, 1967). It was founded with a capital of less than £250.

110 Frost, *Forty Years*, pp. 339–55; Brown, *Victorian News*, p. 267; Curran, 'The Press', p. 71.

111 See for instance the support given by the Liberal *Daily News* to the newly formed National Agricultural Labourers' Union. Arch, *Joseph Arch*, pp. 83–4; Lee, *Origins of the Popular Press*, p. 196.

112 T. Wright, 'The Press and the People', in *Our New Masters* (London, 1873), p. 316.

113 *Ibid.*, p. 316.

114 V. Berridge, 'Popular Sunday Papers and Mid-Victorian Society', in Boyce *et al.*, *Newspaper History*, p. 256. Also Curran, 'The Press as an Agency of Social Control'.

115 By 1900 the paper had fallen out with the ILP, but it continued to carry Labour news and was at least 'benevolently neutral': A. J. Lee, 'The Radical Press', in A. J. A. Morris (ed.), *Edwardian Radicalism 1900–1914* (London, 1979), p. 52.

116 D. Hopkin, 'The Socialist Press in Britain, 1890–1910', in Boyce *et al.*, *Newspaper History*, p. 295.

117 Kenney, *Westering*, p. 24. Also Jackson, *Solo Trumpet*, pp. 62–3; J. Paton, *Proletarian Pilgrimage* (London, 1935), pp. 95–6; L. Thompson, *Robert Blatchford* (London, 1951), pp. 129–31.

118 J. Sexton, *Sir James Sexton, Agitator* (London, 1936), pp. 128, 187–8; D. Howell, *British Workers and the Independent Labour Party 1888–1906* (Manchester, 1983), pp. 129–31.

119 C. Levy, 'Education and Self-Education: Staffing the Early ILP', in C. Levy (ed.), *Socialism and the Intelligentsia 1880–1914* (London, 1987), p. 144.

120 R. Blatchford, *My Eighty Years* (London, 1931), p. 193; Thompson, *Blatchford*, pp. 81–5.

121 F. Reid, 'Keir Hardie and the *Labour Leader*, 1893–1903', in J. Winter (ed.), *The Working Cmass in Modern British History* (Cambridge, 1983), p. 20.

122 Levy, 'Education and Self-Education', p. 149.

123 Howell, *British Workers*, pp. 283–338, 379–80; S. Pierson, *British Socialists* (Cambridge, Mass., 1979), pp. 35, 46.

124 Reid, 'Keir Hardie', p. 40.
125 Although its own national weekly, the *Labour Leader*, did achieve sales of over 40,000 by 1911: Curran, 'Capitalism and Control', p. 216.
126 Holton, 'Daily Herald', pp. 349–74; G. Lansbury, *My Life* (London, 1928), pp. 170–4. The *Citizen*, by contrast, which was under the joint control of the Labour Party and the ILP, raised £26,000. Despite their problems, the circulation of both papers reached peaks of 250,000 before the war.
127 Haslam, *Press and the People*, p. 5. See also the similar verdict of Robert Roberts on nearby Salford. Roberts, *Classic Slum*, p. 167.
128 Gramsci, *Prison Notebooks*, pp. 6, 12, 340.
129 Burt, *Thomas Burt*, p. 49. He was writing about the mid 1840s.
130 W. Hudson, 'How a Railway Man Succeeded', *Pearson's Weekly* (5 April 1906), 709.
131 For a more extended discussion of these points, see Vincent, *Bread, Knowledge and Freedom*, ch. 5.
132 Ch. 5, pp. 163–4.
133 Barnes, 'Pushed into Fame', 633.
134 Cited in W. T. Stead, 'The Labour Party and the Books that Helped to Make it', *Review of Reviews*, XXXIII (1906), 574.
135 Above, ch. 3, pp. 54–66.
136 Hodges, *My Adventures as a Labour Leader*, p. 10.
137 W. C. Steadman, 'How I Got On', *Pearson's Weekly* (8 February 1906), 563.
138 *Ibid.*, 563.
139 Barnes, 'Pushed into Fame', p. 633.
140 Citrine, *Men and Work*, p. 37.
141 J. Wilson, 'An Act that Changed a Life', *Pearson's Weekly* (12 April 1906), 725. For a slightly overstated account of the level of self-education amongst this generation of Labour leaders, see Z. Bauman, *Between Class and Elite* (Manchester, 1972), pp. 196–7.
142 Stead, 'Labour Party', pp. 568–80; D. E. Martin, ' "The Instruments of the People"?: The Parliamentary Labour Party in 1906', in D. E. Martin and D. Rubinstein (eds.), *Ideology and the Labour Movement* (London, 1979), pp. 127–31.
143 See above, ch. 4, p. 151.
144 Thorne, *Life's Battles*, p. 63. Also pp. 46–7.
145 Lawson, *A Man's Life*, pp. 63–4.
146 *Ibid.*, 119. See also Burt, *Thomas Burt*, p. 145.
147 Garratt, *A Man in the Street*, p. 102. Also W. Crooks, 'How I Got On', *Pearson's Weekly* (22 February 1906), 597.
148 Stamper, *So Long Ago*, pp. 172–3. On inquiry the speaker turned out to belong to 'The Clarion crowd, Blatchford's mob'.
149 C. Duncan, 'How I Got On', *Pearson's Weekly* (15 February 1906), 577.
150 Snell, *Men, Movements*, p. 30.
151 Cf. Tony Judt's account of the continuing prevalence of reading aloud and public discussion in the cafes of late-nineteenth-century France: 'The Impact of the Schools, Provence 1871–1914', in Graff, *Literacy and Social Development*, p. 267.
152 Hodges, *Adventures*, p. 24.
153 On the importance of oratory in the labour politics of the 1890s, and the challenge of acquiring the necessary skills, see Levy, 'Education and Self-Education', pp. 168–9.
154 A. Henderson, 'From Errand Boy to M.P.', *Pearson's Weekly* (8 March 1906), 633.
155 For other accounts of the value of training as a lay preacher, see Barr, *Climbing the Ladder*, p. 26; Edwards, *From Crow-Scaring to Westminster*, pp. 36, 42; W. Johnson, 'How I Got On', *Pearson's Weekly* (1 March 1906), 613; Mitchell, 'Autobiography and Reminiscences', p. 121; Stamper, *So Long Ago*, p. 174; Lawson, *A Man's Life*, p. 119; Arch, *Joseph Arch*, p. 48. See also R. Moore, *Pit-Men, Preachers and Politics* (Cambridge, 1974), pp. 145, 170–1.
156 Roberts, *Classic Slum*, p. 177.
157 Burt, *Thomas Burt*, p. 137.
158 Roberts, *Classic Slum*, p. 183.
159 Levy, 'Education and Self-Education', p. 171.

160 Wright, *Habits and Customs*, p. 11.
161 Lawson, *A Man's Life*, p. 108.
162 Scott-James, *Influence of the Press*, p. 219.
163 A point argued by R. McKibbin in 'Why was there no Marxism in Great Britain?', *English Historical Review*, XCIX (April 1984), 325–6.
164 D. Geary, 'Working Class Culture in Imperial Germany', in R. Fletcher (ed.), *Bernstein to Brandt* (London, 1987), pp. 11–16.
165 The sudden swell of support for the secularists when the *Freethinker* was prosecuted for blasphemy in 1882 indicated the dangers which lay in store for the State if it widened an attack on free speech. Royle, *Radicals, Secularists and Republicans*, p. 273.
166 Thorne, *My Life's Battles*, p. 47.
167 Vincent, *Bread, Knowledge and Freedom*, p. 154.
168 Turner, *About Myself*, p. 37.
169 Cf. Keir Hardie, who claimed 'my mother's song made the strongest impression upon me, combined with the tales and romances of my grandfather': Stead, 'Labour Party', p. 570. About two-thirds of the Labour MPs who responded to Stead's inquiry claimed to have been influenced by fiction or poetry.
170 Turner, *About Myself*, p. 50.
171 *Ibid.*, p. 49.
172 *Ibid.*, p. 169.
173 *Ibid.*, p. 358.

8 LITERACY AND ITS USES

1 R. Hoggart, *The Uses of Literacy* (Harmondsworth, 1958).
2 Scott-James, *Influence of the Press*, p. 185.
3 Hoggart, *Uses of Literacy*, p. 324.
4 Roberts, *Classic Slum*, p. 176.
5 In particular Critcher in 'Sociology', pp. 17–20.
6 Gardner, *Lost Schools*.
7 Sutherland, *Ability, Merit and Measurement*.
8 Pattison, *On Literacy*, p. 115.
9 Swindells, *Victorian Writing*, pp. 117–35.
10 Sykes, *Slawit in the 'Sixties*, p. 86.

APPENDIX A

1 O. Anderson, 'The Incidence of Civil Marriage in Victorian England and Wales', *Past and Present*, 69 (November 1975), 50–87.
2 W. A. Armstrong, 'Social Structure from the Early Census Returns', in E. A. Wrigley, *An Introduction to English Historical Demography* (London, 1966).

BIBLIOGRAPHY

i Archives

Berkshire Record Office
Cheshire Record Office
Dudley Public Library
Greater London Record Office
Horace Barks Library, Hanley
John Johnson Collection, Bodleian Library, Oxford
Madden Collection, Cambridge University Library
Modern Records Centre, Warwick University
Newcastle Election Broadsides, University of Keele Library
Post Office Arcnive
St Bride Printing Library
Sheffield City Library
Shropshire Record Office
Staffordshire Record Office
Suffolk Record Office (Ipswich)
Tipton Public Library
Warwick County Record Office
Webb Collection, London School of Economics
Worcester County Record Office

ii Unpublished sources

Child, J. 'The Autobiography of a Dedicated Gardener', transcribed by I. V. Child, TS
Errington, A., MS Autobiography
Green, E., MS Autobiography, *c.* 1880
Marsh, G., 'A Sketch of the Life of George Marsh, Yorkshire Collier. 1834–1921', TS
Mayett, J. Unpublished MS Autobiography, Buckinghamshire Record Office, n.d.
Price, H. E., 'Diary', MS, 1904
Robinson, E. G., 'I Remember', MS

iii Official papers

Hansard
Report from the Committee on . . . the Apprentice Laws of the Kingdom, PP 1812–13, IV

Second Report from the Select Committee on the Education of the Lower Orders, PP 1818, IV

Report of the Select Committee on Artizans and Machinery, PP 1824, V

Report from the Select Committee on the State of Education, PP 1834, IX

Report from the Select Committee on Arts and Manufacture, PP 1835, V; PP 1836, IX

Second Report from the Select Committee on Postage, PP 1837–8, XX

Second Annual Report of the Registrar General, PP 1840, XVII

Minutes of the Committee of Council on Education 1840–41, 1841

Third Annual Report of the Registrar General, PP 1841, VI

Children's Employment Commission. *Appendix to First Report*, PP 1842, XVI

Report from the Select Committee on Postage, PP 1843, VIII

Report of the Select Committee on the Post Office, PP 1844, XIV

Report of the Select Committee on Public Libraries, PP 1849, XI

Report from the Select Committee on the School of Design, PP 1849, XVIII

Report from the Select Committee on Newspaper Stamps, PP 1851, XVII

Report of the Committee of Council on Education 1851–52, 1852

Report upon the Post Office (1854)

First Annual Report of the Postmaster General on the Post Office (1855)

Fourth Annual Report of the Postmaster General on the Post Office (1858)

Report of the Commissioners Appointed to Inquire into the State of Popular Education in England, PP 1861, XXI, pt III

Seventh Annual Report of the Postmaster General on the Post Office (1861)

Ninth Annual Report of the Postmaster General on the Post Office (1863)

Tenth Annual Report of the Postmaster General on the Post Office (1864)

Eleventh Annual Report of the Postmaster General on the Post Office (1865)

Twelfth Annual Report of the Postmaster General on the Post Office (1866)

Twenty-seventh Annual Report of the Registrar General, PP 1866, XIX

Schools Inquiry Commission. Report Relative to Technical Education, PP 1867, XXVI

Report from the Select Committee on Scientific Instruction, PP 1867–8, XV

Copies of Answers from Chambers of Commerce to Queries of the Vice-President of the Council as to Technical Education, PP 1867–8, LIV

Report of a Committee appointed by the Council of the British Association of Science to consider the best means of promoting Scientific Education in Schools, PP 1867–8, LIV

Eleventh and Final Report of the Royal Commissioners Appointed to Inquire into the Organisation and Rules of Trades Unions and other Associations, PP 1868–9, XXXI

Seventeenth Annual Report of the Postmaster General on the Post Office (1871)

Thirty-second Annual Report of the Registrar General, PP 1871, XV

Report of the Committee of Council on Education, 1872–3, 1873

Twenty-fourth Annual Report of the Postmaster General on the Post Office (1880)

Twenty-sixth Annual Report of the Postmaster General on the Post Office (1880)

Forty-second Annual Report of the Registrar General, PP 1881, XXVII

Twenty-seventh Annual Report of the Postmaster General on the Post Office (1881)

Report of the Committee of Council on Education, 1880–1, 1881
Report of the Committee of Council on Education, 1882–3, 1883
Report of the Committee of Council on Education, 1883–4, 1884
Second Report of the Royal Commissioners on Technical Instruction, PP 1884,
    XXIX, XXXI
Forty-seventh Annual Report of the Registrar General, PP 1886, XVII
*First Report of the Commissioners Appointed to Inquire into the Elementary
    Education Acts, England and Wales*, PP 1886, XXIX
*Final Report of the Commissioners Appointed to Inquire into the Elementary
    Education Acts, England and Wales*, PP 1888, XXV
Thirty-fourth Annual Report of the Postmaster General on the Post Office (1888)
Thirty-seventh Annual Report of the Postmaster General on the Post Office (1891)
First Report of the Royal Commission on Labour, PP 1892, XXXIV
Second Report of the Royal Commission on Labour, PP 1892, XXXV
Forty-seventh Annual Report of the Postmaster General on the Post Office (1901)
*Report as to the Practice of Medicine and Surgery by Unqualified Persons in the
    United Kingdom*, PP 1910, XLIII
Report from the Select Committee on Patent Medicines, PP 1913, X; 1914, IX
Seventy-seventh Annual Report of the Registrar General, PP 1916, V

iv Printed primary sources

Abram, W. A., *Blackburn Characters of a Past Generation*, Blackburn, 1894
    'Social Conditions and Political Prospects of the Lancashire Workman', *Fort-
    nightly Review* (1868)
Ackland, J., 'Elementary Education and the Decay of Literature', *Nineteenth
    Century*, XXXV (1894)
Adams, W. E., *Memoirs of a Social Atom*, London, 1903
*The Administration of the Post Office from the Introduction of Mr. Rowland Hill's
    Plan of Penny Postage up to the Present Time*, London, 1844
Adult Literacy and Basic Skills Unit, *Working Together – An Approach to Func-
    tional Literacy*, London, 1981
'Advertisements', *Quarterly Review*, XCVII (1855)
Allen, A. and Cornwell, J., *A New English Grammar, with very copious exercises
    and a systematic view of the formation and derivation of words*, London, 1841
Allen, W. O. B. and McClure, E., *Two Hundred Years: The History of the Society
    for Promoting Christian Knowledge, 1698–1898*, London, 1898
Anderson, I., *The Life History of Isaac Anderson. A Member of the Peculiar
    People*, n.d.
Arch, J., *Joseph Arch, The Story of His Life, told by Himself*. London, 1898
Armstrong, R., *The Modern Practice of Boiler Engineering*, London, 1856
Arnold, M., *The Twice Revised Code*, London, 1862
Ashby, M. K., *Joseph Ashby of Tysoe 1859–1919*, London, 1974
Ashton, J., *Chapbooks of the Eighteenth Century*, London, 1882
Ashworth, H., *Recollections of Richard Cobden, M.P. and the Anti-Corn Law
    League*, 2nd edn, London, 1878

Aspin, J., *A Picture of the Manners, Customs, Sports and Pastimes of the Inhabitants of England*, London, 1825

Atkinson, J. C., *Forty Years in a Moorland Parish*, London, 1891

'The Autobiography of a Suffolk Farm Labourer', *Suffolk Times and Mercury* (1894–5)

Aveling, S. T., *Carpentry and Joinery. A Useful Guide for the Many*, London, 1871

Bales, T., *The Builder's Clerk. A Guide to the Management of a Builder's Business*, London, 1877

Balfour, M. C., *Examples of Printed Folk-Lore Concerning Northumberland*, London, 1904

Bamford, S., *Early Days*, London, 1893
  Passages in the Life of a Radical, London, 1893
  Walks in South Lancashire, Blackley, 1844

Barker, J., *The History and Confessions of a Man*, London, 1846

Barnes, G. N., *From Workshop to War Cabinet*, London, 1923
  'Pushed into Fame', *Pearson's Weekly* (8 March 1906)

Barr, D., *Climbing the Ladder: the Struggles and Successes of a Village Lad*, London, 1910

Barrett, W. H., *A Fenman's Story*, London, 1965

Basset, J., *The Life of a Vagrant*, London [1850]

The Beehive

Bell, A., *Extract from a Sermon on the Education of the Poor*, 2nd edn, London, 1807

Bell, Lady F., 'What People Read', *Independent Review*, 7, pt 27 (1905)

Bell, R., 'How I Got On', *Pearson's Weekly* (15 February 1906)

Bezer, J. J., 'The Autobiography of One of the Chartist Rebels of 1848', in D. Vincent (ed.), *Testaments of Radicalism*, London, 1977

Billington, W., *Sheen and Shade: Lyrical Poems*, Blackburn and London, 1861

Blacket, J., *Specimens of the Party of Joseph Blacket, with an account of his life*, London, 1809

Blatchford, R., *My Eighty Years*, London, 1931

The Book of Trades, London, 1804

Booth, C., *Life and Labour of the People in London*, vol. 17, London, 1902; 2nd series, vol. 5, London, 1905

Bow Bells

Bowd, J., 'The Life of a Farm Worker', *The Countryman*, 51, pt 2 (1955)

Bower, F., *Rolling Stonemason, An Autobiography*, London, 1936

Bowerman, C. W., 'How I Got On', *Pearson's Weekly* (8 February 1906)

'Bowyer, W.' [Honey, W. Bowyer], *Brought Out in Evidence: An Autobiographical Summing-Up*, London, 1941

Brand, J., *Observations on Popular Antiquities*, Newcastle upon Tyne, 1777

Bray, R. A., *Boy Labour and Apprenticeship*, London, 1911

Brierley, B., *Home Memories and Recollections of a Life*, Manchester, 1886

The British Almanack

The British Medical Association, *Secret Remedies*, London, 1909

Britton, J., *The Autobiography of John Britton, FSA*, London, 1850

Broadhurst, H., *Henry Broadhurst, M.P., the Story of His Life from a Stone-*

mason's Bench to the Treasury Bench. Told by Himself, London, 1901

Brougham, H., 'Taxes on Knowledge', *Edinburgh Review*, LXII (October 1835)

Buckley, J., *A Village Politician: The Life Story of John Buckley*, London, 1897

The Builder's and Contractor's Price-Book, London, 1856

Burn, J., *The Autobiography of a Beggar Boy*, ed. D. Vincent, London, 1978

Burne, C. S., *Shropshire Folk-Lore*, 2 vols., London, 1883

Burnell, G. R., *Rudimentary Treatise on Limes, Cements, Mortars, etc.*, London, 1850

Burstow, H., *Reminiscences of Horsham, being Recollections of Henry Burstow, the celebrated Bellringer and Songsinger*, Horsham, 1911

Burt, T., *Thomas Burt, M.P., D.C.L., Pitman and Privy Councillor. An Autobiography*, London, 1924

Byers, J., 'Quackery – With Special Reference to Female Complaints', *British Medical Journal* (1911)

'The Byways of Literature? Reading for the Million', *Blackwood's Magazine* LXXXIV (1858)

Carpenter, J. E., 'Origin and Progress of the "Penny Reading" Movement', in *Penny Readings in Prose and Verse*, vol. 1, London, 1865

Carter, T., *The Guide to Trade. The Plumber, Painter and Glazier*, London, 1838

The Guide to Trade. The Printer, London, 1838

Memoirs of a Working Man, London, 1845

Catling, T., *My Life's Pilgrimage*, London, 1911

Central Society of Education, *Third Publication*, London, 1839

Chapman, H. S., 'The Newspaper Stamp Return', in J. A. Roebuck (ed.), *Pamphlets for the People*, vol. 1, London, 1835

'Characteristics and Peculiarities of Trades. The Tailor and Shoemaker', *The London Saturday Journal* (April 1839)

'Church and State Education', *The Edinburgh Review*, XCII (1850)

Citrine, W., *Men and Work*, London, 1964

Clare, J., 'Autobiographical Fragments', in E. Robinson (ed.), *John Clare's Autobiographical Writings*, Oxford, 1983

Clare, J., 'Essay on Popularity', in J. W. and A. Tibble (eds.), *The Prose of John Clare*, London, 1951

Selected Poems and Prose of John Clare, ed. E. Robinson and G. Summerfield, London, 1967

The Shepherd's Calendar, ed. E. Robinson and G. Summerfield, Oxford, 1973

'Sketches in the Life of John Clare', in E. Robinson, *John Clare's Autobiographical Writings*, Oxford, 1983

The Clarion

'Clericus Londinensis', 'The Public Press', *The Churchman's Penny Monthly Magazine*, I (1846)

Cobbett, J. M. and Cobbett, J. P., *Selections from Cobbett's Political Works*, London, 1835

Cobbett, W., *A Grammar of the English Language in a Series of Letters Intended for the use of Schools and of Young Persons in General; but more especially for the use of Soldiers, Sailors, Apprentices and Plough-Boys*, London, 1835

A Spelling Book with Appropriate Lessons in Reading and with A Stepping-Stone to English Grammar, London, 1831

Coffin, A. I., *A Botanic Guide to Health*, Leeds, 1845

Collar, G. and Crook, C. W., *School Management and Methods of Instruction*, London, 1900

Collier, M., *Poems on Several Occasions ... with some remarks on her life*, Winchester, 1762

Colquhoun, J. C., *An History of Magic, Witchcraft and Animal Magnetism*, 2 vols., London, 1851

Connon, C. W., *A First Spelling-Book*, London, 1851

Cook, M., *A Sure Guide Against Waste in Dress; or The Woollen Draper's, Man's Mercer's and Tailor's Assistant, Adapted also to the Use of Gentlemen, Tradesmen and Farmers shewing The Exact Quantity of Cloth, &c. necessary to make any Garment from a Child to a full sized Man*, London, 1787

Cooper, G., *The Story of George Cooper – Stockport's Last Town Crier. 1824–1895*, Stockport, 1974

Cooper, T., *The Life of Thomas Cooper*, London, 1872

Cooper, W., *Crown Glass Cutter and Glaziers Manual*, Edinburgh and London, 1835

Copper, B., *Early to Rise. A Sussex Boyhood*, London, 1976

A Song for Every Season, London, 1971

Cornwell, J., *The Young Composer; or, Progressive Exercises in English Composition*, London, 1844

Cowham, J. H., *Cowham's Mulhauser Manual of Writing*, London, 1888

Crawfurd, J., *Taxes on Knowledge*, London, 1836

[Croker, J. W.] 'Post Office Reform', *Quarterly Review*, LXIV (1840)

Crooks, W., 'How I Got On', *Pearson's Weekly* (22 February, 1906)

Cropper, P. J., *The Nottinghamshire Printed Chap-Books*, Nottingham, 1892

Dale, N., *The Eventful Life of Nathaniel Dale*, Kimbolton [*c.* 1871]

Darton and Harvey, *Books for Youth*, London, 1805

Davis, E. G., *Some Passages From My Life*, Birmingham, 1898

Dayus, K., *Her People*, London, 1982

Dearle, N. B., *Industrial Training*, London, 1914

The Destructive

Devlin, J., *The Guide to Trade. The Shoemaker*, London, 1839; part 2, London, 1841

Dobson, E., *A Rudimentary Treatise on Masonry and Stonecutting*, London, 1849

Dodd, G., *The Textile Manufactures of Great Britain*, London, 1844

Duncan, C., 'How I Got On', *Pearson's Weekly* (15 February 1906)

Dunn, H., *Popular Education; or the Normal School Manual*, London, 1837

Dunning, T., 'Reminiscences of Thomas Dunning', in D. Vincent (ed.), *Testaments of Radicalism*, London, 1977

Dyche, T., *A Guide to the English Tongue*, 2nd edn, London, 1710

The Echo

Edwards, G., *From Crow-Scaring to Westminster. An Autobiography*, London, 1922

Edwards, J. P., *A Few Footprints*, 2nd edn, London, 1906

Eldred, J., *I Love the Brooks*, London, 1955

Elson, G., *The Last of the Climbing Boys. An Autobiography*, London, 1900

'Emigration and Industrial Training', *Edinburgh Review*, XCII (1850)

English, R., 'The Price of the Novel, 1750–1894', *The Author*, V (1894)

Escott, T. H. S., *England: Its People, Polity, and Pursuits*, London, 1890

Fairbairn, W., *The Life of Sir William Fairbairn, Bart.*, London, 1877

Farish, W., *The Autobiography of William Farish. The Struggles of a Hand Loom Weaver. With Some of his Writings*, Privately printed, 1889

Field, E. M., *The Child and his Book*, 2nd edn, London, 1892

Fitch, J. G., *Lectures on Teaching*, Cambridge, 1881

Fleming, C. E. S., 'Quackery in Rural Districts', *British Medical Journal* (27 May 1911)

Foley, A. *A Bolton Childhood*, Manchester, 1973

Fox, W., *The Working Man's Model Family Botanic Guide*, 10th edn, Sheffield, 1884

Fripp, C. B., 'Report of an Inquiry into the Condition of the Working Classes of the City of Bristol', *Journal of the Statistical Society*, II (1839)

Frost, T., *Forty Years' Recollections, Literary and Political*, London, 1880

Gamble, R., *Chelsea Childhood*, London, 1979

Garratt, V. W., *A Man in the Street*, London, 1939

Gaskell, W., *The Lancashire Dialect Illustrated in Two Lectures*, London and Manchester, 1854

Gattie, W. M., 'What English People Read', *Fortnightly Review*, 52 (1889)

Gill, A. H., 'Made by Self Help', *Pearson's Weekly* (22 March 1906)

Gill, J., *Introductory Text-Book to School Management*, 2nd edn, London, 1857

Ginswick, J. (ed.), *Labour and the Poor in England and Wales 1849–51*, 1, London, 1983

The Golden Dreamer; Or Dreams Realised, Containing The Interpretation of a Great Variety of Dreams, Glasgow, n.d.

Gosling, H., *Up and Down Stream*, London, 1927

Gosse, E. *Father and Son*, London, 1907

Green, S. G., *The Story of the Religious Tract Society*, London, 1899

Grose, F., *A Provincial Glossary with a Collection of Local Proverbs and Popular Superstitions*, London, 1787

Grossek, M., *First movement*, London, 1937

Gunn, J., *Class Teaching and Management*, London, 1895

Gutteridge, J., *Lights and Shadows in the Life of an Artisan*, London, 1969 edn

Haggard, L. S. (ed.), *I Walked by Night, Being the Life and History of the King of the Norfolk Poachers. Written by Himself*, London, 1948

Hall, E., *Canary Girls and Stockpots*, Luton, 1975

Hall, J., *The Olde Religion*, London, 1628

Hampton, R., *Foolish Dick: An Autobiography of Richard Hampton, the Cornish Pilgrim Preacher*, ed. S. W. Christophers, London, 1873

Harland, J., *Ballads and Songs of Lancashire*, London, 1865

'Songs of the Working Classes', *Manchester Guardian* (4, 10 December 1839)

Harland, J. (ed.), *The Songs of the Wilsons*, London, 1865

Harland, J. and Wilkinson, T. T., 'An Essay on Ballads and Songs', *Trans. Hist. Soc. Lancs. and Ches.*, XI (N.S.), 1870

    Lancashire Folk-Lore, 1882

Harris, H., *Under Oars*, London, 1878

Harris, J., *My Autobiography*, London, 1882

Harrison, J. P., 'Cheap Literature – Past and Present', *Companion to the British Almanack* (1873)

Harvey, E., *A Postman's Round 1858–61*, selected and introduced by Tony Mason, Coventry, 1982

Haslam, J. H., *The Press and the People*, Manchester, 1906

Hazlitt, W. H., *Faiths and Folklore*, London, 1905

Haw, G., *From Workhouse to Westminster. The Life Story of Will Crooks, M.P.*, London, 1911

Heaton, H., 'Postal and Telegraphic Progress under Queen Victoria', *The Fortnightly Review*, CCCLXXVI (June 1897)

Heaton, W., *The Old Soldier; The Wandering Lover; and other poems; together with A Sketch of the Author's Life*, London, 1857

Henderson, A., 'From Errand Boy to M.P.', *Pearson's Weekly* (8 March 1906)

Henderson, W., *Notes on the Folk Lore of the Northern Counties of England and the Border*, London, 1866

Herbert, H., *Autobiography of Henry Herbert, a Gloucestershire Shoemaker, and Native of Fairford*, Gloucester, 1866

Heywood, A., *Three Papers on English Printed Almanacks*, 1904

[Hill, M. D.], 'Post Office Reform', *Edinburgh Review*, LXXX (1840)

    'The Post Office', *Fraser's Magazine*, LXI (1862)

Hill, R., *Post Office Reform, its Importance and Practicability*, London, 1837

    'Results of the New Postage Arrangements', *Quarterly Journal of the Statistical Society of London* (July 1841)

Hill, R., and Hill, G. B., *The Life of Sir Rowland Hill and the History of the Penny Postage*, London, 1880

Hindley, C., *Curiosities of Street Literature*, London, 1871

    The History of the Catnach Press, London, 1887

    The Life and Times of James Catnach, Ballad Monger, London, 1878

Hoare, C. J., 'The Penny Press', *The Englishman's Magazine*, N.S., V (December 1850)

Hodges, F., *My Adventures as a Labour Leader*, London, 1925

Hodgson, W. B., 'Exaggerated Estimates of Reading and Writing', *Transactions of the National Association for the Promotion of Social Science* (1867)

Hogg, T., *The Child's First Book and Sunday School Primer*, London, 1838

Holcroft, T., *Memoirs of the late Thomas Holcroft*, London, 1816

Hole, J., *An Essay on the History and Management of Literary, Scientific, & Mechanics' Institutions*, London, 1853

Hollingworth, B. (ed.), *Songs of the People*, Manchester, 1977

Holloway, J. and Black, J. (eds.), *Later English Broadside Ballads*, 2 vols., London, 1975, 1979

Holyoake, G. J., *Bygones Worth Remembering*, 2 vols., London, 1905
   Sixty Years of an Agitator's Life, 2 vols., London 1900
Hone, W., *The Every-Day Book and Table Book*, London, 1838
   The Year Book, London, 1839
Hood, T. (ed.), *Cassell's Penny Readings*, London, 1871
Hopkinson, J., *Victorian Cabinet Maker. The Memoirs of James Hopkinson 1819–1894*, ed. J. B. Goodman, London, 1968
Horler, M., *The Early Recollections of Moses Horler*, Radstock, 1900
Howell, G., 'Trade Unions, Apprentices, and Technical Education', *The Contemporary Review*, XXX (June–November 1877)
Howitt, W., *The Rural Life of England*, London, 1838
Hudson, J. W., *The History of Adult Education*, London, 1851
Hudson, W., 'How A Railway Man Succeeded', *Pearson's Weekly* (5 April 1906)
Hull, G., *The Poets and Poetry of Blackburn*, Blackburn, 1902
Humphery, G. R., 'The Reading of the Working Classes', *The Nineteenth Century*, XXXIII (1893)
Hunt, R., *Popular Romances of the West of England*, 1916
Huntingdon, W., *Memoirs of the Reverend William Huntingdon, S.S. The Coalheaver, late Minister of Providence Chapel, Gray's Inn Lane*, 2nd edn, London 1813
Hutton, C., *A Treatise on Mensuration, both in theory and practice*, Newcastle upon Tyne, 1770; 4th edn, London, 1812
Inman, P., *No Going Back. An Autobiography*, London, 1952
Innes, H., *The British Child's Spelling Book*, London, 1835
   The Rhetorical Class Book, or The Principles and Practice of Elocution, London, 1834
Ireson, A., 'Reminiscences', in J. Burnett (ed.), *Destiny Obscure*, London, 1982
Jackson, T. A., *Solo Trumpet, Some Memories of Socialist Agitation and Propaganda*, London, 1953
Jermy, L., *The Memories of a Working Woman*, London, 1934
Jerrold, D., 'The Postman' and 'The Ballad Singer', in *Heads of the People*, I, London, 1878 edn
'John Dicks', *The Bookseller* (3 March 1881)
Johnson, C. W., *The English Rural Spelling-Book*, London, 1846
Johnson, W., 'How I Got On', *Pearson's Weekly* (1 March 1906)
Jones, W., *The Jubilee Memorial of the Religious Tract Society*, London, 1850
Kay-Shuttleworth, J., *Four Periods of Public Education*, London, 1862
Keating, J., *My Struggle for Life*, London, 1916
Kenney, T., *Westering. An Autobiography*, London, 1939
Kettle, R., *Strikes and Arbitration*, London, 1866
Kiddier, W., *The Old Trade Unions from Unprinted Records of the Brushmakers*, London, 1930
Kitchen, F., *Brother to the Ox*, Horsham, 1940
Knight, C., *London*, London, 1875–7
   The Old Printer and the Modern Press, London, 1854
Kovalev, Y. V. (ed.), *Anthology of Chartist Literature*, Moscow, 1956

'The Labourers' Reading Room', *Household Words*, III (1851)

Lancaster, J., *Improvements in Education as it Respects the Industrious Classes of the Community*, London, 1803

Lang, A., 'Notes on Ballad Origins', *Folklore*, 14 (1903)

Lang, A. and 'X' A Working Man, 'The Reading Public', *Cornhill Magazine* (1901)

Lansbury, G., *My Life*, London, 1928

Laurie, J. S. *First Steps to Reading*, London, 1862
Laurie's Graduated Series of Reading Lesson Books, London, 1866

Lawson, J., *Letters to the Young on Progress in Pudsey during the Last Sixty Years*, Stanningley, 1887

Lawson, Jack, *A Man's Life*, London, 1932

Leatherland, J. A., *Essays and Poems with a brief Autobiographical Memoir*, London, 1862

Leigh, J. G., 'What Do The Masses Read?', *Economic Review* (1904)

Lewins, W., *Her Majesty's Mails*, 2 vols., London, 1865

Liardet, F., 'State of the Peasantry in the County of Kent', in Central Society of Education, *Third Publication*, London, 1839

'The Literature on the Streets', *Edinburgh Review*, CCCXXXVII (January 1887)

Lithgow, R. A. D., *The Life of John Critchley Prince*, Manchester, 1880

Livesey, J., *Autobiography of Joseph Livesey*, London, 1881

Lloyd, R., *Lloyd's Treatise on Hats*, 2nd edn, London, 1819

Lloyd's Weekly Newspaper

Love, D., *The Life and Adventures of David Love, Written by Himself*, 3rd edn, Nottingham, 1823

Lovett, W., *Life and Struggles of William Lovett*, London, 1876

Lovett, W. and Collins, J., *Chartism. A New Organisation of the People*, London, 1840

Lowery, R., *Robert Lowery, Radical and Chartist*, ed. B. Harrison and P. Hollis, London, 1979

Ludlow, J. M. and Jones, L., *The Progress of the Working Class 1832–1867*, London, 1867

McCarthy, C. H., *Chartist Recollections*, Bradford, 1883

Mackay, C., *Memoirs of Extraordinary Popular Delusions*, 3 vols., London, 1841

MacPherson, J. T., 'How I Got On', *Pearson's Weekly* (1 March 1906)

Magnus, P., *Educational Aims and Efforts 1880–1910*, London, 1910

Malcolm, J. P., *Anecdotes of the Manners and Customs of London*, 2 vols., 2nd edn, London, 1810

Mallock, W. H., *Studies of Contemporary Superstition*, London, 1895

Manchester Statistical Society, 'Report on the Condition of the Working Class in the Town of Kingston-upon-Hull', *Journal of the Statistical Society*, V (1842)
'Report on the State of Education among the Working Classes in the Parish of West Bromwich', *Journal of the Statistical Society*, II (1839)

Mandeville, B., *The Fable of the Bees*, ed. F. B. Kaye, Oxford, 1966 edn

Manual of the System of Primary Instruction Pursued in the Model Schools of the British and Foreign Schools Society, London, 1831

Manual of the System of teaching Reading. Writing, Arithmetick, and Needle-Work in the Elementary-Schools of the British and Foreign Schools Society, London, 1816

Markham, W., *An Introduction to Spelling and Reading English*, 5th edn, London, 1738

Martin, J. E., 'Statistics of an Agricultural Parish in Bedfordshire', *Journal of the Statistical Society*, VI (1843)

Marx, K., *Capital*, Everyman edn, London, 1933

Mayhew, H., *London Labour and the London Poor*, London, 1861

Mayne, F., 'The Literature of the Working Classes', *The Englishwoman's Magazine*, New Series, V (October 1850)

'Mazzini and the Ethics of Politicans', *Westminster Review*, LXXXII (September 1844)

Mazzini, J., *Life and Writings of Joseph Mazzini*, 3 vols., London, 1891

Meek, G., *George Meek. Bath Chair-Man. By Himself*, London, 1910

Milner, G., 'Introductory Essay on the Dialect of Lancashire Considered as a Vehicle for Poetry', in E. Waugh, *Poems and Songs*, ed. G. Milner, Manchester, 1893

Mitchell, G., 'Autobiography and Reminiscences' in S. Price (ed.), *The Skeleton at the Plough*, London, 1874

The Monthly Magazine of Fiction

Mother Bunch's Golden Fortune-Teller, Newcastle upon Tyne, n.d.

Murphy, J. T., *New Horizons*, London, 1941

Myles, J. (ed.), *Chapters in the Life of a Dundee Factory Boy. An Autobiography*, Dundee, 1850

Napoleon's Book of Fate, London and Otley, William Walker, n.d.

National Association for the Promotion of Social Science, *Trades' Societies and Strikes*, London, 1860

Neale, W. B., *Juvenile Delinquency in Manchester*, Manchester, 1840

Neve, R., *The City and County Purchaser, and Builder's Dictionary*, 2nd edn, London, 1726

'New and Cheap Forms of Popular Literature', *The Eclectic Review*, N.S., XVIII (July 1845)

Newbolt, W. C. E., *Apostles of the Lord*, London, 1901

News of the World

Nicholson, J., *Poems by John Nicholson, The Airedale Poet with a Sketch of his Life and Writings by John James FSA*, Bingley, 1878

Nicholson, P., *The Carpenter's New Guide: Being a Complete Book of Lines for Carpenting and Joinery*, 3rd edn, London, 1801

The Northern Star

Okey, T., *A Basketful of Memories. An Autobiographical Sketch*, London, 1930

Oliver, T., *Autobiography of a Cornish Miner*, Camborne, 1914

Operative Society of Masons, *Fortnightly Returns*

   Revised Black List from September, 1834, to April 1853, Containing the Names of those Who Have Not Paid the Fine for Supplanting our Members During the Strike at the New Houses of Parliament, London, and at other Places, 1853

'Our Schools and Schoolmasters', *Quarterly Review*, 147 (1879)

Pain, W., *The Builder's Companion and Workman's General Assistant*, London, 1758

    The Carpenter's and Joiner's Repository, London, 1778

    The Practical Builder, London, 1774

    The Practical House Carpenter; or, Youth's Instructor, London, 1794

Parker, J., 'On the Literature of the Working Classes', in Viscount Ingestre (ed.), *Meliora, or Better Things to Come*, London, 1853

Parkinson, G., *True Stories of Durham Pit-Life*, London, 1912

Paton, J., *Proletarian Pilgrimage*, London, 1935

Peacock, M., 'The Folklore of Lincolnshire', *Folklore*, XII (1901)

Pearson's Weekly

'Penny Fiction', *Quarterly Review*, 171 (1890)

Place, F., *The Autobiography of Francis Place*, ed. Mary Thale, Cambridge, 1972

    'The Taxes on Knowledge' in J. A. Roebuck (ed.), *Pamphlets for the People*, vol. 1, London, 1835

'The Poetry of Seven Dials', *Quarterly Review* (1867)

The Poor Man's Guardian

'Popular Literature', *British and Foreign Review*, X (1840)

'Popular Superstitions', *Working Man's Friend*, VI (1851)

Porter, G. R., *The Progress of the Nation*, new edn, rev. F. W. Hirst, London, 1912

'The Post Office', *Fraser's Magazine*, XLI (February 1850)

Postal History

Powell, J. H. *Life Incidents and Poetic Pictures*, London, 1865

'The Present Taste for Cheap Literature', *The Bee* (16 March 1833)

Prest, T. P., *The Death Grasp; or, A Father's Curse*, London, 1844

    Evelina, the Pauper's Child; or, Poverty, Crime, and Sorrow. A Romance of Deep Pathos, London, 1851

Preston, T., *The Life and Opinions of Thomas Preston*, London, 1817

Ramsbottom, J., 'Writing in the Dialect', *Country Words* (15 December 1866)

Rawson, R., 'An Enquiry into the Condition of Criminal Offenders in England and Wales, with respect to Education', *Journal of the Statistical Society of London*, IV (1841)

Reach, A. B., 'The Coffee Houses of London', *New Parley Library*, II (13 July 1844)

Redding, C., *Yesterday and Today*, 3 vols., London, 1863

Repplier, A., 'English Railway Fiction', in *Points of View*, Boston, 1891

Reynolds' Weekly Newspaper

Richards, W. F., *Manual of Method for the Use of Teachers in Elementary Schools*, London, 1854

Roberts, R., *The Classic Slum*, Harmondsworth, 1973

Roebuck, J. A., 'On the Means of Conveying Information to the People' and 'Persecution of the Unstamped Press', in J. A. Roebuck (ed.), *Pamphlets for the People*, vol. I, London, 1835

Ross, J. W., 'The Influence of Cheap Literature', *London Journal*, I (1847)

Rounsfell, J. W., *On the Road, Journeys of a Tramping Printer*, ed. A. Whitehead,

Horsham, 1982
Routledge, J., *Chapters in the History of Popular Progress*, London, 1876
Rowe, R., *How Our Working People Live*, London, 1882
Rowntree, B. S. (ed.), *Betting and Gambling*, London, 1905
   Poverty, A Study of Town Life, London, 1903
Rushton, A., *My Life as a Farmer's Boy, Factory Lad, Teacher and Preacher*,
   Manchester, 1909
Rymer, E. A., 'The Martyrdom of the Mine', *History Workshop Journal*, 1, 2
   (Spring, Autumn, 1976)
Rymer, J. M., 'Popular Writing', *The Queens' Magazine* (June 1842)
Sadler, M. E. and Edwards, J. W., 'Public Elementary Education in England and
   Wales 1870–1895', in Education Department, *Special Reports on Educational
   Subjects 1896–7*, London, 1897
St John, J. A., *The Education of the People*, London, 1858
Sala, G. A., *The Life and Adventures of George Augustus Sala, written by himself*,
   London, 1895
Salmon, E. G., 'What the Working Classes Read', *Nineteenth Century*, XX (1886)
Sanger, G., *Seventy Years a Showman*, London, 1926
Saunders, J., *The Reflections and Rhymes of an Old Miller*, London, 1938
Scott-James, R. A., *The Influence of the Press*, London, 1913
'Sensation Novels', *Quarterly Review*, 113 (1863)
Sexton, J., *Sir James Sexton, Agitator*, London, 1936
Shackleton, D. J., 'Unemployment Brought Success', *Pearson's Weekly* (15 March
   1906)
Sharp, C. J., *English Folk Song, Some Conclusions*, 4th edn, Wakefield, 1964
Shaw, C., *When I Was A Child*, London, 1903
Shaw, S., *Guttersnipe*, London, 1846
Shuckburgh, R. S. (ed.), *The ABC Both in Latyn & English*, London, 1889
Sketches of Obscure Poets, London, 1833
Smith, C. M., *Curiosities of London Life*, London, 1853
   'The Press of the Seven Dials', in *The Little World of London*, London, 1857
   The Working Man's Way in the World, London, 1857
Snell, H., *Men, Movements, and Myself*, London, 1936
Southgate, W., *That's the Way it Was*, London, 1982
Spencer, F. H., *An Inspector's Testament*, London, 1938
Staffordshire Potteries Board of Arbitration, *Minutes of Evidence Taken and
   Award of Arbitration Held at the Queen's Hotel, Hanley. 9th and 10th January,
   1877, before J. E. Davis Esq. (Umpire), On Notice Given by Employers of a
   Ten Per Cent Reduction in Workmen's Prices*, 1877
   Award of Thomas Brassey, M.P., 1880
   *Appeal of Workmen for an increase of Ten per cent and Appeal of Manufacturers
   for a reduction of Ten per cent in wages. Evidence and Award. Umpire, H. T.
   Hinckes, Esq., M.P.*, 1891
Stamper, J., *So Long Ago . . .*, London, 1960
Stead, W. T., 'The Labour Party and the Books that Helped to Make it', *Review of
   Reviews*, XXXIII (1906)

Steadman, W. C., 'How I Got On', *Pearson's Weekly* (8 February 1906)

Stevens, E. T. and Hole, Rev. C., *The Grade Lesson Books in Six Standards Especially adapted to meet the Requirements of the New Code*, London, 1871

Story, R., *The Poetical Works of Robert Story*, London, 1857

'Street Ballads', *The National Review*, XXVI (July 1861)

Sturt, G., *A Small Boy in the Sixties*, Cambridge, 1932

    The Wheelwright's Shop, Cambridge, 1963

Summerbell, T., 'From Barber's Shop to Parliament', *Pearson's Weekly* (22 March 1906)

Sykes, J., *Slawit in the 'Sixties: Reminiscences of the Moral, Social and Industrial Life of Slaithwaite and District in and about the year 1860*, Huddersfield, 1926

Talbot, J., *The Christian School-Master*, new edn, London, 1811

The Taylor's Complete Guide . . . The Whole Concerted and Devised By a Society of Adepts in the Profession, London, 1796

Taylor, A. D., 'Hodge and his Parson', *The Nineteenth Century*, XXXI (March 1892)

Taylor, J. H., 'The Practice of Medicine and Surgery by Unqualified Persons', *British Medical Journal* (27 May 1911)

Thompson, F., *Lark Rise to Candleford*, Harmondsworth, 1982 edn

Thoms, W., 'Folk-Lore', *The Athenaeum*, 982 (22 August 1846)

Thomson, C., *The Auotbiography of an Artisan*, London, 1847

Thorne, W., *My Life's Battles*, London, 1925

Tilke, S. W., *An Autobiographical Memoir*, London, 1840

The Times

Tinsley, W., *Random Recollections of an Old Publisher*, 2 vols., London, 1900

Tomlinson, C., *Cyclopaedia of the Useful Arts*, London, 1854

Tredgold, T., *Elementary Principles of Carpentry*, London, 1820

Tremewan, T., *Cornish Youth. Memories of a Perran Boy (1895–1910)*, Truro, 1968

Trimmer, S., *The Charity School Spelling Book*, 9th edn, London, 1805

    The Oeconomy of Charity, London, 1801

Turner, B., *About Myself*, London, 1930

Union Postale Universelle, *Statistique générale du Service Postale, Année 1890*, Berne, 1892

    Statistique générale du Service Postale, Année 1900, Berne, 1902

'Unqualified Practice Through the Post', *British Medical Journal* (27 May 1911)

Vasey, G., *The Excelsior Reading Made Easy, or Child's First Book*, London, 1855

Vaux, J. E., *Church Folklore*, London, 1894

Waite, A. B., 'By-ways of Periodical Literature', *Walford's Antiquarian*, XXII (1887)

Wallis, T. W., *Autobiography of Thomas Wilkinson Wallis*, London, 1899

Ward, J., 'The Rise of a Ploughboy', *Pearson's Weekly* (15 March 1906)

Wardle, G. J., 'How I Got On', *Pearson's Weekly* (22 February 1906)

Waugh, E., *Home-Life of the Lancashire Factory Folk During the Cotton Famine*, London, 1867

Weale, J., *Catalogue of Books on Architecture and Engineering, Civil, Mechanical, Military, and Naval, New and Old*, London, 1854

Webb, S. and B., *Industrial Democracy*, London, 1902

Weekly Dispatch

Weld, C. R., 'On the Condition of the Working Classes in the Inner Ward of St. George's Parish, Hanover Square', *Journal of the Statistical Society*, VI (1843)

   'On the Popular Penny Literature of the Day', *The Athenaeum*, 643 (1840)

Whittaker, T., *Life's Battles in Temperance Armour*, London, 1884

Whittock, R., *The Complete Book of Trades*, London, 1837

Wilderspin, S., *A System for the Education of the Young*, London, 1840

Wilkinson, T. T., 'On the Popular Customs and Superstitions of Lancashire', *Trans. Hist. Soc., Lancs. and Ches.*, XI (1858–9)

Williams, A., *Life in a Railway Factory*, London, 1915

Wilson, J. 'An Act that Changed a Life', *Pearson's Weekly* (12 April 1906)

Wood, J., *Autobiography of John Wood, an old and well known Bradfordian, Written in the 75th Year of his Age*, Bradford, 1877

Wright, T., *The Great Unwashed*, London, 1868

   Habits and Customs of the Working Classes, London, 1867

   'On a Possible Popular Culture', *Contemporary Review*, 40 (1881)

   'Working Class Education and mis-Education' and 'The Press and the People', in *Our New Masters*, London, 1873

Wroot, H. E., 'A Pioneer in Cheap Literature. William Milner of Halifax', *The Bookman*, 66 (1897)

Wynter, A., *Our Social Bees*, London, 1861

   Peeps into the Human Hive, London, 1874

Younger, J., *Autobiography of John Younger, Shoemaker. St. Boswells*, Kelso, 1881

v Secondary sources

Allen, D. E., *The Naturalist in Britain*, London, 1976

Allen, V. L., 'The Origins of Industrial Conciliation and Arbitration', *International Review of Social History*, IX, pt 2 (1964)

Alliston, N., 'Pictorial Post Cards', *Chambers Journal* (October 1899)

Altick, R. D., *The English Common Reader*, Chicago, 1957

   'The Sociology of Authorship', *Bulletin of the New York Public Library*, 66 (1962)

Anderson, M., *Family Structure in Nineteenth Century Lancashire*, Cambridge, 1971

Anderson, O., 'The Incidence of Civil Marriage in Victorian England and Wales', *Past and Present*, 69 (November 1975)

Anderson, R. D., *Education and Opportunity in Victorian Scotland*, Oxford, 1983

   Education in France 1848–1870, Oxford, 1975

Armstrong, W. A., 'Social Structure from the Early Census Returns', in E. A. Wrigley (ed.), *An Introduction to English Historical Demography*, London, 1966

Armytage, W. H. J., *A. J. Mundella 1825–1897*, London, 1951

Asquith, I., 'The Structure, Ownership and Control of the Press 1780–1855', in Boyce *et al.*, *Newspaper History*

Austen, B., *English Provincial Posts 1633–1840*, London, 1978

Bailey, P., *Leisure and Class in Victorian England*, London, 1978

Baker, W. P., 'Parish Registers and Literacy in East Yorkshire', *East Yorks Local History Society* (1961)

Bantock, G. H., *Industrialisation and Education*, London, 1968

Barrow, L., *Independent Spirits*, London, 1986

Baumann, G. (ed.), *The Written Word*, Oxford, 1986

Bee, H., *The Developing Child*, 3rd edn, New York, 1981

Behagg, C., 'Secrecy, Ritual and Folk Violence: The Opacity of the Workplace in the First Half of the Nineteenth Century', in R. E. Storch (ed.), *Popular Culture and Custom in Nineteenth Century England*, London, 1982

Bennett, T., *Popular Culture: Themes and Issues*, Milton Keynes, 1981

Bennett, T., Martin, G., Mercer, C. and Woollacott, J. (eds.), *Culture, Ideology and Social Process*, London, 1981

Berridge, V., 'Popular Sunday Papers and Mid-Victorian Society', in Boyce *et al.*, *Newspaper History*

Blagden, C., 'Thomas Carman and the Almanack Monopoly', *Studies in Bibliography*, XIV (1961)

Bowley, M., *The British Building Industry*, Cambridge, 1966

Bowman, M. J. and Anderson, C. A., 'Concerning the Role of Education in Development', in C. Geertz (ed.), *Old Societies and new States*, New York, 1963

Boyce, G., Curran, J. and Wingate, P. (eds.), *Newspaper History from the Seventeenth Century to the Present Day*, London, 1978

Bratton, J. S., *Victorian Popular Ballads*, London, 1975

Braverman, H., *Labor and Monopoly Capital*, New York, 1974

Brewer, J., *Party Ideology and Popular Politics at the Accession of George III*, Cambridge 1976

Brooks, J., *When Russia Learned to Read*, Princeton, 1985

Brown, L., *Victorian News and Newspapers*, Oxford, 1985

Brown, P. S., 'Medicines Advertised in Eighteenth-Century Bath Newspapers', *Medical History*, 20 (1976)

Buchan, D., *The Ballad and the Folk*, London, 1972

Buckley, J. H., *The Triumph of Time*, London, 1967

Buday, G., *The History of the Christmas Card*, London, 1964

Budd, S., *Varieties of Unbelief*, London, 1977

Bullock, A., *A Language for Life*, London, 1975

Burchill, F., and Ross, R., *A History of the Potters' Union*, Hanley, 1977

Burgess, K., *The Origins of British Industrial Relations*, London, 1975

Burke, P., *Popular Culture in Early Modern Europe*, London, 1978

Burke, P. and Porter, R. (eds.), *The Social History of Language*, Cambridge, 1987

Burnett, J., Vincent, D. and Mayall, D., *The Autobiography of the Working Class, Vol. I, 1790–1900*, Brighton, 1984

Bushaway, B., *By Rite. Custom, Ceremony and Community in England 1700–1880*,

London, 1982

Calhoun, C., *The Intelligence of a People*, Princeton, 1973

Camp, J., *Magic, Myth and Medicine*, London, 1973

Capp, B., *Astrology and the Popular Press. English Almanacks 1500–1800*, London, 1979

Cartwright, F. F., *A Social History of Medicine*, London, 1977

Chadwick, O., *The Victorian Church*, 2 vols., London, 1970

Chancellor, V. E., *History for their Masters*, Bath, 1970

Chartier, R., 'Culture as Appropriation: Popular Cultural Uses in Early Modern France', in S. L. Kaplan (ed.), *Understanding Popular Culture*, Berlin, 1984

Cipolla, C. M., *Literacy and Development in the West*, Harmondsworth, 1969

Clair, C., *A History of Printing in Britain*, 1965

Clanchy, M. T., *From Memory to Written Record*, London, 1979

Cliff, P. B., *The Rise and Development of the Sunday School Movement in England 1780–1980*, Redhill, 1986

Clinton, A., *Post Office Workers*, London, 1984

Cohen, M., *Sensible Words. Linguistic Practice in England 1640–1785*, Baltimore, 1977

Cole, M. and Scribner, S., 'Culture, Learning and Memory', in M. Cole and S. Scribner (eds.), *Culture and Thought*, New York, 1974

Collison, R., *The Story of Street Literature*, London, 1973

Colls, R., ' "Oh Happy English Children": Coal, Class and Education in the North-East', *Past and Present*, 73 (1976)

Coltham, S., 'The *Bee-hive* Newspaper: Its Origin and Early Struggles', in A. Briggs and J. Saville (eds.), *Essays in Labour History*, London, 1967

Cook-Gumpertz, J. and Cook-Gumpertz, J. J., 'From Oral to Written Culture: The Transition to Literacy', in M. F. Whiteman (ed.), *Writing*, New Jersey, 1981, vol. I

Cooter, R., 'Interpreting the Fringe', *The Society for the Social History of Medicine Bulletin*, 29 (1981)

Corrigan, P., and Sayer, D., *The Great Arch*, Oxford, 1985

Cotgrove, S., *Technical Education and Social Change*, London, 1958

Cranfield, G. A., *The Development of the Provincial Newspaper 1700–1760*, Oxford, 1962

Cremer, W. H., *St. Valentine's Day and Valentines*, London, 1971

Cressy, D., *Literacy and the Social Order*, Cambridge, 1980

Critcher, C., 'Sociology, Cultural Studies and the Post-War Working Class', in J. Clarke, C. Critcher and R. Johnson (eds.), *Working Class Culture*, London, 1979

Cross, N., *The Common Writer. Life in Nineteenth-Century Grub Street*, Cambridge, 1985

Crossick, G., 'The Emergence of the Lower Middle Class in Britain: A Discussion', in G. Crossick (ed.), *The Lower Middle Class in Britain*, London, 1977

Cruikshank, M. J., 'From Mechanics' Institution to Technical School 1850–92', in D. S. L. Cardwell (ed.), *Artisan to Graduate*, Manchester, 1974

Curran, J., 'Capitalism and Control of the Press 1800–1975', in J. Curran, M.

Gurevitch and J. Woollacott (eds), *Mass Communication and Society*, London, 1977
'The Press as an Agency of Social Control: an Historical Perspective', in Boyce *et al.*, *Newspaper History*
Daunton, M. J., *Royal Mail*, London, 1985
Davies, S., *A History of Macclesfield*, 1961
Davis, N. Z., *Society and Culture in Early Modern France*, London, 1975
Deacon, G., *John Clare and the Folk Tradition*, London, 1983
Demos, J. N., *Entertaining Satan*, Oxford, 1982
Denning, M., *Mechanic Accents. Dime Novels and Working-Class Culture in America*, London, 1987
Devlin, J., *The Superstitious Mind. French Peasants and the Supernatural in the Nineteenth Century*, New Haven, 1987
Digby, A., and Searby, P., *Children, School and Society in Nineteenth-Century England*, London, 1981
Dobson, C. R., *Masters and Journeymen*, London, 1980
Dodd, P., 'Englishness and the National Culture', in R. Colls and P. Dodd (eds.), *Englishness. Politics and Culture 1880–1920*, London, 1986
Dorson, R. M., *The British Folklorists*, London, 1968
Dunning, T., 'Reminiscences of Thomas Dunning', in D. Vincent (ed.). *Testaments of Radicalism* (London, 1977)
Dunkerley, D., *The Foreman*, London, 1975
Eisenstein, E. L., *The Printing Press as an Agent of Change*, Cambridge, 1980
Elbourne, R., *Music and Tradition in Early Industrial Lancashire 1780–1840*, Woodbridge, 1980
Ellis, A., *Books in Victorian Elementary Schools*, London, 1971
Educating Our Masters, Aldershot, 1985
A History of Children's Reading and Literature, Oxford, 1968
Epstein, J. A. 'Feargus O'Connor and the Northern Star', *International Review of Social History* (1976)
Evans-Pritchard, E. E. 'The Morphology and Function of Magic', in J. Middleton (ed.), *Magic, Witchcraft and Curing*, New York, 1967
Finnegan, R., *Oral Poetry. Its Nature, Significance and Social Content*, Cambridge, 1977
The Oral Tradition, Cambridge, 1977
Fisher, C., *Custom, Work and Market Capitalism*, London, 1981
Flanders, A., *Industrial Relations*, London, 1965
Flinn, M. W., 'Medical Services under the New Poor Law', in D. Fraser (ed.), *The New Poor Law in the Nineteenth Century*, London, 1976
Flora, P., 'Historical Processes of Social Mobilisation: Urbanisation and Literacy 1850–1965', in S. N. Eisenstadt and S. Rokhan (eds.), *Building States and Nations*, Beverly Hills, 1973
Fox, A., *History and Heritage*, London, 1985
Fox Bourne, H. R., *English Newspapers*, New York, 1966
Friere, P., *Cultural Action for Freedom*, Harmondsworth, 1972
The Pedagogy of the Oppressed, Harmondsworth, 1972

Furet, F. and Ozouf, J., *Reading and Writing: Literacy in France from Calvin to Jules Ferry*, Cambridge, 1982

Fyson, R., 'The Crisis of 1842: Chartism, the Colliers' Strike and the Outbreak in the Potteries', in J. Epstein and D. Thompson (eds.), *The Chartist Experience*, London, 1982

Galenson, D. W., 'Literacy and Age in Pre-industrial England: Quantitative Evidence and Implications', *Economic Development and Cultural Change*, 29, no. 4 (July 1981)

Gardner, P., *The Lost Elementary Schools of Victorian England*, London, 1985

Garside, W. R. and Gospel, H. F., 'Employers and Managers: Their Organisational Structure and Changing Industrial Strategies', in Wrigley, *Industrial Relations*

Geary, D., 'Working Class Culture in Imperial Germany', in R. Fletcher (ed.), *Bernstein to Brandt*, London, 1987

Geertz, C., 'Thick Description: Toward an Interpretative Theory of Culture', in C. Geertz (ed.), *The Interpretation of Cultures*, London, 1975

Gilding, B., *The Journeyman Coopers of East London*, Oxford, 1971

Gillis, J. R., *Youth in History*, New York, 1974

Glasgow, E., 'The Establishment of the *Northern Star* Newspaper', *History*, XXXIX (1954)

Golby, J. M. and Purdue, A. W., *The Civilisation of the Crowd*, London, 1984

Goldstrom, J. M., *The Social Content of Education, 1808–1870*, Shannon, 1972

Goodwin, A., *The Friends of Liberty*, London, 1979

Goody, J., *The Domestication of the Savage Mind*, Cambridge, 1977

Goody, J. and Watt, I., 'The Consequences of Literacy', in J. Goody (ed.), *Literacy in Traditional Societies*, Cambridge, 1968

Gore, V., 'Rank and File Dissent', in Wrigley, *Industrial Relations*

Gosden, P. H. J. H., *Self Help*, London, 1973

Graff, H. J., *The Legacies of Literacy*, Bloomington, 1987
  The Literacy Myth, London, 1979

Graff, H. J. (ed.), *Literacy and Social Development in the West: A Reader*, Cambridge, 1981

Grainger, M., *John Clare: Collector of Ballads*, Peterborough, 1964

Gramsci, A., *Selections from the Prison Notebooks of Antonio Gramsci*, ed. and trans. Q. Hoare and G. Nowell Smith, London, 1971

Gray, W. S., *The Teaching of Reading and Writing*, Paris and London, 1956

Grayson, J., 'Literacy, Schooling and Industrialisation: Worcestershire, 1760–1850', in W. B. Stephens (ed.), *Studies in the History of Literacy: England and North America*, Leeds, 1983

Green, D., *Great Cobbett. The Noblest Agitator*, Oxford, 1985

Greenslade, M. W., and Stuart, D. G., *A History of Staffordshire*, 2nd edn, Chichester, 1984

Hackwood, F., *William Hone. His Life and Times*, London, 1912

Haggar, R. G., 'Pottery', in M. W. Greenslade and J. G. Jenkins (eds.), *A History of the County of Stafford*, II, Oxford, 1967

Haig, A., *The Victorian Clergy*, London, 1984

Haining, P., *The Penny Dreadful*, London, 1975

Hamer, D. A., *The Politics of Electoral Pressure*, Hassocks, 1977

Hand, W., 'The Folk Healer; Calling and Endowment', *Journal of the History of Medicine*, XXVI (1971)

Hanham, H. J., *Elections and Party Management*, London, 1959

Hall, S., 'Culture and the State', in *The State and Popular Culture*, Milton Keynes, 1982

Harris, M., 'Astrology, Almanacks and Booksellers', *Publishing History*, VIII (1980)

Harrison, J. F. C., *Learning and Living*, London, 1961
    The Second Coming, London, 1979

Harrison, R., Woolven, G. B. and Duncan, R., *The Warwick Guide to British Labour Periodicals*, Hassocks, 1977

Harrison, R., and Zeitlin, J. (eds.), *Divisions of Labour*, Brighton, 1985

Harrop, S. A., 'Literacy and Educational Attitudes as Factors in the Industrialisation of North-East Cheshire, 1760–1830', in W. B. Stephens (ed.), *Studies in the History of Literacy: England and North America*, Leeds, 1983

Hartley, V. A., 'Literacy at Northampton 1761–1900', *Northamptonshire Past and Present*, 4 (1966)

Harvey Darton, F. J., *Children's Books in England*, 3rd edn, Cambridge, 1982

Henderson, W., *Victorian Street Ballads*, London, 1937

Hicks, J. R., 'The Early History of Industrial Conciliation in England', *Economica*, X (1930)

Hobsbawm, E. J., 'Customs, Wages and Work-Load' and 'The Tramping Artisan', in *Labouring Men*, London, 1968

Hobsbawm, E. J., and Ranger, T. (eds.), *The Invention of Tradition*, Cambridge, 1984

Hobsbawm, E. J. and Rudé, G., *Captain Swing*, Harmondsworth, 1973

Hodgkinson, R. G., *The Origins of the National Health Service*, London, 1967

Hoggart, R., *The Uses of Literacy*, Harmondsworth, 1958

Hole, C., *Witchcraft in England*, London, 1945

Hollis, P., *The Pauper Press*, Oxford, 1970

Holton, R. J., 'Daily Herald v. Daily Citizen, 1912–15', *International Review of Social History* (1974)

Hopkin, D., 'The Socialist Press in Britain, 1890–1910', in Boyce *et al.*, *Newspaper History*

Houston, R. A., 'The Development of Literacy: Northern England, 1640–1750', *Economic History Review*, 35, no. 2 (1982)
    'Literacy and Society in the West 1500–1850', *Social History*, 8, no. 3 (1983)
    Scottish Literacy and the Scottish Identity, Cambridge, 1985

Howell, D., *British Workers and the Independent Labour Party 1888–1906*, Manchester, 1983

Hudson, D., *Munby, Man of Two Worlds*, London, 1972

Hudson, K., *Working to Rule*, Bath, 1970

Humphries, S., *Hooligans or Rebels?*, Oxford, 1981

Hunt, E. H., *British Labour History 1815–1914*, London, 1981

348   *Bibliography*

Hunter, C. St. J. and Hunter, D., *Adult Illiteracy in the United States*, New York, 1979

Hurt, J. S., *Bringing Literacy to Rural England: The Hertfordshire Case*, Chichester, 1972

   Elementary Schooling and the Working Classes 1860–1918, London, 1979

Inkeles, A. and Smith, D. H., *Becoming Modern*, London, 1974

Irwin, R., 'The English Domestic Library in the Nineteenth Century', *The Library Association Record* (1954)

Jahoda, G., *The Psychology of Superstition*, London, 1969

James, L., *Fiction for the Working Man*, Harmondsworth, 1974

   Print and the People 1819–1851, Harmondsworth, 1978

Johansson, E., 'The History of Literacy in Sweden, in comparison with some other countries', *Educational Reports, Umea*, 12 (1977)

Johnson, P., *Saving and Spending*, Oxford, 1985

Jones, A. H. and Charnley, H. A., *Adult Literacy*, London, 1980

Jones, M. G., *The Charity School Movement*, Cambridge, 1938

Joyce, P., *Society Signified. Popular Conceptions of the Social Order*, forthcoming

Joyce, P. (ed.), *The Historical Meanings of Work*, Cambridge, 1987

Judt, T., 'The Impact of the Schools, Provence 1871–1914', in Graff, *Literacy and Social Development*

Kelly, T., *A History of Public Libraries in Great Britain 1845–1965*, London, 1973

Landes, D. S., *Revolution in Time*, Cambridge, Mass., 1983

Lane, J. 'The Provincial Practitioner and his Services to the Poor, 1750–1800', *The Society for the Social History of Medicine, Bulletin*, 28 (June 1981)

Laqueur, T., 'The Cultural Origins of Popular Literacy in England, 1500–1800', *Oxford Review of Education*, 11, no. 3 (1976)

   'Literacy and Social Mobility in the Industrial Revolution', *Past and Present*, 64 (1974)

   Religion and Respectability. Sunday Schools and Working Class Culture, New Haven, 1976

   'Working Class Demand and the Growth of English Elementary Education 1750–1850', in L. Stone (ed.), *Schooling and Society*, Baltimore, 1976

Larner, C., *Witchcraft and Religion. The Politics of Popular Belief*, Oxford, 1984

Learner, D., *The Passing of Traditional Society*, Glencoe, 1958

Lee, A. J., *The Origins of the Popular Press in England 1855–1914*, London, 1976

   'The Radical Press', in A. J. A. Morris (ed.), *Edwardian Radicalism 1900–1914*, London, 1979

   'The Structure, Ownership and Control of the Press, 1855–1914', in Boyce *et al.*, *Newspaper History*

Leith, D., *A Social History of English*, London, 1983

Levine, D., 'Education and Family Life in Early Industrial England', *Journal of Family History*, 4, no. 4 (Winter 1979)

Levine, K., *The Social Context of Literacy*, London, 1986

Levy, C., 'Education and Self-Education: Staffing the Early ILP', in C. Levy (ed.), *Socialism and the Intelligentsia 1880–1914*, London, 1987

Littler, C. R., *The Development of the Labour Process in Capitalist Societies*,

London, 1982

Lloyd, A. L., *Folk Song in England*, London, 1975

Lockridge, K. A., *Literacy in Colonial New England*, New York, 1974

Loudon, I. S., *Medical Care and the General Practitioner. 1750–1850*, Oxford 1986

Lowther Clark, W. K., *A History of the S.P.C.K.*, London, 1959

Luria, A. R., *Cognitive Development. Its Cultural and Social Foundations*, Cambridge, Mass., 1976

McCann, P. (ed.), *Popular Education and Socialisation in the Nineteenth Century*, London, 1977

McClelland, D. C., 'Does Education Accelerate Economic Growth?', *Economic Development and Cultural Change*, XIV, no. 3 (1966)

McClelland, K., 'Time to Work, Time to Live: Some Aspects of Work and the Reformation of Class in Britain, 1850–1880', in Joyce, *Historical Meanings of Work*

McClelland, K. and Reid, A., 'Wood, Iron and Steel: Technology, Labour and Trade Union Organisation in the Shipbuilding Industry, 1840–1914', in Harrison and Zeitlin, *Divisions of Labour*

McCord, N., *The Anti-Corn Law League 1838–1846*, London, 1958

McKendrick, N., 'Josiah Wedgwood and Factory Discipline', *Historical Journal*, IV, no. 1 (1961)

McKenna, F., *The Railway Workers 1840–1970*, London, 1980

McKenzie, D. F., 'The Sociology of a Text: Oral Culture, Literacy and Print in Early New Zealand', in Burke and Porter, *Social History of Language*

McKibbin, R., 'Why was there no Marxism in Great Britain?', *English Historical Review*, XCIX (April 1984)

'Working-Class Gambling in Britain 1880–1939', *Past and Present*, 82 (1979)

McLeod, H., *Religion and the Working Class in Nineteenth-Century Britain*, London, 1984

McLuhan, M., *The Gutenberg Galaxy*, London, 1962

Madoc-Jones, B., 'Patterns of Attendance and their Social Significance', in McCann, *Popular Education*

Maidment, B. E., 'Class and Cultural Production in the Industrial City' in A. J. Kidd and K. W. Roberts (eds.), *City, Class and Culture*, Manchester, 1985

'Essayists and Artisans – The Making of Victorian Self-Taught Poets', *Literature and History*, IX (Spring 1983)

The Poorhouse Fugitives, Manchester, 1987

Malcolmson, R. W., *Popular Recreation in English Society 1700–1850*, Cambridge 1973

Marcham, A. J., 'The Revised Code of Education 1862: Reinterpretations and Misinterpretations', *History of Education*, 10, no. 2 (1981)

Martin, B., *A Sociology of Contemporary Cultural Change*, Oxford, 1981

Martin, D. E., ' "The Instruments of the People"?: The Parliamentary Labour Party in 1906', in D. E. Martin and D. Rubinstein (eds.), *Ideology and the Labour Movement*, London, 1979

Mason, T., *Association Football and English Society 1863–1915*, Brighton, 1980

Mather, F. C., *Public Order in the Age of the Chartists*, London, 1959

Matthews, M. M., *Teaching to Read, Historically Considered*, Chicago, 1966

Meller, H. E., *Leisure and the Changing City, 1870–1914*, London, 1976

Melling, J., ' "Non-Commissioned Officers": British Employers and their Supervisory Workers, 1880–1920', *Social History*, 5, no. 2 (May 1980)

Mitchell, B. R., *Abstract of European Historical Statistics*, 2nd edn, London, 1981

Mitchell, B. R. and Deane, P., *Abstract of British Historical Statistics*, Cambridge, 1971

Moore, R., *Pit-Men, Preachers and Politics*, Cambridge, 1974

More, C., *Skill and the English Working Class, 1870–1914*, London, 1980

Morgan, D. H., 'The Place of Harvesters in Nineteenth-Century Village Life', in R. Samuel (ed.), *Village Life and Labour*, London, 1975

Muir, W., *Living with Ballads*, London, 1965

Muller, W. D., *The 'Kept Men'?*, Hassocks, 1977

Musgrave, P. W., 'The Definition of Technical Education: 1860–1910', *The Vocational Aspect*, 34 (1964)

Technical Change, the Labour Force and Education, Oxford, 1967

Neuburg, V. E., 'The Literature of the Streets', in H. J. Dyos and M. Wolff (eds.), *The Victorian City*, London, 1973, vol. I

Popular Literature. A History and Guide, London, 1977

The Reading of the Victorian Freethinkers, London, 1973

Obelkevich, J., 'Proverbs and Social History', in Burke and Porter, *Social History of Language*

Religion and Rural Society, Oxford, 1976

O'Brien, P., 'Transport and Economic Development in Europe, 1789–1914', in P. O'Brien (ed.), *Railways and the Economic Development of Western Europe, 1830–1914*, London, 1983

O'Dea, W. T., *The Social History of Lighting*, London, 1958

Olson, D. R., Torrance, N. and Hildyard, A., *Literacy, Language, and Learning*, Cambridge, 1985

Ong, W. J., *Orality and Literacy*, London, 1982

Oxenham, J., *Literacy. Writing, Reading and Social Organisation*, London, 1980

Parker, G., 'An Educational Revolution? The Growth of Literacy and Schooling in Early Modern Europe', *Tijdschrift voor Geschiedenis*, XCIII (1980)

Parry, N., and Parry, J., *The Rise of the Medical Profession*, London, 1976

Pattison, R., *On Literacy*, Oxford, 1982

Pearl, M. L., *William Cobbett, A Bibliographical Account of his Life and Times*, Oxford, 1953

Perkin, H., *The Origins of Modern English Society 1780–1880*, London, 1969

The Age of the Railway, London, 1971

Pethybridge, R., *The Social Prelude to Stalinism*, London, 1974

Phillips, K. C., *Language and Class in Victorian England*, Oxford, 1984

Pickering, M., *Village Song and Culture*, London, 1982

Pickstone, J. V., 'Medical Botany. (Self-Help Medicine in Victorian England)', *Memoirs of the Manchester Literary and Philosophical Society*, 119 (1976–7)

Pierson, S., *British Socialists*, Cambridge, Mass., 1979

Plant, M., *The English Book Trade*, 2nd edn, London, 1965

Pollard, S., 'Factory Discipline in the Industrial Revolution', *Economic History Review*, 16 (1963)

Porter, E., *Cambridgeshire Customs and Folklore*, London, 1969

Porter, J. H., 'The Iron Trade', in Wrigley, *Industrial Relations*
   'Wage Bargaining under Conciliation Agreements, 1860–1914', *Economic History Review*, 2nd series, XXIII (1970)

Porter, R., 'Before the Fringe', in R. Cooter, *Alternative Essays in the Social History of Irregular Medicine*, London, 1987
   'The Language of Quackery in England, 1660–1800', in Burke and Porter, *Social History of Language*
   'Laymen, Doctors and Medical Knowledge in the Eighteenth Century: The Evidence of the *Gentleman's Magazine*', in R. Porter (ed.), *Patients and Practitioners. Lay Perceptions of Medicine in Pre-Industrial Society*, Cambridge, 1986
   'Medicine and the Decline of Magic', unpublished paper, 1986

Postgate, R., *The Builders' History*, London, 1923

Preston, B., *Occupations of Father and Son in Mid-Victorian England*, Reading, 1977

Price, R., *'Labour' in British Society*, London, 1986
   Masters, Unions and Men, Cambridge, 1980

Priestley, P., *Victorian Prison Lives*, London, 1985

Prothero, I., *Artisans and Politics in Early Nineteenth-Century London*, London, 1981

Pye, L. W. (ed.), *Communications and Political Development*, Princeton, 1963

Radbill, S. X., 'Whooping Cough in Fact and Fancy', *Bulletin of the History of Medicine*, XIII (1943)

Radice, G. and L., *Will Thorne. Constructive Militant*, London, 1974

Redford, A., *Labour Migration in England 1800–1850*, 3rd edn, Manchester, 1976

Ree, J., *Proletarian Philosophers*, Oxford, 1984
   'Socialism and the Educated Working Class', in Levy, *Socialism and the Intelligentsia*

Reid, A., 'Intelligent Artisan and Aristocrats of Labour: The Essays of Thomas Wright', in J. Winter (ed.), *The Working Class in Modern British History*, Cambridge, 1983

Reid, D. A., 'The Decline of Saint Monday 1766–1876', *Past and Present*, 71 (1976)
   'Interpreting the Festival Calendar: Wakes and Fairs as Carnivals', in R. D. Storch (ed.), *Popular Culture and Custom in Nineteenth-Century England*, London, 1982

Reid, F., 'Keir Hardie and the *Labour Leader*, 1893–1903', in J. Winter (ed.), *The Working Class in Modern British History*, Cambridge, 1983

Resnick, D. P. and Resnick, L. B., 'The Nature of Literacy: An Historical Exploration', *Harvard Educational Review*, 47, no. 3 (August 1977)

Riesman, D., 'The Oral and Written Traditions', in E. Carpenter and M. McLuhan (eds.), *Explorations in Communication*, London, 1970

Roberts, W., 'Lloyd's Penny Bloods', *Book-collectors' Quarterly*, XVIII (1935)

Robertson, P. L., 'Technical Education in the British Shipbuilding and Marine Engineering Industries 1863–1914', *Economic History Review*, 2nd series XVII (1974)

Robinson, H., *Britain's Post Office*, London, 1953

Roderick, G. W., and Stephens, M. D. (eds.), *Scientific and Technical Education in Nineteenth Century England*, Newton Abbot, 1972

Rogers, P., 'Classics and Chapbooks', in *Literature and Popular Culture in Eighteenth Century England*, Brighton, 1985

Rogers, P. G., *Battle in Bossenden Wood*, London, 1961

Royle, E., 'Mechanics' Institutes and the Working Classes, 1840–1860', *The Historical Journal* (1971)

   Radicals, Secularists and Republicans, Manchester, 1980

Rudé, G., *Wilkes and Liberty*, Oxford, 1962

Rule, J., *The Experience of Labour in Eighteenth-Century Industry*, London, 1981

   'Methodism, Popular Beliefs and Village Culture in Cornwall', in R. D. Storch (ed.), *Popular Culture and Custom in Nineteenth-Century England*, London, 1982

   'The Property of Skill in the Period of Manufacture', in Joyce, *Historical Meanings of Work*

Sales, R., *English Literature in History. 1780–1830, Pastoral and Politics*, London, 1983

Sambrook, J., *William Cobbett*, London, 1973

Samuel, R., 'The Workshop of the World: Steam Power and Hand Technology in Mid-Victorian Britain', *History Workshop*, 3 (1977)

Sanderson, M., *Educational Opportunity and Social Change in England*, London, 1987

   'Literacy and Social Mobility in the Industrial Revolution in England', *Past and Present*, 56 (1972)

   'Social Change and Elementary Education in Industrial Lancashire 1780–1840', *Northern History*, 3 (1968)

Schofield, R. S., 'Dimensions of Illiteracy in England 1750–1850', in H. Graff (ed.), *Literacy and Social Development in the West*, Cambridge 1981

   'The Measurement of Literacy in Pre-Industrial England', in J. Goody (ed.), *Literacy in Traditional Societies*, Cambridge, 1968

Scribner, R. W., *For the Sake of Simple Folk. Popular Propaganda for the German Reformation*, Cambridge, 1981

Scribner, S. and Cole, M., *The Psychology of Literacy*, Cambridge, Mass., 1981

Segalen, M., *Love and Power in the Peasant Family*, Oxford, 1983

Sewell, W. H., *Structure and Mobility*, Cambridge, 1985

   Work and Revolution in France, Cambridge, 1980

Sharp, I. G., *Industrial Conciliation and Arbitration in Great Britain*, London, 1950

Shepard, L., *The History of Street Literature*, London, 1973

Simon, B., 'Systemisation and Segmentation in Education: The Case of England', in D. F. Muller, F. Ringer and B. Simon, *The Rise of the Modern Educational System*, Cambridge, 1987

Smith, A., *The Established Church and Popular Religion 1750–1850*, London, 1981

Smith, F., *A History of English Elementary Education 1760–1902*, London, 1931

Smith, F. B., 'Health', in J. Benson (ed.), *The Working Class in England 1875–1914*, London, 1985

The People's Health, London, 1979

Smith, O., *The Politics of Language*, Oxford, 1984

Smith, R., 'Education, Society, and Literacy: Nottinghamshire in the Mid-Nineteenth Century', *University of Birmingham Historical Journal*, 12 (1969)

Soltow, L. and Stevens, E., *The Rise of Literacy and the Common School in the United States*, Chicago, 1981

Spater, G., *William Cobbett, The Poor Man's Friend*, Cambridge, 1982

Spufford, M., 'First Steps in Literacy: the Reading and Writing Experiences of the Humblest Seventeenth-century Spiritual Autobiographers', *Social History*, 4, no. 3 (October 1979)

Small Books and Pleasant Histories, London, 1981

Staff, F., *The Picture Postcard and its Origins*, London, 1966

'The Valentine' and its Origins, London, 1969

Start, K. B. and Wells, B. K., *The Trend of Reading Standards*, Windsor, 1972

Stedman Jones, G., *Languages of Class*, Cambridge, 1983

Steedman, C., *Policing the Victorian Community*, London, 1984

Steinberg, S. H., *Five Hundred Years of Printing*, 3rd edn, Harmondsworth, 1974

Stephens, E., 'Literacy and the Worth of Liberty', *Quantum*, 34 (1985)

Stephens, W. B., *Education, Literacy and Society, 1830–1870*, Manchester, 1987

'Elementary Education and Literacy, 1770–1870', in D. Fraser (ed.), *A History of Modern Leeds*, Manchester, 1980

'Illiteracy and Schooling in the Principal Towns, 1640–1870: A Comparative Approach', in D. A. Reeder (ed.), *Urban Education in the Nineteenth Century*, London, 1977

'Schooling and Literacy in Rural England 1800–1914', *History of Education Quarterly*, I (1982)

Stephens, W. B. (ed.), *Studies in the History of Literacy: England and North America*, Leeds, 1983

Stock, B., *The Implications of Literacy*, Princeton, 1983

Stone, L., 'Literacy and Education in England 1640–1900', *Past and Present*, 42 (1969)

Storch, R. D., 'The Problem of Working-Class Leisure. Some Roots of Middle-class Moral Reform in the Industrial North: 1825–50', in A. P. Donajgrodski (ed.), *Social Control in Nineteenth Century Britain*, London, 1977

Street, B. V., *Literacy in Theory and Practice*, Cambridge, 1984

Stubbs, M., *Language and Literacy. The Sociolinguistics of Reading and Writing*, London, 1980

Sturt, M., *The Education of the People*, London, 1867

Sutherland, G., *Ability, Merit and Measurement*, Oxford, 1984

Swindells, J., *Victorian Writing and Working Women*, London, 1985

Tannen, D., 'The Myth of Orality and Literacy', in W. Frawley (ed.), *Linguistics and Literacy*, New York, 1982

Thomas, K., 'The Meaning of Literacy in Early Modern England', in Baumann,

The Written Word
'Numeracy in Early Modern England', *Transactions of the Royal Historical Society*, 5th series, 37 (1987)
Religion and the Decline of Magic, Harmondsworth, 1973
Thompson, D., *The Chartists*, London, 1984
Thompson, E. P., 'The Crime of Anonymity', in D. Hay *et al., Albion's Fatal Tree*, Harmondsworth, 1977
The Making of the English Working Class, Harmondsworth, 1968
'Time, Work-Discipline, and Industrial Capitalism', *Past and Present*, 38 (1967)
Thompson, L., *Robert Blatchford*, London, 1951
Thwaite, M. F., *From Primer to Pleasure in Reading*, 2nd edn, London, 1972
Todd, E., *The Causes of Progress*, Oxford, 1987
Townsend, J. R., *Written for Children*, Harmondsworth, 1967
Trimmer, E., 'Medical Folklore and Quackery', *Folklore*, 76 (Autumn 1965)
Turner, E. S., *The Shocking History of Advertising*, London, 1952
Twyman, M., *Printing 1770–1970*, London, 1970
Unesco, *The Experimental World Literacy Programme, a Critical Assessment*, Paris, 1976
Literacy 1965–1967, Paris, 1980
Literacy 1972–1976, Paris, 1980
Unicef, *The State of the World's Children 1984*, Oxford, 1984
Vansina, J., *Oral Tradition*, Harmondsworth, 1973
Vaughan, P., *Doctors' Commons*, London, 1959
Verne, E., 'Literacy and Industrialisation – The Dispossesion of Speech', in E. Bataille (ed.), *A Turning Point for Literacy*, Oxford, 1976
Vicinus, M., *The Industrial Muse*, London, 1974
Vincent, D., *Bread, Knowledge and Freedom*, London, 1981
'Communication, Community and the State', in C. Emsley and J. Walvin (eds.), *Artisans, Peasants and Proletarians, 1790–1860. Essays Presented to Gwyn A. Williams*, London, 1985
'The Decline of the Oral Tradition in Popular Culture', in R. Storch (ed.), *Popular Culture and Custom in Nineteenth Century England*, London, 1982
'Love and Death and the Nineteenth Century Working Class', *Social History*, 5, no. 2 (May, 1980)
'Reading in the Working Class Home', in J. K. Walton and J. Walvin (eds.) *Leisure in Britain 1780–1939*, London, 1983
' "To inform my famely and the world": Autobiography and Ancestry in the Nineteenth Century', in English Genealogical Congress, *Selected Papers Given at the Congresses of 1978 and 1984*, London, 1986
Victorian Eccleshall, Keele, 1982
Waddington, I., *The Medical Profession in the Industrial Revolution*, Dublin, 1984
Wadsworth, A. P., *Newspaper Circulations, 1800–1945*, Manchester, 1955
Walvin, J., *Leisure and Society 1830–1950*, London, 1978
Watson, I., *Song and Democratic Culture in Britain*, London, 1983
Webb, R. K., 'Working Class Readers in Early Victorian England', *English Historical Review*, 65 (1950)

Weber, E., *Peasants into Frenchmen*, London, 1977

Wells, G., *Language Development in the Pre-school Years*, Cambridge, 1985

West, E. G., 'Literacy and the Industrial Revolution', *Economic History Review*, 2nd series XXXI (1978)

Whipp, R., ' "A time to every purpose": an essay on time and work', in Joyce, *Historical Meanings of Work*

Wickwar, W. H., *The Struggle for the Freedom of the Press*, London, 1928

Wiener, J. H., *A Descriptive Finding List of Unstamped British Periodicals 1830–1836*, London, 1970

Williams, R., *Culture and Society 1780–1950*, Harmondsworth, 1971

   The Long Revolution, Harmondsworth, 1965

   'The Press and Popular Culture: An Historical Perspective', in Boyce *et al.*, *Newspaper History*

Woodward, J. and Richards, D., *Health Care and Popular Medicine in Nineteenth Century England*, London, 1977

Wrigley, C., 'The Government and Industrial Relations', in C. Wrigley (ed.), *A. History of British Industrial Relations 1875–1914*, Brighton, 1982

Yeo, E., 'Some Practices and Problems of Chartist Democracy', in J. Epstein and D. Thompson (eds.), *The Chartist Experience*, London, 1982

Yeo, S., 'Notes on Three Socialisms – Collectivism, Statism and Associationsim', in C. Levy (ed.), *Socialism and the Intelligentsia 1880–1914*, London, 1987

Yeo, E. and Yeo, S. (eds.), *Popular Culture and Class Conflict 1590–1914*, Brighton, 1981

Youngson, A. J., *The Scientific Revolution in Victorian Medicine*, London, 1979

Zeitlin, J., 'Engineers and Compositors: A Comparison', in Harrison and Zeitlin, *Divisions of Labour*

   'From Labour History to the History of Industrial Relations', *Economic History Review*, 2nd series, XL, 2 (1987)

vi Unpublished theses

Belfiore, G. M., 'Family Strategies in Essex Textile Towns 1860–1895: The Challenge of Compulsory Elementary Schooling', D.Phil. thesis, Oxford University, 1987

Berridge, V. S., 'Popular Journalism and Working Class Attitudes 1854–1886: A Study of Reynolds' Newspaper, Lloyd's Weekly Newspaper and the Weekly Times', Ph.D. thesis London University, 1976

Campbell, M. J., 'The Development of Literacy in Bristol and Gloucestershire 1755–1870', D.Phil. thesis, Bath University, 1980

Looney, J. J., 'Advertising and Society in England 1720–1820; A Statistical Analysis of Yorkshire Newspaper Advertisements', Ph.D. thesis, Princeton University, 1983

Mitch, D., 'The Spread of Literacy in Nineteenth-Century England', Ph.D. thesis, University of Chicago, 1982

Thomson, R. S., 'The Development of the Broadside Ballad Trade and its Influence upon the Transmission of English Folksongs', Ph.D. thesis, Cambridge University, 1974

INDEX

abortifacients, 168, 170
actors, travelling, 221
Acts of Parliament
  Hardwick's Marriage (1754), 3, 53
  Seditious Meetings (1817), 137, 230
  'Six Acts' (1819), 233, 245, 248
  First Reform (1832), 240
  Registration of Births, Deaths and Marriages (1836), 3, 128
  Stamp (1836), 234
  Medical Registration (1858), 167
  Second Reform (1867), 240
  Education (1870), 54, 67, 92, 97, 224, 270
  Ballot (1872), 237
  Sale of Food and Drugs (1875), 167
  Education (1876), 69
  Definition of Time (1880), 182
  Education (1880), 28, 67, 90, 92, 97, 241-2
  Corrupt Practices (1883), 237
  Fees (1891), 72
  National Insurance (1911), 170
Adams, William Edwin, 182, 196
advertising, 42, 166-71, 192, 253
Aesop's Fables, 89
Age of Reason, Tom Paine, 178
Allen, William, 142
Ally Sloper's Half-Holiday, 223, 225
almanacs, 12, 169, 192-3
Amalgamated Society of Engineers, 124, 142, 145, 149, 253
Anglicanism, *see* Church of England
anthropology, 8
Anti-Corn Law League, 38, 239
apprenticeship, 14, 56, 107-15, 117-18, 120-1, 135-6, 142, 261
arithmetic, 2, 10, 11, 70, 72, 78, 87, 106, 116, 259
Arnold, Matthew, 270
astrologers, astrology, 172, 173, 192
authors, authorship, 200-1, 203, 208-9, 214-17, 219-20, 227

autobiography, 7, 19, 61, 63, 157, 188, 191, 223, 268, 274, 277
Aveling, Edward, 267

Ballad of Chevy Chase, 61
ballads, 61-2, 181, 197, 200, 202-3, 206, 209, 211, 217, 223, 225, 237, 245-6, 252
ballad singers, 199, 202-3, 211, 245
Ballantyne, R. M., 62
Bamford, Samuel, 45, 61-2
Barker, Joseph, 158
Barnes, George, 260, 261
battledores, 68
Battle of Bossenden Wood (1838), 85, 174
Bebel, August, 267
The Bee-Hive, 124, 255
Bell, Lady, 28, 192, 212, 213
Bell, Andrew, 10, 77
The Bible, 1, 6, 9, 12, 58-9, 62, 64-5, 69, 72, 75, 77, 78, 79, 85-6, 176-7, 179, 223
bible and key ceremony, 176-7
Billington, William, 214-16, 227
black lists, 140, 276
blackmail, 168
blasphemy, 236
Blatchford, Robert, 59, 60, 257-8, 262, 266
Boer War, 256
boggards, 158
books
  ownership, 16, 64, 174
  prices, 61, 208, 210-13
  sellers, 202
  shops, 61
stalls, 59, 62, 214
Booth, Charles, 191
botany, 160-2
Bowd, James, 64, 165
Bradlaugh, Henry, 178, 262
Brand, Joseph, 6
Brierley, Benjamin, 7
British and Foreign Bible Society, 178

356

British and Foreign School Society, 53–4, 64, 69, 75, 76, 77, 79, 85, 87, 106, 120, 173, 188, 233
British Medical Association, 168
British Medical Journal, 169
Broadhurst, Henry, 124, 148, 150
broadsides, 174, 197–9, 203–9, 211, 223, 226, 237–8, 245, 252, 253, 257, 275
sellers, 202, 252, 275
Brougham, Henry, 110, 223
Buchan, David, 197
Builder's Price Books, 110
Bullock Report (1975), 16
Burdett, Sir Francis, 245
Burgess, Joseph, 257
Burke, Peter, 4, 210
Burne, Charlotte, 157, 177
Burns, John, 145
Burt, Thomas, 259, 264
Byron, George Gordon, Lord, 89, 221

Carlyle, Thomas, 261
Castlereagh, Lord, 234
Catholicism, *see* Roman Catholic Church
Catnach, James, 45, 174, 197, 199–200, 203–4, 208, 222, 245–6
Caxton, William, 11
census, 17
Central Society of Education, 85
Cervantes, 222, 224
chapbooks, 12, 61–2, 175, 177, 198, 204–5, 221, 226, 245, 275
chapmen, 12, 62, 175, 197
Chartism, chartists, 83, 85, 169, 174, 186–8, 230–31, 239, 243–51, 254, 267, 268
Chaucer, Geoffrey, 214
child-rearing, 54–66
children's literature, 61–3, 68
Christmas cards 45–6, 51, 185
Church of England, 3, 6, 7, 173–5, 178–9; *see also* clergy; National Society for Promoting the Education of the Poor
cinema, 4, 271
Citrine, Walter, 261
City and Guilds, 116–17, 118
Civil Service examinations, 132–3
Clare, John, 58–9, 62, 181–4, 199, 207, 215, 221
Clarion, 242, 257–8, 262, 266
Cleave, John, 247
Cleave's Weekly Police Gazette, 247, 252
clergy, 87, 173–5, 177, 179, 180, 185, 276
clerks, 36, 132, 134, 212
Cobbett, William, 56, 68, 81–2, 233, 243–6, 248, 250, 252, 254, 258
Cobbett's Grammar, 68, 81

Cobbett's Political Register, 242, 246, 248, 250, 252
Cobbett's Spelling Book, 68
Cobden, Richard, 36, 38, 239
cognitive development, 75, 82–3
Cole, Henry, 45, 60
Cole, Michael, 9
Collier, Mary, 67
Committee of Council on Education, 71, 77
composition, 89, 90, 218, 224–5
conciliation and arbitration, 145–52
Cook, Captain, 59, 222
Cooper, James Fenimore, 89
Cooper, Thomas, 56, 183
Counter-Reformation, 2
courtship, 29, 45
Croker, J. W., 36
Culpeper's Herbal, 161
Culture and Anarchy, Matthew Arnold, 270
cunning men, 172–3, 175
customs, 12, 44, 181
trade, 14, 136–7, 184–6

Daily Citizen, 258, 266
Daily Herald, 242, 258, 266, 269
Dayus, Kathleen, 50
debating societies, 260, 268
Defoe, Daniel, 209
Demos, John, 180
Department of Science and Art, 114, 118
Despard, Colonel, 230
Destructive, 246
dialect, dialect movement, 206–7, 227, 268, 269
Dicey, William, 108, 226
Dickens, Charles, 44, 223, 224
Dicks, John, 209, 210
doctors
qualified, 164–71, 180, 276
unqalified, 162–3, 167–71
Doyle, Sir Arthur Conan, 62
dream books, 175–6
drunkenness, 63, 66, 70, 215, 216–7
Dryden, John, 214, 221
Duncombe, Thomas, 231–2
Dyche, Thomas, 76

education, *see* schools
Edwards, George, 64–5, 151, 152, 177
Edwards, Passmore, 70
Eldon, Lord, 233
elections, 237–40, 245
Eliot, George, 222–3
emigration, 37
English, standardisation of, 80
Errington, Anthony, 57, 64

Evangelicals, 173
Evelina, the Pauper's Child, J. Prest, 218–20
evening classes, 260–1, 262, 268

family history, ancestry, 57, 58–9
First World War, 4, 51
Foley, Alice, 60
folklore, 6, 60, 159, 183, 268
folklorists, folklore movement, 12, 156–8, 186, 198, 199, 226
folk-song, 12
football, 190
foreman, 115, 127
fortune-tellers, 173, 175–7, 179
France, 2, 6, 11, 113, 175
free-and-easies, 202
French Revolution, 7, 186
friendly societies, 143, 164, 186, 276
Furet, François, 2, 10, 43

gambling, 190, 194–5, 272
Gardner, P., 272
Geertz, Clifford, 4
geography, 78
geometry, 106–7, 114
George IV, king of England, 245
George, Henry, 261
Germany, 266–7
ghosts, 159
Gibbon, Edward, 187
Goldsmith, Oliver, 224
Goody, Jack, 228
Gosse, Edmund, 55
gothic novel, 218
Graff, Harvey, 2, 125
grammar, 81, 187, 261
grammars,, 13, 81, 82, 245
Gramsci, Antonio, 228, 229, 259, 267
Great Exhibition (1851), 113
Greenwich Mean Time, 182
Grose, Francis, 205
Guilliver's Travels, Jonathan Swift, 221, 222–3
Gutteridge, Joseph, 57, 161–4

Hall, Bishop J., 6
Hamid, Abdul, 34
Hampden Clubs, 248
Hardie, Keir, 257–8, 262
Harland, John, 199, 207
Harris, John, 60
harvest festivals, 184–5
Heaton, J. H., 34, 46
Heaton, William, 67
Henderson, Arthur, 260, 263
Henson, Gravener, 34, 35, 42, 139
herbal medicine, 163, 170

heresy, 5
Hetherington, Henry, 231, 246–7, 250
Hill, Matthew, 34
Hill, Rowland, 34–8, 40, 44, 45, 46, 48, 51, 230, 239
history, historical writings, 187–8, 261, 268, 274
  in schools, 59, 186–7, 236
History of Mother Bunch, 62, 175
Hodges, Frank, 260, 261, 262–3
Hodgson, Joseph, 208
Hodgson, W. B., 7–8, 9–10, 18, 79
Hoggart, Richard, 270, 271, 272, 276
Holcroft, Thomas, 197
Hone, William, 158–9, 184, 186, 245
horse racing, 190, 194–5
Hours with the Muses, J. C. Prince, 215
houses of call, 124
Hume, David, 187
Hunt, Henry, 230
Hyndman, Henry, 267

ill-health, 64, 160, 162–71
Independent Labour Party, 242, 256–8, 262–3, 265, 267, 268, 269
Industrial Revolution, 3, 7, 8, 11, 37, 47–8, 95, 98–100, 105–19, 127–8, 130, 153–4
Inman, Philip, 58, 63
Institute of Civil Engineers, 111
intelligence, 15, 82–4, 91–2
Ireson, Alfred, 55–7
Irving, Washington, 89

Jack the Giant Killer, 61
Jackson, Thomas, 223, 225
Jerrold, Douglas, 35
Johnson's Dictionary, 80
Jone o' Grinfilt, 207
journalism, journalists, 125, 234–6, 243–5, 247–8, 250–2, 254, 256–8, 269
Justice, 242

Kay-Shuttleworth, James, 6, 76, 87, 189
Kettle, Sir Rupert, 146, 147, 150
Knight, Charles, 38, 202

Labour Leader, 257, 262
Labour Party, 229, 252, 257–8, 265, 267–9
Labour Representation Committee, 256, 263
Lancaster, Joseph, 10, 70–1, 188
language, 77–82
Laqueur, T. W., 97
Latin, 81, 163
Lawson, Jack, 61, 261
lay-preachers, 177, 180, 263
learning to read, 1, 10, 56, 66–72, 74–94

learning to talk, 55
learning to work, 14–15, 55–6, 104–19
Leatherland, J. A., 62
Lerner, D., 8
letter carriers, *see* postmen
Liberal Party, 31, 36, 256, 258
libraries
  children's, 61
  public, 59, 61, 190, 191, 212, 213, 214
  school, 79
Liebknecht, Karl, 267
The Life of Guy Earl of Warwick, 177
lighting, domestic, 213
literacy rates, 1–4, 11, 16, 21, 22–41, 46–9,
  53–4, 92, 279
  by age, 26
  by gender, 24–6, 28, 29, 33, 53–4, 101–4,
    126, 277
  by occupation, 30, 32, 33, 89–90, 95, 96–
    102, 125, 151, 233
  by place, 24, 25, 33, 41, 48, 98–100, 103–
    104, 125
  of witnesses, 22–3, 29, 31–2, 283–5
Lloyd, Edward, 175, 197, 200, 204, 235
Lloyd's Weekly News 179, 191, 201, 251–3,
  255, 266
London Corresponding Society, 268
long song sellers, 200
'Look and Say', 84–5, 93
Lovett, William, 59, 61, 231
Lowe, Robert, 233
Luria, A. R., 8

Macaulay, Lord, 89, 187, 232
Macdonald, Alexander, 139
magic, 159–60, 176, 187, 268
Magnus, Philip, 116
Maidment, Brian, 208
mail order, 42, 167–8
Mallock, W. H., 157
Manchester Statistical Society, 78
Mandeville, Bernard, 7, 85
Mann, Tom, 262
manuals
  teaching, 6, 13, 73, 75–7, 80, 84, 93
  work 107–12
marriage, 21–2
marriage registers, 3, 16–18, 21, 29, 30, 32,
  33, 53–4, 56, 274, 279, 281–2
The Martyrdom of the Mine, E. A. Rymer,
  150
Marx, Eleanor, 145, 267
Marx, Karl, 119, 258
Marxism, 9
Mayett, Joseph, 1, 69
Mayhew, Henry, 178, 200, 203, 210
Mazzini, Joseph, 231

mechanics' institutes, 107, 111
medical botanists, 163–4, 170
medicines, 165–71
Meek, George, 240–2
memory, remembering, 8, 55, 60–1, 62, 182–
  4, 188, 194, 206
Merrie England, Robert Blatchford, 257
Methodism, 177, 178, 179, 180, 263
migrants, migration, 35, 37, 41, 45
Mill, John Stuart, 261
Milner, William, 209–10
Milton, John, 89, 213, 214, 221, 223, 224,
  279
modernisation, 3–4, 8, 13
monitors, monitorial system, 10, 77, 79, 120,
  127
Monthly Magazine of Fiction, 220
Morris, William, 258, 262, 267
Mother Bunch's Golden Fortune-Teller, 176
Mother Shipton's Legacy, 62
Munby, A. J., 96
Mundella, A. J., 114, 116, 120, 127, 146, 150
Murray, Lindley, 81
music, 202–3
music halls, 202, 211
Mysteries of London, G. W. M. Reynolds,
  210, 217

Napoleonic Wars, 33, 35, 207, 230, 232
Napoleon's Book of Fate, 175
National Association for the Promotion of
  Social Science, 7
National Charter Association, 250
National Secular Society, 178
National Society for Promoting the Edu-
  cation of the Poor in the Principles of
  the Established Church, 53–4, 57, 64,
  74, 75, 76, 85, 87, 106, 120, 173, 188,
  233, 260, 268
National Typographical Association, 142
National Union of Gas Workers, 145
National Union of the Working Classes,
  243, 246
naturalists, nature study, 57, 59
Nelson's Royal Readers, 89, 94
Newbery, John, 61
Newcastle Commission, 10, 69, 82, 86–7
Newnes Penny Library of Famous Books, 211
News of the World, 179, 250
newspaper delivering, 132, 200, 202
newspapers, 10, 11, 26, 89, 166–7, 202, 212,
  240, 241–58, 261, 263–8, 274–6
  penny, 202, 235, 251–6
  provincial, 214–15, 225–6
  sporting, 190–1, 194–5, 212
  Sunday, 169, 178–80, 190–1, 200, 251–6,
    277

trade union, 255, 276
unstamped, 192, 234, 242–5, 248–9, 257, 267
newspaper stamp, 233–6
Nicholson, John, 67, 215– 17
Nonconformity, 173, 179–80
Northern Star, 169, 243–4, 246–51, 253
numeracy, *see* arithmetic

O'Connor, Feargus, 243, 244, 247–52
The Oeconomy of Charity, Sarah Trimmer, 73
Old Moore's Almanack, 193
Ong, W. J., 181
Operative Society of Masons, 136, 139–41, 144
oral tradition, 5–6, 12, 60, 157, 171, 181, 184, 185, 186, 188, 202, 223, 268, 270
Oxford Movement, 173
Ozouf, J., *see* Furet, François

Paine, Tom, 233, 258
Paradise Lost, John Milton, 183
Paris International Exhibition (1867), 113
patterers, 200, 203
penny dreadfuls, 174, 200–1, 204, 209, 218, 220, 226
penny fiction, 220, 223–5, 266, 277
Pilgrim's Progress, John Bunyan, 62, 69, 89, 179, 209, 222
Pitts, John, 197
Place, Francis, 58
play, 55–7, 59–63, 67
Playfair, Lyon, 113
The Pleasant and Delightful History of Jack and the Giants, 205
poets, working-class, 60, 62, 67, 181, 191, 208, 214–17, 225, 277
police, 123
poor law, workhouses, 37, 53, 60, 65, 70, 114, 241, 249
Poor Man's Guardian, 242, 243–4, 246, 249, 256
Pope, Alexander, 209, 213, 214, 221, 224
Post, Penny, 33, 35, 37–9, 44–6, 48, 89, 122, 167, 175, 182, 192, 210, 230, 235, 236, 239
postal espionage, 230–2, 251
postal flows, 17, 33, 34, 38–40, 44, 46–9, 274
postal workers, 96, 122–23, 127, 132, 154
post boxes, 39, 40
postcards, 39, 46, 49, 51, 276
post coaches, 182
Postmaster General, 33, 39, 42, 44, 45, 46, 122
postmen, letter carriers, 35, 41, 43–4, 49, 176
Post Office, 34, 39, 40, 44, 206, 230

Potter, George, 255
poverty, 16, 57–8, 59–60, 64, 66, 71, 172, 200, 218, 274, 278
Prest, Thomas, 218–20
Preston, Thomas, 228, 229
primers, 2, 6, 13, 68, 70, 76, 77, 78, 80, 82, 84, 203–4
Prince, John Critchley, 215–16
printers, 11, 197, 201, 237–8
printing, 11, 13, 76, 109, 132, 201, 266
prisons, prisoners, 16, 125
professions, 11, 279
Progress and Poverty, Henry George, 261
pronunication, elocution, 13, 80–2, 211, 225
prostitutes, 95
Protestantism, 157, 158
psychology, 7, 8, 55, 77
publishers, publishing, 11, 199–204, 206–9, 214–15, 217, 225–7

Queen Caroline, 245–6
Queen's Scholarships, 127

radio, 4, 271, 273
railway fiction, 211–12
railways, 12, 47–9, 182, 185, 202, 239, 250
railway workers, 96, 123, 126, 127, 132, 154
recreation, *see* play
Reeves' Associations, 232
Reformation, 2, 6, 12, 177, 204
Registrar General, 3, 5, 17, 21, 22, 24, 26, 53–4, 92, 96
religion, 9, 64–5, 74, 85–6, 87, 92, 171–80
Religious Tract Society, 174–5, 178
remembering, *see* memory
Revised Code, 7, 10, 16, 17, 21, 43, 79, 87–91, 92–3, 116, 120, 127, 154, 187, 217–18, 224, 236, 265
Reynolds, G. W. M., 197, 210, 217, 219, 252–4
Reynolds' News, 167, 179, 180, 241–2, 251–6, 266, 268
Roberts, Robert, 28, 153, 263–4, 271
Robinson Crusoe, Daniel Defoe, 62, 221
Roman Catholic Church, 6, 157, 158, 173, 179, 265–6
Rowntree, Seebohm, 190
Ruskin, John, 258, 261
Rymer, J. M., 206

Saint Monday, 189
Sanderson, Michael, 97, 99, 128
Schofield, Roger, 3, 23, 98
school attendance, 16, 47, 66–7, 69, 71–2, 87–8, 89–90
school attendance officers, 241
school inspectors, 72, 73, 76, 77–8, 79–80,

81, 82, 93, 236
school textbooks, 59, 77, 78
schools, schooling, education, 2, 6, 7, 8, 12, 15, 26, 44, 61, 101, 272, 273, 279
schools, types of
  board, 12, 70, 72, 79, 90, 104
  charity, 6, 7, 10, 52, 73, 75, 80, 106, 116
  church, 70, 72, 73–5, 77–8, 84, 85, 87–8, 92, 104, 203
  dame, 56, 69–70, 268
  elementary, 2, 11, 14, 53–4, 75–94, 173–4, 178, 201, 221, 252, 258–60, 268
  grammar, 163
  half-time, 122
  infant, 73
  private adventure, 14, 65, 69–72, 77, 78, 87
  secular Sunday, 258
  Sunday, 1, 10, 57, 58, 65, 69, 74, 101, 177, 185, 250, 260
  technical, 117
  workhouse, 71
schoolteachers, 5, 12, 13, 15, 56, 65, 68, 70, 71–2, 76, 77, 78, 84, 122, 125–6, 133, 165, 236, 260, 265, 271, 276
  parents, relatives as, 67–9
  pupil, 127
  Sunday, 65
science, 5, 110–11, 113–15, 172, 268
Scott, Sir Walter, 214, 223
Scott-James, R. A., 229, 265–6, 270
Scribner, S., 9
seaside, 46, 49, 185
Second World War, 15, 16
Secret Remedies, 169
secularism, freethought, 85–6, 157, 177–8, 236
self-education, 258–63
self-improvement societies, 190, 260, 262, 267–8
Seven Champions of Christendom, 61, 62, 198
Shakespeare, 90, 183, 196, 209, 214, 224, 279
Sharp, Cecil, 12
Shaw, Charles, 58, 65
The Shepherd's Calendar, John Clare, 181, 184
skill, 107–13, 118–19
Smith, Charles Manby, 140, 221
Smith, W. H., 237
Snell, Henry, 64, 65, 160, 164, 178, 262
Social Democratic Federation, 256
Social Democratic Party (Germany), 266–7
socialism, 157, 252, 261–3
social mobility, 30–1, 126–34, 275–6
Society for the Diffusion of Useful Knowledge, 85, 110–11, 192

Society for the Promotion of Christian Knowledge, 85, 174, 178
songbooks, 198, 200, 211
Southgate, Walter, 41
Spa Fields riots (1816), 229
spas, 40
spelling books, 68, 78
Spence, Thomas, 245
Spencer, F. H., 79–80
Spenser, Edmund, 89, 214, 234
Stalin, 8
Stamper, Joseph, 262
State, 7, 73, 75, 77, 114, 118, 152, 155, 197, 220, 229–41, 248, 251, 265–7, 272, 273
Statute of Artificers, 107–8
Steadman, W. C., 260
Stephens, W. B., 99, 104
Story, Robert, 7
story-telling, 12, 58, 60–1
Sturt, George, 113
Sue, Eugene, 210
'superstition', 6, 156–9, 162, 163, 172, 177, 178, 181, 183, 193, 268
Sutherland, Gillian, 272
Sweeney Todd, 209
Sykes, John, 43, 160, 280

Talbot, James, 74, 80
teachers, *see* schoolteachers
teacher training colleges, 75, 80
teaching methods, 77–85, 88–93
technical education, 113–19
telephones, 52
television, 4, 271, 273
Thistlewood, Arthur, 230
Thompson, Flora, 45, 50, 72, 89, 94
Thomson, James, 223
Thorne, Will, 145, 151, 152, 267
time, 150, 180–95
The Times, 11, 201, 231, 236, 253
Tom Hickathrift, 61
Tooke, Horne, 230
Tories, 36
tracts, 174–5, 178
trade union officials, leaders, 64, 124, 180, 263, 265, 268, 273, 275
trade unions, 38, 115, 118, 123–5, 135–56, 186, 254, 276
tramping, 35, 124–5, 135, 138
Trimmer, Sarah, 6, 73, 75, 78
Turner, Ben, 268

unemployment, 37
Unesco, 2, 15, 156
Universal Postal Union, 17, 33, 46
universities, 56, 274

Uses of Literacy, Richard Hoggart, 270, 272

valentines, 44–5, 46, 51
Victoria, Queen, 46

wall-song sellers, 200
Watson, James, 230
Watts, Ian, 229
Waugh, Edwin, 200
weather-forecasting, 180
Webb, R. K., 10
Weekly Times, 251
Wesley, John, 177
West, E. G., 97
White, Gilbert, 224

Whittaker, Thomas, 171
whooping cough, 162, 166, 169, 276
Wilderspin, Samuel, 73
Wilkes, John, 237
Williams, Alfred, 127
The Winning Post, 195
wise men, *see* cunning men
wise women, 170, 175, 276
witches, witchcraft, 61, 159, 171–3, 175, 176, 180
work discipline, 121–2, 140–3, 154, 189
Workman's Times, 242, 257, 269
Wright, Thomas, 134, 135, 221, 231, 256, 264–5
writers, writing, *see* authors, composition

Printed in the United Kingdom
by Lightning Source UK Ltd.
100341UKS00001B/91-93